European Review
of Social Psychology

European Review of Social Psychology

Editorial Board

About the editors

Wolfgang Stroebe has published widely on the topics of attitudes, group processes and health psychology. A former president of the European Association of Experimental Social Psychology and a fellow of the British Psychological Society, the Society for the Psychological Study of Social Issues, and the Society of Personality and Social Psychology, he has recently received an honorary doctorate from the University of Louvain. Having held academic positions in England, USA and Germany he is currently Professor of Social, Organizational and Health Psychology at the University of Utrecht (The Netherlands).

Miles Hewstone has published widely on the topics of social cognition and intergroup relations. He was awarded the British Psychological Society's Spearman Medal in 1987 and its Presidents' Award for Distinguished Contributions to Research in 2001. He was a Fellow at the Center for Advanced Study in the Behavioral Sciences, Stanford, California from 1987–1988 and 1999–2000, and is an Academician of the Academy of Learned Societies in the Social Sciences, and a Fellow of the British Academy. He is Professor of Social Psychology and Fellow of New College, University of Oxford.

European Review of Social Psychology

Volume 14

Edited by

Wolfgang Stroebe
Utrecht University, The Netherlands

and

Miles Hewstone
Oxford University, UK

Routledge
Taylor & Francis Group

LONDON AND NEW YORK

First published 2003 by Psychology Press Ltd

Published 2018 by Routledge
2 Park Square, Milton Park, Abingdon, Oxon, OX14 4RN
52 Vanderbilt Avenue, New York, NY 10017

First issued in paperback 2018

Routledge is an imprint of the Taylor & Francis Group, an informa business

British Library Cataloguing in Publication Data
A catalogue record for this book is available from the British Library

Cover design by Jim Wilkie
Typeset in the UK by Elite Typesetting Techniques Ltd, Eastleigh, Hants.

ISBN 13: 978-1-138-87792-4 (pbk)
ISBN 13: 978-1-84169-941-7 (hbk)
ISSN 1046-3283

Contents

List of contributors

Manuela Barreto, *Social and Organisational Psychology, Leiden University, PO Box 9555, 2300 RB Leiden, The Netherlands*

Mara Cadinu, *DPSS, University of Padova, Via Venezia, 8, 35130 Padova, Italy*

Woo Young Chun, *1147 Biology/Psychology Building, University of Maryland, College Park, MD 20742, USA*

Naomi Ellemers, *Social and Organisational Psychology, Leiden University, PO Box 9555, 2300 RB Leiden, The Netherlands*

Hans Peter Erb, *Klinik und Poliklinik für Psychiatrie und Psychotherapie, Psychiatrische Universitätsklinik, HalleJulius-Kühn Strasse 7, D-06097 Halle/Saale, Germany*

Jason Faulkner, *Department of Psychology, University of British Columbia, 2136 West Mall, Vancouver BC V6T 1Z4, Canada*

Agneta H. Fischer, *University of Amsterdam, Department of Psychology, Roetersstraat 15, 1018 WB Amsterdam, The Netherlands*

Jamin Halberstadt, *Department of Psychology, University of Otago, P.O. Box 56, Dunedin, New Zealand*

Jolanda Jetten, *School of Psychology, University of Exeter, Exeter EX4 4QG, UK*

Cheryl R. Kaiser, *Department of Psychology, Michigan State University, East Lansing, MI 48824, USA*

Arie W. Kruglanski, *1147 Biology/Psychology Building, University of Maryland, College Park, MD 20742, USA*

Anne Maass, *DPSS, University of Padova, Via Venezia, 8, 35130 Padova, Italy*

Brenda Major, *Department of Psychology, University of California, Santa Barbara, Ca 93106-9660, USA*

Lucia Mannetti, *Dipartimento di Psicologia dei Processi di Sviluppo e Socializzazione, (Department of Development and Socialization Processes), University of Rome "La Sapienza", Via dei Marsi, 78, 00185 Roma, Italy*

Shannon K. McCoy, *Health Psychology Program, Department of Psychiatry, 3333 California Street, Suite 465 Box 0848, San Francisco, CA 94143-0848, USA*

Paula M. Niedenthal, *LAPSCO/UFR Psychologie, Université Blaise Pascal, 34, avenue Carnot, 63037 Clermont-Ferrand Cedex, France*

Allison Ottenbreit, *Department of Psychology, University of Maryland, College Park, Maryland 20742, U.S.A.*

Justin Park, *Department of Psychology, University of British Columbia, 2136 West Mall, Vancouver BC V6T 1Z4, Canada*

Antonio Pierro, *Dipartimento di Psicologia dei Processi di Sviluppo e Socializzazione, (Department of Development and Socialization Processes), University of Rome "La Sapienza", Via dei Marsi, 78, 00185 Roma, Italy*

Wendy Quinton, *Psychology Department, California State University, Long Beach, 1250 Bellflower Blvd, Long Beach, CA 90840, USA*

Mark Schaller, *Department of Psychology, University of British Columbia, 2136 West Mall, Vancouver BC V6T 1Z4, Canada*

Russell Spears, *School of Psychology, Cardiff University, PO Box 901, Cardiff, Wales, CF10 3YG*

Scott Spiegel, *406 Shermerhorn Hall, Columbia University, 1190 Amsterdam Avenue, Mail Code 5501, New York City, NY 10027, USA*

Charles Stangor, *Department of Psychology, University of Maryland, College Park, Maryland 20742, U.S.A.*

Katherine van Allen, *Department of Psychology, University of Maryland, College Park, Maryland 20742, U.S.A.*

Acknowledgements

We would like to thank the following reviewers who helped us and the authors to shape these chapters into their final versions:

Dominic Abrams	Alice Eagly	Kate Reynolds
Manuela Barreto	Klaus Fiedler	Bernard Rimé
Nyla Branscombe	Susan Fiske	Mark Snyder
Marilynn Brewer	Jeff Greenberg	Steve Spencer
Rupert Brown	Michael Hogg	Fritz Strack
Richard J. Crisp	Anne Maass	Jim Tanaka
Faye Crosby	Brenda Major	Norbert Vanbeselaere
Kay Deaux	Tony Manstead	Vincent Yzerbyt
Michael Diehl	Paula Niedenthal	
Jack Dovidio	Brian Parkinson	

EUROPEAN REVIEW OF SOCIAL PSYCHOLOGY, 2003, *14*, ix–x

Preface

The *European Review of Social Psychology* was conceived when one of us (Wolfgang Stroebe) was President of the European Association of Experimental Social Psychology. The idea was to create a series that would reflect the dynamism of social psychology in Europe and the attention paid to European ideas and research. Even though the *European Review* has always been intended as a publication of the *European Association of Experimental Social Psychology*, it took more than a decade for the Association to accept this idea. We are therefore delighted that since 2002 we have made this link official, and now the *European Review of Social Psychology* is an official publication of the European Association of Experimental Social Psychology.

From this volume onwards, the *European Review of Social Psychology* will be published as an electronic journal. With each paper being published as soon as the editorial process has been completed, this will not only considerably reduce the publication lag, making the papers available immediately, rather than awaiting publication at the end of the year, but it will also allow libraries to subscribe to the Review, rather than having to order volume by volume via standing orders. However, subscribers will not have to do without the familiar blue volumes, because at the end of the year, the set of chapters for that year will be published as a printed volume.

In the past decade, the *European Review of Social Psychology* has been widely accepted as one of the major international series in social psychology and we are confident that these changes will only further this image. Social Psychology is an international endeavour and this fact underpinned our decision to make the *European Review of Social Psychology* an international review publishing outstanding work of authors from all nations rather than restricting it to Europeans. However, even though the *European Review of Social Psychology* is worldwide in terms of the nationality of its authors, it is European in terms of the nationality of the editors who select the contributions and shape the editorial policies. With the help of an editorial board consisting of senior scholars from various European countries, Australasia, and North America, the editors invite outstanding researchers to contribute to these volumes. Invitations are based either on suggestions from editorial board members or made in response to proposals submitted to the editors and approved by the editorial board. The emphasis of these contributions is on critical assessment of major areas of research and of substantial individual programmes of research as well as on topics and initiatives of contemporary interest and originality. Volumes contain three types of contributions:

(1)   Reviews of the field in some specific area of social psychology, typically one in which European researchers have made some special contribution;
(2)   Reports of extended research programmes which contribute to knowledge of a particular phenomenon or process;
(3)   Contributions to a contemporary theoretical issue or debate.

All manuscripts are externally reviewed and typically extensively revised. The final decision on whether to publish a given manuscript is subject to a positive outcome of the review and editorial process. Thanks to the quality of the authors as well as of the editorial process (assisted by our editorial board as well as outside reviewers), the *European Review* has become internationally renowned.

Wolfgang Stroebe
Miles Hewstone

EUROPEAN REVIEW OF SOCIAL PSYCHOLOGY, 2003, *14*, 1–47

Searching for commonalities in human judgement: The parametric unimodel and its dual mode alternatives

Hans-Peter Erb
Universität Jena, Germany

Arie W. Kruglanski and Woo Young Chun
University of Maryland, USA

Antonio Pierro and Lucia Mannetti
University of Rome "La Sapienza", Italy

Scott Spiegel
Columbia University, USA

We outline a uniform model of human judgement wherein individuals combine situational information with relevant background knowledge to form conclusions. Several judgemental parameters are identified whose specific intersections determine whether given situational information would affect judgements. Abstraction of features from surface manifestations and focus on underlying commonalities afford theoretical integration across judgemental domains and across processes previously assumed to qualitatively differ. The resulting "unimodel" is juxtaposed conceptually and empirically to popular dual-mode frameworks, and implications are drawn for a general rethinking of human judgement phenomena.

The judgement of people and events is a pervasive human activity that over the years has received a great deal of research attention. Scientific investigations of this topic have centred either on a specific *domain* of phenomena, such as persuasion (e.g., Chaiken, Liberman, & Eagly, 1989; Petty & Cacioppo, 1986), attribution (e.g., Kelley, 1967; Trope & Alfieri,

Address correspondence to: Hans-Peter Erb, Universität Jena, Lehrstuhl Sozialpsychologie, Humboldtstr. 26, D-07743, Jena, Germany.

This work was supported by NSF Grant (SBR-9417422) to Arie W. Kruglanski, NIMH pre-doctoral fellowship (1F31MH12053) to Scott Spiegel, and Korea Research Foundation post-doctoral fellowship to Woo Young Chun.

http://www.tandf.co.uk/journals/titles/99998080.asp   DOI: 10.1080/10463280340000009

1997), person perception (e.g., Fiske, Lin, & Neuberg, 1999), judgement under uncertainty (e.g., Kahneman, Slovic, & Tversky, 1982) etc., or around a specific *phenomenon* such as base-rate neglect (e.g., Borgida & Brekke, 1981), dispositional attribution (Trope & Gaunt, 1999), group perception (e.g., Hamilton, Sherman, & Maddox, 1999), stereotyping (e.g., Neuberg & Fiske, 1987), and many others. Over the last several decades, this work has yielded invaluable insights into judgemental mechanisms potentially operative in diverse settings. Yet such insights have been scattered across judgemental topics and, outwardly at least, have had little in common. A possible reason for this is that the theoretical frameworks guiding judgemental research have been typically domain-specific and largely foreign to each other in both emphasis and terminology.

Admittedly, there exists one feature that numerous judgemental models do share. Preponderantly, they distinguish between two qualitatively distinct modes of making judgements. This commonality only compounds the fractionation, however, because each judgemental model identifies a different, unique, pair of judgemental modes (for a source-book, see Chaiken & Trope, 1999). In the field of persuasion, distinctions were drawn between heuristic and systematic modes (Chaiken et al., 1989), or peripheral and central routes (Petty & Cacioppo, 1986); research on judgement under uncertainty distinguished between extensional and intuitive reasoning (Tversky & Kahneman, 1983), or rational and experiential systems (e.g., Epstein & Pacini, 1999); yet other dualistic distinctions have been put forth in domains of dispositional attribution (Trope & Gaunt, 1999), person perception (Fiske et al., 1999), and so on. The picture these models paint of human judgement is quite heterogeneous and fragmented. It conveys the impression that each judgemental domain is governed by its own, qualitatively separate, processes that somehow add up to precisely two in number.

For "something completely different", we presently describe an integrative model of human judgement that cuts through the conceptual diversity extant in the field today. This model unifies the two judgemental modes *within* the separate dual-process models and, by the same token, effects a unification *between* models. Accordingly, we call it the *unimodel*. Our analysis suggests that the same property that gave rise to the dual-mode notion in the first place is also responsible for proliferation of the dual-process models. This property is the characteristic *content-bounded-ness* of most dual-process models. Dispensing with that feature merges each pair of (allegedly) distinct modes into one, affording a within-model integration, while at the same time rendering the content-free model applicable across judgemental topics, affording a between-models integration. Our alternative emphasis on the fundamental factors affecting all judgements affords, additionally, a between-factors integration that has been missing thus far.

Our re-conceptualisation differs radically from "business as usual" in the human judgement field and at the same time is strangely familiar. It differs radically because we propose to replace a considerable number of models and processes by just one. But we do not do it by invoking mysterious novel entities or magical psychological forces. Quite to the contrary, our fundamental constructs are relatively mundane and familiar to researchers in the field. Yet their role in the judgemental process may have been obscured by their inadvertent confounding in prior frameworks with a plethora of content elements.

THE JUDGEMENTAL PROCESS

The concept of evidence

How does a person form a judgement? According to the lay epistemic theory (Kruglanski, 1989, 1990), he or she first comes up with some kind of information to serve as *evidence* for his or her assessment. Nearly anything can serve as evidence under the appropriate circumstances: *What* was being said (read or observed), the *tone* (facial expression, posture) in which it was said, *who* said it, whether *others* agreed with it, the *phenomenal experience* (Schwarz & Clore, 1996) it fostered, etc. In order that a given bit of information serve as evidence, it should form part of a subjective syllogism. It should serve as a minor premise that combines with a previously held major premise, or inference rule, to jointly afford a conclusion. For instance, one might encounter the information "Laura is a graduate of MIT". This might serve as evidence for a conclusion "Laura is an engineer" if it instantiates an antecedent of a major premise in which the individual happened to believe, e.g., "All MIT graduates are engineers", or "If an MIT graduate, then an engineer". In general then, information would form a basis for judgement only whenever background knowledge allowed one to draw conclusions from it. Such background knowledge may come in a variety of representations. It may contain stereotypic beliefs such as "MIT grads are intelligent", attitudinally relevant knowledge about consumer products such as "Low fat foods are healthy", self-relevant meta-cognitive notions such as "If I feel good, I must be a generally happy person" (e.g., Schwarz & Clore, 1983), and so forth.

In describing the judgemental process as syllogistic we hardly mean to imply that individuals necessarily engage in *explicit* syllogistic reasoning (e.g., Newell & Simon, 1972). Nor do we mean to imply that knowledge is always represented as an abstract rule of the "All X are Y" or "If X then Y" variety,[1] that it is consciously accessed in that form from working memory, or that individuals who use it (everyone, by present surmise) are familiar with the intricacies of formal logic, a proposition belied by over 30 years of research on the Wason (1966) card problem, among others. For instance, people might incorrectly treat an implicational "If a, then b" relation as an equivalence relation ("*Only if* a, then b") implying also that "If b, then a". We also accept that often people may be able to better recognise the "correct" implicational properties of concrete statements in familiar domains rather than those of abstract, unfamiliar, statements (Evans, 1989). None of this is inconsistent with the notion that persons generally reason from subjectively relevant rules of the "if-then" format (see also Mischel & Shoda, 1995) that may or may not coincide with what some third party (e.g., the experimenter) had intended, or pronounced as correct.

Fundamental parameters of judgement formation

The notion of *judgemental parameters* is central to the present analysis. These are dimensional continua whose specific intersections determine the impact a given piece of information exerts on a requisite judgement. The several judgemental parameters are now described in turn.

Subjective relevance.   The syllogistic nature of judgement formation was outlined earlier. Viewed against this backdrop, our first parameter is that of relevance, meaning the degree to which the individual believes in a linkage between the antecedent and the consequent terms in the major premise. For

---

[1]In cognitive psychology, considerable debate ensued about whether human reasoning is rule-based in the Newell and Simon (1972) sense of the term "rule" denoting a highly abstract statement, containing symbols, characterised by a great degree of generality, and applied consciously. As an alternative, some researchers (for a review see Medin & Ross, 1989) have put forth "instance models" involving the retrieval of specific instances from memory that are then used as analogues to reach judgements about other instances. Other theorists (see Schank, 1982) put forth case-based models wherein particular cases are stored in memory along with information about how these exemplars can be generalised, etc. Our concept of rule is intended in a broad enough sense to be compatible with all those various proposals. Thus, we do not assume that the rule must be represented symbolically, that it must be abstract, general, or consciously and deliberately applied. All we are saying is that current information is used for judgemental purposes only if it fits a contingent background statement. This is our general sense of the "rule" concept. Thus, a former instance (e.g., experiencing an electric shock upon touching one's hair dryer) may be recorded in memory as a contingent expectancy linking the touching of that specific dryer with being electrocuted. This would lead to the judgement that Mary who uttered a shrill cry upon touching the dryer, did so because of the electric shock she suffered. In our analysis, this represents an instance wherein touching the dryer constituted *evidence* that Mary will be shocked, because of the background knowledge linking the two events in a contingent fashion.

example, one may believe strongly or only weakly in the proposition "All MIT graduates are engineers", with all the different shades of belief or disbelief in between. A strong belief renders the antecedent category and the information that instantiates it (in our example, the knowledge that "Laura is an MIT graduate") highly relevant to the conclusion. In contrast, complete disbelief renders the information (instantiating the antecedent term) irrelevant as evidence. Consider the statement "All persons weighing above 150 lb. are medical doctors". We all disbelieve this particular statement, and hence consider the information that a target weighs 162 lb. completely irrelevant to the judgement of whether she is a doctor. Degrees of belief in a linkage between the antecedent and the consequent terms in a given inference rule (a major premise) constitute a continuum defining the parameter of perceived relevance a given bit of information possesses regarding a given conclusion. We assume, quite unsurprisingly, that the greater the perceived relevance of the evidence to the conclusion, the greater its impact on judgements.

The subjective relevance parameter is of pivotal importance to the judgement process. It is the "jewel in the parametric crown", in reference to which the remaining judgemental parameters (described below) are auxiliary. As we shall see, the latter parameters refer to various *enabling conditions* affording the full realisation of the *relevance potential* of the "information given" *to*, or actively wrested *by*, the individual. These enabling parameters are considered next.

Experienced difficulty of the judgemental task. The first parameter described in this category is experienced difficulty of the judgemental task. Its value may depend on such factors as the length and complexity of the information confronted by the individual, the information's ordinal position in the informational sequence, its saliency, accessibility from memory of the pertinent inference rules, and our evolutionarily evolved capacity to deal with various information types (such as frequencies vs ratios, cf., Cosmides & Tooby, 1996; Gigerenzer & Hoffrage, 1995; but see Evans, Handley, Perham, Over, & Thompson, 2000).

Within the unimodel, perceived difficulty is treated as a parameter ranging from great ease (e.g., when the information appears early, is simple, brief, salient, and fitting a highly accessible inference rule) to considerable hardship (e.g., when the information is late-appearing, lengthy, complex, non-salient, and/or fitting only a relatively inaccessible rule). Generally, the ease of information processing enables a quick, and relatively effortless realisation of its degree of judgemental relevance, whereas the difficulty of processing hinders such a realisation.

Magnitude of processing motivation. The magnitude of motivation to engage in extensive information processing en route to judgement is determined variously by the individual's information-processing goals, such as accuracy (Chaiken et al., 1989; Petty & Cacioppo, 1986), accountability (Tetlock, 1985), need for cognition (Cacioppo & Petty, 1982), the need to evaluate (Jarvis & Petty, 1996), or the need for cognitive closure (Kruglanski & Webster, 1996; Webster & Kruglanski, 1998). For instance, the higher the magnitude of accuracy motivation or need for cognition, the greater the degree of processing motivation. By contrast, the higher the magnitude of need for closure, the lesser the degree of such motivation.

Magnitude of processing motivation may be additionally determined by the desirability of initially forming beliefs. If such beliefs were desirable, the individual would be disinclined to engage in further information processing, lest the current conclusions be undermined by further data. On the other hand, if one's current beliefs were undesirable, the individual would be inclined to process further information that hopefully would serve to alter the initial, undesirable, notions (Ditto & Lopez, 1992).

We assume, again unsurprisingly, that the higher the degree of processing motivation, the greater the individual's readiness to invest effort in information processing, and hence the greater her or his readiness to cope with difficult-to-process information. Thus, if some particularly relevant information was presented in a format that rendered it difficult to decipher, a considerable amount of processing motivation would be needed to enable the realisation of its relevance.

Cognitive capacity.   Another factor assumed to affect individuals' processing efforts is their momentary cognitive capacity, determined by such factors as cognitive busyness, i.e., the alternative tasks they are attempting to execute in parallel, as well as by their degree of alertness and energy vs exhaustion or mental fatigue (e.g., Webster, Richter, & Kruglanski, 1998). We assume that a recipient whose cognitive capacity is depleted would be less successful in decoding complex or lengthy information, and hence less impacted by such information as compared to an individual with a full cognitive capacity at his or her disposal. Capacity drainage will also favour the use of highly accessible as well as simple decision rules (and related evidence) over less accessible and/or more complex rules that are more difficult to retrieve from background knowledge (e.g., Chaiken et al., 1989). In short, the less is one's cognitive capacity at a given moment, the less will be one's ability to process information, particularly if doing so appeared difficult, complicated, and laborious.

Motivational bias.   Occasionally, individuals do not particularly care about the judgemental outcome—i.e., the conclusion they may reach—or about the judgemental process whereby it was reached. Where they do so care, we speak of motivational bias (see also Dunning, 1999; Kruglanski, 1989,

1990, 1999; Kunda, 1990; Kunda & Sinclair, 1999). In principle, all possible goals may induce such bias under the appropriate circumstances, rendering judgements congruent with the goal desirable and those incongruent with the goal undesirable. Thus, the *ego defensive*, *ego enhancing*, and *impression management* goals discussed by Chaiken et al. (1989) may induce motivational biases, but so many sundry other goals would render the use of specific information (e.g., the use of specific, conversationally appropriate inference rules, Grice, 1975) or specific conclusions particularly desirable to the individual, e.g., prevention and promotion goals (Higgins, 1997), goals of competence, autonomy, or relatedness (Ryan, Sheldon, Kasser, & Deci, 1996), etc. Motivational biases may enhance the realisation (or use) of subjectively relevant information yielding such conclusions, and hinder the realisation of subjectively relevant information yielding the opposite conclusions (cf. Dunning, 1999; Kunda & Sinclair, 1999). Again, we view the degree of motivational bias as lying on a continuum ranging from an absence of bias to considerable bias with regard to a given judgemental topic.

Processing sequence. This parameter concerns the sequence in which the information is considered by the individual. Specifically, conclusions derived from prior processing can serve as evidential input, in which terms subsequent inferences are made. Thus, for example, several prior conclusions can combine to form a subsequent, aggregate, judgement (Anderson, 1971; Fishbein & Ajzen, 1975). In addition, prior conclusions can affect the construction of specific inference rules whereby subsequent, ambiguous, information is interpreted. Given that a source has been classified as "intelligent", for example, her or his subsequent, ambiguous, pronouncements may be interpreted as "clever". Given that an actor has been classified as a "middle-class housewife" the epitaph "hostile" may be interpreted as referring to "verbal aggressiveness", whereas given that she has been classified as a "ghetto resident", "hostile" may be interpreted to mean "physical aggression" (cf. Duncan, 1976).

The parameters' properties: Continua vs dichotomies. The present parametric approach is distinct in major ways from the prevalent dual-process paradigm. A critical difference is that the dual-process models assume *qualitative dichotomies* (e.g., between central and peripheral processes, heuristic and systematic processes, heuristic and extensional reasoning, or category-based and individuating processing), whereas all our parameters represent *continua* (e.g., recipients may have differing degrees of processing motivation, or of cognitive capacity, they may experience greater or lesser difficulty in addressing a given judgemental task, or they may perceive the information given as more or less relevant to the judgemental topic). As Reber (1997, p. 52) recently commented: "Psychologists just can't seem to resist dichotomies … we seem ineluctably drawn to setting up poles rather than recognizing continua. Alas, this tendency often functions as a hindrance to doing good science." We agree.

Admittedly, some dual-process models explicitly incorporate continua into their formulations. Most notably, Petty and Cacioppo (1986) discuss a continuum of elaboration likelihood that runs from brief elaboration to extensive and thorough elaboration "received by the message" (p. 129). However, as shown later, the "brief and shallow" processing at one end of the continuum targets peripheral cues, whereas the thorough and extensive elaboration targets issue and message arguments. Thus, the elaboration likelihood model blends together the degree of elaboration and the information being elaborated (cues vs message arguments). Similarly, Fiske and Neuberg (1990) propose a "continuum" model that extends from the early consideration of one type of content (i.e., "social categories") to subsequent consideration of another content ("individuating" or "attribute" information), given sufficient motivation and capacity. Hence, once again, the quantitative continuum of processing sequences from "early" to "late" processed information is intimately bound here with *contents* of the information processed (categories vs attributes), and it is the contents of information that lend the air of qualitative difference to Fiske and Neuberg's (1990) dual modes. In short, whereas the dual-process models assume (content-laden) *qualitative* differences in the ways judgements are reached, the unimodel accounts for variability in judgements in thoroughly *quantitative* terms related to the parameter values.

The parameters' role in judgement formation

What specific role do the foregoing parameters play in judgement formation? As already noted, our key parameter is subjective relevance. All the remaining parameters define conditions allowing the subjective relevance parameter to take effect. Thus, where the information-processing task is difficult, the information's relevance may not be accurately realised unless the individual had an appropriately high degree of processing motivation and cognitive capacity to handle the difficulty. The more difficult the task, the more motivation and capacity would be required to discern the information's (subjective) relevance to the judgement. Similarly, the ordinal position parameter may supply "grist" for the "relevance mill" by yielding on-line conclusions serving as evidence for subsequent inferences, e.g., of combinatorial (cf. Anderson, 1971; Fishbein & Ajzen, 1975) or interpretative nature. It is in the foregoing sense that the parameters of motivation, capacity, task difficulty, and ordinal position play an *auxiliary* or *enabling* role with respect to the crucial parameter of subjective relevance.

Over the years, different judgemental models highlighted distinct judgemental parameters out of the present set. For example, the "probabilogical" models of McGuire (1960, 1968) or Wyer (1970) emphasised the syllogistic relation between evidence and conclusions, related to the present relevance parameter. Motivational bias was highlighted in models of cognitive dissonance (Festinger, 1957) or motivated reasoning (Kunda, 1990; Kunda & Sinclair, 1999). It was also accorded some attention in contemporary dual-process models (e.g., Chaiken et al., 1989; Petty & Cacioppo, 1986), although these models emphasised in particular the factors of nondirectional motivation and cognitive capacity, to the relative neglect of evidential relevance considerations. Most judgemental models in the social psychological literature paid relatively little attention to perceived difficulty of the judgemental task, and none of the prior models to our knowledge attempted to elucidate the full set of judgementally relevant parameters. As a consequence, much judgemental research failed to control for some of these parameters, leaving the door open to rival alternative interpretations of the findings.

For instance, in research claiming support for a qualitative difference in the processing of heuristic or peripheral cues vs message arguments (Chaiken et al., 1989; Petty & Cacioppo, 1986) one would need to control for the difficulty of processing these two types of information, their degree of perceived relevance to the judgemental topic, the desirability of conclusions each may yield given the participants' momentary motivation, etc. The same holds for research claiming support for a qualitative difference in the processing of social category vs individuating attribute information (Fiske & Neuberg, 1990), statistical vs heuristic information (Tversky & Kahneman, 1974), or behavioural identity vs dispositional trait information (Trope & Alfieri, 1997). Such controls have been conspicuous in their absence from large bodies of judgemental work. Instead, such work typically confounded *informational contents* with *parameter values*; hence, the latter provide a general alternative interpretation of results often cited in support of various dual-process models.

In what follows, we consider such a reinterpretation in four major areas of dual-process work: (1) persuasion, (2) attribution, (3) impression formation, and (4) biases and heuristics. Space considerations make it impossible to exhaustively consider all of the various dual-process models in the literature. Extrapolation of the present reasoning to alternative dual-process models is straightforward, however, and can be readily undertaken.

PERSUASION

The elaboration likelihood model and the heuristic-systematic model

Influential dual-process models in the realm of persuasion have been (1) Petty and Cacioppo's (1983, 1986) elaboration likelihood model (ELM), and (2) Chaiken's (1980; Chaiken et al., 1989) heuristic-systematic model

(HSM). Although distinct from each other in several respects (for discussions, see Eagly & Chaiken, 1993; Petty, 1994) these models' fundamental view of persuasion shared significant commonalities: Both approached it from a cognitive perspective (cf. Greenwald, 1968; Petty, Ostrom, & Brock, 1981) and located persuasive "action" within the recipient's ongoing mental processes. Relatedly, both assigned an important role to recipients' processing motivation and cognitive capacity. Finally, and of special present interest, both drew a distinction between *two* qualitatively different informational inputs impinging upon the recipient. One of these, common to the ELM and the HSM, consisted in the processing of information contained in the message arguments or otherwise related to the issue or topic under consideration. The second, conceptualised somewhat differently in the two models, consisted of the processing of information unrelated to the topic or the issue, yet capable of fostering persuasion under some circumstances.

In the HSM, the latter information went under the label of "heuristic cues" assumed to call to mind "simple decision rules" to which a recipient may subscribe (Eagly & Chaiken, 1993, p. 327). In the ELM it was referred to as "peripheral cues" that, while not formally defined, referred to a host of factors extraneous to the issue, such as source expertise, consensus information, number of arguments provided, speed of the communicator's speech, recipient's mood, etc. (for discussion, see Petty & Cacioppo, 1986, p. 130). In both the ELM and the HSM then, "peripheral cues" or "heuristics" have been pervasively juxtaposed to message arguments or issue-related information.

A major common feature of the ELM and the HSM has been their integration of the motivation/capacity factors with the informational distinction between message arguments and cues or heuristics. It was that integration, specifically, that defined the two qualitatively distinct modes of persuasion, of pivotal importance to both models: According to their analysis, when motivation and capacity are plentiful, persuasion is accomplished via the "central" (in the ELM) or the "systematic" mode (in the HSM), consisting of the extensive elaboration and processing of *message or issue information*. By contrast, when motivation and/or capacity are scarce, persuasion is accomplished via the "peripheral" (in the ELM) or the "heuristic" (in the HSM) mode consisting of a relatively brief and shallow processing of various ("peripheral" or "heuristic") *cues*.

Empirical research in the dual-mode paradigm

In a typical dual-mode persuasion experiment, the peripheral or heuristic cues are presented up-front, and the message arguments come subsequently. Moreover, the message arguments are typically lengthier and more complex than the heuristic or peripheral cues. Kruglanski and Thompson (1999) recently reviewed the persuasion literature and found this to be so in the preponderance of cases. Either length, complexity, and/or the order of presentation could have rendered the message arguments more difficult to process than the heuristic cues. In terms of the present analysis, past persuasion research within the dual-mode framework might have confounded the contents of persuasive information (i.e., cues vs message arguments) with values on the processing difficulty parameter. That could be the reason why the cues typically exerted their persuasive effect under low processing motivation or cognitive capacity, whereas the message arguments typically did so under high motivation and capacity. If so, controlling for processing difficulty of cues and message arguments should eliminate the statistical interactions between information type and motivation or cognitive capacity, which heretofore constituted one of the most robust bulwarks of evidence for the dual-modes notion in the persuasion domain.

Unimodel-based persuasion research

Impact of lengthy source information under high issue involvement. We proceeded to explore the above notions in several studies. Thus, in an early experiment (Kruglanski & Thompson, 1999, Study 1) we presented the source information lengthily rather than briefly (as was typically done in prior research). It consisted of a curriculum vitae which indicated that the source was either competent or not. After having received the source information, all participants were given the same one-page essay in which the communicator presented arguments in favour of the attitude topic (comprehensive exams). Orthogonally to the expertise information, we manipulated participants' involvement in the issue. We found that only the involved, but not the uninvolved, participants were persuaded more by the expert vs the inexpert source. It appears then that it is not the content or type of information that matters, but rather its processing difficulty. At any rate, the motivational factor of issue involvement seems to have a similar effect on ("heuristic") information about the source as it was shown to have on message argument information in prior research.

In subsequent research (Kruglanski & Thompson, 1999, Study 3), we found that long expertise information had a persuasive effect only in the absence of distraction, mimicking message argument effects in prior research (Petty, Wells, & Brock, 1976). By contrast, short expertise information had an effect only in the presence of distraction, consistent with the dual-mode prediction for peripheral or heuristic information in general. In yet another study (Erb, Pierro, Mannetti, Spiegel, & Kruglanski, 2003, Study 1), we manipulated the length of the expertise information orthogonally to the degree of involvement. We found that the short expertise information had greater impact under low involvement, replicating the expertise effects of prior research, whereas the long expertise information had greater impact under high involvement, mimicking the message argument effects of prior research (see Figure 1).

Kruglanski and Thompson (1999, Study 4) obtained the same effects for brief (and up-front) vs lengthy (and later-appearing) message argument information. Specifically, the brief initial arguments had greater impact under low involvement, mimicking the typical findings with "peripheral" or "heuristic" information, whereas the subsequent lengthy arguments had greater impact under high involvement, replicating the typical message argument effects.

Need for closure augments the impact of early source or message information.   In a typical persuasion study, the heuristic or peripheral information comes before the message information. Thus, a confounding

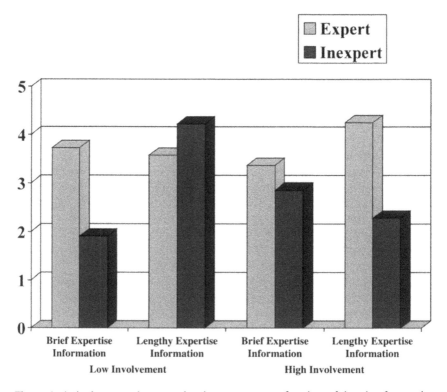

Figure 1. Attitudes towards comprehensive exams as a function of length of expertise information and involvement.

exists between order of presentation (and thus the processing sequence parameter) and information type (message argument or heuristic/peripheral information). It is possible that part of the reason why the peripheral/ heuristic source information exerted its effect primarily under low processing motivation is that the processing sequence matters, and under low magnitude of processing motivation participants were *motivated to stop soon*, and hence to base their judgements on the early information. Consistent with this analysis, we (Erb et al., 2003) found that the need for closure, a variable known to effect the "seizing" and "freezing" on early information (Kruglanski & Webster, 1996; Webster & Kruglanski, 1998), enhanced the impact of the source, *or* the message information where it appeared early in the informational sequence, i.e., prior to the alternative information type (i.e., message and source information, respectively). These data are summarised in Figure 2.

Biased processing of persuasive information. Both the ELM and the HSM hold that central-route or systematic processing can occasionally be biased by heuristic or peripheral cues (e.g., Bohner, Ruder, & Erb, 2002; Chaiken & Maheswaran, 1994; Erb, Bohner, Schmälzle, & Rank, 1998; Petty, Schuman, Richman, & Strathman, 1993). Significantly, within the dual-process models, the biasing hypothesis is *asymmetrical*: It is the heuristic or peripheral cues that are presumed capable of biasing subsequent systematic or central processing, but not vice versa. The reason for the asymmetry is obvious: Because in prior persuasion studies "cues" typically appeared before the message arguments, it does not make much sense to ask whether their processing might be biased by the ("central" or "systematic") processing of message arguments. But the unimodel removes the constraint on processing sequence, hence it affords the question whether *any* information type might be capable of biasing the processing of subsequent information provided one was sufficiently motivated to consider the latter. How might that occur?

Simply, the early information could make accessible certain conclusions serving as evidence for further inference rules in whose light the subsequent information might be interpreted (Higgins, Rholes, & Jones, 1977). We conducted two experiments to test this idea (Erb et al., 2003). In the first, we looked at the biasing effects of early message arguments on processing subsequent message arguments, and in the second, at biasing effects of early message arguments on processing subsequent source information.

Thus, in the first study participants were given information consisting entirely of message arguments. The initial argument was of either high or low quality. The subsequent five arguments were constant for all the participants and were all of moderate quality. Orthogonally to the quality of initial arguments, we manipulated processing motivation (high vs low) via

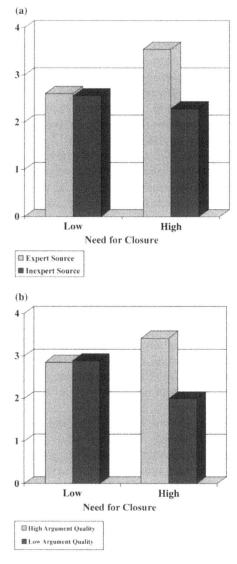

Figure 2. (a) Attitudes towards comprehensive exams as a function of early-appearing source information and need for closure. Figure adopted from Kruglanski, A. W., Sleeth-Keppler, D., Erb, H.-P., Pierro, A., Mannetti, L., Fishbach, A., & Spiegel, S. (2002). All you need is one: The persuasion unimodel and its dual-mode alternatives. *New Review of Social Psychology*, *1*, 62–71. (b) Attitudes towards comprehensive exams as a function of early-appearing message argument information and need for closure. Figure adopted from Kruglanski, A. W., Sleeth-Keppler, D., Erb, H.-P., Pierro, A., Mannetti, L., Fishbach, A., & Spiegel, S. (2002). All you need is one: The persuasion unimodel and its dual-mode alternatives. *New Review of Social Psychology*, *1*, 62–71.

accountability instructions. We found that attitudes towards the aspects highlighted in the subsequent arguments (those constant for all the participants) were biased by the initial message argument, but this occurred only when recipients were sufficiently motivated to process the subsequent arguments (high accountability). Specifically, in the high motivation condition attitudes towards those aspects of the issue mentioned in the subsequent arguments were significantly more positive when the initial argument was of high vs low quality. In the low motivation condition this difference disappeared (see Table 1a).

We also found that the thought listings generated in response to the subsequent (constant) arguments were affected by initial argument quality, but only under high processing motivation. In that condition, thoughts generated in response to those arguments were more positive when the initial argument quality was high vs low.

Path analyses additionally demonstrated that under high (but not under low) processing motivation, persuasion was mediated by the biased processing of the subsequent arguments in light of the earlier arguments.

TABLE 1
Biased processing of persuasive information

| | (a) Motivation | | | |
| | Low | | High | |
Initial argument	Weak	Strong	Weak	Strong
Attitudes towards message aspects	6.29	6.66	5.93	6.76
Cognitive responses towards message aspects	+ 0.17	− 0.02	− 0.04	+ 0.21

| | (b) Order of presentation | | | |
| | After | | Before | |
Argument quality	Weak	Strong	Weak	Strong
Perceived expertise	6.04	6.08	5.22	6.92
Cognitive responses towards communicator description	+ 0.06	+ 0.08	− 0.18	+ 0.17

(a) Attitudes towards subsequent message aspects and cognitive responses towards subsequent message aspects as a function of motivation and the quality of the initial argument quality. (b) Perceived expertise of the communicator and cognitive responses towards the communicator description as a function of order of presentation and the quality of the brief argument. Higher numbers indicate more favourable attitudes (range from 1, *unfavourable*, to 9, *favourable*) and more favourable thoughts (range from − 1, *exclusively unfavourable thoughts listed*, to + 1, *exclusively favourable thoughts listed*).

Sobel test analyses confirmed that in the high motivation condition, the effect of the initial argument on attitude judgements was mediated by biased processing of the subsequent arguments. Under low motivation the valence of the initial argument determined the thoughts about this particular argument, which in turn determined attitude judgements. There was no mediation here by thoughts about the subsequent arguments; hence, no evidence for biased processing.

Our second study reversed the typical order of presentation by placing in one condition message arguments (of high or low quality) *before* (rather than after) the source information (of moderate expertise, constant for all participants). In the second condition, source information came first, followed by the (high or low quality) message argument. All participants were placed under high processing motivation. The results revealed that the perceived expertise of the communicator was appropriately biased by the argument's quality but only when the argument preceded, and not when it succeeded, the source information (Table 1b). In turn, biased processing of the source information mediated the brief argument's effect on attitude judgements, when it preceded but not when it succeeded the source information.

Taken as a body, the research reviewed above suggests that the contents of persuasive information do not matter. What matters are the parameter values (the processing difficulty, processing motivation, and order of presentation parameters). When these are controlled for, prior pervasive *differences* between the peripheral or heuristic processing of "cues" and the central or systematic processing of issue- or message-related information disappear.

Remaining questions about the dual-mode models of persuasion

The place of "cues" and "arguments" on the elaboration continuum. As noted above, in ELM-inspired research the distinction between "cues" and "message arguments" has been confounded with difficulty of information processing. It is of interest to ask, however, whether such confounding is limited merely to the operational level, or whether it represents a more fundamental feature of the theoretical formulation. In a recent statement, Petty, Wheeler, and Bizer (1999, p. 157) denied the latter. As they put it, "In the ELM, content (e.g., source variables, message variables) and process ... are orthogonal. That is, one can engage in effortful scrutiny of source factors, message factors and other factors ...". Nonetheless, note that in the major statement of the model by Petty and Cacioppo (1986, p. 129) the low end of the elaboration continuum is associated with the use of "cues" *as well as* with low processing motivation or capacity, while the high end is associated with processing issue-related information *as well as* with high motivation and capacity. Thus, a theoretical confounding does seem to be implied here between *what* is processed (i.e., "cues" or "message arguments") and *how extensively* it is processed.

Multiple functions of variables in persuasion.   An important assumption of the ELM is that the same variables can serve different persuasive functions. Thus, a source variable can serve in the function of a message argument (e.g., source attractiveness can be an argument in favour of a cosmetic product) and a message can serve in a cue function (Petty, 1994; Petty & Cacioppo, 1986). But the essential question is how exactly do the "cue" and "message" functions *differ*? Clearly, if something was considered to serve a cue function simply because it was processed briefly, and an argument function simply because it was processed extensively, the distinction between cue and argument functions would reduce, simply, to the extent of processing dimension, replacing a qualitative dichotomy by a quantitative continuum (captured by the unimodel's processing motivation and capacity parameters), and hence removing the basis for a dual-mode formulation.

Nor does there seem to be any effective alternative way of conceptually distinguishing between "cue" and "argument" *functions*. Petty et al. (1999) exemplified the "cue function" by the *counting of arguments* and the argument function as *processing the substance of the message*. They insisted on the qualitative difference in modes of processing beyond mere quantitative variation inherent in the notion of the elaboration continuum. As they put it (p. 161), "... the key question ... is whether all persuasion findings can be explained by this quantitative variation. If so, then the qualitative variation postulated by the ELM (and some other dual-route models) would not be necessary." Of course, they concluded that it is necessary and that, *contrary to our present claims*, it is unrelated to differences in informational contents. To demonstrate this point, Petty et al. (1999) cited research by Petty and Cacioppo (1984) wherein counting the arguments (three vs nine) constituted the "cue", juxtaposed to the substance of the "message arguments". But note that the "number of arguments" represents a *content* of information every bit as much as the substance of the arguments, whatever it may be. Just as the substance of arguments may indicate to the recipient that the conclusion is valid, so too can the number of arguments (many vs few) to someone subscribing to the appropriate premise, e.g., "If there are so many arguments it must be good" (as Petty et al., 1999, p. 161, explicitly recognised). Indeed, Petty et al. (1999, p. 161) acknowledged that both the processing of cues and of message arguments "... could reasonably ... (represent) ... some type of if-then reasoning" [parenthesis ours]. This is in accord with our present assumption that the "if-then" premises in the two cases contain different *informational contents* (i.e., "cues" or "message arguments") as the antecedent terms in the appropriate "if-then" statements, defining what the persuasive evidence in each case consists of. Thus, while the notions of "many" vs "few" arguments (the product of counting) and the substance of some message (e.g., "graduates of prestigious colleges get better jobs") are clearly different in their informational contents, they fulfil the very same evidential function in accordance with the appropriate prior if-then rules.

Consequences of heuristic/peripheral vs systematic/central processing. Dual-process theorists have consistently argued that attitudes formed via the systematic or central mode are more persistent and resistant to counter-persuasion than attitudes formed via the heuristic or peripheral mode. Empirical research (see Eagly & Chaiken, 1993, pp. 318–319 and p. 620, for a review) basically found that the more effort invested in processing, the more resistant the attitudes. Although a complete discussion of these studies is beyond the present scope, a unimodel-based analysis can readily be applied to this issue. From our perspective, it is conceivable that resistant attitudes emerge from extensive processing under some conditions, but not necessarily from more extensive *issue-related* (vs cue-related) processing. The present analysis implies that extensive processing of peripheral or cue information may well lead to more persistent and resistant attitudes than shallow processing of message arguments. Besides processing effort (captured by the processing motivation and capacity parameters), we would expect other parameters to affect attitude stability as well. For example, attitudes serving an individual's preferred conclusion (motivational bias), e.g., an ego-enhancing judgement, or attitudes based on (subjectively) highly relevant information, e.g., the information that the message comes from the Pope for a Catholic, are likely to persist over time and resist counter-argumentation. Such effects should be independent of processing effort and independent of whether the evidence is of the cue or the message type. These predictions have not been tested so far, and they await explicit probing for their validation.

How are heuristics to be defined?   In response to our analysis, HSM theorists might argue that "heuristics" are by definition brief and simple (cf. Chaiken et al., 1989), hence our creation of lengthy "heuristic" information in research described above is an oxymoron. However, note that if brevity (or simplicity) alone were the sole yardstick for a "heuristic" status, then the pervasive juxtaposition of "heuristics" and "message arguments" would be unwarranted. After all, message arguments too can be brief and simple. Moreover, if *brevity* is the hallmark of "heuristics", the distinction between "heuristic" and "systematic" processing shades into a quantitative continuum of length (captured by the unimodel's difficulty parameter), rather than a qualitative dichotomy. All things considered then, the dual-mode portrayals of persuasion seem vulnerable on both empirical and theoretical grounds.

DISPOSITIONAL ATTRIBUTIONS

In the attribution domain, Trope and his colleagues (Trope, 1986; Trope & Alfieri, 1997; Trope & Liberman, 1996) proposed an influential dual-process model wherein the contextual constraint information impacts *behaviour identification* and *dispositional inference* in qualitatively different ways. At the identification stage, the incorporation of contextual constraints is said to be relatively effortless, automatic, and independent of cognitive resources. By contrast, at the dispositional inference stage the influence of context is said to be controlled, deliberative, and capacity-demanding (Trope & Alfieri, 1997, p. 663).

Trope and Alfieri (1997) tested their dual-process model in two experiments. In their first study, participants were either submitted or not submitted to cognitive load. They then received information about a target person who had given either an unambiguously or an ambiguously positive evaluation of a fellow employee, and had done so under situational constraints prompting either a positive or a negative evaluation of the target. All participants then indicated (1) how positive was the target person's evaluation of the employee (behaviour identification), and (2) how positively the target person *really felt* towards the employee (dispositional inference). The authors predicted and found that *irrespective of load*, participants rated the unambiguously positive evaluation as very positive, and the ambiguous evaluation as more positive when the situational constraints prompted a positive rather than a negative evaluation (presumably because of an assimilation of the ambiguous evaluation to the constraints). These data were interpreted as supportive of the notion that assimilating a behaviour to the context constitutes a resource-independent, effortless task that anyone can carry out, irrespective of cognitive capacity.

The results also indicated that only participants in the no-load condition, but not those under load, were able to subsequently *discount* the situational constraints from their behavioural identification ratings in inferring how much the evaluator really liked the employee. This finding was interpreted as indicating that, unlike behaviour identification, dispositional inference is effortful and resource-dependent, and that people can perform it only if endowed with adequate cognitive capacity.

Trope and Alfieri (1997) also postulated that the effortless and resource-independent way in which the context affects behaviour identifications renders this process relatively irreversible and inflexible, compared to the effortful and resource-dependent manner in which it affects dispositional inference. In contrast, because incorporating the context information into dispositional inferences is considered resource-dependent, the influence of such information should be reversible or revisable on the basis of subsequent relevant evidence. Trope and Alfieri (1997, Experiment 2) reported data consistent with these predictions. Specifically, even after it was invalidated (!), situational information continued to affect the *identification* of a target's behaviour, but it no longer affected the *dispositional inferences* made from the behaviour.

A unimodel-based analysis of assimilative behaviour identifications and dispositional inferences

"Phenotypically", dispositional inference phenomena seem starkly different from instances of persuasion. They contain neither a message nor a communicator, and their major interpretations (e.g., Gilbert & Osborne, 1989; Trope, 1986) do not distinguish between distinct routes or modes of reaching judgements. Moreover, unlike the dual-process models of persuasion, in which the modes represent different ways (or paths) of forming an attitude or an opinion, Trope's (1986) dual-process model of dispositional inferences is dual in the sense of distinguishing between two *sequential* phases whereby inferences are reached. These apparent differences notwithstanding, each of these phases revolves about a judgement, and hence each is explicable in terms of the very same process identified by the unimodel.

From this perspective, each of the phases addresses a different, content-specific, question. The first is the identification question, "*What is it?*". The second is the causal inference question, "*What caused it?*". According to the unimodel both (and in fact, all) questions are answered on the basis of relevant evidence. In these terms, contextual information may constitute evidence relevant both to the behavioural identification and the dispositional attribution questions. For instance, a person's ambiguous facial expression, interpretable alternatively as "happy" or "sad", might be construed as "happy" if the context of the observation was a party, because of the prior assumption that "people generally try to appear happy at parties" and hence, the inference rule, "if party, then happy-appearing". Similarly, if the context consisted of a funeral, one may interpret the expression as "sad" because of the relevance assumption (or an inference rule) whereby "if funeral, then sad-appearing". Note that *only subjectively relevant* aspects of the context will be used to disambiguate the behaviour. Irrelevant aspects (i.e., ones that the individual does not tie strongly to the requisite judgement) should not impact identification. For instance, the individual may rather doubt the statement "if in Amsterdam then happy/sad". Information that an individual was spotted on the Leidseplein, should not appreciably influence the way in which her Mona-Lisa-like smile was demystified, because that particular knowledge would be considered irrelevant to the smile-identification problem.

In exactly the same way that (for some individuals, subscribing to the appropriate lay theories, or inference rules) certain contextual information may constitute relevant evidence *for* a given identification, it may constitute relevant evidence *against* a dispositional attribution. Again, the individual's belief in an "if-then" connection between the contextual information and the situational attribution is crucial. Thus, departing from the premise that "everybody smiles at parties", an individual may reason that "if X smiles at a party, she behaves like everyone else, i.e., non-uniquely", which is inconsistent with a *dispositional* attribution of the smiling, defined in terms of its uniqueness.

In short, the role of contextual information in behavioural identification and dispositional inference is the same. In both cases it serves as *relevant evidence* for reaching a given, albeit a different, conclusion. Just as with behavioural identification, irrelevant contextual information, e.g., that the smiling occurred in Amsterdam, should have no impact on dispositional attributions because of a lack of a prior subjective "if-then" belief linking Amsterdam to smiling.

The *perceived difficulty of processing* parameter also applies alike to behaviour identification and dispositional attribution judgements. For instance, the contextual constraint information may be presented in a salient manner, and/or the rule linking it to the behavioural identification may be highly accessible. This would render the information relatively easy to process. Alternatively, the information may be presented in a pallid fashion and the inference rule that lends it relevance may be relatively inaccessible; this would render it relatively difficult to process. Other factors affecting the difficulty of processing might be the informational "signal to noise ratio" in the stimulus material, or the degree to which the pertinent evidence is imbedded in diluting information. All such factors are assumed to function identically with respect to behaviour identification and dispositional attribution judgements.

According to the unimodel, the more difficult the judgemental task, the more processing motivation and/or cognitive capacity should be required to properly carry it out. From that perspective, it is quite possible that Trope and Alfieri's (1997) findings pertain to a situation wherein, for some reason, using the contextual information to answer the *identification* question was relatively easy, demanded little cognitive capacity and, consequently, was unaffected by cognitive load, whereas using that same information to answer the *dispositional inference* question was for some reason relatively difficult, demanding, and hence sensitive to load.

That the dispositional inference question can be independent of load in some circumstances has, in fact, already been demonstrated in a series of studies by Trope and Gaunt (2000). Each of their three experiments varied a different knowledge activation factor. One experiment varied the *saliency* of the contextual information, another varied its *accessibility*, and the third varied its *specificity*. As Trope and Gaunt (2000, p. 344) summarised it, this research found, " ... that cognitive load eliminated discounting when situational information was low in salience, accessibility, or specificity. However, when situational information was more salient, accessible, or specific, it produced strong discounting effects even when perceivers were under cognitive load ...". We view these interesting results as at odds with a dual-process model that portrays dispositional inferences (in counter-distinction to behavioural identifications) as *inherently* exigent of resources and hence sensitive to load. But is it the case that assimilative behaviour identifications can be sensitive to load in some circumstances?

We (Chun, Spiegel & Kruglanski, 2002) conducted three separate experiments addressed at that question, all varying the difficulty of information processing in reference to the behaviour identification judgement. These studies were modelled in most pertinent details after the ambiguous behaviour condition of Trope and Alfieri's (1997) research. Cognitive load was manipulated by asking participants to recite an eight-digit number silently to themselves vs not. Consistent with the unimodel, participants' perception of the ambiguous behaviour was independent of cognitive load where the behaviour identification task was made easy (by increasing the saliency of the behavioural or the contextual information), but was significantly dependent on load where this task was difficult (see Figure 3a and b).

Furthermore, where the task was easy, invalidating the contextual information did not affect prior behavioural identifications, replicating Trope and Alfieri (1997). However, where the task was difficult, apparently making the participants self-conscious about the way they reached their judgements, invalidating the contextual constraint information eradicated its effects on behavioural identification (see Figure 4).

In short, the research reviewed above suggests that it is not necessary to posit *qualitatively distinct* judgemental processes for the phases of behaviour identification and dispositional inference. The available evidence suggests that when the parameter of processing difficulty is controlled for (as well it should be), the putative processing differences between these phases are eliminated.

IMPRESSION FORMATION

Impression formation has constituted a central domain of dual-process theorising. Two influential models in this area have been those of Fiske and

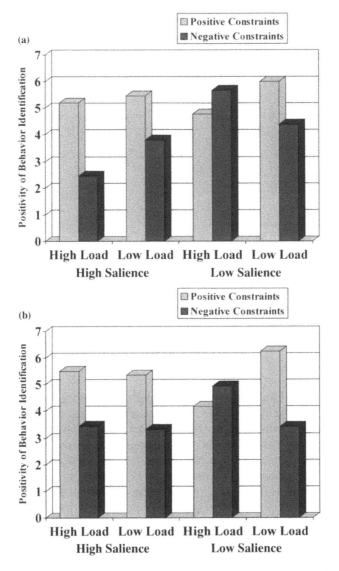

Figure 3. (a) Behaviour identification ratings as a function of situational information, salience of situational constraint information, and cognitive load. Figure adopted from Chun, W. Y., Spiegel, S., & Kruglanski, A. W. (2002). Assimilative behavior identification can also be resource-dependent: A unimodel perspective on personal-attribution phases. *Journal of Personality and Social Psychology*, *83*, 542–555. (b) Behaviour identification ratings as a function of situational constraint information, behaviour saliency, and cognitive load. Figure adopted from Chun, W. Y., Spiegel, S., & Kruglanski, A. W. (2002). Assimilative behavior identification can also be resource-dependent: A unimodel perspective on personal-attribution phases. *Journal of Personality and Social Psychology*, *83*, 542–555.

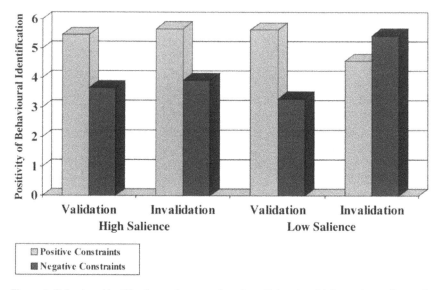

Figure 4. Behaviour identification ratings as a function of situational information, salience of situational constraints and behavioural information, and situational validation. Figure adopted from Chun, W. Y., Spiegel, S., & Kruglanski, A. W. (2002). Assimilative behavior identification can also be resource-dependent: A unimodel perspective on personal-attribution phases. *Journal of Personality and Social Psychology, 83,* 542–555.

Neuberg (1990: Fiske et al., 1999) and of Brewer (1988). Although these conceptualisations differ in some important regards, they nonetheless share striking features, crucial from the unimodel's perspective: Perhaps most important among these is that they both distinguish between category-based and attribute-based processing and view them as qualitatively different. Category-based processing is assumed to be "top-down" and attribute-based processing "bottom-up" (Brewer, 1988, p. 4; Fiske & Neuberg, 1990, p. 60).

Both models also assume that impression formation follows a fixed order whereby it commences with an automatic identification of the target in terms of some general categories. According to Fiske and Neuberg (1990, p. 10) "the category label is more likely to be a social grouping (demographic category, role, job) than a single personality trait". Subsequently, if the incoming information and the individual's self-involvement warrant it, she or he may continue processing information and at the end might process individuating or personal attribute information as well. In Brewer's (1988, p. 23) model, for example, personalisation requires a sufficient degree of self-involvement, which allows "… attributes and behaviors … inconsistent with previously established expectancies [to] be processed extensively and incorporated into the person representation ...". In Fiske and Neuberg's (1990, pp. 5–6) model, if the target is "minimally interesting or personally relevant ... then the perceiver will attend to ... information necessary to form an impression beyond the essentially perceptual, rapid initial categorization ...".

We readily accept the notion of a continuum common to Fiske and Neuberg's (1990) and Brewer's (1988) models. In fact, all our parameters represent quantitative continua on which judgemental situations could vary. We differ from these dual-process models of impression formation, however, with regard to the assumptions that (1) particular contents of information (related, e.g., to social categories) invariably will be processed first, or are assigned greater weight in the overall judgement under some motivational/ cognitive capacity conditions than are other contents, and that (2) judgement based on some types of information (e.g., on social categories) is mediated by a qualitatively different process from judgement based on other types of information (e.g., on attribute information).

Primacy.   According to the unimodel, the sequence in which information is processed and impacts judgement is generally independent of contents *per se.* Instead, primacy depends on whether the information is seen as relevant to the judgement and on the readiness with which such relevance is recognised by the individual (determined by such factors as the information's salience and accessibility and/or accessibility of the rules that lend the information its relevance). The role of subjective relevance was noted by Medin (1988, p. 122). As he put it, "The response should depend on what information is *needed* and how well that information can be predicted from knowledge about who the person is, what groups they can be classified into, or what situation is instantiated ..." [emphasis ours]. Exactly the same point was implied earlier by Bruner (1957) namely that "... a primary determinant of category activation is the search requirements imposed by the perceiver's needs, objectives and task goals ..." (cited in Brewer, 1988, p. 18).

Categories vs attributes?   Furthermore, it is doubtful that a "social category" and a "personal attribute" can be meaningfully distinguished from each other as far as the judgemental process is concerned. In the statement "Judy is a nurse", the term "nurse" (i.e., a social category) can be readily considered one of Judy's attributes, as may the category "friendly person" in the statement "Judy is friendly". As Klatzky and Andersen (1988, p. 98) noted, "Even individualized person concepts have associated attributes and ... these attributes are themselves social categories ...". Medin (1988, p. 122) expanded on this point to say, "if every person were treated as absolutely unique, then there would be no basis at all for generating expectations. This would be analogous to the situation of a physician being confronted with a totally new disease unlike any other ...".

To summarise then, the information utilised upon an encounter with a social stimulus may indeed represent a "social" *category* or a "trait/ attribute" *category*, all depending on their subjective relevance ("search requirements", "task goals", or "informational needs") to the judgement at hand. As far as the judgemental process is concerned, "social categories" and "traits" or "attributes" are functionally equivalent in constituting evidence for the requisite judgement.

It seems, furthermore, that impression formation models conceived of a social category in the singular (i.e., *the* category within which the stimulus person is placed during the identification phase) whereas they conceived of the personal attributes in the plural (i.e., the *various* attributes that need to be pieced together, in the "piecemeal" process). However, there is no reason to think of a person as fitting a single category necessarily, or being characterised by multiple attributes necessarily. To reiterate, the distinction between "categories" and "attributes" is essentially one of informational contents and is unrelated to the *number* of categories or attributes that may fit a given individual.

Automaticity. The notion that the *identification stage* (referred to as "categorisation") is necessarily "automatic" and resource-independent was already questioned in connection with the dispositional attribution research described above (Chun et al., 2002). Any information-processing task may be made easy, hence relatively "automatic", or difficult, and hence controlled depending on the circumstances, its degree of routinisation, or the individual's learning history. An identical point was made by E. R. Smith (1988, p. 167) who stated:

> ... the specific dimensions that are classified automatically will depend on people's learning history as well as on context. Practice making particular categorizations or other types of social judgment can lead to automaticity of processing. Thus, there can be no fixed line between dimensions that are processed automatically and those that are not. A new-car salesman who (because of occupational demands) classifies hundreds of people daily as potential customers vs. mere "lookers" may eventually make distinctions along that dimension automatically. In our society race, gender, age and (I would add) socioeconomic status are highly salient determinants of many significant social roles, so they are probably processed automatically by most adults. But this might not hold true in other cultures, while other dimensions (e.g., clan membership) might attain automatic status ...

Bottom-up vs top-down processing? Both Brewer's (1988) and Fiske and Neuberg's (1990) models assume that category-based processing is *top-down* whereas the processing of attribute information is *bottom-up*. But let us take a closer look. Note first that both types of processing involve jointly

(1) contextual information or *data*, and (2) background knowledge or memory *schemata* (cf. Bobrow & Norman, 1975). The distinction between bottom-up and top-down processing refers to the *instigation-provenance* of processing attempts. In the former case the process is instigated by the data (is "data-driven") while in the latter, it is instigated by the schema (is "theory-driven"). Several authors point out that bottom-up and top-down processing co-occur and are inextricably intertwined with each other. Thus, Bobrow and Norman (1975, p. 148) who originally introduced the "bottom-up/top-down" partition noted that, "Both ... processes must go on together; each requires the other." A similar point was made by Ned Jones (1988, p. 86) in his commentary on Brewer's (1988) model. In his words: "There is a suggestion that order of recall will help us maintain the dual process distinction, but I find it hard to believe that this is going to be anything like a truly reliable discrimination since perceivers inevitably go back and forth between the data and its conceptualization ...".

Thus, it may be rather difficult to separate *in any given instance* the occurrence of "bottom-up" from "top-down" processing. Moreover, it should be at least as difficult to substantiate the claim that one type of processing occurs with one type of information (namely with "social categories") and another type of processing with another type of information (namely, "personal attribute" categories).

In summary, careful analysis suggests that, consistent with the unimodel, (1) "social category" information does not need to be generally utilised prior to "personal attribute" information. Rather, each type of information is utilised as a function of its (subjective) relevance to the judgemental problem at hand. More generally, (2) contextually given "category" and "attribute" information types are functionally equivalent as far as the judgemental process is concerned, both serving as "evidence" for requisite judgements. (3) The degree to which given information is processed "automatically" or effortlessly vs effortfully or deliberately is related to its subjective "ease" (determined, e.g., by its degree of routinisation) rather than to its contents (i.e., constituting "social category" or "personal attribute" information). (4) The distinction between "bottom-up" and "top-down" processing may hardly distinguish the differential use of "category" vs "attribute" information. Bottom-up and top-down processing seem inextricably intertwined, and they are involved in the treatment of any type of information (i.e., "category" and "attribute" among others).

Reassessing the empirical evidence for a dual-process model of impression formation

Although the foregoing considerations are consistent with the unimodel, we still need to contend with empirical evidence seemingly corroborating the dual-process models of impression formation. To that end, we consider now two major studies cited in support of Fiske and Neuberg's (1990) dual-process model, namely the Pavelchak (1989) experiment claimed to provide the " ... clearest evidence to date for 2 distinct person evaluation processes: 1 based on liking for person attributes and 1 based on social categorization" (Pavelchak, 1989, p. 354), and the equally important Neuberg and Fiske (1987) study.

The Pavelchak (1989) study.   In the first session of Pavelchak's experiment, participants rated the likeability of 35 academic majors and 50 personality traits. In the second session participants were presented with six stimulus persons, each portrayed via four traits. There were two conditions: *category* and *piecemeal.* In the category condition, participants (1) guessed the targets' academic majors, and (2) rated their likeability. In the piecemeal condition, they rated targets' likeability after exposure to their traits, but *before* guessing their majors. Pavelchak (1989) hypothesised and found that participants in the *category* condition who categorised the targets prior to rating their likeability, rendered likeability ratings that were more congruent with the categories' likeability than with likeability of the traits. Participants in the *piecemeal* condition, by contrast, made likeability ratings that were more congruent with likeability of the traits than of the categories. Pavelchak (1989, p. 361) interpreted these results as offering "clear evidence that there are two distinct modes of person evaluation: one computed from attribute evaluations and one based on category evaluations".

From the unimodel's perspective, however, these results are alternatively explicable in terms of a *differential accessibility* of the "category" information in Pavelchak's (1989) two experimental conditions. Recall that in the *category* condition participants received the information about the target's traits, then guessed her or his major (the category in question), and then rated her or his likeability. Because the category information was generated (guessed at) just prior to rendition of the likeability judgements, it was probably highly accessible to participants due to its recency of activation (cf. Higgins et al., 1977; Srull & Wyer, 1979). As a consequence, it may have readily figured as a basis for participants' likeability judgements rendered immediately afterwards. By contrast, in the *piecemeal* condition, participants rated the target's likeability immediately following their exposure to the target trait descriptions—these were then highly accessible at the moment of rating, and hence constituted a ready basis for likeability judgements. The "category" (i.e., the participant's major) must have been quite inaccessible at that moment; it may even have been *unavailable* in participants' memory (cf. Higgins, King, & Mavin, 1982) as they did not have any particular reason to infer those categories unless specifically instructed to do so by the experimenter (which in the *piecemeal* condition occurred only *after* participants had made the likeability ratings). Thus, it is not surprising that the category in the piecemeal condition exercised limited influence on likeability judgements. Should one reverse the order and activate the trait information closer to the moment of judgement (hence rendering it more accessible) than the category information, the trait information might well then exert the stronger influence upon judgements. These notions could be profitably probed in subsequent research.

The Neuberg and Fiske (1987) study. In the procedure employed by Neuberg and Fiske (1987) participants believed they would interact with a former schizophrenic named Frank. Participants expected to work with Frank in an outcome-dependent or independent fashion. They then read a personal profile (the individuating information) allegedly provided by Frank. Half the participants received a stereotypically and affectively neutral profile, the other half received a profile inconsistent with the schizophrenic label. The main dependent variable was participants' liking for Frank. Neuberg and Fiske (1987) predicted that in the absence of outcome dependency (Experiment 1) or accuracy motivation (Experiment 2), and where the individuating information was neutral, participants should not be particularly motivated to process the information and hence should rely on the category label and evaluate Frank negatively. However, where the individuating information was inconsistent with the category, or where participants were outcome dependent on Frank, they should be motivated to process the individuating information and hence base their liking judgements on such information—that is, render relatively neutral judgements where the individuating information was neutral and relatively positive judgements where the individuating information was positive.

Results of the Neuberg and Fiske (1987) experiments yielded the predicted pattern, which the authors interpreted as support for the dual-process model, and especially for the notion that processing motivation (induced either via outcome dependency, informational inconsistency, or accuracy motivation) encourages attribute-based processing or individuation, whereas the absence (or relatively low level) of processing motivation encourages category-based processing.

But a close look at the Neuberg and Fiske (1987) procedure suggests an alternative interpretation. Specifically, the category information that Frank is a former schizophrenic was presented very briefly (via a single line of text stating that "Frank, ... entered St. Mary's around a year ago as a schizophrenic"; Neuberg & Fiske, 1987, p. 435) and up-front. By contrast, the individuating information was presented subsequently and rather extensively (namely, via a "one page personal profile ostensibly written by Frank about himself", ibid.). It is thus possible that the reason why the category information had greater influence on likeability judgements under low processing motivation is that it was easier to process than the lengthier, more complex, and subsequent individuating information. By the same token, the latter information may have been processed more extensively, and hence exerted greater influence on judgements where the participants' motivation was heightened by the outcome dependency or by a glaring inconsistency between the category and the individuating information.

To explore these notions, we (Chun & Kruglanski, 2003a) created two experimental conditions: one in which, much as in the Neuberg and Fiske (1987) studies, the category information that Frank had been hospitalised as a schizophrenic was presented briefly and up-front, whereas the (positive) individuating information came subsequently and was relatively lengthy. In the second, novel, condition, the individuating information came first and was relatively brief (albeit equated for positivity with that of the lengthy individuating information). It was followed by a relatively lengthy description of the routine life of Frank in a hospital where he had been hospitalised, at the end of which participants learned that the reason for the hospitalisation was schizophrenia (the category information). Orthogonally, we manipulated cognitive load. The results yielded the predicted two-way interaction between informational sequence and load. Where the category information was presented up-front, its relative effect on likeability judgements was *enhanced* under cognitive load (vs the absence of load). In this condition, likeability ratings of Frank were lower under load (vs no load) reflecting the fact that the category "schizophrenic" had negative connotations for our participants. However, where the category information was presented last, its effect on likeability judgements was *undermined* by load, in that the likeability ratings of Frank were higher under load (vs no load) reflecting the reduced relative effect under load of the category vs the individuating information. These results are shown in Figure 5.

Thus, it appears that, just as with any other type of information, category information need not be relied on more where the individual's processing resources are low. Rather, the degree to which any information (including category information) is relied on depends, among others, on the relation of its processing difficulty (determined, e.g., by its length, complexity, and sequential position) to the individual's processing resources.

BIASES AND HEURISTICS

A vastly influential research programme in the psychology of judgement has been the "biases and heuristics" approach launched by a seminal series of papers by Amos Tversky and Daniel Kahneman (e.g., Kahneman & Tversky, 1973; Tversky & Kahneman, 1974, 1983). According to their view,

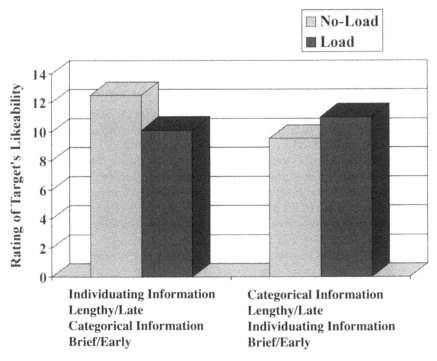

Figure 5. Effects of individuating and categorical information as a function of its length/ complexity and cognitive load.

shared by many researchers to date, people often do not follow the laws of probability calculus but instead apply rules of thumb or heuristics that often lead to judgemental errors, sometimes labelled as *cognitive biases* or *illusions*. This "heuristics and biases" view implies that there is something *qualitatively distinct* about the way people use heuristics vs statistics; reflecting a qualitative difference between what Tversky and Kahneman (1983) referred to as "extensional" vs "intuitive" reasoning. Although no elaborate theory was put forth in support of this distinction, the heuristics and biases view suggested that, much like visual illusions, cognitive illusions too *cannot* be overridden by conscious effort or formal training (for a thorough discussion, see Sedlmeier, 1999).

A very different perspective on the heuristics and biases work is offered by the unimodel. According to this view, "heuristics" and "statistics" represent two content categories of inferential rules whereby judgements may be reached. Other than that, their use and impact is governed by the very same process embodied in the judgemental parameters elaborated earlier.

Subjective relevance of "representativeness" vs "base-rate" rules. Consider the famous "lawyer and engineer" problem used to demonstrate the putatively ubiquitous *base-rate neglect* by lay individuals. In a typical experiment claiming this effect, participants are provided with individuating (or "indicative") information about a target as well as with information about the base-rates of engineers and lawyers in the sample. In judging whether the target is an engineer, for example, the participant might use a "representativeness" rule whereby "If target has characteristic a, b, and c, then he or she is likely/unlikely to be an engineer". Alternatively, the participant might use a "base-rate" rule whereby "If the base-rate in the sample is X, the target is likely/unlikely to be an engineer". In the original demonstrations by Tversky and Kahneman, participants were much more likely to base their likelihood judgement on the representativeness rule rather than on the base-rates, evidencing considerable base-rate neglect. The question is why.

From the unimodel's perspective, a straightforward possibility is that the *constellation of parametric values* in original "base-rate neglect" studies may have favoured for some reason the "representativeness" over the base-rate rule. For instance, it could be that participants perceived the "representativeness" rule as more relevant to the judgement at hand than the "base-rate" rule. Research has indeed established that framing the lawyer–engineer problem as "statistical" or "scientific" appreciably reduced the base-rate neglect (Schwarz, Strack, Hilton, & Naderer, 1991; Zukier & Pepitone, 1984). In present terms, framing might have increased the momentary perceived relevance of the statistical information to the judgement at hand. Another way of accomplishing the same effect would be to alter the "chronic" relevance of the statistical information. This might be accomplished by teaching statistical rules to individuals, hence increasing their belief in an "if-then" statement linking the base-rates, for example, to the likelihood judgements. Indeed, research (Nisbett, Cheng, Fong, & Lehman, 1987; Sedlmeier, 1999) has established that statistical reasoning can be taught and that it can result in the increased use of statistical information. As Sedlmeier recently put it (1999, p. 190): "The pessimistic outlook of the heuristics and biases approach cannot be maintained ... Training about statistical reasoning can be effective ...".

The notion that the use of the base-rates depends on their perceived relevance to the individual is not exactly new (cf. Borgida & Brekke, 1981). As Bar-Hillel (1990, p. 201) aptly remarked:

> ... base-rates are by and large neglected if and when they are considered to be irrelevant to the prediction at hand ... (furthermore) in the ... tasks that dominate laboratory studies of base-rate neglect – base-rates provide only a general informational background on which other information, which typically pertains

more directly or specifically to the target case, is added ... Such information ...
tends to render the arbitrary base-rates subjectively irrelevant ...

Also, "different people may differ in the extent to which they judge base-rates as irrelevant and hence in the extent to which they are inclined to ignore them ..." (ibid., p. 202).

According to Bar-Hillel (1983), in some cases the subjective relevance of base-rates to the prediction task may be indeterminate *even for the statistically sophisticated* (!). In her words (Bar-Hillel, 1983, pp. 58–59), "It would seem ... that any use of base-rates could be justified, provided one can come up with the proper scenario ... [hence] we may need to relax out concept of a 'normative solution' ... [as] intuition is often sensitive to considerations that are not captured by simplistic formal models ...". Thus, even to the statistically enlightened, base-rates need not appear more relevant than alternative ("intuitive") inference rules.

In other words, the parameter of subjective relevance applies equally to statistical and "heuristic" information. Whichever one of these two appears the more relevant to the judgement at hand, is likely to be used as the evidence for the judgement. Ginosar and Trope (1980) found, for example, that when the individuating sketch was non-diagnostic with regard to the engineer–lawyer problem (and hence was considered irrelevant) participants did utilise the base-rates. As Ginosar and Trope (1980, p. 240) noted, "when the individuating information is useless as a guide to prediction attention is shifted ... to the base-rate frequencies ...". Of course, the perceived relevance of any information type, i.e., statistical or "heuristic", to a given judgement is a matter of degree. In one of our studies, we included a condition in which the "representativeness" information was mixed; some was consistent with the engineer stereotype and some with the lawyer stereotype, lowering the subjective relevance of such information to judgement of the target's profession. As compared with the "pure" "representativeness" information, consistent with the engineer stereotype, the "mixed" condition reduced participants' tendency to view the target as an engineer, while enhancing the effect of base-rates (see Figure 6).

Difficulty of information utilisation: Accessibility effects. According to the unimodel, subjective relevance is hardly the sole parameter affecting the use of information. Another such parameter is processing difficulty, related, *inter alia*, to accessibility of the judgemental rule that lends the given information its relevance. Consider the children's riddle "Why is more grass consumed by white sheep than by black sheep?". While many respondents are perplexed by this question, the answer is extremely simple: because there are more white sheep than black sheep. As Bar-Hillel noted (1983, p. 206), "... the sheep riddle works not because people are unaware that a large

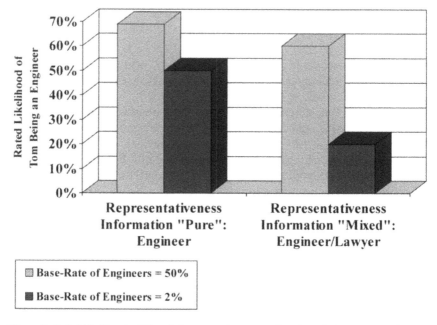

Figure 6. Rated likelihood of Tom being an engineer as a function of the representativeness (subjective relevance) of the individuating information and base-rate information.

population eats more than a smaller one but because *they do not think of the population* when asked the riddle" [emphasis ours]. In other words, although the inference rule "If a population is large, it eats more" may be *available* in the individual's mental repertory, it may be quite *inaccessible* to an individual at the moment of judgement (Higgins et al., 1982). Somewhat analogously, the "psychological" context of most early base-rate neglect studies might have rendered the statistical rules not only less subjectively relevant to participants but also less accessible. This should render their use more difficult, and hence unlikely.

In a study we performed to address this issue (Erb, Fishbach, & Kruglanski, 2003), participants were first primed with words that called to mind statistical information. They were asked to rank order the frequency of occurrence in ordinary speech of 15 words (for details of the procedure, see Erb, Bioy, & Hilton, 2002). In the priming condition the list included words such as "random", "percentage", and "ratio". In the non-priming condition these words were replaced by similar words not representing statistical concepts (e.g., "patio"). In a ostensibly unrelated "second study" we presented the lawyer and engineer problem and varied base-rate information at two levels, either 2% of the sample were engineers and 98% lawyers, or the figures were 50% for each category. As shown in Figure 7, in the no-priming control condition, the base-rate neglect found in the original demonstrations was robustly replicated. However, in our statistical priming condition, sensitivity to base-rates was much increased, in that participants now significantly distinguished between the two percentages (see Figure 7).

Difficulty of information processing: Informational length and complexity. Just as with the processing of message and cue information in persuasive contexts, the processing of statistical and representativeness information may be affected by their length and complexity. In the original demonstrations of base-rate neglect the base-rates were presented briefly, via a single sentence, and up-front. The case information followed and was conveyed via a relatively lengthy vignette. If we assume that participants in those studies had sufficiently high magnitude of processing motivation and cognitive capacity, it is plausible that they were inclined to process the lengthier, more difficult to digest, information and hence may have given it considerable weight, just as in persuasion studies the lengthier, later-appearing information was given considerable weight under high motivation or cognitive capacity conditions.

But if processing difficulty matters, we should be able to increase or decrease the use of statistical information, for example, by varying its processing difficulty orthogonally to participants' capacity or motivation. In

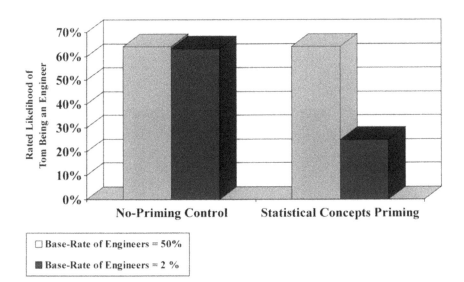

Figure 7. Rated likelihood of Tom being an engineer as a function of priming statistical concepts and base-rate information.

a recent study designed to do so (Chun & Kruglanski, 2003b, Study 1) we presented participants in one condition with the usual sequence of brief base-rate information followed by extensive case information. In another condition, we presented brief case information followed by extensive statistical base-rate information. This novel, *short case-information long base-rate* condition, read:

> We collected data regarding a group of people. One member of the group is Dan. His hobbies are home carpentry, sailing, and mathematical puzzles. He was drawn randomly from that group of people. The group included 14% criminal lawyers, 6% trade lawyers, 9% mechanical engineers, 4% patent lawyers, 10% human rights lawyers, 11% electrical engineers, 12% public defence lawyers, 8% divorce lawyers, 10% nuclear engineers, 16% tax lawyers.

Additionally, we manipulated cognitive load. Finally, the base-rates too were varied, consisting of 30% engineers in one condition, and 70% in the other condition. As shown in Figure 8, when the base-rate information was presented briefly and up-front, its use actually increased under cognitive load (!). But when it came later and was lengthy and more difficult to process, it was utilised only in the absence of load.

Finally, if difficulty of processing matters, we should be able to reproduce the foregoing results juxtaposing two types of *representativeness information*, one brief and up-front (i.e., easy to process), the other lengthy and late-

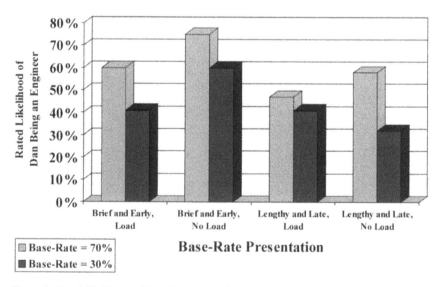

Figure 8. Rated likelihood of Dan being an engineer as a function of base-rate presentation, cognitive load, and base-rate information.

appearing (hence, more difficult to process), rather than pitting (as has been typically the case) base-rate *against* representativeness information. To test this idea we (Chun & Kruglanski, 2003b, Study 2) created two informational sequences: one in which brief information representative of the lawyer stereotype was followed by lengthier information representative of an engineer stereotype, the other in which brief information representative of the engineer stereotype was followed by lengthier information representative of the lawyer stereotype. Orthogonally, we manipulated cognitive load. The results, shown in Figure 9, indicate that where the engineer information was presented briefly and up-front, participants' likelihood judgements that the target was an engineer were enhanced by cognitive load. However, where the engineer information was lengthy and came late, the judged likelihood that the target was an engineer was lower under load. In short, the processing of statistical and heuristic (in this case "representativeness") information seems to be affected identically by values of the parameters of processing difficulty and processing capacity.

Motivational biases.   If judgements based on statistical and heuristic information are governed by the same process, they should be affected similarly by the parameter of motivational bias (known also to affect attributions; for a review, see Kunda, 1990), and the elaboration of persuasive information (Kruglanski & Thompson, 1999). Cumulative

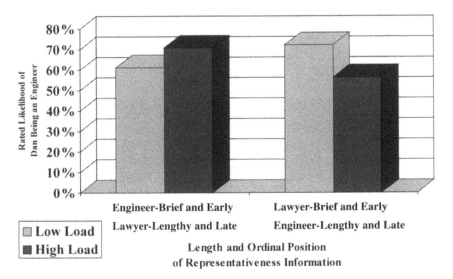

Figure 9. Rated likelihood of Dan being an engineer as a function of the relative length/ordinal position of the engineer versus lawyer representativeness information and cognitive load.

research evidence supports this prediction. Thus, work by Sanitioso and Kunda (1991) demonstrated that the use of the statistical rule, whereby predictability increases sharply with sample size, was greater where it allowed the participants to conclude what they wished to conclude, namely that their sample of observations was large enough for their predictions. A similar conclusion was reached by Ginosar and Trope (1987) where the use of base-rate information increased in conditions where the conclusion it yielded was motivationally desirable to participants. In a different line of work Sanitioso, Freud, and Lee (1996) found that the use of stereotypic or "representativeness" information, too, was affected by participants' directional motivation. Specifically, where the gender stereotype implied that the participant's partner is competent, the participant used the stereotype more, and where it implied that the partner is incompetent the participant used it less.

In summary, it appears that the use of "heuristics" and of statistics is affected identically by the judgemental parameters identified earlier. These are the same parameters that govern the use of message arguments and peripheral/ heuristic cues in persuasion settings, or the use of contextual constraint information in behavioural identification or dispositional inference judgements. Note, furthermore, that in the early "biases and heuristics" research, the parameter values on which the statistical and heuristic information types might have differed were not controlled for. Thus, the statistical information might have been less accessible, less subjectively relevant, and/or earlier-appearing, and hence less likely to be processed than the heuristic information. The findings reviewed above suggest, however, that when those parameter values are controlled for, the previously claimed differences between the use of "heuristic" and statistical information disappear.

RECAPITULATION AND CONCLUSION

People form judgements on a plethora of topics, and use to that end a plethora of evidence types. Nonetheless, all instances of judgement share critical features in common. It is these common features, furthermore, that afford an answer to the fundamental question about the kind of information that may impact judgements, and, about the circumstances under which it may do so. Specifically, we have argued that all human judgement is determined by an intersection of several dimensional parameters, present at some of their values in the judgemental context. The empirical data reviewed above support the notion that such parametric intersections explain large bodies of prior findings in diverse domains of human judgement. Moreover, our parametric framework affords new predictions that receive consistent support in empirical research.

The essence of the unimodel

The gist of our conception holds that judgements are based on information serving as evidence in accordance with its fit within pre-existing rules of the "if-then" variety. The parameter of subjective relevance represents the individual's degree of belief in a given such rule, so that the greater the degree of subjective relevance, the greater the information's impact on judgement. That on condition, of course, that the individual *realises* the degree of subjective relevance a given information affords, which depends, in turn, on difficulty of the judgemental task at hand, on the individual's (cognitive and motivational) *readiness* to cope with the difficulty, and so forth.

A major assumption of the unimodel is that informational contents, though necessarily present in every instance of judgement, do not ultimately matter as far as the information's judgemental impact is concerned. What matters instead are the parametric intersections to which given judgemental contents may be attached. Diverse judgemental contents may be attached to the same parametric intersections, and it is the latter rather than the former that ultimately determine the information's impact upon judgement.

We applied our unimodel to four major domains of social judgement, namely to: (1) persuasion, (2) attribution, (3) impression formation, and (4) biases and heuristics. In all these areas the unimodel's predictions were corroborated when pitted against the implications of pertinent dual-mode frameworks. It appears that various dual-process models have typically confounded informational contents with parametric intersections (e.g., the *contents* of information with its *processing difficulty* in a given instance). Once the two had been "unconfounded", however, it became apparent that the informational contents *per se* do not matter, contrary to implications of the dual-process models.

Associationistic vs rule-following conceptions of human judgement

However pervasive, differentiation between processing modes in content-related terms is not the exclusive manner in which such distinctions have been made. A particularly well-known alternative is Sloman's (1996) distinction between two "reasoning systems" one "associative", the other "rule-based" (see also Smith & DeCoster, 2000). It may be well to consider this distinction closely in light of the present analysis. First, note that Sloman (1996, p. 11) himself admits that "any apparently associative process can be described as rule based because of the representational power of rules". Yet based on a subjective feeling, Sloman is led to suspect that there is a distinction. As he put it (1996, p. 3):

> Associative thought *feels* like it arises from a different cognitive mechanism than does deliberate, analytical reasoning. Sometimes conclusions simply appear at some level of awareness, as if the mind goes off, does some work, and then comes back with a result, and sometimes coming to a conclusion requires doing the work oneself, making an effort to construct a chain of reasoning...

Obviously a subjective feeling of *some* difference is not a conclusive argument for a fundamental difference in *process*. Hence, Sloman (1996) settles on a demarcation criterion that he views as crucial in warranting a qualitative distinction in process. This is his *Criterion S* described as follows (1996, p. 11) "A reasoning problem satisfies *Criterion S* if it causes people to simultaneously believe two contradictory responses." Take Sloman's own example, the statement that a "whale is a mammal". Whales are commonly perceived to resemble fish more than typical mammals like a cow or a horse. Thus, an individual may need to deal in this case with two contradictory beliefs, one derived from the whale's outward similarity to fish and one derived from the "academic" knowledge that classifies whales as mammals. But from the unimodel perspective, all we have here are two distinct *rules* yielding opposite conclusions. One rule is based on similarity, or the "representativeness" heuristic (and heuristics, after all, constitute rules by definition), e.g., "If X looks like a fish, swims like a fish, and lives like a fish, then X *is* a fish". The other rule may be based on other criteria for classification in the mammal category, e.g., "breast feeding of offspring", or indeed the source *heuristic* "If a biology text book claims X (e.g., that whales are mammals), then X is the case".

Perhaps the most striking of Sloman's (1996) examples of a confusion between rule contents and qualitatively distinct processes concerns the Müller-Lyer illusion. Here, perception provides the answer that the lines are of unequal length, and a ruler furnishes an incompatible answer, that they are equally long. Once again, however, it is easy to understand this phenomenon in terms of two rules in which the individual happens to strongly believe, and that happen to yield disparate conclusions. One of these rules is that one's visual perceptions are valid ("If my eyes inform me that X, then X it is"); the other, that application of a ruler yields valid answers.

Note that not every single person necessarily upholds both these rules. For instance, individuals hampered by a limited eyesight may probably harbour considerable doubt about the veracity of their perceptual experiences. Similarly, members of a culture devoid of length-measuring instruments may not trust the ruler much. Suppose, finally, that on two different occasions an individual measured the same line with different rulers, one of which was biased (e.g., having an inch represented by 2.5 cm, rather than the normal 2.3 cm). In one instance, the conclusion might be that the line's length is less than some X, and in the other instance, that it is more than X. Clearly then, the use of the very same rule-based "reasoning system" (here application of a ruler) may lead to two contradictory conclusions, satisfying Sloman's Criterion S for system distinctiveness.

In summary then, Sloman's (1996) criterion S (of incompatible, strongly held beliefs) is in fact highly compatible with the unimodel notion whereby different rules (major premises) applied to the same evidence (minor premises) may yield completely different conclusions. This does not seem to warrant the assumption of a qualitative difference in reasoning processes.

This is not to deny the pervasive occurrence of associationistic phenomena, but rather to adopt a different perspective on *their role in judgement*. According to the unimodel, semantic associations refer to knowledge activation, but not all activated knowledge is relevant to the judgement at hand. Imagine that you observed John smile. This may evoke the associations "friendly", and also the memory of a teeth-bleaching ad claiming to improve the brilliance of one's smile. Only the former but not the latter association, of course, would affect the judgement that John is friendly because of the subjective relevance of "smiling" to "friendliness". The moral of the story is that associations would affect judgements only if they activated (subjectively) relevant "if-then" rules and not otherwise. According to this argument, associationistic processes do not constitute a qualitative alternative to a rule-following process assumed by the unimodel. Associations may activate certain constructs, but only those among the activated constructs that are also subjectively relevant would be used in judgement formation.

Human judgement according to the unimodel

Beyond its ability to explain prior data and concepts, the unimodel offers a number of advantages for conceptualising human judgement. Two are particularly important. They are the unimodel's integrative power and generative potential. We consider them in turn.

Integrative power.   The unimodel affords three types of integration: (1) A *within-models* integration of the dual modes, based on the notion that judgemental phenomena addressed by these models are better explicable in terms of parametric intersections of several quantitative continua rather than in terms of qualitative dichotomies. (2) A *between-models* integration, based on the notion that different content domains of judgement, for which disparate conceptual models have been proposed, are actually governed by the same set of principles, related to workings of the parametric intersections. (3) A *between-parameters* integration, based on the notion that they all work interactively and that the impact of information on human judgement is determined jointly by an intersection of parametric values at a given instance of judgements. By contrast, prior judgemental models typically (if implicitly) focused on a single parameter, or a subset of parameters, be it processing capacity and motivation (implicit, e.g., in Petty & Cacioppo's, 1986, elaboration likelihood continuum), subjective relevance of evidence for the typical individual (implicit, e.g., in Tversky & Kahneman's, 1974, notions of reliance on [subjectively relevant] heuristics rather than statistics), and McGuire's (1960), and Wyer's (1970, 1974) classic analyses of probabilogical judgement, or be it motivational bias (addressed, e.g., in models of motivated reasoning; Dunning, 1999; Kunda, 1990; Kunda & Sinclair, 1999).

Generative potential.   The unimodel has considerable potential for generating further research on judgemental phenomena across domains. The present paper reviewed some initial efforts in this vein, but ample further unimodel-based research could (and should) be carried out. Novel experimental studies, meta-analyses of prior research and conceptual reviews should be possible wherein previous notions and findings are examined and re-interpreted from the present theoretic perspective. Last, but not least important, the unimodel offers a more *flexible* portrayal of human judgements than did its predecessors (cf. Strack, 1999). Accordingly, no judgemental content (such as social categories or stereotypes) necessarily defines the departure point of judgemental deliberations, no judgemental content (e.g., various statistical notions) is necessarily doomed for misuse or neglect. According to that view, any informational content can either have or lack judgemental impact depending on the constellation of parameters to which it happens to be attached. Liberation from contents has important implications for further inquiry and theory development on the topic of human judgement. It suggests, specifically, that we should re-focus our modelling efforts on a more precise elaboration of the judgemental parameters, their interrelations, and their conjoint impact on people's impressions, opinions, or estimates.

REFERENCES

Anderson, N. H. (1971). Integration theory and attitude change. *Psychological Review, 78*, 171–206.

Bar-Hillel, M. (1983). The base-rate fallacy controversy. In R.W. Scholz (Ed.), *Decision making under uncertainty*. Amsterdam: Elsevier.

Bar-Hillel, M. (1990). Back to base-rates. In R. M. Hogarth (Ed.), *Insights in decision making*. Chicago, IL: University of Chicago Press.

Bobrow, D. G., & Norman, D. A. (1975). Some principles of memory schemata. In D. G. Bobrow & A. Collins (Eds.), *Representation and understanding: Studies in cognitive science* (pp. 131–149). New York: Academic Press.

Bohner, G., Ruder, M., & Erb, H.-P. (2002). When expertise backfires: Contrast and assimilation effects in persuasion. *British Journal of Social Psychology, 41,* 495–519.

Borgida, E., & Brekke, N. (1981). The base rate fallacy in attribution and prediction. In J. H. Harvey, W. Ickes, & R. F. Kidd (Eds.), *New directions in attribution research* (Vol. 3, pp. 63–95). Hillsdale, NJ: Lawrence Erlbaum Associates Inc.

Brewer, M. B. (1988). A dual process model of impression formation. In T. K. Srull & R. S. Wyer Jr. (Eds.), *Advances in social cognition* (Vol. 1, pp. 1–36), Hillsdale, NJ: Lawrence Erlbaum Associates Inc.

Cacioppo, J. T., & Petty, R. E. (1982). The need for cognition. *Journal of Personality and Social Psychology, 42,* 116–131.

Chaiken, S. (1980). Heuristic versus systematic information and the use of source versus message cues in persuasion. *Journal of Personality and Social Psychology, 39,* 752–756.

Chaiken, S., Liberman, A., & Eagly, A. H. (1989). Heuristic and systematic processing within and beyond the persuasion context. In J. S. Uleman & J. A. Bargh (Eds.), *Unintended thought* (pp. 212–252). New York: Guilford Press.

Chaiken, S., & Maheswaran, D. (1994). Heuristic processing can bias systematic processing: Effects of source credibility, argument ambiguity, and task importance on attitude judgments. *Journal of Personality and Social Psychology, 66,* 460–473.

Chaiken, S., & Trope, Y. (Eds.). (1999). *Dual-process theories in social psychology.* New York: Guilford Press.

Chun, W. Y., & Kruglanski, A. W. (2003a). *When increasing cognitive load reduces stereotypical judgments.* Unpublished data. University of Maryland, College Park, USA.

Chun, W. Y., & Kruglanski, A. W. (2003b). *Distraction from biased reasoning: The case of judgment from base-rates.* Unpublished data. University of Maryland, College Park, USA.

Chun, W. Y., Spiegel, S., & Kruglanski, A. W. (2002). Assimilative behavior identification can also be resource-dependent: A unimodel perspective on personal-attribution phases. *Journal of Personality and Social Psychology, 83,* 542–555.

Cosmides, L., & Tooby, J. (1996). Are humans good intuitive statisticians after all? Rethinking some conclusions from the literature on judgment under uncertainty. *Cognition, 58,* 1–73.

Ditto, P. H., & Lopez, D. F. (1992). Motivated skepticism: Use of differential decision criteria for preferred and nonpreferred conclusions. *Journal of Personality and Social Psychology, 63,* 568–584.

Duncan, B. L. (1976). Differential social perception and attribution of intergroup violence: Testing the lower limits of stereotyping of blacks. *Journal of Personality and Social Psychology, 34,* 590–598.

Dunning, D. (1999). A newer look: Motivated social cognition and the schematic representation of social concepts. *Psychological Inquiry, 10,* 1–11.

Eagly, A. H., & Chaiken, S. (1993). *The psychology of attitudes.* Fort Worth, TX: Harcourt Brace Jovanovich College Publishers.

Epstein, S., & Pacini, R. (1999). Some basic issues regarding dual-process theories from the perspective of cognitive-experiential self-theory. In S. Chaiken & Y. Trope (Eds.), *Dual process theories in social psychology* (pp. 462–482). New York: Guilford Press.

Erb, H.-P., Bioy, A., & Hilton, D. J. (2002). Choice preferences without inferences: Subconscious priming of risk attitudes. *Journal of Behavioral Decision Making, 15,* 251–262.

Erb, H.-P., Bohner, G., Schmälzle, K., & Rank, S. (1998). Beyond conflict and discrepancy: Cognitive bias in minority and majority influence. *Personality and Social Psychology Bulletin, 24,* 620–633.

Erb, H.-P., Fishbach, A., & Kruglanski, A. W. (2003). *The effects of rule priming on social judgment.* Unpublished draft. University of Jena, Germany.

Erb, H.-P., Pierro, A., Mannetti, L., Spiegel, S., & Kruglanski, A. W. (2003). *Persuasion according to the unimodel.* Unpublished manuscript. University of Jena, Germany.

Evans, J. St. B. T. (1989). *Bias in human reasoning: Causes and consequences*. Hove, UK: Lawrence Erbaum Associates Ltd.

Evans, J. St. B. T., Handley, S. J., Perham, N., Over, D. E., & Thompson, V. A. (2000). Frequency versus probability formats in statistical word problems. *Cognition, 77*, 197–213.

Festinger, L. (1957). *A theory of cognitive dissonance*. Evanston, IL: Row, Peterson.

Fishbein, M., & Ajzen, I. (1975). *Belief, attitude, intention, and behavior: An introduction to theory and research*. Reading, MA: Addison-Wesley.

Fiske, S. T., Lin, M., & Neuberg, S. L. (1999). The continuum model: Ten years later. In S. Chaiken & Y. Trope (Eds.), *Dual process theories in social psychology* (pp. 231–254). New York: Guilford Press.

Fiske, S. T., & Neuberg, S. L. (1990). A continuum model of impression formation, from category-based to individuating processes: Influences of information and motivation on attention and interpretation. In M. P. Zanna (Ed.), *Advances in experimental social psychology* (Vol. 23, pp. 1–74). New York: Academic Press.

Gigerenzer, G., & Hoffrage, U. (1995). How to improve Bayesian reasoning without instruction: Frequency formats. *Psychological Review, 102*, 684–704.

Gilbert, D. T., & Osborne, R. E. (1989). Thinking backward: The curable and incurable consequences of cognitive busyness. *Journal of Personality and Social Psychology, 57*, 940–949.

Ginosar, Z., & Trope, Y. (1980). The effects of base rates and individuating information on judgments about another person. *Journal of Experimental Social Psychology, 16*, 228–242.

Ginosar, Z., & Trope, Y. (1987). Problem solving in judgment under uncertainty. *Journal of Personality and Social Psychology, 52*, 464–474.

Greenwald, A. G. (1968). Cognitive learning, cognitive response to persuasion, and attitude change. In A. G. Greenwald, T. C. Brock, & T. M. Ostrom (Eds.), *Psychological foundations of attitudes* (pp. 147–170). San Diego, CA: Academic Press.

Grice, H. P. (1975). Logic and conversation. In P. Cole & J. L. Morgan (Eds.), *Syntax and semantics 3: Speech acts* (pp. 41–58). San Diego, CA: Academic Press.

Hamilton, D. L., Sherman, S. J., & Maddox, K. B. (1999). Dualities and continua: Implications for understanding perceptions of persons and groups. In S. Chaiken & Y. Trope (Eds.), *Dual-process theories in social psychology* (pp. 606–626). New York: Guilford Press.

Higgins, E. T. (1997). Beyond pleasure and pain. *American Psychologist, 52*, 1280–1300.

Higgins, E. T., King, G. A., & Mavin, G. H. (1982). Individual construct accessibility and subjective impressions and recall. *Journal of Personality and Social Psychology, 43*, 35–47.

Higgins, E. T., Rholes, W. S., & Jones, C. R. (1977). Category accessibility and impression formation. *Journal of Experimental Social Psychology, 13*, 141–154.

Jarvis, W. B. G., & Petty, E. E. (1996). The need to evaluate. *Journal of Personality and Social Psychology, 70*, 172–194.

Jones, E. E. (1988). Impression formation: What do people think about? In T. K. Srull & R. S. Wyer Jr. (Eds.), *Advances in social cognition* (Vol. 1, pp. 83–90). Hillsdale, NJ: Lawrence Erlbaum Associates Inc.

Jones, E. E., & Davis, K. E. (1965). From acts to dispositions: The attribution process in person perception. In L. Berkowitz (Ed.), *Advances in experimental social psychology* (Vol. 2, pp. 219–266). San Diego, CA: Academic Press.

Kahneman, D., Slovic, P. & Tversky, A. (1982). *Judgment under uncertainty: Heuristics and biases*. Cambridge: Cambridge University Press.

Kahneman, D., & Tversky, A. (1973). On the psychology of prediction. *Psychological Review, 80*, 237–251.

Kahneman, D., & Tversky, A. (1982). On the study of statistical intuitions. *Cognition, 11*, 123–141.

Kelley, H. H. (1967). Attribution theory in social psychology. In D. Levine (Ed.), *Nebraska Symposium on Motivation* (Vol. 15, pp. 192–240). Lincoln, NE: University of Nebraska Press.

Klatzky, R. L., & Andersen, S. M. (1988). Category-specificity effects in social typing and personalization. In T. K. Srull & R. S. Wyer Jr. (Eds.), *A dual process model of impression formation. Advances in social cognition* (Vol. 1., pp. 91–101). Hillsdale, NJ: Lawrence Erlbaum Associates Inc.

Kruglanski, A.W. (1989). *Lay epistemics and human knowledge: Cognitive and motivational bases.* New York: Plenum Press.

Kruglanski, A.W. (1990). Lay epistemic theory in social cognitive psychology. (Target article for peer commentary.) *Psychological Inquiry, 1*, 181–197.

Kruglanski, A. W. (1999). Motivation, cognition, and reality: Three memos for the next generation of research. *Psychological Inquiry, 10*, 54–58.

Kruglanski, A. W., & Thompson, E. P. (1999). Persuasion by a single route: A view from the unimodel. (Target article for peer commentary.) *Psychological Inquiry, 10*, 83–109.

Kruglanski, A. W., & Webster, D. M. (1996). Motivated closing of the mind: "Seizing" and "freezing". *Psychological Review, 103*, 263–283.

Kunda, Z. (1990). The case of motivated reasoning. *Psychological Bulletin, 108*, 480–498.

Kunda, Z., & Sinclair, L. (1999). Motivated reasoning with stereotypes: Activation, application, and inhibition. *Psychological Inquiry, 10*, 12–22.

McGuire, W. J. (1960). A syllogistic analysis of cognitive relationships. In C. I. Hovland & M. J. Rosenberg (Eds.), *Attitude organization and change: An analysis of consistency among attitude components* (pp. 65–111). New Haven, CT: Yale University Press.

McGuire, W. J. (1968). Personality and attitude change: An information processing theory. In A. G. Greenwald, T. C. Brock, & T. M. Ostrom (Eds.), *Psychological foundations of attitudes* (pp. 171–196). San Diego, CA: Academic Press.

Medin, D. L. (1988). Social categorization: Structures, processes, and purposes. In T. K. Srull & R. S. Wyer Jr. (Eds.), *A dual process model of impression formation. Advances in social cognition* (Vol. 1, pp. 119–126). Hillsdale, NJ: Lawrence Erlbaum Associates Inc.

Medin, D. L., & Ross, B. H. (1989). The specific character of abstract thought: Categorization, problem solving, and induction. In R. J. Sternberg (Ed.), *Advances in the psychology of human intelligence* (Vol. 5). Hillsdale, NJ: Lawrence Erlbaum Associates Inc.

Mischel, W., & Shoda, Y. (1995). A cognitive-affective system theory of personality: Reconceptualizing situations, dispositions, dynamics and invariance in personality structure. *Psychological Review, 102*, 246–268.

Neuberg, S. L., & Fiske, S. T. (1987). Motivational influences on impression formation: Outcome dependency, accuracy-driven attention, and individuating processes. *Journal of Personality and Social Psychology, 53*, 431–444.

Newell, A., & Simon, H. A. (1972). *Human problem solving.* Englewood Cliffs, NJ: Prentice-Hall.

Nisbett, R. E., Cheng, P. W., Fong, G. T., & Lehman, D. (1987). *Teaching reasoning.* Unpublished manuscript. University of Michigan, USA.

Pavelchak, M. A (1989). Piecemeal and category-based evaluation: An idiographic analysis. *Journal of Personality and Social Psychology, 56*, 354–363.

Petty, R. E. (1994). Two routes to persuasion: State of the art. In G. d'Ydewalle, P. Eelen, & P. Berteleson (Eds.), *International perspectives on psychological science* (Vol. 2, pp. 229–247). Hillsdale, NJ: Lawrence Erlbaum Associates Inc.

Petty, R. E., & Cacioppo, J. T. (1983). Central and peripheral routes to persuasion: Applications to advertising. In L. Percy & A. Woodside (Eds.), *Advertising and consumer psychology* (pp. 3–23). Lexington, MA: Heath.

Petty, R. E., & Cacioppo, J. T. (1984). The effects of involvement on response to argument quantity and quality: Central and peripheral routes to persuasion. *Journal of Personality and Social Psychology, 46,* 69–81.

Petty, R. E., & Cacioppo, J. T. (1986). The elaboration likelihood model of persuasion. In L. Berkowitz (Ed.), *Advances of experimental social psychology* (Vol. 19, pp. 123–205). San Diego, CA: Academic Press.

Petty, R. E., Ostrom, T. M., & Brock, T. C. (Eds.). (1981). *Cognitive responses in persuasion.* Hillsdale, NJ: Lawrence Erlbaum Associates Inc.

Petty, R. E., Schumann, D. W., Richman, S. A., & Strathman, A. J. (1993). Positive mood and persuasion: Different roles for affect under high- and low-elaboration conditions. *Journal of Personality and Social Psychology, 64,* 5–20.

Petty, R. E., Wells, G. L., & Brock, T. C. (1976). Distraction can enhance or reduce yielding to propaganda: Thought disruption versus effort justification. *Journal of Personality and Social Psychology, 34,* 874–884.

Petty, R. E., Wheeler, S. C., & Bizer, G. Y. (1999). Is there one persuasion process or more? Lumping versus splitting in attitude change theories. *Psychological Inquiry, 10,* 156–163.

Reber, A. S. (1997). Implicit ruminations. *Psychonomic Bulletin and Review, 4,* 49–55.

Ryan, R. M., Sheldon, K. M., Kasser, T., & Deci, E. L. (1996). All goals are not created equal: An organismic perspective on the nature of goals and their regulation. In P. M. Gollwitzer & J. A. Bargh (Eds.), *The psychology of action.* New York: Guilford Press.

Sanitioso, R., Freud, K., & Lee, J. (1996). The influence of self-related goals on the use of stereotypical and individuating information. *European Journal of Social Psychology, 26,* 751–761.

Sanitioso, R., & Kunda, Z. (1991). Ducking the collection of costly evidence: Motivated use of statistical heuristics. *Journal of Behavioral Decision Making, 4,* 161–176.

Schank, R. C. (1982). *Dynamic memory: A theory of learning in people and computers.* Cambridge: Cambridge University Press.

Schwarz, N., & Clore, G. L. (1983). Mood, misattribution, and judgments of well-being: Informative and directive functions of affective states. *Journal of Personality and Social Psychology, 45,* 513–523.

Schwarz, N., & Clore, G. L. (1996). Feelings and phenomenal experiences. In E. T. Higgins & A. W. Kruglanski (Eds.), *Social psychology: A handbook of basic principles* (pp. 433–465). New York: Guilford Press.

Schwarz, N., Strack, F., Hilton, D. J., & Naderer, G. (1991). Base-rates, representativeness, and the logic of conversation. *Social Cognition, 9,* 67–84.

Sedlmeier, P. (1999). *Improving statistical reasoning: Theoretical models and practical implications.* Mahwah, NJ: Lawrence Erlbaum Associates Inc.

Sloman, S. A. (1996). The empirical case for two systems of reasoning. *Psychological Bulletin, 119,* 3–22.

Smith, E. R. (1988). Impression formation in a general framework of social and nonsocial cognition. In T. K. Srull & R. S. Wyer (Eds.), *Advances in social cognition* (Vol. 1, pp. 165–176). Hillsdale, NJ: Lawrence Erlbaum Associates Inc.

Smith, E. R., & DeCoster, J. (2000). Dual-process models in social and cognitive psychology: Conceptual integration and links to underlying memory systems. *Personality and Social Psychology Review, 4,* 108–131.

Srull, T. K. & Wyer, R. S., Jr. (1979). The role of category accessibility in the interpretation of information about persons: Some determinants and implications. *Journal of Personality and Social Psychology, 37,* 1660–1672.

Strack, F. (1999). Beyond dual-process models: Toward a flexible regulation system. *Psychological Inquiry, 10,* 166–170.

Tetlock, P. E. (1985). Accountability: A social check on the fundamental attribution error. *Social Psychology Quarterly*, *48*, 227–236.

Trope, Y. (1986). Identification and inferential processes in dispositional attribution. *Psychological Review*, *93*, 239–257.

Trope, Y., & Alfieri, T. (1997). Effortfulness and flexibility of dispositional judgment processes. *Journal of Personality and Social Psychology*, *73*, 662–674.

Trope, Y., & Gaunt, R. (1999). A dual-process model of overconfident attributional inferences. In S. Chaiken, & Y. Trope (Eds.), *Dual process theories in social psychology* (pp. 161–179). New York: Guilford Press.

Trope, Y., & Gaunt, R. (2000). Processing alternative explanations of behavior: Correction or integration. *Journal of Personality and Social Psychology*, *79*, 837–852.

Trope, Y., & Liberman, A. (1996). Social hypothesis testing: Cognitive and motivational mechanisms. In E. T. Higgins & A. W. Kruglanski (Eds.), *Social psychology: Handbook of basic principles* (pp. 239–270). New York: Guilford Press.

Tversky, A., & Kahneman, D. (1974). Judgment under uncertainty: Heuristics and biases. *Science*, *185*, 1124–1130.

Tversky, A., & Kahneman, D. (1980). Causal schemas in judgment under uncertainty. In M. Fishbein (Ed.), *Progress in social psychology* (pp. 13–34). Hillsdale, NJ: Lawrence Erlbaum Associates Inc.

Tversky, A., & Kahneman, D. (1983). Extensional versus intuitive reasoning: The conjunction fallacy in probability judgment. *Psychological Review*, *91*, 293–315.

Wason, P. C. (1966). *Reasoning*. In B. M. Foss (Ed.), *New horizons in psychology* (pp. 113–135) Harmondsworth, UK: Penguin.

Webster, D. M., & Kruglanski, A. W. (1998). Cognitive and social consequences of the need for cognitive closure. In W. Stroebe & M. Hewstone (Eds.), *European review of social psychology* (Vol. 8, pp. 133–141). Chichester, UK: Wiley.

Webster, D. M., Richter, L., & Kruglanski, A. W. (1998). On leaping to conclusions when feeling tired: Mental fatigue effects on impression formation. *Journal of Experimental Social Psychology*, *32*, 181–195.

Wyer, R. S., Jr. (1970). Quantitative prediction of belief and opinion change: A further test of a subjective probability model. *Journal Personality and Social Psychology*, *16*, 559–570.

Wyer, R. S., Jr. (1974). *Cognitive organization and change: An information processing approach.* Hillsdale, NJ: Lawrence Erlbaum Associates Inc.

Zukier, H., & Pepitone, A. (1984). Social roles and strategies in prediction: Some determinants of the use of base rate information. *Journal of Personality and Social Psychology*, *47*, 349–360.

EUROPEAN REVIEW OF SOCIAL PSYCHOLOGY, 2003, *14*, 49–76

Top-down influences in social perception

Paula M. Niedenthal

University of Clermont-Ferrand, France

Jamin B. Halberstadt

University of Otago, Dunedin, New Zealand

The present chapter makes a case for the importance of the study of social perception as a phenomenon separate from impression formation and social categorisation, and of great significance for social psychology. We claim specifically that the development of tasks for studying perception is critical for addressing the question of whether top-down processes influence perception. Three series of studies conducted by the authors, and which relied on newly developed tasks, are presented. The first two series examine the effects of emotion and adult attachment orientation on the perception of facial expression of emotion. The third examines the influences of emotion concepts on perceptual memory for facial expression. The studies together provide good support for influences of emotional state, personality factors, and prior knowledge on the perception of facial expression of emotion, and call, we hope, for greater attention to perceptual processes in social psychology.

Most social psychologists who study "social perception" and "person perception" actually study cognition. That is, if the relationship between perception and cognition is a continuum, then the study of social perception, as it exists in the literature, lies at the cognition end. This is the case because the tasks usually used to investigate social perception are susceptible to many intervening processes, such as attention, categorisation, and correction (Brauer, Wasel, & Niedenthal, 2000). As result, it is hard to know what a person actually "perceived". Of course, this is not a problem if, as is often true, the process of interest is not perception in the first place. After all, when social psychologists use the term "social perception" they often mean, and actually care about, impression formation or social judgement, which are based on *perceptual* properties of other people (Heider, 1944; Schneider, Hastorf, & Ellsworth, 1979). So in many cases the nature of the information

---

Address correspondence to: Paula M. Niedenthal, LAPSCO/UFR Psychologie, Université Blaise Pascal, 34, avenue Carnot, 63037 Clermont-Ferrand, Cedex France. E-mail: Paula.Niedenthal@srvpsy.univ-bpclermont.fr.

http://www.tandf.co.uk/journals/titles/99998080.asp   DOI: 10.1080/10463280340000018

(perceptual versus conceptual, for example) under study, is confused with the process (perceptual or conceptual) that is measured. If the impact of a perceptual feature of another individual (e.g., his or her attractiveness) is under investigation, it is still the burden of the task used to measure the dependent variable to demonstrate convincingly that *perception* has been affected by that variable. If perceptual features are varied, but cognitive processes are measured, then conclusions can only be drawn about cognition, not about perception

We have been interested in the perception end of the social perception continuum, and particularly the extent to which top-down processes such as emotions, schemas, and concepts might influence what is taken in from the external environment (e.g., Niedenthal, 1992). We have been motivated by an intellectual interest in different versions of the Whorfian hypothesis (e.g., Whorf, 1941/1956), models of the interactions between cognition and perception (e.g., Schyns & Rodet, 1997), and the intuitive belief that, because people rely on their perceptions as faithful and compelling representations of reality, an understanding of perception strongly facilitates the understanding of behaviour.

In the present chapter we review three research programmes in which we have looked at top-down influences in social perception, specifically the perception of, and perceptual memory for, facial expression of emotion. The first and second research programmes examine the role of emotion and attachment style, respectively, in the perception of emotional expression. The third examines the idea that the use of emotion concepts to interpret facial expressions during encoding alters perceptual memory for the expressions themselves. We have developed some new stimuli and tasks just for the purpose of such exploration, and we describe these methods in some detail. Throughout the chapter we discuss the importance of exploring top-down influences in perception. Before describing the research, we briefly review the importance of facial expressions in social psychology.

WHY STUDY FACIAL EXPRESSION?

In social interaction, individuals use facial expressions as cues to the expressor's attitudes, which often importantly guide social interaction (Salovey & Mayer, 1990). For example, if a speaker makes an assertion of his own attitude during a conversation and a listener's face changes from a smile to a scowl, the speaker, guessing that the listener does not agree with him, might change the topic of conversation to avoid offence. The speaker might even try to change the apparently offensive statement itself as he detects the changes in the facial expression of the listener. We have all had the experience of talking to someone who, we suddenly realise, holds a vastly different attitude from ours. In mid-sentence, just as we are bemoaning, say, the recent election of someone whom we consider to be a blithering idiot, we detect the change in the facial expression of the person with whom we are conversing and spontaneously try to alter the extremity of our expressed opinion.

We also closely monitor the facial expression of someone whose emotional state we are trying to influence. For example, we might tell jokes to cheer up a friend who is sad, monitoring her facial expression to gauge our success. We take an emerging smile as a sign that we are succeeding, and an exaggeration of her sad expression that perhaps we should stop our attempts altogether. Thus, in their signalling of emotional states and attitudes, facial expressions are very useful and important social stimuli, and our monitoring of them has important consequences for the unfolding and outcome of social interactions.

Perceivers, however, are not free of bias, and many studies have revealed systematic inaccuracies in the "decoding" (in the sense of categorisation) of facial expressions. One quite robust predictor of accuracy is gender. On average, women decode facial expression of emotion more accurately than men (see Hall, 1984, for a review). (An exception is the facial expression of anger, which men seem to decode more accurately, and sometimes faster, than women, particularly if the expressor is male; Wagner, MacDonald, & Manstead, 1986; but see also Hess, Blairy, & Kleck, 1997.) Most demonstrations of bias are, as noted above, demonstrations of *judgemental* bias, even if perceivers themselves argue that they really *saw* the emotion they reported. Therefore, an interesting and unanswered question is whether the *perception* of facial expressions is subject to stable and transient influences. In particular, one possibility that has interested us, given that emotional expressions are potent elicitors of emotional reactions, is whether ambient emotional states influence the way the emotional expressions of others are perceived (Niedenthal, 1992; see also recent work showing that extraversion moderates amygdala responses to happy faces; Canli, Silverse, Whitfield, Gotlib, & Gabrieli, 2002).

EFFECTS OF EMOTIONAL STATE ON THE PERCEPTION OF FACIAL EXPRESSIONS

Although the literature on basic processes in face perception is quite extensive (e.g., Bruce, 1988; Farah, 1996), and quite a bit is known about the perception of emotional expressions (e.g., Ellison & Massaro, 1997; Etcoff & Magee, 1992; Young et al., 1997), much less is known about top-down influences on these processes, and even less about how perceivers' emotions influence their perception of facial expressions.

Probably the earliest research designed to examine emotion as a moderator of the perception of emotional expression tested the psychoanalytic notion of *projection*. In projection individuals prevent consciousness of their own anxiety-producing impulses by perceiving the same impulses in other people. Feshbach and colleagues found evidence of two types of projection, "supplementary" and "complementary". In supplementary projection, as in the conventional account of projection, the emotional state of the individual is "connected to contemporaneous perceptions and ideation. One might describe this process as the infusion of cognition with affect ..." (Feshbach & Singer, 1957, p. 283). For example, in several studies, experimentally frightened participants reported that more fear was expressed by a target individual, compared to control participants, particularly if the participants were instructed to repress their feelings of fear (Feshbach & Feshbach, 1963). In complementary projection, the individual perceives on the face of another person the expression that caused his or her, the perceiver's, own emotions. For example, a fearful person might perceive anger expressed by others. Feshbach also observed complementary projection in subsequent research, particularly when the relationship between the perceiver and the target afforded such a process (e.g., the perceiver was a child and the target was an adult; Feshbach & Feshbach, 1963).

One of the few studies directed specifically at the question of the influences of emotional state on the interpretation of facial expressions of emotion, and that was not inspired by psychoanalytic theory, was reported by Schiffenbauer (1974). Participants in the study heard an audio-taped message that induced feelings of either disgust or amusement. Control participants heard nothing or else were exposed to white noise. During the manipulation participants saw pictures of faces with different expressions and were asked to generate a word label for each. For analysis, labels were coded as positive or negative, and were also categorised as belonging to specific emotion categories (happy, surprise, fear, disgust, sadness, and anger). Findings indicated that participants in the disgust condition used fewer positive labels than did control participants, who in turn used fewer positive labels than participants in the amusement condition. Participants in the disgust condition also used disgust labels more often than the other groups of participants. Schiffenbauer concluded that people tend to see displayed on other's faces the same emotion that they themselves are feeling, consistent with process of supplementary projection.

However, once again we cannot conclude from this work that emotions influence the perception of emotional expression, because the dependent measures were judgement scales or verbal labels, which are not measures of perception. Emotional states have been shown to increase the efficiency with which emotion-congruent words are processed (e.g., Niedenthal & Setterlund, 1994; Niedenthal, Setterlund, & Jones, 1994). Thus, assuming that emotion-congruent labels were more accessible or judged more probable, a response bias interpretation (Manis, 1967) or a verbal priming interpretation (Bower, 1981) could also account for Fechbach's and Shiffenbauer's findings.

A morph task for measuring the perception of facial expression of emotion

Given the small number and the ambiguity of existing studies, the principal aim of our first programme of research was to re-examine influences of emotion in the perception of facial expression, using a method that could more clearly assess what participants were seeing. The method we developed utilised morphing technology. Specifically, photographs of actors displaying happiness and sadness were digitally blended, or morphed, with a photograph of the same actor expressing neutral emotion to create 100-frame movies in which faces initially expressing an emotion became gradually neutral. Six frames of one such stimulus movies can be seen in Figure 1, top panel.

Experimental participants could then play these movies and, for example, stop them at the frame at which the initial facial expression no longer appeared (to them) to be present on the face. One dependent variable we could assess with these movies, then, was the frame of "offset" of the initial facial expression. A critical advantage of this technique is that it requires a nonverbal response—the perceived offset of an emotional expression—which we have argued assesses individuals' perception of the emotional expression rather than their use of labels to categorise it. Of course we cannot dismiss the possibility that participants implicitly label the faces when they perform this task, but their self-reports argue against this

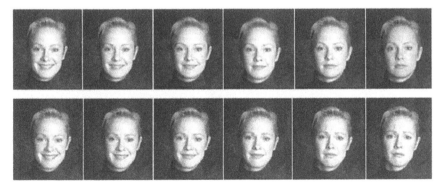

Figure 1. Six frames of a happy-to-neutral morph movie and six frames of a happy-to-sad morph movie used in the present experiments. (Adapted from Niedenthal et al., 2001.)

alternative explanation. No participant in any post-experimental question-naire has ever mentioned any verbal strategies for performing the task. At the very least we can say that the procedure used in this study does not require verbal labels or verbalised judgements, and that explicit or implicit labelling and judgement do not appear to occur naturally when the task is performed.

One could also interpret the morph procedure as a task that measures the perceived boundaries of facial expression categories. Such a description seems to us to be an overinterpretation of what the task actually measures, however, since participants are not given specific facial expression categories to use as criteria. The task *could* be used to measure the implicit expansion and constriction of category boundaries, but given the instructions that we use it in our studies, we think that the simplest way to say this is that the task measures the detection (or not) of evidence of a facial expression present on the face. This may have the effect of changing category boundaries of course.

Furthermore, as in studies of categorical perception (e.g., Calder, Young, Perrett, Etcoff, & Rowland, 1996), frames from the types of morphs that we have constructed can be extracted and compared in same–different judgement tasks, for example, in order to evaluate even finer-grained changes in perception due to emotional state.

Emotion congruence in the morph task: Evidence and mechanism

If past research findings on the categorisation of facial expression of emotion actually do have a perceptual basis, then perceivers in happy emotional states should perceive happy expressions as lasting longer in a morph movie than perceivers in sad states. Conversely, sad perceivers should perceive sad expressions as lasting longer than perceivers in happy states. Control participants should see the offset of both expressions at about the same point in the movies.

In the first experiment we conducted (Niedenthal, Halberstadt, Margolin, & Innes-Ker, 2000), which involved 96 participants, this is just what we observed. In the experiment, we induced happiness, sadness, or neutral emotions in participants, using a combination of film and music (see, for example, Halberstadt & Niedenthal, 1997, for details). Participants then viewed morph movies in which faces of men and women that initially expressed happiness or sadness became neutral. Analysis of the perceived frame of emotion offset revealed the predicted interaction between emotional state and initial facial expression. Happy participants perceived happy expressions to be present on an increasingly neutral face for a longer time into the movie than did sad perceivers. Sad participants saw sad expressions to be present on an increasingly neutral face for a longer time than did happy perceivers.

One interpretation of emotion congruence in the perception of emotional expression depends on an associative network account of memory (e.g., Bower, 1981; Teasdale, 1983). According to this model, each emotion is represented as a central unit of information in memory that is connected by semantic pointers to other causally linked events and information. When a unit is activated above threshold (e.g., by exposure to an emotional stimulus), activation spreads to other units that generate the autonomic and expressive behaviour characteristics of the emotion. In addition, ideas and events that have been associated with the emotion are activated, so that these representations are more likely to come to mind and to influence subsequent information processing (e.g. Bower, 1981). In terms of this model, emotion-congruent perception of emotional expressions occurs when the participant's emotion activates the corresponding emotion unit in memory, which in turn primes all information related to that emotion. Because of this additional activation, ambiguous expressions in the emotion movies will more likely be interpreted as consistent with the participant's own emotional state.

There is, however, another mechanism that could influence the perception of facial expression. This is mimicry on the part of the perceiver. Evidence that mimicry accompanies perception of a facial expression of emotion was reported by Dimberg (1982; see also Bush, Barr, McHugo, & Lanzetta, 1989), who showed that electromyographic (EMG) activity in the zygomatic muscle increases when individuals observe a smiling face, and that activity in the corrugator muscle increases during the observation of an angry face. Furthermore, Adolphs, Damasio, Tranel, Cooper, and Damasio (2000) recently showed that clinical patients with lesions in somatosensory cortex categorised facial expressions less accurately than did control participants without such lesions. This latter finding indicates that simulating a perceived emotional expression, and experiencing the somatosensory feedback such simulation produces, facilitates the process of recognition. Thus it appears that facial mimicry occurs spontaneously in the perception of facial expression, and that the motor responses of the perceiver guide recognition of it (see also Carr, Iacoboni, Dubeau, Mazziotta, & Lenzi, 2001). Importantly, the imitation of another's facial expression is likely to interact with the emotional state of the perceiver. It is easier and perhaps more natural for a perceiver to mimic expressions that are emotionally congruent (for other demonstrations of top-down influences on imitation, see Decety et al., 1997). Other motivations being equal, happy individuals probably mimic happy faces more readily and easily than sad individuals, and vice versa.

Differences in facial feedback from mimicry may account for Niedenthal et al.'s (2000) findings as follows: Happy-condition participants mimicked the happy expressions more efficiently and for a longer time than did sad-condition participants. They thus received facial feedback indicating the offset of the perceived (happy) expression later than the sad-condition participants did. And the converse was true of sad-condition participants looking at sad faces. Furthermore, since the expressions became neutral over time, no new facial information appeared to compete with a congruence effect. This mimicry account fits easily within recent theories of social cognition as *embodied simulations* of perceived and imagined social information (e.g., Gallese, 2003; Barsalou, Niedenthal, Barbey, & Ruppert, 2003). These theories assume that the perception of emotional information involves partial use of the sensory-motor routines typical of that emotion, thus for them perception of facial expression is not just influenced by mimicry, but it is fundamentally reliant on that process. That is, as Adolphs and colleagues' (2000) work shows, imitation is actually a fundamental part of perception (see also, Calder, Keane, Manes, Antoun, & Young, 2000; Carr et al. 2001). Furthermore, according to theories of embodied simulation, the specific simulations already prepared by the experience of an ambient emotional state will make imitation of another's facial expression more or less successful.

Note that while both approaches, an associative network model and an embodied simulation model, can account for mimicry as a mechanism that produces emotion congruence, only an embodied simulation model makes the prediction *a priori* that mimicry plays any role in this effect (see Barsalou, 2003, and Barsalou et al., 2003, for discussion).

Mimicry and emotion congruence in face perception

The role of mimicry in the Niedenthal et al. (2000) result was investigated in two studies by Niedenthal, Brauer, Halberstadt, and Innes-Ker (2001). In their first study, participants in whom happy, sad, or neutral emotion had been induced using a combination of films and music, viewed morph movies in which faces changed from happy to sad, or sad to happy (see Figure 1, bottom panel). When a face changes from an emotion-congruent to an incongruent expression, the mimicry account predicts perceptual effects opposite to those found when an emotion-congruent expression becomes neutral. Specifically, when an emotional expression changes from congruent to incongruent, individuals can readily mimic the initial expression, and detect change in it quickly because it produces a noticeable shift in their own facial expression (and its feedback). In contrast, when an emotional expression changes from incongruent to congruent, individuals do not readily mimic the initial expression, and considerably less change in facial feedback due to concurrent mimicry is experienced. They are thus less sensitive to change in the target face, and perceive change later.

If mimicry plays no role in the perception of emotion change, then the results should replicate those of the Niedenthal et al. (2000) study, in which faces changed from happy or sad to neutral and emotion congruence was observed. In fact, the results of the study, which appear in Figure 2, showed that the offset of an emotion-congruent expression changing into a categorically different expression is perceived *earlier* than the offset of an emotion-incongruent expression changing into a congruent one.

The results of this experiment therefore suggest that mimicry may be involved in previously observed influences of emotion in the perception of emotional expression. However, this initial experiment provides indirect evidence at best. Thus, in a second experiment participants again looked for the offset of faces changing from one emotional expression to another. In this second experiment, however, the participants' emotional states were not manipulated. Rather, half of the participants were instructed to hold a pen between their lips and teeth during the viewing task. The manipulation disrupted efficient mimicry of the stimulus faces without forcing the posing

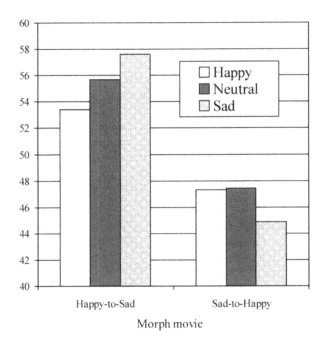

Figure 2. Mean frame of offset of expressions in happy-to-sad and sad-to-happy morph movies by individuals in happy, sad, and control emotion conditions. (Adapted from Niedenthal, Brauer, Halberstadt, & Innes-Ker, 2001.)

of a specific facial expression task (cf. Strack, Martin, & Stepper, 1988). A group of control participants were free to mimic the expressions conveyed by the stimulus faces. The reasoning here was that individuals who can mimic the faces freely are similar to individuals who are in an emotional state and observing an emotion-congruent expression. This is because in theory both sets of individuals can mimic the initial expression efficiently.

Individuals who cannot mimic are similar to individuals observing an expression inconsisent with their emotional state. This is because neither can efficiently mimic the expression. If the mimicry account of perceiving faces during emotional states is correct, then individuals who can freely mimic the faces should see facial expressions offset earlier than individuals who are prevented from mimicking the expressions. Findings indicated that participants who could mimic the faces indeed saw the offset of the initial expressions earlier than did participants who were not able to mimic the expressions, paralleling the results of the first study.[1]

The findings of this second set of studies are provocative in suggesting a close relationship between motor behaviour and perception. Although these specific studies will need to be replicated and extended, they are certainly consistent with other recent work that demonstrates the same types of relations (e.g., Adolphs et al., 2000; Carr et al., 2001). Our findings are also consistent with the conceptualisation of interaction between perception and cognition that is suggested in theories of embodied cognition which, as we discuss in detail later, may provide us with a much more compelling models of cognition – perception interactions (e.g., Barsalou et al., 2003).

In any event, it is clear from the studies just reviewed that perceivers' momentary emotional states can cause systematic, and potentially important influences in the perception of others' facial expressions of emotion. Of course, factors other than emotional state, such as individuals' chronic attitudes and motivations, are also likely to influence emotion perception. One such plausible and highly consequential factor is adult attachment style, a factor we consider in the next section.

ATTACHMENT AND THE PERCEPTION OF FACIAL EXPRESSION

Individuals differ not only in their emotional reactions to the same stimuli, but also in how they manage their own emotions and respond to the emotions of others. These differences appear strongly related to their

---

[1]Although it could be argued that participants who held a pencil in their mouths were more distracted than the other participants, we suspect that distraction would have led to the perception of offset later rather than earlier in the movies, and therefore consider it an unlikely alternative explanation.

attachment orientations, represented as mental models that "guide perceptions and trigger characteristic emotions, as well as defensive mechanisms, or rules for regulating emotion and for processing or failing to process certain kinds of attachment relevant information" (Cooper, Shaver, & Collins, 1998, p. 1381). As such, attachment orientation is a plausible moderator of the perception of emotional information, especially emotional expressions.

Bartholomew and Horowitz (1991) proposed a four-category conceptualisation of attachment orientation that was derived theoretically by fully crossing the content of individuals' "mental models", that is their representations of *self* versus *other*, with the valence associated with those representations (i.e., *positive* versus *negative*). The resulting scheme contains a *secure* category of people who have positive views of self and other; a *preoccupied* category of individuals who feel that others are available to them, but that they themselves are not worthy of receiving intimacy; a *fearful avoidant* category, which describes individuals who hold a negative view of self and a negative view of the supportiveness and availability of others; and a *dismissive avoidant* category in which individuals have a positive view of the self as worthy of caring for, but more negative view of others as essentially unavailable to them. Importantly, the four categories can and have been accounted for by a two-dimensional structure representing the extent to which an individual exhibits *anxious* (about abandonment) and *avoidant* (of intimacy) attachment-related behaviours (see Bartholomew & Shaver, 1998; Brennan, Clark, & Shaver, 1998; Fraley & Waller, 1998, for reviews). However, the present discussion and predictions largely utilise the categorical approach to remain consistent with much previous work on attachment style and emotion regulation (e.g., Feeney, 1998; Mikulincer & Florian, 1998).

Attachment, emotional experience, and emotion regulation

Attachment orientation has been shown to be associated with specific patterns of emotional responses and emotion regulation strategies (e.g., Mikulincer & Orbach, 1995; Simpson & Rholes, 1994). *Securely attached* individuals appear to cope well with their own emotions. They also respond effectively to displays of emotion expressed by attachment figures (e.g., Kobak, Cole, Ferenz-Gillies, Fleming, & Gamble, 1993). Furthermore, secure individuals seek intimacy and, when distressed, expect and accept support from intimate others (Mikulincer, & Florian, 1998; Simpson, Rholes, & Nelligan, 1992). In contrast, *dismissing avoidant* individuals consciously deny the need for intimate relationships. They tend to repress or otherwise rid themselves of negative emotions that stem from rejection (e.g.,

Shaver & Hazan, 1993), often by orienting attention away from conflict and negative attachment issues (Simpson, Rholes, & Philips, 1996). *Preoccupied* individuals have a strong need for intimacy. They are highly sensitised to negative emotional signals from attachment figures, and are concerned about the meaning of those cues for the stability and quality of the intimate relationship (Bowlby, 1980). Consequently, these individuals respond intensely to negative emotional input, and cope poorly with their own emotional responses, perhaps by directing too much attention to them (Shaver & Hazan, 1993). Finally, *fearful avoidants* try to stay clear of intimate relationships altogether, fearing that positive reactions from others will not be forthcoming and that negative reactions are all too probable. They are thought to try to minimise intimacy in order to minimise the pain of disappointment and rejection (Bartholomew & Horowitz, 1991).

Attachment and the perception of facial expression

The vulnerabilities to emotions and strategies for managing emotions that characterise different attachment orientations suggest specific ways in which attachment might affect the perception of facial expressions of emotion. Facial expressions convey not only the emotional state of the person expressing the emotion (Ekman & Friesen, 1975), but also the behavioural requirements of that state for the *perceiver* (for discussions of the affordances signalled by facial expressions, see e.g., Buck, 1991, 1999; McArthur & Baron, 1983). For instance, sadness signals a need to be taken care of, which places the perceiver in a care-taker role; anger signals the necessity to handle conflict, which places the perceiver in either an attack or a negotiating role; and so on. We can therefore ask how attachment style is related to the encoding of such invitations to social interaction. What is already known about attachment style and emotion regulation provides a rather good basis for prediction. Specifically, if it is assumed that individuals who fear interpersonal interactions (e.g., fearfuls) show evidence in processing of this fear at the level of perception, then they should avoid processing cues that invite such interactions. In the context of the morph task this means that they would see the offset of a facial expression that invites such an interaction earlier than an individual without the fear of engaging in such interactions. The complementary prediction would be made for individuals who vigilantly seek out interpersonal interaction (e.g., preoccupieds); they would more efficiently process evidence that invites such interaction. The evidence of this would be a tendency to see the offset of such expressions later in the movie.

Niedenthal, Brauer, Robin, and Innes-Ker (2002a, Study 1) conducted a study to test these basic hypotheses. Participants in the study were approximately 25 individuals from each of the four attachment orientations.

The study was described as an investigation of the categorisation of faces, and the experimental task consisted of 60 trials, composed of two repetitions each of 10 happy, 10 sad, and 10 angry morph movies, in which faces became neutral in expression. At the end of the session, participants completed the 36-item Experiences in Close Relationships scale (ECR; Brennan et al., 1998). For final analysis, participants' attachment orientation was recalculated using Brennan et al.'s (1998) scoring instructions for the ECR. First an Avoidance score and an Anxiety score was calculated for each participant. Then, participants were assigned to one of the four attachment orientations based on equations involving the classification coefficients (Fisher's linear discriminant functions) generated from a sample of $N = 1082$ US American college students (Brennan et al., 1998). The final groups included 28 secures, 32 preoccupieds, 13 dismissives, and 27 fearfuls.

Responses of secure individuals were used as a baseline to which other attachment styles were compared. Results are illustrated in Figure 3. As predicted, preoccupied individuals, who crave closeness and are vigilant to intimacy cues, saw the offset of happy (in happy-to-neutral movies) and angry (in angry-to-neutral movies) emotional expressions at a later point in the morph movies than did secures. In contrast, fearful individuals, who avoid intimacy and invitations to closeness, saw the offset of expressions earlier than secures. Dismissive individuals, like fearfuls, typically report that attachment concerns are not important to them, but, like preoccupied individuals, often reveal heightened concern with intimacy on implicit measures (e.g., Mikulincer, Florian, & Tolmacz, 1990). On the present task, dismissives indeed behaved like preoccupied individuals in that they saw the offset of happy and angry faces as occurring later in the morph movies than the secures.

Unexpectedly, there was no observed influence of attachment orientation on the perception of the offset of sad expressions. We had suggested that sadness signals the need to be taken care of, and predicted that, as with happy and angry expressions, the offset of this expression would be perceived differently by individuals with different attachment orientations. It is possible that sadness is a less ambiguous signal than happiness and anger, and that the behavioural requirements on the part of the perceiver are more stereotyped and less emotionally taxing. However, the present finding should be replicated before it is strongly interpreted.

In interpreting the results of this first study it is important to recognise that according to attachment theory (e.g., Bowlby, 1969) the attachment system evolved to motivate adaptive behaviours in times of distress or threat. Therefore the influence of attachment orientation on the processing of facial expressions may be moderated by the distress level of the perceiver, because the signal value of the face changes when the perceiver is distressed. Specifically, for a distressed perceiver, facial expression conveys information

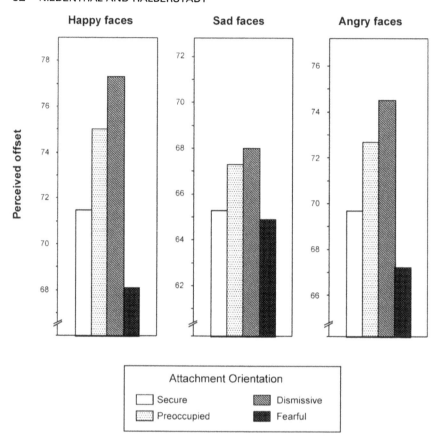

Figure 3. Mean offset scores for happy, sad, and angry faces, grouped by attachment orientation. (Adapted from Niedenthal et al., 2002a, Study 1.)

about the availability of the *expressor of the emotion* to provide support to the perceiver. In this case sadness and anger both signal unavailability, due to self-preoccupation and hostility, respectively. This unavailability is of special concern to insecurely attached individuals. Thus, if individuals were distressed, we would make different predictions from those tested in the study just described. Indeed, Niedenthal and colleagues (2002a) conducted a second study, which was a replication of the first except that a manipulation of distress was added.

The predictions were that, first, all insecure groups would see the offset of the negative facial expressions of emotion later than the secure group because of their concern, under distress, that a "safe haven" does not exist for them. This was thought to be particularly likely for the fearfuls who have neither feelings of worthiness nor feelings that others can be depended upon. Although preoccupied and dismissive individuals are also strongly motivated to be vigilant to negative facial cues, distress might actually reduce the processing efficiency of these individuals. Preoccupied individuals do not manage negative emotions well, and when feeling distress they may actually direct processing resources to their own emotional state at the expense of the efficient encoding of external stimuli. This would counteract somewhat the effect of their distress-heightened vigilance, yielding a perceived offset later than secures, but still earlier than the fearful group. At the same time, equally consuming emotion management strategies by dismissive individuals could also impair the efficiency of their processing of facial expression information. Specifically, it could be that dismissives devote processing resources to dissipating or repressing their ambient feelings of distress at the expense of efficient processing of external stimuli (Fraley, Davis, & Shaver, 1998; Simpson et al., 1996). Thus Niedenthal and colleagues (2002a) predicted that dismissives and preoccupieds would behave similarly to each other (albeit for different reasons) in their tendency to see negative facial expressions lasting longer on the face than would secure individuals, but not as long as the fearful individuals.

The procedure for inducing distress used in this second experiment was based on a method developed by Simpson et al. (1992), involving an alleged two-study paradigm. The "first" study was described to participants as a simple computer task concerned with face categorisation, and the "second" as a physiological study, which required that a baseline pulse be taken. After the pulse was taken, the experimenter continued the distress induction by reading a description, based on that used by Simpson et al. (1992), which indicated that the second study typically evoked heightened anxiety and distress in participants, but which failed to disclose details about the procedure of the study. After the paragraph was read to the participants, they were encouraged to look into the room where the procedures were supposedly going to take place. The "distressing room" was a dimly lit cubicle at the end of a hall. A large machine that measured heart rate and blood pressure was placed in between a TV monitor and computer on a desk. There were unattached wires covering the machine and tabletop so that the equipment appeared not fully set-up. An old wooden chair with wires attached to it was placed in front of the desk. The experimenter mentioned that the equipment was not ready yet, but would be by the time they had completed the computer task. After participants had taken a look, they followed the experimenter into a cubicle where they received further instructions and performed practice morphing trials. They then continued with the morphing experiment.

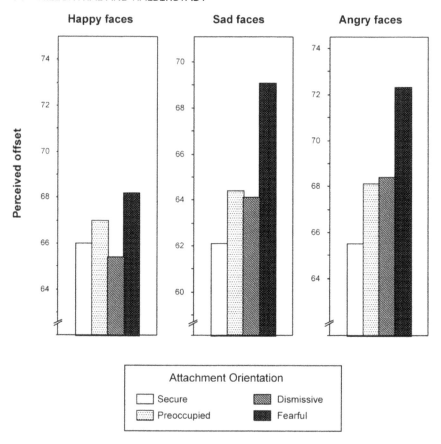

Figure 4. Mean offset scores for happy, sad, and angry faces, grouped by attachment orientation. (Adapted from Niedenthal et al., 2002a, Study 2.)

The hypothesised relations between attachment orientation and the perception of offset of facial expressions were supported by the findings, which are illustrated in Figure 4. As can be seen, compared to secure individuals, insecure individuals saw negative facial expressions of sadness and anger as lasting significantly longer on the faces. Moreover, compared even to preoccupied and dismissive individuals, this was particularly true for fearfuls, as would be expected. Furthermore, there were no differences between the groups in their perception of the offset of the expression of happiness from the face.

The results of this second series of experiments make the advantages of the morph task, and the importance of studying perception, quite clear. The task can capture differences in the nature of a facial expression that is seen by one type of individual as constituting evidence of an emotional expression, and by another type of individual as expressing neutral emotion. This difference has important implications for the interpersonal interaction that follows the facial gesture. For example, the perception (perhaps by a non-distressed dismissive individual) that another person no longer needs to be taken care of, because their sadness has passed, will perhaps lead the individual to redirect themselves away from the care-taking role to some other activity. The perception (perhaps by a distressed preoccupied individual) that another person is still angry will lead the individual to persist in appeasement behaviours that could be irritating and destructive. Thus, clearly the investigation of the perception of offset of facial expression provides greater insight into the processes underlying attachment behaviour, and goes well beyond the description of the emotional experiences and behaviours that characterise adults—and infants—with different attachment orientations.

This second series of studies complements the first in showing systematic top-down influence on the perception of facial expression of emotion. Such a result, combined with those observed in the first set of studies described earlier, hint at a new way of conceptualising the development and processing of attachment orientation. Although many descriptions of the parenting behaviours that are correlated with different attachment orientations currently exist in the literature (e.g., Roberts & Noller, 1998), much less is known about the mechanism, or the process by which these behaviours influence and become represented by the child. Recently, motor imitation, particularly of all types of emotional communication, indeed, "affective tuning" (Stern, 1985), has been proposed as the "missing link" in the process of empathy and the understanding of intention (Gallese, 2003; Iacoboni et al., 1999; Moore & Decety, 2003). And extension of these ideas to the development of an attachment orientation is quite natural. It may be, for example, that parents who perform the kinds of behaviour linked to different attachment styles already documented in the literature, also (and fundamentally) communicate emotions in very particular ways in the visual, tactile, and vocal channels. If such communications are repeatedly imitated by their children, the children will develop representations of the emotional communications of significant others—some of which may be potentially biased or maladaptive—and even inaccurate or unhealthy ways of responding to them (see Barsalou et al., 2003, for details of this processing). Thus, it could be that motor imitation is the primary vehicle of attachment orientation. In this sense, attachment orientation and emotional state may have not similar, but mechanistically identical types of effects on the perceptual processing of facial expression.

EFFECTS OF EMOTION CONCEPTS ON PERCEPTUAL MEMORY FOR EMOTIONAL EXPRESSIONS

Thus far we have demonstrated two factors that affect perceptions of others' emotional expressions: the perceiver's emotional state and their attachment orientation. We believe the demonstrations are particularly compelling because the tasks that we used involve a nonverbal response format. Participants viewed realistic, dynamic changes in targets' emotional expressions, just as they would in real social interactions, and assessed the visual displays directly. At the same time, however, the nonverbal nature of the task also distinguishes it from many real social interactions. Social perceivers of real emotional expressions and interactions *do* talk about them. A fundamental social task is to explain emotional events and expressions, probably because, as discussed above, different characterisations of the same facial expressions motivate and justify different types of behaviour.

Ironically, the very language that people use to communicate about others' emotional expressions may influence their perception of those expressions. Verbal explanations of emotion naturally invoke concepts, which we already know to guide perceptual memory for nonsocial stimuli (e.g., Carmichael, Hogan, & Walter, 1932). Tests of accentuation theory (e.g., Krueger, 1991; Tajfel & Wilkes, 1963), in which the assignment of category labels *per se* increases intra-category similarity, provide a psychophysical basis for social categorical distortions such as outgroup homogeneity (Linville, Fischer, & Salovey, 1989) and minimal-group discrimination (Brewer, 1979). In the domain of emotion perception researchers have analogously found that judgements of emotional facial expressions vary with the conceptual labels accompanying the faces. In the first study of this type, for example, Goodenough and Tinker (1931) found that perceivers were more ambivalent about what an emotional expression was communicating when it was accompanied by a verbal description associated with a different emotion than when it was accompanied by a consistent description (see also Fernandez-Dols & Carroll, 1997; Wallbott, 1988).

We believe, however, that it is not just the content of an explanation of emotion, but also the explanation itself, that influences perception. A growing literature suggests that language is a poor tool for encoding and remembering faces (e.g., Schooler & Engstler-Schooler, 1990). Schooler and Engstler-Schooler (1990), for example, showed a videotape of a staged bank robbery to participants, some of whom were subsequently asked to describe the perpetrator's face. Participants who verbalised the face were less accurate than controls at recognising it in a line-up situation.

A likely reason for the so-called "verbal overshadowing" effect is that the translation of a stimulus into a verbal or pre-verbal form interferes with "configural" processing. The fact that faces are processed configurally—that is, as nondecomposable wholes and/or featural relationships, rather than independent features—has been established, among other ways, by the disproportionate effect of face inversion on face perception and recognition (see Valentine, 1988, for review). Inverting a face in theory deprives perceivers of the configural information they would normally use to encode it, and forces reliance on relatively poor featural processing. Support for the role of configurality in verbal overshadowing includes the findings that verbalisation also interferes with memory for other configural stimuli, such as colour swatches (Schooler & Engstler-Schooler, 1990, Study 3), music (Houser, Fiore, & Schooler, 1996), and wine (Melcher & Schooler, 1996), but does *not* interfere with memory for inverted faces.

If verbal explanations of facial expressions indeed "decompose" them into their component features, then the expressions should be particularly vulnerable to being reintegrated with concepts that happen to be available at encoding. The most salient plausible concept will likely be contained in the explanation itself. Therefore, an emotion concept used to interpret an ambiguous facial expression should bias encoding of the expression in the direction of that concept. For example, a person explaining why someone's face looks sad should actually perceive, and therefore remember, the face *as* more sad than a person who explained the same face in terms of anger. This is particularly true if explanation involves simulation of the state, and its expressive aspects, by the perceiver themself (e.g., Niedenthal, Ric, & Krauth-Gruber, 2002b).

In a series of studies designed to test this hypothesis, Halberstadt and Niedenthal (2001) developed a novel recognition measure based on their morph movie methodology. Typically participants in face recognition research encode a real face under some experimental conditions and then later attempt to identify that face from among a set of similar foils. In contrast, Halberstadt and Niedenthal (2001) exposed participants to emotion *blends* extracted from various frames of their emotion movies and later asked them to reconstruct the blend online using the movie player described above. In the context of emotion recognition this procedure is more ergonomic than traditional forced-choice paradigms, in the sense of mimicking the common social task of monitoring gradual and subtle emotional changes. It is also more precise, quantifying bias in terms of the difference between the remembered emotional expression and the frame to which the participant was actually exposed. Finally, as noted above, the morphing task avoids the explicit use of labels and therefore isolates perceptual from labelling and response biases.

In one key experiment (Halberstadt & Niedenthal, 2001, Study 2), for example, participants viewed ambiguous angry – happy expressions. Each image was determined through pretesting to lie at the psychological midpoint of the angry–happy movie from which it was extracted. Participants were given one of three sets of instructions: In the control condition participants simply viewed the faces for 1 minute each without any additional information; in the "label" condition the statement, "this person is happy" appeared below half of the faces, and the statement, "this person is angry" appeared below the other half; in the critical "explanation" condition the instruction, "explain why this person is happy [angry]" appeared below the faces. Participants were told to explain the emotional expressions "in your head", because pretesting indicated no difference between explicit and implicit verbalisation. After 30 minutes of an unrelated filler task, all participants viewed the morph movies from which the target faces were generated and, using the movie viewer described above, attempted to identify the facial expressions they had seen at encoding. The dependent measure was memory bias, defined as the signed difference (in frames) between the remembered and the seen emotional expressions.

The results, which appear in Figure 5, supported the hypothesis that explanation enhances the perceptual bias associated with the emotion concepts used to interpret ambiguous emotional expressions. Participants remembered faces as marginally more angry when they were paired with "angry" labels than when they were paired with "happy" labels, but this influence was significantly enhanced when participants were asked to explain why the labels applied to the faces. Control participants, who had viewed the faces without additional information, demonstrated no bias at all. An examination of the absolute differences between remembered and seen faces indicated that controls also remembered the faces more accurately than the other two groups. Paradoxically, although explanation presumably increased attention to the target face at encoding, the content of the categories used in the explanation led to less accurate memory.

Thus, the same ambiguous blend of anger and happiness was perceived and remembered differently depending on the emotion concepts invoked to explain it. Anger and happiness, however, are unlikely to occur together in real social situations. Scherer and Tannenbaum (1986), in a large telephone survey, in fact found that anger and happiness are the only emotions that are *not* necessarily blended with other emotions. If our participants had previously encountered few anger–happy expressions, and had very little experience disambiguating them, then their interpretations of those expressions may have been particularly flexible and particularly vulnerable to verbal and conceptual biases.

Therefore, in a follow-up study Halberstadt and Niedenthal (2001, Study 3) replicated their results using anger–sadness blends, one of the two most common blends reported in Scherer and Tannenbaum's (1986) survey (the other was fear–sadness). The procedure was identical to that of the first

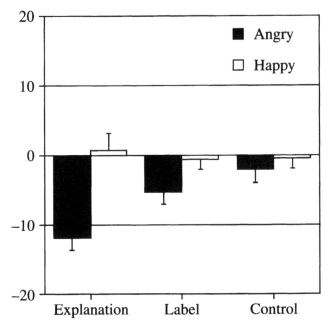

Figure 5. Top panel: Recognition of target faces as a function of categorisation and encoding condition, Study 2. Negative and positive numbers indicate that the face was remembered as more angry and happy, respectively, than it really was. Bottom panel: Recognition of target faces relative to participants' subjective midpoints, as a function of categorisation and encoding condition, Study 2. Error bars represent standard errors of the means. (Adapted from Halberstadt & Niedenthal, 2001, Study 2.)

study. First, a new set of pretest participants generated the midpoints of a set of anger – sadness morph movies, which became the ambiguous target faces presented to independent participants in the main study. Once again, participants were either asked to explain why the targets were angry or why they were sad (within-subject), were simply told the targets *were* angry or sad, or else viewed the faces with no additional information. The results replicated the emotion concept by encoding condition interaction almost perfectly. Participants again remembered as angrier faces described as "angry" than faces described as "sad", but the bias was significantly enhanced for participants who explained the emotions. Once again the control group's memory was relatively accurate.

Thus, participants exposed to both relatively rare angry – happy emotion blends and to extremely common anger – sadness blends perceived and remembered those faces consistent with the emotion concepts available at encoding, particularly when those concepts were part of a verbal explanation of the emotion blend. We believe these influences are indeed perceptual encoding biases, and were unlikely to have occurred at retrieval, for several reasons. First, participants' motivation to remember the concepts with which they were provided does not appear to enhance their effects. For example, the conceptual biases are equivalent whether participants provide their explanation before or after the recognition test, even though in the latter case the concepts provided by the experimenter are more accessible at the time of retrieval (e.g., Halberstadt & Niedenthal, 2001, Study 1). Second, controls remembered the faces more accurately than the explanation group, indicating that in the absence of prior verbal explanation participants have a relatively veridical representation of the face they saw. Why, at retrieval, would concepts invoked at encoding override participants' otherwise accurate perceptual memory?

We have interpreted these influences in terms of a two-stage process of decomposition and reintegration. Verbal explanations decompose emotional facial expressions, which are normally processed as configural wholes, leaving them vulnerable to reintegration with emotion concepts available in the explanation itself. However it is also possible that the process of explanation simply forges a stronger link between the faces and their category labels. Explanation has in fact been associated with increased salience in other social domains, such as judgements of the likelihood of events (e.g., Sherman, Skov, Hervitz, & Stock, 1981). Perhaps existing accentuation theory, with the additional assumption that explanation enhances the association between a facial expression and its category label, could account for the reported results without reference to configurality.

A variation on the main experiments, noted above, in which explanations were given either before or after the recognition test, argues against an account based solely on accentuation effects. Because only the latter group had reason to remember and rehearse their explanations, the timing manipulation served as an implicit manipulation of label salience, yet categorical distortions were equally strong in both conditions (Halberstadt & Niedenthal, 2001, Study 1). However this argument is based on a null result, and is in any case indirect. Much stronger evidence for configural decomposition could be garnered by holding the encoding conditions constant and varying the configurality of the faces. If the effects of explanation are indeed due to configural decomposition of the target faces, explanation should only enhance conceptual influences for configural stimuli. If the stimuli are processed featurally even in the absence of explanation, participants' perception should not be more biased by explanation of the emotion concepts than by presentation of the emotion labels alone. Importantly, the accentuation account, in which explanation increases the association between a face and its label, predicts explanation-enhanced distortion regardless of the configurality of the stimulus.

As noted above, face inversion is known to interfere with configural processing of faces by disrupting the familiar relationships among their features. Therefore we re-ran the explanation and label conditions of the previous study, varying, as an additional between-subjects factor, whether the target faces were presented upright or inverted. The results supported the configural decomposition account. As before, upright faces associated with anger at encoding were remembered as angrier than the same faces associated with sadness, and this difference was greater for participants who explained the target faces than for those who merely received a label for them. Memory for inverted faces, although also biased by the concepts provided at encoding, did not differ between the two encoding conditions. Furthermore, absolute recognition error was equivalent for upright and inverted faces, indicating that the differences are not simply attributable to poor memory for the latter.

In sum, the current experiments show that categorising an ambiguous emotional expression, a fundamental social task, leads to perceptual memory biases related to the category. Such an influence is caused, we have suggested, by the integration of the emotion concept with the features of the percept, an integration facilitated by verbal explanation of concept's application to the target face. And this interpretation makes the most sense if, again, we consider the use of an emotion concept as the simulation of the sensory-motor aspects of the emotional state and its expressive aspects (Barsalou et al., 2003; Niedenthal et al., 2002b). Thus the findings, in combination with those of the first two programmes of research presented in this chapter, have implications for our understanding of the interaction of language, memory, and emotion processing, of the nature and function of emotional expressions, and of perceivers' social information processing based on memories of emotional interactions. The ensemble of our work shows that there are important moderators of the perception of facial expression of emotion. This suggests that there are similar moderators of the perception of other stimuli as well, particularly stimuli that are of interest to social psychologists.

CONCLUSIONS

Von Hippel, Sekaquaptewa, and Vargas (1995) asserted that "nearly all of the effects of stereotypes take place at encoding ...," but they bemoaned the fact that "social psychological research is only rarely conducted in a manner that would allow one to determine at what point in the encoding process the effects take place" (von Hippel et al., 1995). Although social psychologists feel convinced, and often assert, that high-order processes of stereotyping, conceptualisation, and emotion affect perception, they have rarely tested that proposal empirically. What we have tried to do in this chapter is to provide some better evidence in support of this assertion. We also suggest that tasks can be developed and used, hand and hand with more precise perceptual tasks (such as word naming; Niedenthal, Halberstadt, & Setterlund, 1997) to detect the location in processing in which interesting, but clearly complex, effects are taking place, or are starting.

We have suggested throughout this chapter that recent embodied cognition/simulation accounts of conceptual processing suggest much more compelling ways to think about how cognition – perception interaction takes place. Because in such theories concepts are grounded in perceptual symbols, and entail sensory-motor simulation, this means that cognition and perception rely on the same (perceptual) representations (Barsalou, 1999a). Thus, many types of top-down processes in perception can be conceptualised as the preparation for perception by the prior perceptual simulation. In this case, theorists will not need to rely on some magical translation process by which abstract, amodal symbols that represent thoughts influence the altogether different representations used in perception (see, e.g., Prinz, 2002, for discussion).

The importance of such an approach is not entirely, indeed not even largely, in its possible impact on models of cognition, for cognitive psychologists. We think that this is perhaps most important for social psychologists. Thus, we concur with the recent thinking of Gallese (2003) when he wrote:

> When faced with the problem of understanding the meaning of others' behaviour, adult human beings must *necessarily* translate the sensory information about the observed behaviour into a series of *mental representations* that share, with language, the propositional format. This enables one to ascribe to others intentions, desires, and beliefs, and therefore to understand the *mental antecedents* of their overt behaviour ... I think that the view heralded by classic cognitivism, according to which our capacity of understanding the intentions determining others' behaviour is *solely determined* by meta representations created by ascribing propositional attitudes to others, is biologically implausible ... I think there is now enough empirical evidence to reject a disembodied theory of mind as biologically implausible.

REFERENCES

Adelmann, P. K., & Zajonc, R. B. (1987). Facial efference and the experience of emotion. *Annual Review of Psychology, 40*, 249 – 280.

Adolfs, R., Damasio, H., Tranel, D., Cooper, G., & Damasio, A. R. (2000). A role for somatosensory cortices in the visual recognition of emotion as revealed by three-dimensional lesion mapping. *Journal of Neuroscience, 20*, 2683 – 2690.

Barsalou, L. W. (1999a). Perceptual symbol systems. *Behavioral and Brain Sciences, 22*, 577 – 609.

Barsalou, L. W. (1999b). Language comprehension: Archival memory or preparation for situated action? *Discourse Processes, 28*, 61 – 80.

Barsalou, L. W. (2003). Situated simulation in the human conceptual system. *Language and Cognitive Processes, 18*, 513–562.

Barsalou, L. W., Niedenthal, P. M., Barbey, A., & Ruppert, J. (2003). Social embodiment. In B. Ross (Ed.), *The psychology of learning and motivation* (Vol. 43, pp. 43–92). San Diego, CA: Academic Press.

Bartholomew, K., & Horowitz, L. M. (1991). Attachment styles among young adults: A test of a four-category model. *Journal of Personality and Social Psychology, 61*, 226–244.

Bartholomew, K., & Shaver, P. R. (1998). Methods of assessing adult attachment: Do they converge? In J. A. Simpson & W. S. Rholes (Eds.), *Attachment theory and close relationships* (pp. 25–45). New York: Guilford Press.

Bower, G. H. (1981). Mood and memory. *American Psychologist, 36*, 129–148.

Bowlby, J. (1969). Disruption of affectional bonds and its effects on behavior. *Canada's Mental Health Supplement, 59*, 12.

Bowlby, J. (1980). By ethology out of psycho-analysis: An experiment in interbreeding. *Animal Behaviour, 28*, 649–656.

Brauer, M., Wasel, W., & Niedenthal, P. M. (2000). Implicit and explicit components of prejudice. *Review of General Psychology, 4*, 1–22.

Brennan, K. A., Clark, C., & Shaver, P. R. (1998). Self-report measurement of adult attachment: An integrative overview. In J. A. Simpson & W. S. Rholes (Eds.), *Attachment theory and close relationships* (pp. 46–76). New York: Guilford Press.

Brewer, M. B., (1979). In-group bias in the minimal intergroup situation: A cognitive-motivational analysis. *Psychological Bulletin, 86*, 307–324.

Bruce, V. (1988). *Recognizing faces*. Hove, UK: Lawrence Erlbaum Associates Ltd.

Buck, R. (1991). Social factors in facial display and communication: A reply to Chovil and others. *Journal of Nonverbal Behavior, 15*, 155–162.

Buck, R. (1999). The biological affects: A typology. *Psychological Review, 106*(2), 301–336.

Bush, L. K., Barr, C. L., McHugo, G. J., & Lanzetta, J. T. (1989). The effects of facial control and facial mimicry on subjective reactions to comedy routines. *Motivation and Emotion, 13*, 31–52.

Calder, A. J., Keane, J., Manes, F., Antoun, N., & Young, A. W. (2000). Impaired recognition and experience of disgust following brain injury. *Nature Neuroscience, 3*, 1077–1078.

Calder, A. J., Young, A. W., Perrett, D. I., Etcoff, N., & Rowland, D. (1996). Categorical perception of morphed facial expressions. *Visual Cognition, 3*, 81–117.

Canli, T., Silvers, H., Whitfield, S. L., Gotlib, I. H. & Gabrieli, J. D. E. (2002). Amygdala response to happy faces as a function of extraversion. *Science, 296* (21 June), 2192.

Carmichael, L., Hogan, H. P., & Walter, A. A. (1932). An experimental study of the effect of language on the reproduction of visually perceived forms. *Journal of Experimental Psychology, 15*, 73–86.

Carr, L., Iacoboni, M., Dubeau, M-C., Mazziotta, J. C., & Lenzi, G. L. (2001). *Observing and imitating emotion: Implications for the neurological correlates of empathy*. Paper presented at the First International Conference of Social Cognitive Neuroscience, Los Angeles, 24–26 April.

Cooper, M. L., Shaver, P. R., & Collins, N. L. (1998). Attachment styles, emotion regulation, and adjustment in adolescence. *Journal of Personality and Social Psychology, 74*, 1380–1397.

Decety, J., Grézes, J., Costes, N., Perani, D., Jeannerod, M., Procyk, E., et al. (1997). Brain activity during observation of actions: Influence of action content and subject's strategy. *Brain, 120*, 1763–1777.

Dimberg, U. (1982). Facial reactions to facial expressions. *Psychophysiology, 19*, 643–647.

Ekman, P., & Friesen, W. V. (1975). *Unmasking the face*. Englewood Cliffs, NJ: Prentice-Hall.

Ellison, J. W., & Massaro, D. W. (1997). Featural evaluation, integration, and judgment of facial affect. *Journal of Experimental Psychology: Human Perception and Performance, 23,* 213–226.

Etcoff, N. L., & Magee, J. J. (1992). Categorical perception of facial expressions. *Cognition, 44,* 227–240.

Farah, M. J. (1996). Is face recognition "special"? Evidence from neuropsychology. *Behavioural Brain Research, 76,* 181–189.

Feeney, J. A. (1998). Adult attachment and relationship-centered anxiety: Responses to physical and emotional distancing. In J. A. Simpson & W. S. Rholes (Eds.), *Attachment theory and close relationships* (pp. 189–218). New York: Guilford Press.

Fernandez-Dols, J. M., & Carroll, J. M. (1997). Is the meaning perceived in facial expression independent of its context ? In J. A. Russell & J. M. Fernandez-Dols (Eds.), *The psychology of facial expression. Studies in emotion and social interaction.* New York: Cambridge University Press.

Feshbach, S., & Feshbach, N. (1963). Influence of the stimulus object upon the complementary and supplementary projection of fear. *Journal of Abnormal Social Psychology, 66,* 498–502.

Feshbach, S., & Singer, R. D. (1957). The effects of fear arousal and suppression of fear upon social perception. *Journal of Abnormal & Social Psychology, 55,* 283–288.

Fraley, R. C., Davis, K. E., & Shaver, P. R. (1998). Dismissing-avoidance and the defensive organization of emotion, cognition, and behavior. In J. A. Simpson & W. S. Rholes (Eds.), *Attachment theory and close relationships* (pp. 249–279). New York: Guilford Press.

Fraley, R. C., & Waller, N. G. (1998). Adult attachment patterns: A test of the typological model. In J. A. Simpson & W. S. Rholes (Eds.), *Attachment theory and close relationships* (pp. 77–114). New York: Guilford Press.

Gallese, V. (2003). The manifold nature of interpersonal relations: The quest for a common mechanism. *Philosophical Transactions of the Royal Society, B, 358,* 517–528.

Goodenough, F., & Tinker, M. A. (1931). The relative potency of facial expression and verbal description of stimulus in the judgment of emotion. *Comparative Psychology, 12,* 365–370.

Halberstadt, J. B., & Niedenthal, P. M. (1997). Emotional state and the use of stimulus dimensions in judgment. *Journal of Personality and Social Psychology, 72,* 1017–1033.

Halberstadt, J. B., & Niedenthal, P. M. (2001). Effects of emotion concepts on perceptual memory for emotional expressions. *Journal of Personality and Social Psychology, 81,* 587–598.

Hall, J. (1984). *Nonverbal sex differences: Communication accuracy and expressive style.* Baltimore: Johns Hopkins University Press.

Heider, F. (1944). Social perception and phenomenal causality. *Psychological Review, 51,* 358–374.

Hess, U., Blairy, S., & Kleck, R. E. (1997). The intensity of emotional facial expressions and decoding accuracy. *Journal of Nonverbal Behavior, 21*(4), 241–257.

Houser, T., Fiore, S. M., Schooler, J. W. (1996). *Verbal overshadowing of music memory: What happens when you describe that tune?* Unpublished manuscript, University of Pittsburgh, Learning Research and Development Center.

Iacoboni, M., Woords, R. P., Brass, M., Bekkering, H., Mazziotta, J. C., & Rizzolatti, G. (1999). Cortical mechanisms of human imitation. *Science, 286,* 2526–2528.

Kobak, R. R., Cole, H. E., Ferenz-Gillies, R., Fleming, W. S., & Gamble, W. (1993). Attachment and emotion regulation during mother-teen problem solving: A control theory analysis. *Child Development, 64,* 231–245.

Krueger, J. (1991). Accentuation effects and illusory change in exemplar-based category learning. *European Journal of Social Psychology, 21,* 37–48.

Linville, P. W., Fischer, G. W., & Salovey, P. (1989). Perceived distributions of the characteristics of in-group and out-group members: Empirical evidence and a computer simulation. *Journal of Personality and Social Psychology, 57*, 165–188.

Manis, M. (1967). Context effects in communication. *Journal of Personality and Social Psychology, 5*, 326–334.

McArthur, L. Z. & Baron, R. M. (1983). Toward an ecological theory of social perception. *Psychological Review, 90*, 215–238.

Melcher, J. M., & Schooler, J. W. (1996). The misremembrance of wines past: Verbal and perceptual expertise differentially mediate verbal overshadowing of taste memory. *Journal of Memory and Language, 35*, 231–245.

Mikulincer, M., & Florian, V. (1998). The relationship between adult attachment styles and emotional and cognitive reactions to stressful events. In J. A. Simpson & W. S. Rholes (Eds.), *Attachment theory and close relationships* (pp. 143–165). New York: Guilford Press.

Mikulincer, M., Florian, V., & Tolmacz, R. (1990). Attachment styles and fear of personal death: A case study of affect regulation. *Journal of Personality & Social Psychology, 58*, 273–280.

Mikulincer, M., & Orbach, I. (1995). Attachment styles and repressive defensiveness: The accessibility and architecture of affective memories. *Journal of Personality and Social Psychology, 68*, 917–925.

Niedenthal, P. M. (1992). Affect and social perception: On the psychological validity of rose-colored glasses. In R. F. Bornstein & T. S. Pittman (Eds.), *Perception without awareness* (pp. 211–235). New York: Guilford Press.

Niedenthal, P. M., Brauer, M., Halberstadt, J. B., & Innes-Ker, Å. H. (2001). When did her smile drop? Contrast effects in the influence of emotional state on the detection of change in emotional expression. *Cognition and Emotion, 15*, 853–864.

Niedenthal, P. M., Brauer, M., Robin, L., & Innes-Ker, Å. H. (2002a). Adult attachment and the perception of facial expression of emotion. *Journal of Personality and Social Psychology, 82*, 419–433.

Niedenthal, P. M., Halberstadt, J. B., Margolin, J., & Innes-Ker, Å. H. (2000). Emotional state and the detection of change in facial expressions of emotion. *European Journal of Social Psychology, 30*, 211–222.

Niedenthal, P. M., Halberstadt, J. B., & Setterlund, M. B. (1997). Being happy and seeing "happy": Emotional mediates visual word recognition. *Cognition and Emotion, 11*, 403–432.

Niedenthal, P. M., Ric, F., & Krauth-Gruber, S. (2002b). Explaining emotion congruence (and its absence) in terms of perceptual simulation. [Comment on J. Forgas, "Feeling and Doing: Affective influences on interpersonal behavior"] *Psychological Inquiry, 13*, 80–83.

Niedenthal, P. M., & Setterlund, M. B. (1994). Emotion congruence in perception. *Personality and Social Psychology Bulletin, 20*, 401–410.

Niedenthal, P. M., Setterlund, M. B., & Jones, D. E. (1994). Emotional organization of perceptual memory. In P. M. Niedenthal & S. Kitayama (Eds.), *The heart's eye: Emotional influences in perception and attention* (pp. 87–113). San Diego, CA: Academic Press.

Prinz, J. J. (2002). *Furnishing the mind: Concepts and their perceptual basis.* Cambridge, MA: MIT Press.

Roberts, N., & Noller, P. (1998). The associations between adult attachment and couple violence: The role of communication patterns and relationship satisfaction. In J. A. Simpson & W. S. Rholes (Eds.), *Attachment theory and close relationships* (pp. 317–350). New York: Guilford Press.

Salovey, P., & Mayer, J. D. (1990). Emotional intelligence. *Imagination, Cognition and Personality, 9*, 185–211.

Scherer, K. R., & Tannenbaum, P. H. (1986). Emotional experiences in everyday life: A survey approach. *Motivation and Emotion, 10*, 295–314.

Schiffenbauer, A. (1974). Effect of observer's emotional state on judgments of the emotional state of others. *Journal of Personality and Social Psychology, 30*, 31–35.

Schneider, D., Hastoft, D. J., & Ellsworth, P. (1979). *Person perception.* New York: Addison-Wesley, Inc.

Schooler, J. W., & Engstler-Schooler, T. Y. (1990). Verbal overshadowing of visual memories: Some things are better left unsaid. *Cognitive Psychology, 22*, 36–71.

Schyns, P. G., & Rodet, L. (1997). Categorization creates functional features. *Journal of Experimental Psychology: Learning, Memory, and Cognition, 23*, 681–696.

Shaver, P. R., & Hazan, C. (1993). Adult romantic attachment: Theory and evidence. In D. Perlman & W. Jones (Eds.), *Advances in personal relationships* (Vol. 4, pp. 29–70). London: Jessica Kingsley.

Sherman, S. J., Skov, R. B., Hervitz, E. F., & Stock, C. B. (1981). The effects of explaining hypothetical future events: From possibility to probability to actuality and beyond. *Journal of Experimental Social Psychology, 17*, 142–158.

Simpson, J. A., & Rholes, W. S. (1994). Stress and secure base relationships in adulthood. In K. Bartholomew & D. Perlman (Eds.), *Attachment processes in adulthood* (pp. 181–204). London: Jessica Kingsley.

Simpson, J. A., Rholes, W. S., & Nelligan, J. S. (1992). Support seeking and support giving within couples in an anxiety-provoking situation: The role of attachment styles. *Journal of Personality and Social Psychology, 62*, 434–446.

Simpson, J. A., Rholes, W. S., & Phillips, D. (1996). Conflict in close relationships: An attachment perspective. *Journal of Personality and Social Psychology, 71*, 899–914.

Stern, D. N. (1985). *The interpersonal world of the infant.* London: Karnac Books.

Strack, F., Martin, L. L., & Stepper, S. (1988). Inhibiting and facilitating conditions of the human smile: A nonobtrusive test of the facial feedback hypothesis. *Journal of Personality & Social Psychology, 54*, 768–777.

Tajfel, H., & Wilkes, A. L. (1963). Classification and quantitative judgement. *British Journal of Psychology, 54*, 101–114.

Teasdale, J. D. (1983). Negative thinking in depression: Cause, effect, or reciprocal relationship, *Advances in Behaviour Research & Therapy, 5*, 3–25.

Valentine, T. (1988). Upside-down faces: A review of the effect of inversion upon face recognition. *British Journal of Psychology, 79*, 471–491.

von Hippel, W. Sekaquaptewa, D., & Vargas, P. (1995). On the role of encoding processes in stereotype maintenance. In M. P. Zanna (Ed.), *Advances in experimental social psychology* (Vol. 27, pp. 177–254). San Diego, CA: Academic Press.

Wagner, H. L., MacDonald, C. J., & Manstead, A. S. (1986). Communication of individual emotions by spontaneous facial expressions. *Journal of Personality and Social Psychology, 50*, 737–743.

Wallbott, H. G. (1988). In and out of context: Influences of facial expression and context information on emotion attributions. *British Journal of Social Psychology, 27*, 357–369.

Whorf, B. L. (1941/1956). Languages and logic. In J. B. Carroll (Ed.), *Language, thought, and reality: Selected papers of Benjamin Lee Whorf* (pp. 233–245). Cambridge, MA: MIT Press.

Young, A. W., Rowland, D., Calder, A. J., Etcoff, N., Seth, A., & Perrett, D. I. (1997). Facial expression megamix: Tests of dimensional and category accounts of emotion recognition. *Cognition, 63*, 271–313.

EUROPEAN REVIEW OF SOCIAL PSYCHOLOGY, 2003, *14*, 77–104

Prejudice and self-esteem: A transactional model

Brenda Major, Shannon K. McCoy, and Cheryl R. Kaiser

University of California at Santa Barbara, USA

Wendy J. Quinton

California State University, Long Beach, USA

This paper reviews three theoretical models of how prejudice affects the self-esteem of its targets. The *stimulus-response* model assumes that prejudice has a direct, negative effect on self-esteem. The *stimulus-perception-response* model recognises that perceptions of prejudice may not directly mirror experiences with prejudice, but predicts that the subjective perception of being a target of prejudice has a direct, negative effect on self-esteem. Both of these models are found to be inadequate. We propose a third, *transactional* model, which assumes that individuals do not respond in uniform way to being the target of prejudice. Rather, this model contends that self-esteem and emotional responses to prejudice are determined by cognitive appraisals of prejudicial events and coping strategies used in response to these events; these processes, in turn, are shaped by personal, situational, and structural factors. Experiments are presented showing that self-esteem in response to perceived prejudice is moderated by presence or absence of threats to personal identity, clarity of prejudices cues in the situation, ingroup identification, dispositional optimism, endorsement of legitimising ideologies, and group status. We argue that a transactional model of responses to prejudice emphasises sources of resistance as well as vulnerability among targets of prejudice.

Identities derived from group memberships are a core component of the self and provide individuals with a sense of belonging, esteem, and proscriptions for behaviour (Tajfel & Turner, 1986). Whereas some social identities are valued, respected, and sought out, others are devalued, disrespected, and avoided. Among these negative social identities, some are devalued only in certain narrow contexts, whereas others are consensually devalued, or stigmatised. Stigmatisation may stem from

Address correspondence to: Brenda Major, Department of Psychology, University of California, Santa Barbara, CA 93106-9660, USA. Email: major@psych.ucsb.edu

Preparation of this article was supported by National Science Foundation Grant #BCS-9983888 to Brenda Major and by National Institute of Mental Health Grant #1F32MH64308-01 to Cheryl Kaiser.

http://www.tandf.co.uk/journals/titles/99998080.asp   DOI: 10.1080/10463280340000027

possession of a tribal stigma, such as membership in a devalued ethnic or religious group, a physical stigma, such as disability or disfigurement, or a character stigma, such as drug addiction (Goffman, 1963). Defining features of stigmatisation include the possibility that one will be a target of prejudice or discrimination, as well as uncertainty about whether one's outcomes are due to discrimination or to some other cause (Crocker, Major, & Steele, 1998).

What are the behavioural and psychological implications of possessing a social identity that is consensually devalued, of being a target of pervasive negative stereotypes, prejudice, and discrimination? Researchers have examined a variety of cognitive, emotional, and behavioural consequences of this predicament, such as self-stereotyping, group identification, collective self-esteem, outgroup-directed hostility, task performance, social interactions, and personal self-esteem (see Crocker et al., 1998, for a review). Each of these outcomes is an important domain of inquiry. Here we focus on how perceiving the social self as a target of prejudice affects personal self-esteem and esteem-related emotions. In Western cultures, personal self-esteem is strongly related to the affective quality of experience, with people who have high personal self-esteem reporting more positive affect, more life satisfaction, less hopelessness, and less depression than people with low self-esteem (see Crocker & Quinn, 2000). Self-esteem is the strongest predictor of life satisfaction in the United States, stronger than all demographic and objective outcomes (such as age, income, education, and marital status) and other psychological variables (Diener, 1984). Self-esteem also is positively related to other significant life outcomes, including perceived control, task persistence and motivation, and social inclusion (see Baumeister, 1998, for a review). Thus, how prejudice affects the personal self-esteem of its targets is an important psychological concern.

In this paper we discuss three different theoretical models of how prejudice might affect the self-esteem of its targets. The *stimulus–response* model assumes that prejudice has a direct, negative effect on the self-esteem of its targets. *The stimulus–perception–response* model recognises that perceptions of prejudice may not directly mirror experiences with prejudice, but predicts that the subjective perception of being a target of prejudice has a direct, negative effect on self-esteem. A third, *transactional* model assumes that individuals do not respond in a uniform way to being the target of prejudice; rather, self-esteem and affective responses to being a target of prejudice are determined by how individuals cognitively appraise the event and the coping strategies they use to deal with the event. These processes, in turn, are a function of characteristics of both the person and the situation. We discuss each of these perspectives, and the evidence in support of them, below.

STIMULUS–RESPONSE MODEL

Many people assume that experiencing stressful life events leads directly to negative physical and mental health outcomes (Allison, 1998). This assumption, for example, guided the development of the Holmes and Rahe Social Readjustment Rating scale (1967), which was designed to determine the impact of number of stressful life events experienced on subsequent health. People whose social identities are consensually devalued are more likely to experience various forms of stressful events in their daily lives than are individuals whose social identities are more valued (Allison, 1998). Hence, the stimulus–response perspective predicts that being a victim of prejudice and discrimination will have a direct, negative effect on targets' self-esteem (see Figure 1). Certainly there is ample evidence that prejudice and discrimination cause targets harm. Prejudice limits targets' access to resources such as employment, income, housing, education, and medical care, and compromises their physical well being (see Allison, 1998; Clark, Anderson, Clark, & Williams, 1999, for reviews). Prejudice also exposes targets to many forms of interpersonal threat, including being ignored, excluded, patronised, belittled, ridiculed, and the target of physical violence (Leary, Tambor, Terdal, & Downs, 1995).

Based on such evidence, a number of scholars have asserted that experiencing pervasive prejudice and discrimination inevitably leaves "marks of oppression" on the personalities and self-esteem of their victims (e.g., self-hatred, neuroticism) (e.g., Allport, 1954/1979; Cartwright, 1950; Erikson, 1956). For example, although Allport (1954) recognised that targets vary in how they respond to prejudice and discrimination, he nonetheless observed that, "One's reputation, whether false or true, cannot be hammered, hammered, hammered, into one's head, without doing something to one's character" (p. 142). Cartwright noted, "To a considerable extent, personal feelings of worth depend on the social evaluation of the group with which a person is identified. Self-hatred and feelings of worthlessness tend to arise from membership in underprivileged or outcast groups" (1950, p. 440). Likewise, in commenting on their observation that a large percentage of African-American children in their study seemed to prefer White skin colouring to Black skin colouring, Clark and Clark (1950) wrote, "They [their data] would seem to point strongly to

Figure 1. Stimulus–response model.

the need for a definite mental hygiene and educational program that would relieve children of the tremendous burden of feelings of inadequacy and inferiority which seem to become integrated into the very structure of the personality as it is developing" (p. 350).

Reflecting this perspective, many studies have compared the self-esteem of members of stigmatised groups to the self-esteem of members of nonstigmatised groups, on the assumption that group differences in self-esteem would be due to group differences in experiences with prejudice and discrimination. As we discuss more fully elsewhere, however, researchers adopting this approach frequently encountered a paradox (see Crocker & Major, 1989). Members of chronically stigmatised groups often do not exhibit lower self-esteem than members of nonstigmatised groups (Crocker & Major, 1989; Porter & Washington, 1979; Rosenberg & Simmons, 1972; Simpson & Yinger, 1985). Indeed, some groups that are exposed to repeated, pervasive, and severe discrimination, such as African-Americans, have higher self-esteem than groups who are rarely targets of prejudice, such as European-Americans (Twenge & Crocker, 2002). Stimulus–response models are inadequate to explain these findings.

STIMULUS–PERCEPTION–RESPONSE MODEL

A second approach to conceptualising how prejudice affects the self-esteem of its targets assumes that perceived prejudice mediates the effects of exposure to prejudice on self-esteem (see Figure 2). According to this perspective, objective prejudice is not always perceived. This difference

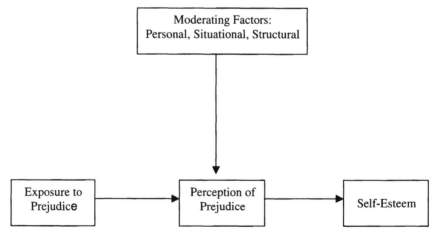

Figure 2. Stimulus–perception–response model.

between objective exposure and subjective perceptions of discrimination can lead to variability in targets' response to objective prejudice. If the self or ingroup is perceived to be a victim of discrimination, however, this perception has a direct, negative effect on self-esteem. In the following sections, we briefly review the evidence with regard to each of the two paths in the S – P – R model: from objective prejudice to perceived prejudice, and from perceived prejudice to self-esteem (for a more complete discussion, see Major, Quinton, & McCoy, 2002b).

From objective to perceived discrimination

Objective exposure to discrimination and subjective perceptions of the self or group as a victim of discrimination often do not correspond (see Crosby, 1982; Feldman-Barrett & Swim, 1998; Stangor, Swim, & Sechrist, this volume). Some individuals who are targets of discrimination fail to realise it, whereas other individuals believe they are victims of discrimination even when they are not. Recent reviews of this literature (Major et al., 2002b; Stangor, et al., this volume) indicate that whether or not people perceive themselves as targets of prejudice depends on a variety of personal, situational, and structural factors. For example, individuals are more likely to perceive discrimination against their group as a whole than against themselves personally (Crosby, 1982; Taylor, Wright, & Porter, 1994), are more likely to detect discrimination when information is presented aggregated across members of a group than on a case-by-case basis (Crosby, Pufall, Snyder, O'Connell, & Whalen, 1989), and are more likely to perceive themselves as targets of discrimination as the intensity of prejudice cues in the environment increases (Major, Quinton, & Schmader, 2003c).

In addition, some individuals are more sensitive to prejudice in their environment than are others. For example, African-American students who scored high on a measure of race-rejection sensitivity prior to beginning college were more likely to perceive negative race-related experiences and discrimination over the course of their first 3 weeks in college (Mendoza-Denton, Purdie, Downey, Davis, & Pietrzak, 2003). Individual differences in stigma-consciousness (i.e., the expectation of being stereotyped and reacted to on the basis of group membership) are positively related to perceptions of being discriminated against both at a personal and group level (Pinel, 1999). Individual differences in identification with the devalued group are also related positively to perceptions of personal and group identification (e.g., Branscombe, Schmitt, & Harvey, 1999; Crosby et al., 1989; Major, Gramzow, McCoy, Levin, Schmader, & Sidanius, 2002a; Sellers & Shelton, 2003), especially when prejudice cues in the environment are attributionally ambiguous (Major et al., 2003c; Operario & Fiske, 2001). For example, Major et al. (2003c) found that in the absence of situational cues indicating that an evaluator was prejudiced, or in the presence of blatant cues, level of gender identification did not predict the extent to which women blamed a poor evaluation on discrimination. However, when prejudice cues were ambiguous, women high in group identification were significantly more likely to blame a poor grade on discrimination than were those who were low in group identification (see Figure 3).

Individual differences in endorsement of beliefs that legitimise status differences in society also influence perceptions of personal and group discrimination. Such beliefs include the belief that status systems are permeable, that hard work is rewarded, and that one's outcomes and status are under one's own control, among others (Major & Schmader, 2001). In three studies, Major et al. (2002a), found that the more strongly low-status participants (Latino/a-Americans; women) endorsed the ideology of individual mobility (e.g., agreed with items such as "Advancement in American society is possible for individuals of all ethnic groups"), the less likely they were to report in general that they personally, or members of their group, were a target of ethnic discrimination. They were also less likely to blame discrimination when a higher-status confederate (European-American; man) rejected them for a desirable role ($\beta = -.45$). In contrast, among members of high-status groups, the more they endorsed the ideology of individual mobility, the more likely they were to blame discrimination when a member of a lower-status group rejected them for a desirable role ($\beta = .52$). This interaction is illustrated in Figure 4.

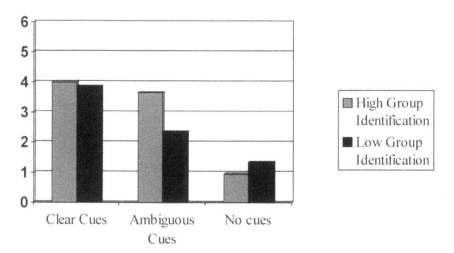

Figure 3.   Attributions to discrimination as a function of clarity of prejudice cues and group identification (from Major et al., 2003c).

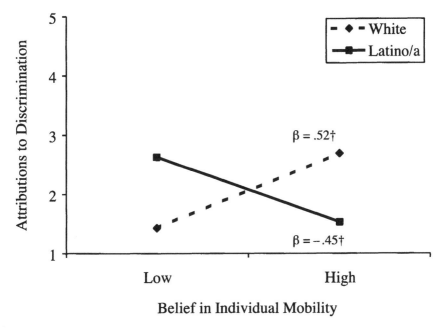

Figure 4. Attributions to discrimination among high- and low-status group members as a function of individual differences in the belief in individual mobility (from Major et al., 2002a).

As the studies by Major et al. (2002a) illustrate, relative group status also influences the extent to which discrimination is perceived. Reflecting their greater exposure to and experiences with discrimination, members of stigmatised groups are more likely than members of nonstigmatised groups to report on questionnaires or interviews that they and members of their group have been victims of discrimination (Major et al., 2002a; Operario & Fiske, 2001). When status differences in exposure are controlled experimentally, however, main effects of group status on attributions to discrimination are often not observed (Inman, 2001; Major et al., 2002a).

To summarise, perceived discrimination against the self (or group) does not always directly match objective exposure to discrimination. This disconnection between exposure and subjective perception may account for some of the variability in individual responses to prejudice. Both vigilance for and denial of discrimination may be associated with psychological costs, but under different circumstances (see Major et al., 2002b, 2003c; Miller & Kaiser, 2001, for a fuller discussion of this issue).

From perceived prejudice to lower self-esteem

The second assumption of the stimulus – perception – response approach is that perceiving oneself as a victim of prejudice and discrimination has a direct, negative effect on personal self-esteem (see Figure 2). This prediction is derived from symbolic interactionist theories of the development of the self, which posit that self-perceptions are based on perceptions of how others see the self (see Crocker & Major, 1989, for a discussion). This prediction is also consistent with theories that propose that psychological well-being is dependent on inclusion by others (Leary, 1990; Williams, 1997), the fulfillment of affiliation needs (Bowlby, 1969), and the perception that one is valued by others (Pyszczynski, Greenberg, & Solomon, 1997). For example, research has shown that ostracism or exclusion by others results in lowered self-esteem (Leary et al., 1995; Williams, Shore, & Grahe, 1998). In addition, perceiving that one's outcomes are due to discrimination requires recognising that others devalue an important and enduring aspect of the self—one's social identity (Branscombe et al., 1999; Schmitt & Branscombe, 2002a). For the stigmatised, discrimination also implies that important outcomes are under the control of powerful others. Consequently, perceiving oneself as a target of discrimination is hypothesised to have a direct, negative effect on self-esteem for members of stigmatised groups.

Consistent with the S – P – R model, a number of correlational studies report a negative relationship among members of disadvantaged groups between perceptions of discrimination and measures of psychological well-being. For example, the more women report being the victim of sexism, the more depression (Kobrynowicz & Branscombe, 1998) and less social self-esteem they report (Swim, Hyers, Cohen, & Ferguson, 2001). Higher general negative affect (hostile, depressed, and anxious affect combined) was also observed among women asked to imagine that they were excluded from a course by a sexist professor than among women asked to imagine that they were rejected by a professor who was a "jerk" (Schmitt & Branscombe, 2002b). Perceptions of personal discrimination are also associated with lower self-esteem among gay men (Diaz, Ayala, Bein, Henne, & Marin, 2001) and African-Americans (Branscombe et al., 1999).

Almost all of the studies cited in support of the existence of a direct, negative effect of perceiving prejudice against the self or group on self-esteem are correlational. As we have discussed extensively elsewhere (Major et al., 2002b), although the negative correlation between perceiving prejudice and self-esteem is reliable, its meaning is unclear for several reasons. First, of course, one cannot infer causation from correlation. It is possible that the causal direction is from self-esteem and depressed affect to perceptions of discrimination rather than the reverse. For example, Sechrist, Swim, and Mark (2003) found that women in whom a negative mood was induced were more likely to perceive themselves, and their group, as victims of discrimination than were women in whom a positive mood was induced, as long as an external attribution for induced mood was not provided.

Second, self-reports of frequently being a victim of discrimination are difficult to interpret. Typically, respondents are asked to indicate the extent (or frequency) with which they have been targets of prejudice in the past, e.g., "I consider myself a person who has been deprived of opportunities because of my gender" (Schmitt, Branscombe, Kobrynowicz, & Owen, 2002). Responses to such questions reflect the frequency (and/or severity) of exposure to objectively discriminatory events as well as subjective interpretations of and explanations for those events. Indeed, some researchers consider responses to questions such as these to reflect the amount of objective discrimination that respondents have experienced (Klonoff & Landrine, 1997) whereas others consider responses to the same questions to reflect attributional processes (Schmitt & Branscombe, 2002a).

Third, the relationship between perceptions of discrimination and self-esteem may be inflated by a "third variable" that biases both measures, such as individual differences in negative affectivity or interpersonal sensitivity (Major, Richards, Cooper, Cozzarelli, & Zubek, 1998). This problem is compounded when researchers ask participants the extent to which they feel like a "victim" (e.g., "I feel like I am personally a victim of society because of my gender", Kobrynowicz & Branscombe, 1997). Mendoza-Denton et al. (2003) found that among African-American participants, sensitivity to race-based rejection was negatively correlated with personal self-esteem, consistent with the S–P–R model. Both variables, however, were also correlated with individual differences in sensitivity to rejection in close relationships. Furthermore, when sensitivity to rejection in close relation-ships was partialled out, the relationship between race-based rejection sensitivity and self-esteem was no longer significant. In contrast, the negative relationship between rejection sensitivity in close relationships and self-esteem remained significant when controlling for race-based rejection sensitivity.

Our argument that individual differences in negative affectivity, rejection sensitivity, and related measures may inflate the relationship between perceived discrimination and self-esteem is not meant to imply that individuals who perceive themselves as targets of discrimination are neurotic or "making it up". Nor is it meant to imply that the relationship is not meaningful. Our point is an empirical one: researchers examining the relationship between perceptions of victimisation (due to any cause, including discrimination) and self-esteem should assess this relationship controlling for individual differences that might bias the correlation among these measures (or use experimental manipulations). In sum, although there is a consistent and reliable negative correlation between perceiving oneself as a frequent victim of discrimination and self-esteem, there is as yet little evidence that it is the perception of prejudice directed against the self or group that directly causes lowered personal self-esteem.

TRANSACTIONAL MODEL OF RESPONSES TO PREJUDICE

A third approach to understanding the impact of prejudice on self-esteem is shown in Figure 5. This approach draws upon transactional stress and coping models (e.g., Lazarus, 1999; Lazarus & Folkman, 1984). Possessing a consensually devalued social identity is a stressor similar to other types of chronic and acute stressors (Allison, 1998; Clark et al., 1999; Miller & Kaiser, 2001; Miller & Major, 2000). Thus, theoretical and empirical insights gained from research on adjustment to stressful events in general can be usefully applied to advance understanding of how people respond to being a target of prejudice. This perspective guides our own research (see Kaiser, Major, & McCoy, in press; Major et al., 2002b; Miller & Kaiser, 2001; Miller & Major, 2000).

Transactional models of stress and coping were designed to explain significant variability across individuals in adaptation and response to stressful events (Bandura, 1977; Lazarus, 1999; Lazarus & Folkman, 1984). A core premise of transactional models is that responses to stressful life events are unlikely to be uniform. Emotional responses to stressful events are assumed to be a function of how individuals cognitively appraise the event and the coping strategies they use to deal with events that are appraised as stressful. Events are appraised as stressful when internal or external demands are seen as taxing or exceeding the adaptive resources of the individual (Lazarus & Folkman, 1984).

Cognitive appraisals are judgements about the relationship between an individual and his or her environment and the implications of this relationship for psychological well-being (Lazarus, 1999; Lazarus & Folkman, 1984). In primary appraisal, a person assesses whether an event has the potential to threaten important, self-relevant goals or values. In

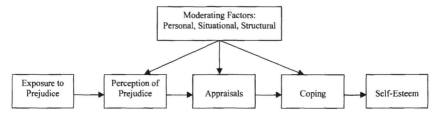

Figure 5. Transactional model.

secondary appraisal, an individual considers whether he or she is capable of remedying a stressful person–environment relationship. Although primary and secondary appraisals can be conceptually distinguished, they are interdependent, and often empirically indistinguishable (Lazarus, 1999). Coping is a goal-directed process aimed at regulating emotion, cognition, behaviour, physiology, and the environment, in response to stressful events or circumstances (Compas, Conner-Smith, Saltzman, Thomsen, & Wadsworth, 2001). Lazarus (1999) observed that although cognitive appraisals and coping are conceptually distinct constructs, it is often difficult to distinguish the two. For example, one method of coping is cognitive reappraisal—redefining an event as less threatening than it was originally appraised as being.

Cognitive appraisals and coping are a function of characteristics of both the person and the situation (Lazarus & Folkman, 1984). Situational factors that affect appraisals and/or coping include, for example, the severity, imminence, and predictability of the stressor, its self-relevance, and whether supportive others are present in the situation (Lazarus, 1999). Person factors include, for example, dispositional optimism, locus of control, and self-esteem (Major et al., 1998; Scheier, Carver, & Bridges, 2001; Taylor, 1989). Structural factors, such as membership in a group with high social status and ample resources, also moderate coping and appraisal processes (Adler & Ostrove, 1999; James, Hartnett, & Kalsbeek, 1983; Sapolsky, 1995). These situational, structural, and personal factors moderate the relationship between stressors and psychological response via their impact on cognitive appraisals and coping.

In the following sections, we use the conceptual model illustrated in Figure 3 as an organising framework for discussing our own research programme addressing targets' self-esteem and esteem-related emotional responses to perceiving discrimination based on their social identity. According to our transactional model, although an event may be perceived as discriminatory, the consequences of that perception for self-esteem are unlikely to be direct or uniform. Rather, they will depend on how the discriminatory event is appraised and coped with; these processes, in turn, are shaped by a variety of personal, situational, and structural factors.

MODERATORS OF THE IMPACT OF PERCEIVED PREJUDICE ON SELF-ESTEEM

The research we present here focuses on factors that moderate the relationship between perceptions of prejudice and self-esteem, presumably through their effects on appraisals and coping strategies. The moderators we address do not by any means exhaust the list of potential moderators, but illustrate the type of factors likely to moderate the relationship between perceived prejudice and self-esteem. We address various ways of coping with perceived prejudice in more detail elsewhere (e.g., Major et al., 2002b; Major, Quinton, McCoy, & Schmader, 2000; Major & Schmader, 1998; Miller & Kaiser, 2001; Miller & Major, 2000).

Threats to personal identity

An important variable that moderates the impact of perceived prejudice on personal self-esteem is whether or not the person has also experienced a threat to his or her personal identity. Personal identity refers to a person's sense of his or her *unique* self; i.e., the self based in an individual's unique characteristics and traits. Personal identity can be distinguished from social identity, i.e., the self derived from membership in social categories or groups, and which is shared to some extent with others. People may experience threat (e.g., rejection; a poor evaluation) based on aspects of their personal identity (for example, their personality or ability) or social identity (for example, their gender or ethnic group membership), or may experience both types of identity threat. For example, a person who is told that their group is lazy (a threat to social identity) may also be told that they are personally incompetent (a threat to personal identity). The impact of a threat to social identity on personal self-esteem is likely to vary depending on whether the person has or has not also experienced a threat to their personal identity.

Several scholars (Crocker & Major, 1989; Dion, 1975; Dion & Earn, 1975; Major & Crocker, 1993) propose that perceiving oneself as a target of prejudice based on one's social identity can help to protect personal self-esteem when individuals are faced with threats to their personal identity. Drawing on Kelley's (1973) discounting principle, Crocker and Major (1989) hypothesised that the perceived availability of prejudice as a plausible external cause of negative outcomes might allow the stigmatised to *discount* their own role in producing those outcomes. Furthermore, Crocker and Major (1989) hypothesised that because prejudice is external to the personal self, attributing negative outcomes to prejudice should protect personal self-esteem relative to making attributions to "internal, stable, and global causes such as lack of ability" (p. 613). They based their hypothesis on theoretical models of emotion positing that attributing negative events to causes external to the self protects affect and self-esteem, whereas attributing negative outcomes to causes internal to the self for which one is responsible, such as one's lack of ability, leads to negative affect and low self-esteem (e.g., Abramson, Seligman, & Teasdale, 1978; Weiner, 1995). In support of their predictions, Crocker, Voelkl, Testa, and Major (1991) found that women who received negative evaluations on an essay from a sexist male evaluator were more likely to attribute it to sexism, reported significantly less depressed affect, and reported marginally higher self-esteem, than women who received negative feedback from a non-sexist evaluator. As we noted elsewhere (Major et al., 2002b), the discounting hypothesis can be considered a reappraisal coping process by which an individual cognitively reframes a threatening situation in a manner that avoids implicating core stable aspects of the personal self as the cause of the event, such as intelligence or personality.

Subsequent statements of the theory differentiated between attributing a negative event to one's social identity and attributing it to *prejudice* against one's social identity (Crocker & Major, 1994; Major et al., 2002b). In order to qualify as discrimination, an event must be perceived as *both* unjust and due to group membership. If an individual perceives herself as treated unjustly, but blames her treatment on her personal, rather than social, identity this is not an attribution to discrimination. More importantly, if an individual attributes his treatment to his social identity, but also believes the treatment was justified, this too does not qualify as an attribution to discrimination. The latter attribution is an attribution to *justifiable differential treatment*. This definitional clarification is important because attributions to justifiable differential treatment lack the self-protective properties sometimes associated with attributions to discrimination. For example, Crocker, Cornwell, and Major (1993) found that overweight women who were rejected as a partner by a man who knew their weight blamed the rejection on their weight, rather than on prejudice. Furthermore, blaming weight was associated with negative emotional consequences for the overweight women. Crocker and Major (1994) argued that rejection on the basis of weight is often seen as justified because weight is presumed to be under personal control.

In more recent refinements, Major and her colleagues (Major et al., 2002b; Major, Kaiser, & McCoy, 2003a) reconceptualised the discounting hypothesis as a theory of the emotional consequences of attributions of *blame* rather than of attributions of causality. According to their self-blame discounting hypothesis, an attribution to discrimination involves attributing responsibility (or blame) for a negative event to another whose actions are unjustified. Furthermore, it is judgements of blame, rather than judgements about the locus of causality (internal vs external) that are the critical determinants of emotion due to negative events (Weiner, 1985). Thus, Major et al. (2002b) argued that attributing a negative event to discrimination protects self-esteem to the extent that it discounts self-blame rather than internal causes. This distinction is important because attributions to prejudice, because they implicate one's group membership, contain an internal as well as an external component (see Schmitt & Branscombe, 2002b). Indeed, Major et al. (2003a) found that attributions to discrimination protect self-esteem to the extent that they discount *self-blame*, but not internal causation, for a negative outcome.

Perceived discrimination is likely to buffer self-esteem primarily when an individual experiences a threat to an internal, stable aspect of the personal self. Recent evidence indicates that although attributing a negative event to discrimination protects self-esteem relative to attributing the event to internal, stable qualities of self, it does not protect self-esteem relative to making purely external attributions (Major et al., 2003a; Schmitt & Branscombe, 2002b). Schmitt and Branscombe (2002b) found that women experienced more negative affect (on a composite measure of depressed, anxious, and hostile affect) if they imagined being rejected from a course by a sexist professor who excluded women than if they imagined being rejected because of purely external factors (i.e., the professor was a "jerk" who excluded everyone). In a replication and extension of this study, Major et al. (2003a) found that women and men who were asked to imagine that they were excluded from a course by a sexist professor were significantly less depressed (but not less angry) than men and women asked to imagine they were excluded because the professor thought they were unintelligent. These experiments indicate that whether an attribution to discrimination is likely to have beneficial or detrimental emotional effects depends on what the alternative attribution to discrimination is likely to be and the specific emotion in question.

When predicting emotional reactions to perceiving the self as a target of prejudice, it is particularly important to differentiate among *self-directed* emotions such as depression and self-esteem and *other-directed* emotions such as anger and hostility (Major et al., 2003a; Major et al., 2002b). Crocker and Major (1989) hypothesised that attributing a negative event to discrimination could protect *self-esteem* and related self-relevant emotions, such as depression. They did not hypothesise, nor would one expect, that attributions to discrimination would protect individuals from experiencing anger. In their initial test of the discounting hypothesis, Crocker and colleagues (1991) found that attributing a negative evaluation to discrimination buffered women from experiencing depressed affect, but not from hostile or anxious affect. The study by Major et al. (2003a) described above observed similar emotional specificity. Furthermore, Branscombe et al. (1999) found perceptions of discrimination among African-Americans to be positively associated with hostility towards Whites. Thus, when researchers combine hostile and depressed affect into a single composite measure (e.g., Schmitt & Branscombe, 2002b) the results are difficult to interpret and likely to produce misleading conclusions.

In sum, research suggests that in the context of a threat to personal identity, perceiving discrimination based on one's social identity can buffer personal self-esteem to the extent that it shifts blame from stable, unique aspects of the personal self to the prejudice of others. It is important to note that blaming specific events on discrimination (e.g., "I failed the test because the grader is sexist") is conceptually and methodologically distinct from self-reports of experiencing pervasive discrimination (e.g., "I am a victim of society because of my gender"). As noted above, self-reports of experiences with discrimination confound attributional processes with frequency and severity of exposure to discrimination. In contrast, experiments that test the prediction that an attribution to prejudice can protect self-esteem from personal threat control for exposure to a negative event across participants and manipulate the plausibility that prejudice could have caused the event. Attributing a negative event to discrimination can be viewed as a coping strategy that mitigates the threat to personal self-esteem that might arise from blaming the event on internal, stable aspects of the self. Self-reported experiences of being a target of pervasive prejudice that are assessed in the absence of a direct personal threat do not serve such a purpose. Thus, we regard the presence of a personal threat as an important contextual factor that moderates the emotional consequences of perceived discrimination.

Clarity of prejudice cues

A second factor that moderates the relationship between perceived prejudice and self-esteem is the clarity, or intensity, of prejudice cues in the environment. Crocker and Major (1989) hypothesised that blatant prejudice protects self-esteem from threat more than prejudice that is hidden or disguised. When one is faced with blatant prejudice, there is no uncertainty about who is to blame for the negative event. In contrast, being exposed to ambiguous prejudice leaves members of stigmatised groups with considerable uncertainty about the causes of negative feedback. Thus, they may be unable to reap the benefits of attributions to discrimination because they cannot fully discount their role in producing negative outcomes. Major, et al. (2003c) tested this hypothesis in a study in which women received negative feedback from a man in the presence of cues indicating that he was either clearly sexist, ambiguously sexist, or no cues to his sexism were revealed. As predicted, women reported significantly higher state self-esteem when the negative feedback came from a clearly sexist man than when the man's sexism was ambiguous or no cues to his sexism were mentioned. In addition, women in the clear cues to sexism condition discounted the negative feedback (i.e., attributed the feedback more to discrimination than to their lack ability) more than did women in the ambiguous cues condition or the no cues condition. Across conditions, the more women discounted their ability as a cause of the feedback, the higher their personal self-esteem.

Internal analyses examining the correlation between attributions to discrimination and self-esteem within experimental conditions revealed that this relationship varied dramatically by context. Blaming discrimination was *positively* associated with self-esteem in the clear cues condition, was *unassociated* with self-esteem in the ambiguous cue condition, and was *negatively* associated with self-esteem when no cues to the man's sexism were present. This interaction is illustrated in Figure 6. These results suggest that correlational studies and experimental studies may sometimes produce such different results because of differences in the clarity of prejudice cues in the situation in which they are assessed. These results also suggest that being overly vigilant for signs of prejudice (i.e., blaming outcomes on discrimination when no cues are present) is negatively associated with self-esteem. So too, however, is denying blatant discrimination (i.e., failing to blame outcomes on discrimination when discrimination is clear). In sum, when clear situational cues to discrimination facilitate the discounting of one's own role in causing a

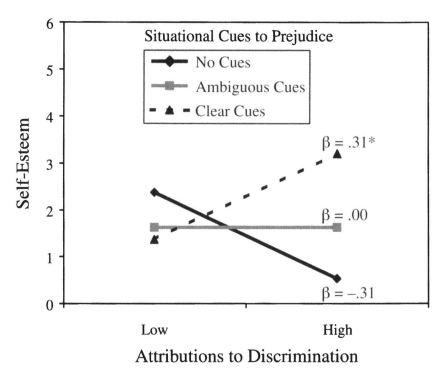

Figure 6. Self-esteem as a function of clarity of prejudice cues and attributions to discrimination (from Major et al., 2003c).

negative outcome, it can buffer personal self-esteem from the consequences of that outcome.

Group identification

A third variable that moderates the impact of perceived discrimination against the group on personal self-esteem is the extent to which the individual is identified with the targeted group. The more identified one is with a group, the greater likelihood that negative group-related events will be appraised as self-relevant. Negative events that are more self-relevant are appraised as more threatening (Lazarus & Folkman, 1984; Patterson & Neufeld, 1987). Thus, the more central and important a particular social identity is to an individual, the more threatening it might be for that individual to perceive discrimination against that social identity. McCoy and Major (2003) tested this hypothesis in two experiments. In their first experiment, women, all of whom had previously completed a measure of gender identification, received negative feedback on a speech from a male evaluator. Thus, all received a threat to their personal identity. On the basis of an exchange of attitude questionnaires, the women learned that the evaluator had clearly sexist or nonsexist attitudes towards women. Women low in gender identification reported less depressed emotion, and higher self-esteem, in the sexist than nonsexist condition. In contrast, among highly gender-identified women, self-esteem and depressed emotions did not differ between the sexist and nonsexist conditions (see Figure 7). This interaction suggests that perceiving prejudice against one's social identity protects personal self-esteem from threat only when that social identity is not a core aspect of self. When social identity is a core aspect of the self, prejudice against that social identity is more self-relevant, and hence more personally threatening. It is important to note that, however, even among women who were highly group identified, the sexist condition did not result in *lower* self-esteem than the nonsexist condition. As discussed above, we believe this occurred because all women experienced a threat to their personal identity in this study.

In McCoy and Major's (2003) second experiment, Latino/a-American students, all of whom had previously completed a measure of ethnic group identification, read an article documenting pervasive prejudice against Latino/as or a control article. Threat appraisals as well as emotional responses were then assessed. Consistent with predictions, group identification also moderated the impact of perceptions of pervasive ingroup prejudice on emotional responses. Among participants in the ingroup prejudice condition, group identification was positively associated with depressed affect, such that participants high in ethnic group identification were more depressed after reading about prejudice against their group than

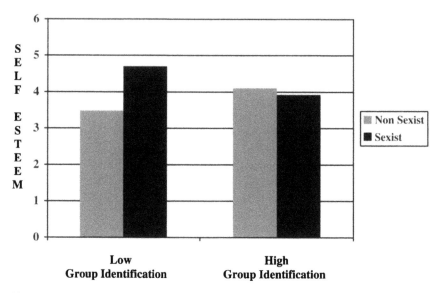

Figure 7. Self-esteem as a function of group identification and prejudice condition (from McCoy & Major, 2003). Note: Graph displays predicted mean values of self-esteem one standard deviation above and below the mean of group identification.

were participants low in ethnic group identification. In contrast, in the control condition, group identification was negatively associated with depressed emotions. Furthermore, group identification also interacted with experimental condition to predict threat appraisals. The more Latino/a-American students in the prejudice condition identified with their ethnic group, the more they reported being personally threatened by racism. These primary appraisals of threat, in turn, fully mediated the positive relationship between group identification and depressed emotion. Collectively these two experiments indicate that individual differences in group identification moderate the impact of perceived prejudice against the group on personal self-esteem. Furthermore, consistent with our transactional model, the second experiment demonstrated that group identification moderated the relationship between perceived prejudice against the group and depressed emotion via its impact on cognitive appraisals of personal threat.

Although identification with a group can increase an individual's vulnerability to perceived threats against the group, identifying with a group can also be an important coping strategy in response to group threat (Allport, 1954/1979). Groups can provide emotional, informational, and instrumental support, social validation for one's perceptions, and social consensus for one's attributions. Turning to the group can facilitate attempts to directly solve the problem of prejudice (e.g., collective action) as well as facilitate attempts to deal with the emotions resulting from perceiving prejudice. Branscombe and colleagues proposed that group identification increases in response to perceived prejudice against the group, and that this increased group identification enhances psychological well-being. They further proposed that this increase in identification with the group partially offsets a direct negative effect of perceived prejudice against the group on self-esteem and psychological well-being. Thus, perceived prejudice has an indirect, positive effect on well-being, mediated by its impact on group identification (Branscombe et al., 1999). Several studies have shown that perceptions of prejudice and group identification are positively associated (e.g., Branscombe et al., 1999; Major et al., 2002a; Operario & Fiske, 2000). Further, Jetten, Branscombe, Schmitt, and Spears (2001) showed experimentally that customers in a piercing salon who read that prejudice existed against body piercers subsequently identified more strongly with that group than customers who read that prejudice against body piercers was decreasing. A number of studies also report a positive association between group identification and self-esteem among stigmatised groups (Bat-Chava, 1994; Branscombe et al., 1999; Munford, 1994; Phinney, 1990; Rowley, Sellers, Chavous, & Smith, 1998). These findings are consistent with the idea that group identification can be an effective coping strategy in response to perceptions of prejudice against the group.

However, not all members of stigmatised groups may cope with discrimination by increasing their identification with the group. Some individuals and groups may cope with perceived prejudice against the group by decreasing their affiliation and identification with a group (e.g., Arndt, Greenberg, Schimel, Pyszczynski, & Solomon, 2002). Research by Ellemers and colleagues suggests that highly identified members of a group respond to threats to the group by increasing their identification with the group, whereas those members who are low in identification decrease their identification even more in response to threats to the group (see Ellemers, Spears, & Doosje, 2002 for a review). In the study described above, McCoy and Major (2003, Exp. 2) observed a significant interaction between prejudice condition and initial levels of group identification on subsequent identification with the group. Specifically, after reading about pervasive discrimination towards their ingroup, Latino/a-American students who had previously reported low levels of ethnic group identification identified even less with their ethnic group, whereas previously highly group identified Latino/a-American students identified even more strongly with their ethnic group. Further research is needed to determine when group identification is a buffer against vs a source of vulnerability to prejudice against the group.

Optimism

Stable characteristics of persons also moderate the relationship between perceived prejudice and self-esteem. Research in the health domain indicates that personal resources, such as dispositional optimism and an internal locus of control, are important moderators of emotional responses to stressors. For example, relative to people with a pessimistic outlook on life, optimistic individuals tend to fare better emotionally in the face of a wide variety of stressful events (see Scheier et al., 2001, for a review). Optimism is theorised to affect adjustment through its impact on cognitive appraisals. People with an optimistic outlook tend to appraise potentially stressful events as less harmful and taxing than people with a pessimistic outlook on life. Their more benign appraisals, in turn, are associated with greater psychological resilience in the face of stressful life events (Major et al., 1998).

Kaiser et al. (in press) examined whether dispositional optimism moderated the impact of perceived prejudice against the group on personal self-esteem, and whether it did so via its impact on cognitive appraisals. In their first study, men and women who had previously completed a measure of dispositional optimism were randomly assigned to read an article about prejudice against their own gender group or one of two control articles (i.e., an article about prejudice against the elderly or a neutral article unrelated to prejudice). Participants then completed measures of self-esteem and depressed emotions. Among men and women who read about pervasive sexism directed towards their own gender group, an optimistic outlook on life was associated with significantly higher self-esteem and less depression. Among participants who read control information, optimism was unrelated to depressed emotions and still significantly, but more weakly, positively related to self-esteem. There was no main effect of the prejudice manipulation on self-esteem or depressed emotions, even though participants in the sexism condition perceived greater prejudice against their gender group than participants in the control conditions.

A follow-up study examined whether cognitive appraisals of personal threat mediated the relationship between optimism and self-evaluative emotions (Kaiser et al., in press, Study 2). Women who were dispositional optimists or pessimists were recruited and asked to read an article documenting pervasive sexism against women. They then completed measures of primary and secondary appraisals, personal self-esteem, and depressed emotions. Again, optimism was positively related to self-esteem and negatively related to depressed emotions. Furthermore, as predicted, this relationship was mediated by cognitive appraisals. Compared to pessimists, optimists appraised prejudice against their group as less personally threatening and believed they were better prepared to cope with prejudice. These more benign appraisals, in turn, were related to higher self-esteem and less depression. In sum, these studies demonstrate that individual differences in personal resources, such as dispositional optimism, moderate the relationship between perceived prejudice against the group and self-evaluative emotions, and that they do so via their impact on cognitive appraisals of threat.

Legitimising ideologies

The accessibility of ideologies that legitimise group status differences also moderates the self-esteem implications of perceived discrimination against the group (Kaiser & Major, in press; Major, Kaiser, & McCoy, 2003b). Legitimising ideologies locate the source of group status differences within individual attributes of group members (e.g., low effort, lack of ability). Endorsing legitimising ideologies helps people to feel that their environments are predictable and controllable, and is positively related to psychological health (Kluegel & Smith, 1986). However, because legitimising ideologies encourage blaming the self for outcomes that may in fact be due to factors outside one's control, endorsing them can also make individuals who are targets of prejudice and discrimination feel like moral failures. For example, Quinn and Crocker (1999) found that overweight women who had been primed with the Protestant work ethic ideology prior to reading about discrimination against the overweight reported lower self-esteem and lower well-being than overweight women primed with an inclusive ideology. The prime had no effect on average weight women.

Major et al. (2003b) demonstrated that this vulnerability is not limited to group membership perceived as controllable, as overweight generally is seen as being. They investigated whether individual differences in endorsement of legitimising ideologies moderated women's self-esteem in response to reading about sexism and Latino/a-Americans' self-esteem in response to reading about racism against Latino/a-Americans. In an initial study, women, all of whom had previously completed measures of individual mobility and self-esteem, read an article describing pervasive sexism against women, or one of 2 control articles. As predicted, women who read that sexism was pervasive and who strongly endorsed the ideology of individual mobility reported decreased self-esteem relative to women who less strongly endorsed this ideology. In contrast, when women read neutral information, endorsement of legitimising ideology tended to be positively associated with self-esteem. There was no main effect of sexism condition on self-esteem, even though women in the sexism condition perceived more discrimination against women than did women in the control conditions.

In another study, Latino-Americans who read that prejudice against their own ethnic group was pervasive reported lower self-esteem the more they endorsed the ideology of individual mobility. In contrast, among Latino-Americans who read about prejudice against a non-self-relevant group, endorsing the ideology of individual mobility was unassociated with self-esteem. Again, there was no main effect of prejudice condition on self-esteem, even though participants in the racism condition perceived more discrimination against Latino/a-Americans than did those in the control condition. Collectively, these studies demonstrate that the extent to which individuals chronically or temporarily endorse ideologies that legitimise their low status moderates the impact of perceived prejudice against the group on personal self-esteem.

Group status

Experiences of being a target of prejudice vary with the social status of one's group. Because they face less frequent and less severe forms of discrimination, members of high-status groups, relative to low-status groups, are likely to appraise the discrimination they do experience as less threatening (Schmitt & Branscombe, 2002a). For these reasons, Schmitt and Branscombe (2002a) argue that attributions to discrimination are less detrimental to the self-esteem and well-being of members of high-status groups, than for low-status groups. They cite evidence that perceptions of discrimination are negatively correlated with psychological well-being among low-status groups but not among higher-status groups in support of their argument (e.g., Kobrynowicz & Branscombe, 1998). However, as we noted above, these studies have several interpretational problems. For example, members of high- and low-status groups may be thinking of examples of discrimination that vary greatly in severity when responding to self-report questions about experience with discrimination. Thus, observed status differences may be due to the effects of objective experiences with discrimination on well-being rather than the effects of attributional processes on well-being.

Does group status moderate the emotional consequences of attributing the *same* negative event to discrimination? Evidence is mixed. In one study, women who imagined being excluded from a course because of prejudice reported more negative affect (a composite of hostile, anxious, and depressed affect) than men who imagined being rejected due to prejudice (Schmitt & Branscombe, 2002b). A replication and extension of this study, however, failed to replicate this gender difference (Major et al., 2003a). Women as well as men in this latter experiment experienced less depressed affect if they were rejected because of prejudice than if they were rejected because of a presumed lack of intelligence.

In sum, a variety of personal, situational, and structural factors moderate the impact of perceived discrimination on personal self-esteem via their impact on appraisals and coping. Our research indicates that perceiving discrimination based on one's social identity is likely to protect personal self-esteem when it occurs in the context of a personal threat and provides a less threatening explanation for a negative self-relevant outcome, and when the contextual cues to prejudice are clear thereby facilitating discounting of self-blame (Major et al., 2003c; Major et al., 2003a). Our research also indicates that personal resources, such as dispositional optimism, can buffer personal self-esteem from perceived prejudice against the group by reducing the extent to which prejudice is appraised as personally threatening (Kaiser et al., in press). In contrast, the personal self-esteem of individuals who identify highly with the targeted group (McCoy & Major, 2003), and who endorse ideologies that legitimise the low status of the targeted group by implicating their lower inputs (Major et al., 2003b), is vulnerable to perceived prejudice against the ingroup. Thus, framing target responses to prejudice within a transactional coping model allows for increased understanding and prediction of self-esteem variability in targets' responses to prejudice.

CONCLUSIONS

We argue that insights from the stress and coping literature can inform research and theory concerning the psychological consequences of being a target of prejudice. In this paper we have presented a transactional model of coping with prejudice. This model contends that self-esteem and affective responses to being a target of prejudice are determined by how individuals cognitively appraise prejudicial events and the coping strategies they use to deal with those events. These processes, in turn, are a function of characteristics of the person, the situation, and the larger social structure. This model assumes variability in the perception of discrimination, as well as variability in the consequences of this perception for targets' self-esteem. We addressed several personal, situational, and structural factors that contribute to this variability through their effects on appraisals and coping. In our view, conceptualising targets' responses to prejudice and discrimination within a transactional model emphasises sources of resistance as well as vulnerability among targets. Such an approach will advance theory and research on how individuals respond cognitively, emotionally, and behaviourally to being a target of prejudice because of their social identity.

We close by noting that although here we conceptualised successful adaptation among the stigmatised in terms of feelings of personal self-worth, successful adaptation can also be conceptualised in other ways. For example, successful adaptation may involve feeling that one's ingroup is worthy, or feeling attached to one's ingroup. Successful adaptation may also involve feeling anger at the injustices faced by their group. Although anger is rarely seen as a healthy emotion, anger may be necessary for people to publicly claim discrimination when it occurs, and to work for social change.

REFERENCES

Abramson, L. Y., Seligman, M. E., & Teasdale, J. D. (1978). Learned helplessness in humans: Critique and reformulation. *Journal of Abnormal Psychology, 87*, 49 – 74.

Adler, N. E., & Ostrove, J. M. (1999). Socioeconomic status and health: What we know and what we don't. In N. E. Adler & M. Marmot (Eds.), *Socioeconomic status and health in industrial nations: Social psychological and biological pathways. Annals of the New York Academy of Sciences, 896* (pp. 3 – 15). New York: New York Academy of Sciences.

Allison, K. W. (1998). Stress and oppressed category membership. In J. K. Swim & C. Stangor (Eds.), *Prejudice: The target's perspective* (pp. 145 – 170). San Diego, CA: Academic Press.

Allport, G. (1954/1979). *The nature of prejudice.* New York: Doubleday Anchor.

Arndt, J., Greenberg, J., Schimel, J., Pyszczynski, T., & Solomon, S. (2002). To belong or not to belong that is the question: Terror management and identification with gender and ethnicity. *Journal of Personality and Social Psychology, 83*, 26 – 43.

Bandura, A. (1977). Self-efficacy: Toward a unifying theory of behavioral change. *Psychological Review, 84*, 191 – 215.

Bat-Chava, Y. (1994). Group identification and self-esteem of deaf adults. *Personality and Social Psychology Bulletin, 20*, 494 – 502.

Baumeister, R. F. (1998). The self. In D. Gilbert, S. T. Fiske, & G. Lindzey (Eds.), *Handbook of social psychology* (4th ed., pp. 680 – 740). Boston, MA: McGraw Hill.

Bowlby, J. (1969). Disruption of affectional bonds and its effects on behavior. *Canada's Mental Health Supplement, 59*, 12.

Branscombe, N. R., Schmitt, M. T., & Harvey, R. D. (1999). Perceiving pervasive discrimination among African Americans: Implications for group identification and well-being. *Journal of Personality & Social Psychology, 77*, 135 – 149.

Cartwright, D. (1950). Emotional dimensions of group life. In M. L. Raymert (Ed.), *Feelings and emotions* (pp. 439 – 447). New York: McGraw Hill.

Clark, K. B., & Clark, M. P. (1950). Emotional factors in racial identification and preference in Negro children. *Journal of Negro Education, 19*, 341 – 350.

Clark, R., Anderson, N. B., Clark, V. R., & Williams, D. R. (1999). Racism as a stressor for African Americans: A biopsychosocial model. *American Psychologist, 54*, 805 – 816.

Compas, B. E., Connor-Smith, J. K., Saltzman, H., Thomsen, A. H., & Wadsworth, M. E. (2001). Coping with stress during childhood and adolescence: Problems, progress and potential in theory and research. *Psychological Bulletin, 127*, 87 – 127.

Crocker, J., Cornwell, B., & Major, B. (1993). The stigma of overweight: Affective consequences of attributional ambiguity. *Journal of Personality & Social Psychology, 64*, 60 – 70.

Crocker, J., & Major, B. (1989). Social stigma and self-esteem: The self-protective properties of stigma. *Psychological Review, 96*, 608 – 630.

Crocker, J., & Major, B. (1994). Reactions to stigma: The moderating role of justifications. In M. P. Zanna & J. M. Olson (Eds.), *The psychology of prejudice: The Ontario Symposium* (Vol. 7, pp. 289 – 314). Hillsdale, NJ: Lawrence Erlbaum Associates Inc.

Crocker, J., Major, B., & Steele, C. (1998). Social stigma. In D. Gilbert, S. T. Fiske, & G. Lindzey (Eds.), *Handbook of social psychology* (4th ed., pp. 504 – 553). Boston, MA: McGraw Hill.

Crocker, J., & Quinn, D. M. (2000). Social stigma and the self: Meanings, situations, and self-esteem. In T. F. Heatherton & R. E. Kleck (Eds.), *The social psychology of stigma* (pp. 153–183). New York: Guilford Press.

Crocker, J., Voelkl, K., Testa, M., & Major, B. (1991). Social stigma: The affective consequences of attributional ambiguity. *Journal of Personality and Social Psychology, 60*, 218–228.

Crosby, F. (1982). *Relative deprivation and working women.* New York: Oxford University Press.

Crosby, F., Pufall, A., Snyder, R. C., O'Connell, M., & Whalen, P. (1989). The denial of personal disadvantage among you, me, and all the other ostriches. In M. Crawford & M. Gentry (Eds.), *Gender's thought: Psychological perspectives* (pp. 79–99). New York: Springer-Verlag.

Diaz, R. M., Ayala, G., Bein, E., Henne, J., & Marin, B. V. (2001). The impact of homophobia, poverty, and racism on the mental health of gay and bisexual Latino men: Findings from 3 US cities. *American Journal of Public Health, 91*, 927–932.

Diener, E. (1984). Subjective well-being. *Psychological Bulletin, 95*, 542–575.

Dion, K. L. (1975). Women's reactions to discrimination from members of the same or opposite sex. *Journal of Research in Personality, 9*, 294–306.

Dion, K. L., & Earn, B. M. (1975). The phenomenology of being a target of prejudice. *Journal of Personality and Social Psychology, 32*, 944–950.

Ellemers, N., Spears, R., & Doosje, B. (2002). Self and social identity. In S. T. Fiske, D. L Schacter, & C. Zahn-Waxler (Eds.), *Annual Review of Psychology, 53*, 161–186.

Erikson, E. H. (1956). The problem of ego identity. *Journal of the American Psychoanalytic Association, 4*, 56–121.

Feldman-Barrett, L., & Swim, J. K. (1998). Appraisals of prejudice and discrimination. In J. K. Swim & C. Stangor (Eds.), *Prejudice: The target's perspective* (pp. 12–37). San Diego: Academic Press.

Goffman, E. (1963). *Stigma: Notes on the management of spoiled identity.* Englewood Cliffs, NJ: Prentice-Hall.

Holmes, T. H., & Rahe, R. H. (1967). The social readjustment rating scale. *Journal of Psychosomatic Research, 11*, 213–218.

Inman, M. L. (2001). Do you see what I see? Similarities and differences in victims' and observers' perceptions of discrimination. *Social Cognition, 19*, 521–546.

James, S. A., Hartnett, S. A., & Kalsbeek, W. D. (1983). John Henryism and blood pressure differences among Black men. *Journal of Behavioral Medicine, 6*, 259–278.

Jetten, J., Branscombe, N. R., Schmitt, M. T., & Spears, R. (2001). Rebels with a cause: Group identification as a response to perceived discrimination from the mainstream. *Personality and Social Psychology Bulletin, 27*(9), 1204–1213.

Kaiser, C. R. & Major, B. (in press). Judgments of deserving and the emotional consequences of stigmatization. In L. Tiedens & C. W. Leach (Eds.), *The social life of emotions.* New York: Cambridge University Press.

Kaiser, C. R., Major, B., & McCoy, S. K. (in press). Expectations about the future and the emotional consequences of perceiving prejudice. *Personality and Social Psychology Bulletin.*

Kelley, H. H. (1973). The processes of causal attribution. *American Psychologist, 28*(2), 107–128.

Klonoff, E. A., & Landrine, H. (1997). Distrust of Whites, acculturation, and AIDS knowledge among African Americans. *Journal of Black Psychology, 23*, 50–59.

Kluegel, J. R., & Smith, E. R. (1986). *Beliefs about inequality: Americans' view of what is and what ought to be.* Hawthorne, NJ: Aldine de Gruyer.

Kobrynowicz, D., & Branscombe, N. R. (1997). Who considers themselves victims of discrimination? Individual difference predictors of perceived gender discrimination in women and men. *Psychology of Women Quarterly, 21*, 347–363.

Lazarus, R. S. (1999). *Stress and emotion: A new synthesis.* New York: Springer.

Lazarus, R. S., & Folkman, S. (1984). *Stress, appraisal, and coping.* New York: Springer.

Leary, M. R. (1990). Responses to social exclusion: Social anxiety, jealousy, loneliness, depression, and low self-esteem. *Journal of Social and Clinical Psychology, 9,* 221–229.

Leary, M. R., Tambor, E. S., Terdal, S. K., & Downs, D. L. (1995). Self-esteem as an interpersonal monitor: The sociometer hypothesis. *Journal of Personality & Social Psychology, 68,* 518–530.

Major, B., & Crocker, J. (1993). Social stigma: The affective consequences of attributional ambiguity. In D. M. Mackie & D. L. Hamilton (Eds.), *Affect, cognition, and stereotyping: Interactive processes in intergroup perception* (pp. 345–370). New York: Academic Press.

Major, B., Gramzow, R., McCoy, S. K., Levin, S., Schmader, T., & Sidanius, J. (2002a). Perceiving personal discrimination: The role of group status and status legitimizing ideology. *Journal of Personality and Social Psychology, 82,* 269–282.

Major, B., Kaiser, C., & McCoy, S. K. (2003a). It's not my fault: When and why attributions to prejudice protect self-esteem. *Personality and Social Psychology Bulletin, 29,* 772–781.

Major, B., Kaiser, C., & McCoy, S. K. (2003b). *Faring well in an unfair world: Ideology endorsement and the impact of prejudice on self-esteem.* Manuscript in preparation.

Major, B., Quinton, W. J., & McCoy, S. K. (2002b). Antecedents and consequences of attributions to discrimination: Theoretical and empirical advances. In M. P. Zanna (Ed.), *Advances in experimental social psychology (Vol. 34,* pp. 251–330). New York: Academic Press.

Major, B., Quinton, W. J., McCoy, S. K., & Schmader, T. (2000). Reducing prejudice: The target's perspective. In S. Oskamp (Ed.), *Reducing prejudice and discrimination. The Claremont Symposium on Applied Social Psychology* (pp. 211–237). Mahway, NJ: Lawrence Erlbaum Associates Inc.

Major, B., Quinton, W. J., & Schmader, T. (2003c). Attributions to discrimination and self-esteem: Impact of group identification and situational ambiguity. *Journal of Experimental Social Psychology, 39,* 220–231.

Major, B., Richards, C., Cooper, M. L., Cozzarelli, C., & Zubek, J. (1998). Personal resilience, cognitive appraisals, and coping: An integrative model of adjustment to abortion. *Journal of Personality and Social Psychology, 74,* 735–752.

Major, B., & Schmader, T. (1998). Coping with stigma through psychological disengagement. In J. K. Swim & C. Stangor (Eds.), *Prejudice: The target's perspective* (pp. 220–243). San Diego, CA: Academic Press, Inc.

Major, B., & Schmader, T. (2001). Legitimacy and the construal of social disadvantage. In J. Jost & B. Major (Eds.), *The psychology of legitimacy: Emerging perspectives on ideology, justice, and intergroup relationships* (pp. 176–204). New York: Cambridge University Press.

McCoy, S. K., & Major, B. (2003). Group identification moderates emotional responses to perceived prejudice. *Personality and Social Psychology Bulletin, 29,* 1005–1017.

Mendoza-Denton, R., Purdie, V. J., Downey, G., Davis, A., & Pietrzak, J. (2003). Sensitivity to status-based rejection: Implications for African-American students' college experience. *Journal of Personality and Social Psychology, 83,* 896–918.

Miller, C. T., & Kaiser, C. R. (2001). A theoretical perspective on coping with stigma. *Journal of Social Issues, 57,* 73–92.

Miller, C. T., & Major, B. (2000). Coping with stigma and prejudice. In T. F. Heatherton, R. E. Kleck, M. R. Hebl, & J. G. Hull (Eds.), *The social psychology of stigma* (pp. 243–272). New York: Guilford Press.

Munford, M. B. (1994). Relationship of gender, self-esteem, social class, and racial identity to depression in Blacks. *Journal of Black Psychology, 20,* 157–174.

Operario, D., & Fiske, S. T. (2001). Ethnic identity moderates perceptions of prejudice: Judgments of personal versus group discrimination and subtle versus blatant bias. *Personality & Social Psychology Bulletin, 27*, 550–561.

Patterson, R. J., & Neufeld, W. J. (1987). Clear danger: Situational determinants of the appraisal of threat. *Psychological Bulletin, 101*, 404–416.

Phinney, J. S. (1990). Ethnic identity in adolescents and adults: Review of research. *Psychological Bulletin, 10*, 499–514.

Pinel, E. C. (1999). Stigma consciousness: The psychological legacy of social stereotypes. *Journal of Personality and Social Psychology, 76*, 114–128.

Porter, J. R., & Washington, R. E. (1979). Black identity and self-esteem: A few studies of Black self-concept. 1968–1979. *Annual Review of Sociology, 5*, 53–74.

Pyszczynski, T., Greenberg, J., & Solomon, S. (1997). Why do we need what we need? A terror management perspective on the roots of human social motivation. *Psychological Inquiry, 8*(1), 1–20.

Quinn, D. M., & Crocker, J. (1999). When ideology hurts: Effects of belief in the Protestant ethic and feeling overweight on the psychological well-being of women. *Journal of Personality & Social Psychology, 77*, 402–414.

Rosenberg, M., & Simmons, R. G. (1972). *Black and white self-esteem: The urban school child.* Washington, DC: American Sociological Association.

Rowley, S. J., Sellers, R. M., Chavous, T. M., & Smith, M. A. (1998). The relationship between racial identity and self-esteem in African-American college and high school students. *Journal of Personality and Social Psychology, 74*, 715–724.

Sapolsky, R. M. (1995). Social subordinance as a marker of hypercortisolism: Some unexpected subtleties. In G. P. Chorousos & R. McCarty (Eds.), *Stress: Basic mechanisms and clinical implications. Annals of the New York Academy of Sciences* (Vol. 771, pp. 626–639). New York: New York Academy of Sciences.

Scheier, M. F., Carver, C. S., & Bridges, M. W. (2001). Optimism, pessimism, and psychological well-being. In E. C. Chang (Ed.), *Optimism and pessimism: Implications for theory, research, and practice* (pp. 189–216). Washington, DC: American Psychological Association.

Schmitt, M. T., & Branscombe, N. R. (2002a). The meaning and consequences of perceived discrimination in disadvantaged and privileged social group. In W. Stroebe & M. Hewstone (Eds.), *European review of social psychology* (Vol. 12, pp. 167–199). Chichester, UK: Wiley.

Schmitt, M. T., & Branscombe, N. R. (2002b). The internal and external causal loci of attributions to prejudice. *Personality and Social Psychology Bulletin, 28*, 620–628.

Schmitt, M. T., Branscombe, N. R., Kobrynowicz, D., & Owen, S. (2002). Perceiving discrimination against one's gender group has different implications for well-being in women and men. *Personality and Social Psychology Bulletin, 28*, 197–210.

Sechrist, G. B., Swim, J. K., & Mark, M. M. (2003). Mood as information in making attributions to discrimination. *Personality and Social Psychology Bulletin, 29*, 524–531.

Sellers, R. M., & Shelton, J. N. (2003) The role of racial identity in perceived racial discrimination. *Journal of Personality and Social Psychology, 84*, 1079–1092.

Simpson, G. E., & Yinger, J. M. (1985). The consequences of prejudice and discrimination. In L. Susskind & L. Rodwin (Series Eds.), *Racial and cultural minorities: An analysis of prejudice and discrimination* (5th ed., pp. 111–136). New York: Plenum Press.

Swim, J. K., Hyers, L. L., Cohen, L. L., & Ferguson, M. J. (2001). Everyday sexism: Evidence for its incidence, nature, and psychological impact from three daily diary studies. *Journal of Social Issues, 57*, 31–53.

Tajfel, H., & Turner, J. C. (1986). The social identity theory of intergroup behavior. In S. Worchel & W. G. Austin (Eds.), *The psychology of intergroup relations* (pp. 7–24). Chicago, IL: Nelson-Hall.

Taylor, D. M., Wright, S. C., & Porter, L. E. (1994). Dimensions of perceived discrimination: The personal/group discrimination discrepancy. In M. P. Zanna, & J. M. Olson, (Eds.), *The psychology of prejudice: The Ontario Symposium* (Vol. 7, pp. 233–255). Hillsdale, NJ: Lawrence Erlbaum Associates Inc.

Taylor, S. E. (1989). *Positive illusions: Creative self-deception and the healthy mind.* New York: Basic Books.

Twenge, J. M., & Crocker, J. (2002). Race and self-esteem: Meta-analysis comparing Whites, Blacks, Hispanics, Asians, and American Indians and comment on Gray-Little and Hafdahl (2000). *Psychological Bulletin, 128,* 371–408.

Weiner, B. (1985). An attributional theory of achievement motivation and emotion. *Journal of Personality and Social Psychology, 92,* 548–573.

Weiner, B. (1995). *Judgments of responsibility: A foundation for a theory of social conduct.* New York: Guilford Press.

Williams, K. D. (1997). Social ostracism. In R. M. Kowalski (Ed.), *Aversive interpersonal behaviors* (pp. 133–170). New York: Plenum Press.

Williams, K. D., Shore, W. J., & Grahe, J. E. (1998). The silent treatment: Perceptions of its behaviors and associated feelings. *Group Processes and Intergroup Relations, 1,* 117–141.

EUROPEAN REVIEW OF SOCIAL PSYCHOLOGY, 2003, *14*, 105–137

Prehistoric dangers and contemporary prejudices

Mark Schaller, Justin H. Park and Jason Faulkner

University of British Columbia, Canada

We review the logical principles that guide the application of evolutionary ideas to psychological problems, and show how these principles can be used to derive novel, testable hypotheses about contemporary prejudice processes. We summarise two recent lines of research employing this approach. One line of research examines prejudices resulting from perceived vulnerability to physical injury. The other examines prejudices resulting from perceived vulnerability to disease. Results from both lines of research support novel psychological hypotheses identifying variables—pertaining to both personality and to local context—that trigger specific prejudices against specific categories of people. We conclude by discussing more broadly some of the useful conceptual and practical implications of this evolutionary approach to prejudice.

"We humans have to grant the presence of some past adaptations, even in their unforgivable extremes, if only to admit they are permanent rocks in the stream we're obliged to navigate."

(Barbara Kingsolver, 1995, p. 8)

The psychological study of prejudice is often motivated not only by scientific goals, but by practical social goals as well. If we can better understand the causes and processes of prejudice, then we might be better prepared to navigate our way around the problems that prejudices pose. And, ideally, we might be able to devise interventions that inhibit the prevalence of these problems.

Consistent with these goals, there are numerous examples of specific ways in which inquiry into the processes that underlie prejudice has led to the development of intervention strategies that actually have some

Correspondence should be addressed to Mark Schaller, Department of Psychology, University of British Columbia, 2136 West Mall, Vancouver, BC V6T 1Z4, Canada, Email: schaller@psych.ubc.ca.

The research reported in this article was supported by a grant from the Social Sciences and Humanities Research Council of Canada, and by a fellowship from the Natural Sciences and Engineering Research Council of Canada.

http://www.tandf.co.uk/journals/titles/99998080.asp   DOI: 10.1080/10463280340000036

positive impact (e.g., Gaertner & Dovidio, 2000; Schaller, Asp, Rosell, & Heim, 1996; Wright, Aron, McLaughlin-Volpe, & Ropp, 1997). For example, the study of social identity processes has led to interventions based on the creation of common ingroup identities, and these interventions can help to reduce intergroup prejudices and conflict (Gaertner, Dovidio, Anastasio, Bachman, & Rust, 1993). These results are encouraging.

But we must be careful not to overgeneralise the practical utility of these sorts of results. In the social psychological laboratory, where it is possible to create stereotypes and prejudices quite quickly, it is also possible to eliminate them more easily than we can in the real world where prejudices often have longer histories and deeper roots. The fracturing of the former Yugoslavia along ethnic and cultural lines reveals, among other things, that deeply held prejudices may not be so easily eliminated by common superordinate identities even when those identities persist across a lifetime or longer. This example does not diminish the importance of social identity processes in our understanding of intergroup prejudice, but it does suggest that many other processes are important as well. If we are to truly understand the prejudices that exist in the world around us—and if we hope to be able to do something about them—then we must be prepared to discover and intellectually embrace any and all of the processes that might contribute to those prejudices.

Our purpose here is to illustrate the utility of applying the tools of evolutionary psychology towards that goal. When applied rigorously, informed speculations about evolutionary prehistory can lead to hypotheses about contemporary prejudice processes—including hypotheses that specify which individuals are especially likely to be prejudiced, circumstances under which individuals are especially likely to be prejudiced, and categories of individuals that are especially likely to become targets of these particular prejudices. While the underlying evolutionary speculations are difficult to verify, the resulting psychological hypotheses can be tested directly with standard research methods. Consequently, this meta-theoretical approach provides a useful means of making novel discoveries about contemporary prejudice processes.

For several different reasons, people are sometimes uncomfortable with evolutionary approaches to prejudice. Some of these reasons are rooted in common misunderstandings about what an evolutionary approach does and does not logically imply when applied to complex psychological phenomena such as prejudice. Therefore, we begin by reviewing the logic that guides the application of evolutionary principles to contemporary prejudice processes. We then describe two recent lines of research informed by this evolutionary logic. These lines of research have identified and supported novel hypotheses about variables that trigger the experience and expression of specific prejudices. We conclude by discussing more broadly some of the useful implications of this evolutionary approach to prejudice.

EVOLUTIONARY PRESSURES AND PSYCHOLOGICAL RESPONSES

Evolutionary psychology as a tool for conceptual discovery

Evolutionary processes operate on populations over very long periods of time, while psychological processes operate on individuals at very specific points in time. These two sets of processes comprise two very different levels of scientific analysis. In recent years, there have been substantial advances in understanding the complex linkages between evolutionary processes and the psychological processes governing the thoughts, emotions, and actions of individuals (Barkow, Cosmides, & Tooby, 1992; Buss, 1995; Crawford & Krebs, 1998; Cummins & Allen, 1998; Gangestad & Simpson, 2000; Marr, 1982; Pinker, 1997; Scher & Rauscher, 2002; Simpson & Kenrick, 1997). These lines of inquiry have revealed clearly defined logical strategies for the application of evolutionary principles towards the development of testable theories about psychological processes.

It is easy to engage in a sort of "backward-thinking" approach to evolutionary psychology—to make up plausible evolutionary scenarios that might explain the origins of phenomena that have already been observed in contemporary human environments. But to be useful to psychological scientists, evolutionary psychology must do more than simply explain the historical origins of existing phenomena; it must produce novel hypotheses pertaining to psychological processes in the here-and-now (Conway & Schaller, 2002; Ketelaar & Ellis, 2000). It is therefore necessary to apply a more "forward-thinking" deductive approach (Murphy, 2003). This approach begins with the specification of well-articulated assumptions about specific problems pertaining to survival and/or sexual reproduction that plausibly existed in the evolutionary past. Because specific problems imposed specific selection pressures on ancestral populations, it is then possible to deduce hypotheses about psychological mechanisms that might have evolved in response to those pressures. These hypotheses about evolutionary processes in the past can, in turn, be used to derive hypotheses about psychological responses that may still operate in the present. Hypotheses derived in this manner are logically no different from any other psychological hypotheses, and they can be tested with the methods of experimental psychology. The evolutionary background adds to the richness of the theoretical structures from which these hypotheses are derived, but the primary value of this meta-theoretical approach ultimately lies in the specification and empirical testing of these evolutionarily informed hypotheses: These tests can lead to novel empirical discoveries about contemporary human cognition and behaviour.

Characteristics of evolved psychological processes

An essential element in most evolutionary approaches to psychology is the assumption that a specific psychological process served some useful function to individuals in ancestral times. Thus, if fear has an evolutionary basis (and it appears that it does; see Öhman & Mineka, 2001, for an extensive discussion), it is because the capacity for fear served an important function during a vast period of human evolutionary history. (It is not the case, however, that evolved responses are necessarily functional in contemporary contexts. The mechanisms of biological evolution proceed much more slowly than cultural change, and psychological mechanisms that evolved in response to ancestral environments may be counter-productive in many contemporary environments.)

The functional logic of evolutionary psychology typically leads to the specification of pan-human psychological mechanisms. These universal mechanisms pertain primarily to the basic psychological structures through which information is perceived and processed, and through which cognitive, affective, and behavioural "outputs" are generated. For example, in general, people have the capacity to experience fear when they perceive information indicating the proximity of some imminent danger. Rarely, however, does the specification of these universal mechanisms imply equivalence across individuals in psychological outputs. There are vast individual differences in fear responses (e.g., some people are more chronically fearful than others) that result from the many additional, more proximal, influences on individual information processing. These influences include additional biological processes that promote genetic diversity within human popula-tions, as well as the effects of local environments and social learning processes. (Individual differences are not irrelevant to evolutionary psychology, however. Regardless of their origin, many individual difference variables can serve as perceptual inputs that influence the operation of evolved psychological processes. We discuss this point at greater length below.)

As with other psychological processes, evolved psychological processes are highly flexible. Most of these processes (particularly those of most relevance to the study of social cognition) provide for the capacity to respond in specific ways to specific categories of perceptual input. Thus, the evolved mechanisms underlying fear provide the capacity for a fear response to be triggered in response to specific perceptual cues (such as an unexpected loud noise) that appear to indicate the proximity of some imminent danger.

The process whereby individuals respond to perceptual cues provides one of several points at which social learning mechanisms intersect importantly with evolved psychological mechanisms. While there may be an evolved, pan-human tendency to respond with fear to cues connoting imminent danger, individuals must learn many of the specific stimulus cues that connote danger (Öhman & Mineka, 2001). There may be innate predispositions to quickly learn certain kinds of stimulus-response linkages (see Garcia, 1981, for discussion of one classic example), but other linkages may be based more fully on learning processes. Consequently, even for psychological processes that very clearly have some basis in evolutionary biology—such as those pertaining to human emotions—there may be differences between individuals, and between cultures, in the sets of cues that trigger these processes (Park, Faulkner, & Schaller, 2003).

The engagement of adaptive responses often conforms loosely to some sort of implicit cost–benefit analysis (if cues indicate the presence of some dangerous thing, then the costs associated with a fear response are likely to be outweighed by the benefits precipitated by that response), but this does not mean that they are engaged only after rational consideration. Often these psychological responses are reflexive—triggered spontaneously and automatically by the simple perception of cues (Schaller, 2003). The automaticity of the fear response is such that a fear response may be triggered by a perceptual cue (e.g., loud noise) even when the perceiver is explicitly aware that no danger is present. Consequently, these processes are fallible (Haselton & Buss, 2000). Because many evolved psychological processes respond reflexively to heuristic cues, they may be triggered under circumstances in which, from a rational perspective, they serve no real function.

Because evolved psychological mechanisms are responsive to information that informs an implicit cost–benefit analysis, the strength of association between eliciting stimulus and adaptive response may be moderated by additional "background" variables that bear on that implicit—and fallible—cost–benefit analysis. Thus, stimuli that typically elicit fear may elicit more fear when individuals already feel especially vulnerable to harm, and may elicit less fear when they feel personally invulnerable. Some of this background information may be provided by chronic individual difference variables. Individuals who are generally more fearful and wary of danger— for whatever reason—are likely to have a lower threshold for the "triggering" of the evolved mechanisms whereby fear is elicited in response to some perceptual cue (such as a loud noise). Many evolutionary psychological theories yield hypotheses implying relations between specific individual difference variables and the strength of specific psychological responses (e.g., Gangestad & Simpson, 2000).

Other background information is provided by temporary contextual cues that connote the potential costs or benefits of response. A fearful reaction to loud noises, for example, is especially pronounced under conditions of ambient darkness, a contextual cue that heuristically connotes vulnerability to harm (Grillon, Pellowshi, Merikangas, & Davis, 1997). Many evolutionary psychological theories yield hypotheses implying causal effects of specific environmental and social contexts on the strength of specific psychological responses (e.g., Burnstein, Crandall, & Kitayama, 1994).

EVOLUTIONARY MODELS OF CONTEMPORARY PREJUDICE PROCESSES

In recent years, a number of theoretical models have suggested ways in which contemporary group stereotypes and prejudices may be consequences of psychological mechanisms that evolved a long time ago (Fox, 1992; Krebs & Denton, 1997; Kurzban & Leary, 2001; Neuberg, Smith, & Asher, 2000; Schaller, 2003). The common evolutionary logic underlying these perspectives is summarised by Kurzban and Leary (2001): The contemporary human mind evolved in response to the adaptive problems imposed by the environments in which ancestral populations lived; for the past several million years of this evolutionary history, ancestral populations lived in social groups; specific adaptive problems associated with group life may have given rise to specific psychological mechanisms that influenced evaluative perceptions of and reactions to individuals associated with specific sorts of groups. In other words, certain prejudicial ways of thinking and acting may have conferred adaptive benefits within ancestral environments, and now—even though contemporary environments are very different in very many ways—those prejudicial ways of thinking and acting may persist.

Within this broad evolutionary framework, there are a number of conceptually distinct theoretical models identifying links between specific adaptive problems of the past and specific prejudice processes in the present. For instance, one model links the adaptive utility of status hierarchies with contemporary tendencies to express domination over others (Pratto, Sidanius, & Stallworth, 1993). Another model links the adaptive utility of cooperative social exchange behaviours with contemporary prejudices against individuals who, either because of disinclination or disability, tend to contribute fewer resources than they receive (Kurzban & Leary, 2001; Neuberg et al., 2000). These theoretical models add a level of historical depth and richness to our understanding of well-known prejudice phenomena. More importantly, though, these evolutionary analyses are beginning to yield novel answers to questions that are not easily addressed by other models of prejudice. For instance, Neuberg and Cottrell (2002) draw on evolutionary logic to make predictions—supported by empirical data—about the specific affective contents of negative attitudes towards different outgroups. The results reveal that prejudices that appear identical in terms of overall evaluative valence are in fact qualitatively distinct in predictable ways. This research highlights important, under-researched questions about the specific contents of prejudices, and provides answers to these questions through the deduction of novel hypotheses.

In our own recent research, we have focused on two specific evolutionarily informed models of prejudice processes, each of which yields novel predictions about the specific variables that trigger specific prejudices against specific peoples. One of these processes focuses on vulnerability to physical injury. The other focuses on vulnerability to disease. In the sections that follow, we describe the evolutionary logic underlying these models and summarise some of the recent empirical evidence supporting novel psychological hypotheses derived from each model.

PERCEIVED VULNERABILITY TO PHYSICAL INJURY AND ITS EFFECTS ON PREJUDICE

For sensible reasons, we are wary around others who pose some real danger of inflicting physical injury upon us, and we harbour negative attitudes towards exactly these sorts of people. Less rationally, however, it appears that perceived vulnerability to physical injury may be linked to prejudices against categories of people who do not pose any objective danger or threat, and that these prejudices may be moderated by cues that heuristically connote increased (or decreased) vulnerability.

Conceptual background

The conceptual logic underlying this linkage is summarised within a theoretical structure that we have been calling "intergroup vigilance theory". The key assumption underlying this theory pertains to a specific evolutionary pressure operating on populations during that long stretch of evolutionary history in which individuals lived in small tribal units. Within this tribal context, there may have been real physical risks associated with unexpected interactions with "outsiders"—strangers who were not part of the tribal ingroup. Cognitive structures that motivated the vigilant avoidance of potentially injurious intergroup encounters would have been adaptive. Consequently, innate psychological mechanisms may have emerged that facilitated the learning and consequent activation of cognitive associations linking tribal outsider status with expectations of dangerous intent. Given reciprocal relations between cognition and culture (Kenrick, Li, & Butner, 2003; Schaller & Crandall, 2003), these cognitive mechanisms are likely to have an impact on—and in turn to be supported by—the emergence of specific kinds of cultural norms, such as myths and legends illustrating the dangers posed by strange peoples.

The cognitive association linking outsiders with danger is expected to be responsive to perceptual cues (facial features, linguistic labels, etc.) that connote "tribal" outgroup status. The exact nature of these cues may vary, of course, depending on local cultural conditions and learning environments. In many contemporary cultural contexts, cues clearly connoting ethnic and/or national outgroup status may trigger the activation of cognitions indicating dangerous intent.

The activation of these cognitions (along with an associated fearful response) is expected to be moderated by additional background variables— including both chronic individual differences and temporary circumstances—that heuristically indicate functional costs or benefits of responding in a prejudicial manner. Especially relevant are variables connoting personal vulnerability to harm (e.g., a high likelihood of unexpected and potentially dangerous intergroup contact). Individuals who chronically feel vulnerable to harm are especially likely to perceive tribal outgroups as dangerous. In addition, this specific prejudicial perception of outgroups is likely to be facilitated under temporary circumstances that connote personal vulnerability. The operation of an implicit cost – benefit analysis also implies that there may be interactive effects among multiple background variables. For example, the facilitating effects of any one variable may be muted if another variable clearly connotes safety and invulnerability, whereas the facilitating effects may be strengthened if another variable indicates the need for wariness.

Implications and empirical evidence

On the basis of this analysis, intergroup vigilance theory yields a number of implications and predictions about the specific nature of intergroup prejudice, and the moderators of that prejudice.

One implication is that individuals who are perceived to be outsiders— members of outgroups that fit a tribal template—inspire the sort of threat-related emotional and cognitive reactions that typically motivate vigilant avoidance. Empirical research bears this out. Encounters with members of ethnic outgroups are associated with self-reported and physiological indicators of fear and anxiety (Blascovich, Mendes, Hunter, Lickel, & Kowai-Bell, 2001; Phelps et al., 2000). Ethnic outgroups also inspire negative stereotypes and attitudes consistent with those emotional responses (Phelps et al., 2000; Stephan, Diaz-Loving, & Duran, 2000; Stephan, Ybarra, Marinez, Schwarzwald, & Tur-Kaspa, 1988).

A second implication is that these kinds of prejudicial responses are likely to be especially strong among individuals who feel chronically vulnerable to interpersonal danger. Altemeyer (1988) developed a useful self-report questionnaire assessing individual differences in "belief in a dangerous world" (BDW). The BDW scale includes 12 items of the following sort: "There are many dangerous people in our society who will attack someone out of pure meanness, for no reason at all" and "Despite what one hears about 'crime on the street,' there probably isn't any more now than there ever has been". The items all pertain to perceptions of interpersonal danger in general; not a single item pertains specifically to perceptions of outgroups. Nevertheless, Altemeyer (1988) found that individuals with higher levels of BDW also expressed higher levels of prejudice against outgroups.

It is worth noting that the internally coherent BDW scale correlates substantially with measures designed to assess the multiple psychological constructs that comprise "the authoritarian personality" (Adorno, Frenkel-Brunswik, Levinson, & Sanford, 1950; Altemeyer, 1988). This may help us understand better why authoritarianism predicts prejudice. At a psychologically fundamental level, the effect may be based not so much on political ideology, beliefs about authority, or cognitive rigidity—all of which are conceptually distinct facets of the authoritarian personality style—but on an irrational feeling of vulnerability to danger. Suedfeld and Schaller (2002) have argued that it is this particular fear-based facet of authoritarianism that is most useful in understanding the complicated relationship between authoritarianism and complicity in extreme acts of prejudice, such as genocide.

A third implication is that prejudicial responses are likely to be facilitated by transient cues connoting increased vulnerability to harmful encounters with outgroups. Some of these contextual variables are obvious. For instance, stereotypical associations with danger and prejudicial beliefs are expected to be magnified by information indicating increased likelihood of intergroup conflict or competition. This clearly is the case. Information connoting intergroup conflict leads stereotypic beliefs to coalesce around danger-relevant characteristics and images (Alexander, Brewer, & Herrmann, 1999). Information connoting conflict or threat leads individuals to perceive outgroups as more stereotypically homogeneous (Judd & Park, 1988; Rothgerber, 1997), and amplifies tendencies toward ingroup favouritism and outgroup derogation (Brewer, 1979).

Other background variables may more indirectly connote a heightened risk of potentially injurious intergroup contact. The relative size of ingroup and outgroup is one such variable. The greater the relative size of an outgroup, the more vulnerable individuals are to an injurious inter-group encounter. Consistent with this reasoning, there is considerable evidence that the increased size of an outgroup is associated with increased prejudice (Mullen, Brown, & Smith, 1992).

Perhaps more interestingly, intergroup vigilance theory implies that the same sorts of prejudicial consequences may also be influenced by other danger-connoting contextual variables, even if those variables are logically irrelevant to groups or intergroup relations. This follows from the assertion that these evolutionarily influenced prejudice processes are facilitated by any kind of background information that heuristically connotes personal vulnerability to harm (even if, rationally, one recognises that there is no danger of harmful intergroup encounter). One such a cue is ambient darkness. We recently conducted a series of studies examining the causal effects of ambient darkness on the activation of content-specific prejudicial beliefs. These studies provide particularly strong tests of hypotheses derived from intergroup vigilance theory. In addition, because no previous theory or research has linked ambient darkness to the psychology of prejudice, these studies illustrate the value of this theory as a tool for the discovery of novel phenomena.

Study 1: Effects of ambient darkness on prejudicial trait ratings

The onset of darkness can arouse anxiety and fear. This makes considerable adaptive sense given that in darkness there is a diminution of visual information—a major liability for a species that relies heavily on vision to navigate physical and social landscapes and to avoid dangers lurking within those landscapes. Thus, whereas ambient light may be reassuring, the onset of darkness may serve as a heuristic cue indicating vulnerability to physical danger (Grillon et al., 1997). As a result, ambient darkness may lead individuals to be especially wary of potential dangers implicitly associated with ethnic outgroups.

A preliminary test of the impact of ambient darkness on intergroup prejudice emerged from the results of a very simple pilot study conducted in 1998. Participants were 17 high-school students from Vancouver, British Columbia (Canada). Participants were assigned to one of two experimental sessions; one session comprised the Light condition, and the other comprised the Dark condition. In both conditions, participants were seated in a windowless room, and given blank sheets of paper on which they were instructed to write down answers to a brief set of questions that they were asked by the experimenter. Participants were asked to rate "people from Iraq" and "people from Canada" on four trait dimensions (*hostile, ignorant, trustworthy, open-minded*); each rating was made by writing down a number from 1 to 10 on the blank sheet of paper. In the Light condition, the experimenter simply proceeded to recite the questions to which participants recorded their responses on the blank sheets of paper. In the Dark condition, immediately prior to reciting the questions, the experimenter turned off the lights that had been illuminating the room (participants were informed that they would be given an explanation at the conclusion of the study). These participants listened to the questions and recorded their responses in the dark. They had no difficulty in making legible rating responses, even though they could not see the paper on which they were writing.

Based on prior research (Rothbart & Park, 1986) and our own pre-testing, we determined that two of these traits (hostile, ignorant) were approximately equally negatively valenced, but differed in the extent to which they connoted danger. The two other traits (trustworthy, open-minded) were approximately equally positively valenced but also differed in danger-relevance. Consequently, after reverse-scoring ratings on the negatively valenced traits, we computed separate two-item composite indices indicating evaluations of ingroup and outgroup on (a) traits high in danger-relevance, and (b) traits low in danger-relevance. (Table 1 summarises these means.) We then subtracted ratings of the outgroup from the ingroup, to create two measures of ingroup favouritism—one indicating ingroup favouritism on high danger-relevance traits, and the other indicating ingroup favouritism on low danger-relevance traits. Figure 1 depicts the degree of ingroup favouritism that emerged on each index, separately within the Light and Dark experimental sessions. On highly danger-relevant traits, ingroup favouritism was higher in the dark than in the light, but no such difference was observed on low danger-relevance traits. Results from a 2×2 repeated measures ANOVA indicate that, despite the small sample size, sampling error cannot readily account for any such Darkness × Index interaction, $F(1, 15) = 3.38, p = .086$. Note that this

TABLE 1
Effects of darkness on evaluations of ingroup and outgroup (Study 1)

		Light	Dark
High danger-relevance traits			
Rating of ingroup	Mean	6.95	7.36
	(SD)	(1.30)	(1.22)
Rating of outgroup	Mean	5.35	4.65
	(SD)	(1.20)	(1.22)
Low danger-relevance traits			
Rating of ingroup	Mean	6.15	6.79
	(SD)	(1.13)	(1.29)
Rating of outgroup	Mean	4.85	5.61
	(SD)	(1.13)	(1.66)

Ratings of ingroup and outgroup are scaled in such a way that higher values indicate more favourable evaluations.

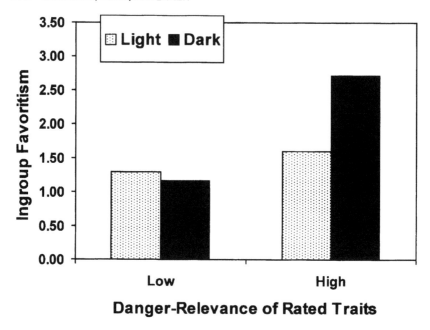

Figure 1. Effect of ambient darkness on ingroup favouritism reflected in trait ratings (Study 1).

probability value is based on a non-directional test of the null hypothesis, and so is conservative; the likelihood is lower that sampling error alone could produce the specific interaction predicted and observed here, $p = .043$.

Study 2: Interactive effects of darkness and "belief in a dangerous world" on prejudicial trait ratings

Before drawing conclusions from the results of that preliminary study, it is important to consider also the results from an additional study with similar methods. This study (conducted in 1999) was more rigorous, and also tested the moderating effect of an additional background variable. Specifically, this study examined the interactive effects of ambient darkness and beliefs in a dangerous world. The rationale follows from intergroup vigilance theory: Among individuals who chronically worry that harm might befall them, ambient darkness may be especially likely to facilitate the activation and expression of prejudicial beliefs (particularly beliefs about dangerous intent). But among individuals who chronically feel safe from harm, the effects of darkness may be muted.

The procedures were similar to those described above. Participants were 69 students from the University of British Columbia. Several participants at a time participated in each experimental session, through which they were randomly assigned to either the Light condition or the Dark condition. Participants sat in a windowless room that was well-lit by electric fluorescent lights, and completed several questionnaires, including the "belief in a dangerous world" questionnaire described above (BDW; Cronbach's alpha in this sample was .81).

Participants were then given blank sheets of paper and instructions on how to record their ratings on these sheets. The experimenter explained that future instructions and questions would be provided by a pre-recorded voice on audiotape. The experimenter then turned on the audiotape player. After the voice on the tape gave a few preparatory instructions, the experimenter paused the audiotape and ascertained that the voice was audible to all participants.

In the Light condition, the experimenter restarted the audiotape and further instructions were provided by the voice on tape.

In the Dark condition, the experimenter followed the same procedures, with one exception: Just prior to restarting the audiotape (and after announcing to participants that they would be given an explanation later) the experimenter turned off the lights that had been illuminating the room. The participants listened to the audiotaped instructions and recorded their ratings in the dark.

Participants were asked to rate "men from Iraq" and "men from Canada" on four trait dimensions (*hostile, ignorant, trustworthy, openminded*) by writing down a number from 1 to 10. In addition—as a global measure of perceived intra-group homogeneity—they also rated how similar to each other Iraqis are, and how similar to each other Canadians are. (As in Study 1, participants had no difficulty recording legible ratings, even in the Dark condition in which they could not see the paper on which they were writing.)

Following the same computational procedures used in Study 1, we computed composite indices reflecting the ratings of Canadians and Iraqis on low and high danger-relevance traits. (Table 2 summarises mean ratings on these two indices, broken down according to whether participants scored low or high on BDW—based on a median split for illustrative purposes—and whether they participated in the Light or Dark condition.) These values were then used to compute two indices of ingroup favouritism: One index assessed ingroup favouritism on highly danger-relevant traits; the other assessed ingroup favouritism on low danger-relevance traits.

The effects of BDW and Darkness on each of these two indices were tested with regression analyses. Darkness and BDW were first transformed into z-scores. The multiplicative product of these two z-scores was computed, representing the BDW × Darkness interaction. The standardised

TABLE 2
Interactive effects of darkness and belief in a dangerous world (BDW) on evaluations of ingroup and outgroup (Study 2)

		Low BDW		High BDW	
		Light	Dark	Light	Dark
High danger-relevance traits					
Rating of ingroup	Mean	7.08	6.88	6.68	7.18
	(SD)	(1.10)	(1.34)	(1.32)	(1.13)
Rating of outgroup	Mean	5.17	5.79	4.97	3.94
	(SD)	(1.69)	(1.70)	(1.52)	(1.47)
Low danger-relevance traits					
Rating of ingroup	Mean	7.31	7.00	5.68	6.91
	(SD)	(1.26)	(1.49)	(1.40)	(1.29)
Rating of outgroup	Mean	5.42	5.12	4.00	5.00
	(SD)	(1.81)	(1.36)	(1.52)	(1.15)

Ratings of ingroup and outgroup are scaled in such a way that higher values indicate more favourable evaluations.

BDW and Darkness variables and the interaction variable were entered as predictors in a pair of regression analyses. There were no meaningful effects on the low danger-relevance index. In contrast, effects did emerge on the high danger-relevance index of ingroup favouritism. There was a main effect of BDW (*beta* = .27, p = .019), and this main effect was qualified by a BDW × Darkness interaction (*beta* = .31, p = .008). There was essentially no relation between BDW and danger-relevant ingroup favouritism in the Light (r = −.03), but there was a substantial relation in the Dark (r = −.56). A different depiction of the interaction is provided in Figure 2 (in which, strictly for the sake of illustration, high- and low-BDW categories were based on a median split). This figure reveals that darkness facilitated ingroup favouritism (on highly danger-relevant traits) among high-BDW individuals, but not among low-BDW individuals.

There were no meaningful effects of BDW and Darkness on rated similarity within the ingroup, but there was some evidence of an interactive effect on ratings of within-outgroup similarity. The rating of similarity among Iraqis was entered as a dependent variable in a regression analysis following the same format as those described above. Three predictor variables were included, representing the main and interactive effects of BDW and Darkness. The result of greatest interest was a weak, but potentially meaningful, BDW × Darkness interaction effect (*Beta* = .20, p = .095; this probability value is based on a conservative, non-directional test of the null hypothesis; a directional

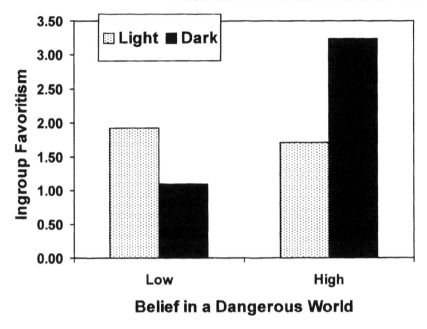

Figure 2.   Interactive effect of ambient darkness and belief in a dangerous world on ingroup favouritism reflected in ratings on highly danger-relevant traits (Study 2).

test yields $p = .048$). Deeper examination of this effect revealed that BDW predicted ratings of within-outgroup similarity in the Dark ($r = .39$, $p = .021$) but not in the Light ($r = .01$). A different depiction of the interaction is provided in Figure 3 (in which, strictly for the sake of illustration, high- and low-BDW categories were based on a median split). This figure reveals that among high-BDW individuals—but not low-BDW individuals—darkness led to greater perceived homogeneity within the outgroup.

Results illustrated in Figures 2 and 3 suggest that, while ambient darkness facilitates prejudicial responses among high-BDW individuals, it may actually have the opposite effect among those low in BDW. Further research is required to determine whether this apparent reversal among low-BDW individuals is a truly meaningful effect. If it is, it will demand consideration of additional explanatory constructs (e.g., specific personality processes that contribute to—or are correlated with—low BDW) which complement those specified by intergroup vigilance theory.

Two other aspects of the results are of more immediate conceptual note. First, under conditions in which BDW and darkness exerted their

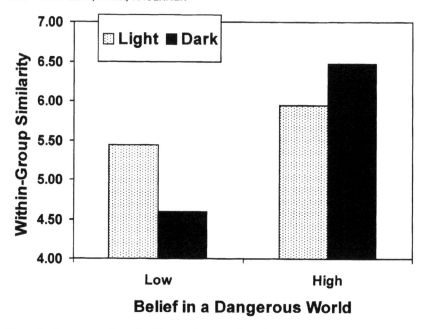

Figure 3. Interactive effect of ambient darkness and belief in a dangerous world on the extent to which members of outgroup are perceived to be similar to each other (Study 2).

effects on prejudicial beliefs, the effects were driven more by perceptions of outgroups than by perceptions of ingroups (see the means presented in Table 2). These results indicate that the effects are psychologically distinct from other processes—such as those pertaining to social identity—that influence intergroup prejudice primarily through their influence on perceptions of ingroups. Second, the effects occurred only on danger-relevant prejudicial beliefs; no effects were observed on equally derogatory beliefs that were connotatively irrelevant to danger. These results are not only consistent with the processes specified by intergroup vigilance theory, they are inconsistent with potential alternative explanations that might be otherwise be offered by many other well-established psychological phenomena. For instance, it is possible that the sudden onset of darkness may enhance autonomic arousal, uncertainty, deindividuation, and feelings of personal anonymity; and there are conceptually distinct processes through which these constructs could lead to exaggerated expressions of prejudice. But those processes imply effects that should be observed across all evaluative domains of prejudice. They cannot provide adequate explanations for the domain-specific effects observed in these studies.

Interactive effects of ambient darkness and BDW on stereotype activation

Further evidence supporting the predictions of intergroup vigilance theory is found in the results of two studies reported by Schaller, Park, and Mueller (2003), in which BDW and ambient darkness exerted interactive effects on the activation of ethnic stereotypes—specifically stereotypes connoting danger. In both studies, participants were non-Black university students in Canada, and the methods were designed to assess the implicit activation of stereotypes about Black people.

In one study (Schaller et al., 2003, Study 1), participants—who had earlier completed the BDW questionnaire—watched a slide show designed to make Black people salient to participants. The slide show consisted of nine photos of individual young African-American men, projected onto a blank wall of the room. Depending on experimental condition, participants were presented with these photos under conditions of either dim lighting, or near-total darkness. After the slide show, participants completed a trait-rating measure on which they rated the extent to which they perceived various traits to be part of the popular cultural stereotype of Black people. (Rather than rating their own beliefs, they rated their perceptions of others' beliefs—a method that has been used previously to infer the activation of stereotypical knowledge structures.) A subset of these traits connoted danger (e.g., criminal, untrustworthy), and was used to comprise a high danger-relevance stereotype index. Another subset of traits was also derogatory and stereotypical but was less relevant to danger (e.g., lazy, ignorant), and so was used to comprise a low danger-relevance stereotype index. Results on the high danger-relevance stereotype index revealed an interaction between BDW and ambient darkness: Stereotypes connoting danger were especially strongly activated among high-BDW individuals in the dark (see Figure 4). Effects on the low danger-relevance index were weaker.

In the other study (Schaller et al., 2003, Study 2), participants again completed the BDW measure, and were induced to think about Black people under conditions of either ambient light or ambient darkness. Stereotype activation was assessed with a computer-based reaction-time measure—the "implicit association test" (IAT; Greenwald, McGhee, & Schwartz, 1998)— that assesses differential cognitive association of social categories with semantic information. Participants completed two IAT tasks, the order of which was counterbalanced. One IAT task was designed to assess the implicit cognitive association between the social category "African" and the semantic category "danger". The other IAT task assessed the implicit association between "African" and "unpleasant". Results on the African/ danger IAT revealed the familiar interactive effects of BDW and ambient darkness; results on the African/unpleasant IAT were weaker.

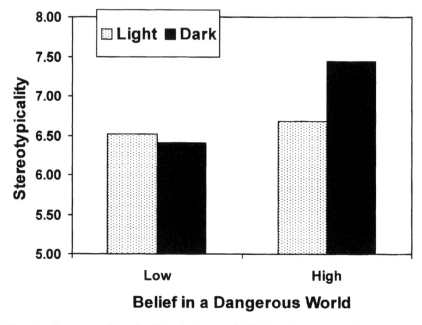

Figure 4. Interactive effect of ambient darkness and belief in a dangerous world on the extent to which danger-relevant traits are perceived to be stereotypical of Black people (Schaller et al., 2003).

These results not only further substantiate the interesting interactive effects of BDW and ambient darkness, they also indicate that these effects occur implicitly, with a minimum of cognitive effort or awareness. The automaticity of these responses is consistent with the processes specified by intergroup vigilance theory.

Summary remarks

The results of these various studies are consistent with the thesis that a specific psychological process contributing to intergroup prejudice emerged as an adaptive response to social environments in which outgroups actually posed some threat of physical injury. More interestingly, these studies reveal that this prejudice response can be triggered by contemporary cues and contexts—like ambient darkness—that heuristically connote vulnerability to danger.

Several of these studies reveal that the prejudices triggered by these variables are specific to functionally relevant domains of judgement. This domain-specificity is notable for several reasons. First, domain-specificity of exactly this sort is predicted by intergroup vigilance theory, and is a hallmark of many other psychological processes that have an evolutionary basis (Kenrick, Sadalla, & Keefe, 1998; Kurzban & Leary, 2001; Neuberg & Cottrell, 2002). Second, it cannot be easily explained by many of the other processes that social psychologists commonly identify as the causes of intergroup prejudice—such as processes based on social identity and self-concept. Therefore, these results signal the need to consider the role of additional prejudice processes that complement those with which we are already so familiar.

PERCEIVED VULNERABILITY TO DISEASE AND ITS EFFECTS ON PREJUDICE

Contact with other people may pose a health risk even if those people don't intend physical harm. Potential peril also lurks in the unintentional communication of disease. Thus, for sensible reasons, people prefer to avoid others who are known to be carriers of parasites and pathogens (Crandall & Moriarty, 1995). In addition, perceived vulnerability to disease may be linked to prejudices against categories of people who are objectively non-contagious, but who have features that—at a purely heuristic level—connote disease. These latent prejudices may themselves be responsive to background variables signalling personal vulnerable to disease.

Conceptual background

The conceptual logic underlying this disease-avoidance theory of prejudice has been summarised by Kurzban and Leary (2001), and begins with the specification that one survival problem that our ancestors faced was the avoidance of communicable pathogens and parasites. Because many of these disease-causing agents were communicated through interpersonal contact with other individuals, behavioural tendencies that facilitated the avoidance of contagious individuals would have been adaptive, as would affective reactions (e.g., disgust) and cognitive structures that motivated this sort of avoidance behaviour. Consequently, specific psychological mechanisms have evolved—and specific cultural norms may have emerged as well—to facilitate these negative psychological responses to any individual marked by features that heuristically connote disease.

The psychological mechanism linking individuals with disease is expected to be responsive to a wide range of disease-connoting features. Some of these features are the sorts of specific physical symptoms and behavioural tics that historically have been, and continue to be, correlated with the presence of contagious disease—skin lesions, coughing spasms, and so forth. It is unlikely that a disease-avoidance mechanism could have evolved to make the sort of fine distinctions that separate actual symptoms of contagious disease from a much broader category of superficially similar physical and behavioural features, many of which may be unrelated to any sort of contagious agent (Zebrowitz & Collins, 1997). Consequently, evolved disease-avoidance mechanisms may be sensitive to a wide range of physical or behavioural features that are judged to be normatively unusual. The exact nature of these cues may vary depending on local environments.

This analysis has interesting implications for present-day prejudice and discrimination. Unusual-looking people who are objectively known not to be carriers of contagious disease may nonetheless arouse disgust, and may elicit disease-connoting cognitive and behavioural reactions. Furthermore, these reactions may be triggered most strongly under conditions in which background variables—including both chronic individual differences and temporary contexts—indicate some high personal vulnerability to contagious disease. In our recent research, we have applied this analysis to derive hypotheses about specific variables that may predict prejudices towards people with disabilities, and towards subjectively foreign ethnic outgroups.

Prejudicial reactions to individuals with physical disabilities

Individuals may appear physically unusual in a number of different ways. Some people have asymmetric features, for instance, and perceivers are perceptually sensitive to these asymmetries. Asymmetrical individuals are typically judged to be less attractive, and one explanation is that asymmetry is a cue connoting ill-health (Gangestad & Buss, 1993; Moller, 1992). More obvious forms of physical unusualness include disfigurement and disability. There is a large literature revealing prejudicial reactions to individuals stigmatised by some sort of physical disability. These reactions tend to be defined behaviourally by avoidance and physical distancing—the same sorts of reactions directed towards individuals who actually are diseased (e.g., Snyder, Kleck, Strenta, & Mentzer, 1979; for a review, see Park et al., 2003).

If indeed prejudicial reactions to physical disability are based, in part, on some implicit concern with disease, then these negative reactions are likely to be more pronounced among individuals who chronically feel vulnerable to disease. Park et al. (2003) report results from two studies that offer some support for this hypothesis. In both studies, participants completed an individual difference measure designed to assess "perceived vulnerability to disease" (PVD). The PVD measure contains two types of items that comprise two distinct factors. One factor reflects aversive reactions to situations in which germs are likely to be transmitted (e.g., "It really bothers me when people sneeze without covering their mouths"). The second factor reflects more general beliefs about personal susceptibility to contagious diseases (e.g., "In general, I think I am very susceptible to colds, flu, and other infectious diseases"). Results from one study revealed that individuals who scored more highly on the overall PVD measure were less likely to have friends with physical disabilities ($r = -.26$).

The second study assessed implicit cognitive associations with physically disability. These implicit stereotype associations were assessed with an implicit association test (IAT) modelled after those used to assess the activation of stereotypes and attitudes bearing on ethnic groups (e.g., Greenwald et al., 1998). Participants completed two IAT tasks, the order of which was counterbalanced. One IAT task was designed to assess the implicit cognitive association between the social category "disabled" and the semantic category "disease"; the other was designed to assess the implicit association between "disabled" and "unpleasant". The results revealed that, among individuals socialised in a European culture that emphasises germs as a mode of disease transmission, scores on the germ-aversion factor of the PVD scale predicted stronger implicit associations linking disabled individuals to the connotative concept "disease" as well as stronger implicit associations linking disabled individuals to the evaluative concept "un-pleasant". These effects are illustrated by means summarised in Table 3 (in which—for the sake of simple illustration—participants have been categorised depending on whether their PVD subscale scores were below or above the mean). Interestingly, no such effect was found among individuals who were socialised in an East Asian culture that traditionally emphasises rather different (not germ-based) means of contracting disease. Nor did the second PVD factor—the one assessing more general and explicit beliefs—predict these implicit associations (for details, see Park et al., 2003).

Although very preliminary, these results are generally consistent with the evolutionarily informed model of disease-based prejudice elicited by the perception of physical disability. The results from the IAT study indicate

TABLE 3

Relation between perceived vulnerability to disease (PVD – Germ Aversion Subscale) and implicit associations with physical disability (Park et al., 2003)

		Low PVD	High PVD
Implicit association between	Mean	311.42	473.65
disability and "disease"	(SD)	(157.15)	(215.38)
Implicit association between	Mean	233.54	416.77
disability and "unpleasant"	(SD)	(218.55)	(144.90)

Strength of implicit association is derived from a computer-based reaction-time task, and is measured in milliseconds. (This pattern of results was found only among participants of European cultural heritage.)

that the activation of prejudicial cognitions is based not so much on a thoughtful consideration of susceptibility to disease, but perhaps more on an affective response—probably disgust—to information connoting this form of vulnerability. This affective response may precipitate a wide range of negative cognitive associations, including associations that directly connote the implied threat (disease), as well as more diffuse evaluative associations that justify discriminatory behaviour (Haidt, 2001). These results also illustrate that, even if an underlying psychological mechanism has been sculpted by evolutionary pressures, it may still be—indeed usually is—highly responsive to social learning processes, and so may be facilitated by somewhat different sets of background variables across different cultural contexts.

Prejudicial attitudes toward unfamiliar ethnic outgroups

An evolved disease-avoidance mechanism may also play some role in prejudices against members of unfamiliar ethnic outgroups. There are several reasons why unfamiliar ethnicity may have emerged as a marker connoting threat of contagion. First, as much human epidemiological history reveals, contact with previously unknown populations brings increased risk of encountering contagious diseases for which one has no acquired immunity (Diamond, 1999). Second, individuals from non-local cultures are more likely to engage in subjectively strange customs violating local customs that help to inhibit transmission of disease (e.g., customs pertaining to hygiene, food preparation, and sexual activity). Thus, over the course of human history, avoidance and social exclusion of subjectively foreign peoples may have been functional in the avoidance of disease. Consistent with this analysis, Schiefenhövel (1997) notes that people often display disgust reactions when speaking about other ethnic groups, and Rozin, Haidt, McCauley, and Imada (1997, p. 73) suggest that "disgust in humans serves as an ethnic or outgroup marker".

If so, then—following the same line of reasoning summarised above— background variables connoting personal vulnerability to disease may facilitate prejudicial reactions to unfamiliar ethnic outgroups. Exactly such an effect was found across a series of studies that tested the predicted relation between individual differences in perceived vulnerability to disease (PVD) and prejudicial attitudes towards outgroups (Faulkner, Schaller, Park, & Duncan, 2003).

Several of these studies assessed University of British Columbia students' attitudes towards potential immigrants, and examined the relation between these attitudes and PVD. In two studies, PVD predicted less favourable attitudes towards an immigrant group from Eastern Africa. One of these studies was particularly noteworthy because it assessed not only attitudes towards African immigrants (a population that participants perceived to engage in unfamiliar customs and habits), but also towards immigrants from Eastern Europe and Eastern Asia (populations that, given local demographics, were perceived to be more highly familiar). PVD predicted less favourable attitudes towards Africans ($r = -.38$) but not towards the culturally familiar immigrant groups. The third study revealed that the effects of PVD are not specific to attitudes about Africans; PVD also predicted less favourable attitudes to immigrants from three additional geographical locations (Peru, Qatar, and Sri Lanka) that were perceived to be subjectively foreign.

Particularly notable is the fact that the predictive effects of PVD mirror the subjective perception of cultural unfamiliarity. Table 4 summarises means on an index—with a possible range from 1 to 9—indicating the extent to which six different immigrant groups were judged by a separate sample of participants to have unfamiliar customs and habits. Table 4 also summarises the correlations, obtained across the two studies summarised above, between PVD and participants' attitudes favouring immigration of each group to Canada. The covariation between these two sets of numbers is extraordinarily strong.

Additional data from these studies revealed that, although PVD correlates moderately highly with BDW (rs are typically in the .3 to .4 range), the predictive effects of PVD on prejudicial reactions were largely independent of any effects of BDW. Thus, prejudice processes linked to the threat of disease seem to be psychologically distinct from prejudice processes linked to the threat of physical injury.

Prejudicial attitudes towards foreign peoples may be predicted not only by chronic worries about disease, but also by situational contexts that make

TABLE 4

Perceived cultural unfamiliarity of six immigrant groups, and the extent to which perceived vulnerability to disease (PVD) predicts attitudes supporting their immigration (Faulkner et al., 2003)

Geographical origin of immigrants	Cultural unfamiliarity		Correlation between PVD and attitude
	Mean	(SD)	
Eastern Europe	3.60	(1.40)	.16
Eastern Asia	4.04	(1.46)	.15
Eastern Africa	5.84	(1.96)	−.38
Peru	5.83	(1.76)	−.30
Qatar	5.93	(1.74)	−.36
Sri Lanka	6.13	(1.96)	−.53

the threat of contagious diseases temporarily salient. Faulkner et al. (2003) report results from two additional experimental studies that provide preliminary evidence consistent with this hypothesis. In both experiments, participants were randomly assigned to watch one of two different slide shows, each of which was designed to make a particular health threat salient. One slide show portrayed a threat that was irrelevant to disease; it contained a series of pictures that conveyed the ease with which physical accidents occur in everyday life. The other slide show was specifically designed to make diseases salient; it contained a series of pictures that conveyed the ease with which germs and diseases are transmitted in everyday life. Results from one study showed that—compared to the control condition in which accidents were salient—when diseases were made salient, participants were relatively less favourable towards immigrants from Nigeria (a subjectively foreign group), but not less favourable towards immigrants from Scotland (a familiar group). In the other experiment, participants indicated the percentage of a special federal budget that should be spent to recruit immigrants from each of eight countries. Immigrants from four of these countries (Nigeria, Mongolia, Brazil, and Peru) had been pre-rated as subjectively foreign; immigrants from four other countries (Scotland, Taiwan, Poland, and Iceland) had been pre-rated as subjectively familiar. Budget allocations to the four foreign locations were combined into a single index, and budget allocations to the four familiar locations were combined into a separate index. When accidents were salient, participants allocated almost equal amounts to recruit foreign and familiar immigrants; but when diseases were salient, participants allocated relatively less of the budget to recruit immigrants from foreign locations, and relatively more of the budget to recruit immigrants from familiar locations (see Figure 5).

Summary remarks

The results of these studies reveal that several quite different categories of people might be targets of prejudices that are based on some underlying concern with the transmission of disease. These prejudices are expressed more strongly by perceivers who feel more chronically vulnerable to the transmission of diseases. Preliminary evidence also indicates that these prejudices can be triggered more strongly by transient contextual cues connoting vulnerability to disease. It is also likely that these prejudices—like those based on fear of physical injury—may be responsive to complex interactions between different kinds of background variables that connote vulnerability or invulnerability to disease. These disease-based prejudices are also likely to be linked to specific affective reactions (disgust), and to imply specific kinds of cognitive and behavioural responses (especially behavioural

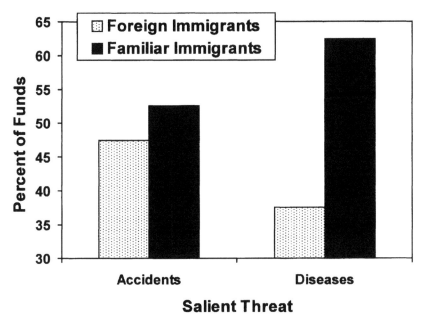

Figure 5. Effect of temporarily salient threats on allocation of funds to recruit immigrants from subjectively foreign or familiar locations (Faulkner et al., 2003).

avoidance and cognitions that compel avoidance). Research exploring these implications has just begun; there are many logically implied hypotheses that remain to be tested. That fact, more than anything, reveals the heuristic hypothesis-generating value of this evolutionary approach to prejudice.

BROADER IMPLICATIONS

Any evolutionarily informed theory of psychological processes contains conceptual models at two levels of analysis. At one level of analysis, there is a model of historical events, which specifies how specific evolutionary pressures led to the emergence of specific adaptive mechanisms. The evolutionary processes specified within these historical models are exceptionally difficult to verify, and this fact surely contributes to many individuals' discomfort with evolutionary psychology (Conway & Schaller, 2002). But the scientific utility of these historical models rests not merely on their merits as theories of evolutionary origin; it rests also on their capacity to generate, through deduction, a second conceptual model that operates at a very different level of analysis: A model of contemporary psychological events. These models should specify testable relations between psychological variables operating in the here-and-now. The veracity and utility of these models is what matters most within the psychological sciences.

The two evolutionarily informed theoretical frameworks reviewed above contain models of contemporary psychological events that are consistent with existing empirical data within the prejudice literature. More importantly, these models have provided a basis for the deduction of new hypotheses and the discovery of previously undocumented influences on contemporary prejudices. These conceptual models, and the results that support them, suggest some broader implications as well—which are worth considering further if we wish to understand the problems of prejudice more completely, and to address these problems more effectively.

Conceptual prominence of outgroup derogation

A defining feature of intergroup prejudice is the tendency to treat ingroups more charitably than outgroups—such as when Canadians rate their fellow Canadians more positively than they rate Iraqis. The mere fact of this bias begs a deeper question: Does the bias reflect a special benevolence towards the ingroup, a derogation of the outgroup, or both? Several theoretical perspectives on prejudice imply that the psychological "action" lies primarily in evaluations of the ingroup; careful reviews of the social psychological literature reveal that there is greater empirical evidence of ingroup favouritism than outgroup derogation (Brewer, 1979; Hewstone, Rubin, & Willis, 2002). We might be wise, however, not to draw too quick or over-general a conclusion on the basis of these past results. The existing empirical literature may not accurately portray the full breadth of prejudice processes that operate in the real world. For a variety of reasons both conceptual and methodological, a substantial chunk of the psychological literature on stereotypes and prejudice focuses on beliefs about specific social categories that are functionally unique (e.g., men and women) or have minimal functional implication (e.g., engineers and artists). Another chunk of the literature focuses on ad-hoc "minimal" groups that are created in the laboratory; inevitably, the results of these studies reflect prejudice processes that emerge from mere categorisation in the absence of any additional functional context. The apparent absence of outgroup derogation in the empirical literature may under-represent its actual prevalence in the real world (Hewstone et al., 2002).

The evolutionary frameworks summarised here imply clearly that outgroup derogation may play a larger role in prejudice processes than is currently revealed in the social psychological literature. These theories begin with assumptions about members of specific outgroups and the formerly functional purposes served by derogatory beliefs about those groups. The conceptual consequences are hypotheses about contemporary acts of outgroup derogation and the circumstances under which this derogation is especially likely to occur. Under these predictable circumstances, the "action" underlying acts of prejudice may be primarily that of outgroup derogation.

The results of several of the studies reviewed above are consistent with this conceptual emphasis on outgroup derogation. The broader implication is this: By pursuing more thoroughly the implications of these and other evolutionary theories, we may rediscover the significance of outgroup derogation in the psychology of prejudice. It is an unpleasant phenomenon to focus on, but it may be necessary to a complete understanding of prejudice.

Effects of threats on prejudices

The psychology of threat is another unpleasant, but apparently necessary, focus of these evolutionary approaches to prejudice. The concept of threat has long been associated with prejudice, and has shown up in a variety of very different guises (Adorno et al., 1950; Allport, 1954; Esses, Jackson, & Armstrong, 1999; Fein & Spencer, 1997; Harmon-Jones, Greenberg, Solomon, & Simon, 1996; Stephan et al., 1998). The evolutionary perspective instructs us to pay special attention to specific kinds of threats that pertain directly to bodily health. Psychological processes designed to protect against specific threats to bodily health can have important influences on prejudice— and can even influence prejudices against people that, at a rational level, pose no realistic threat at all. This conclusion is also compelled by a perusal of various forms of real-world propaganda used to justify and inflame others to engage in acts of prejudice. Suedfeld and Schaller (2002) noted that Nazi propaganda abounded with text and images that linked Jews to disease and to the threat of malicious harm. Contemporary organisations devoted to the incitement of ethnic prejudice employ similar rhetorical devices. A website maintained by one such Canadian organisation displays banners bearing slogans such as "Immigration can kill you!" and regularly features stories linking non-White immigrants to various sorts of violent crime, and to diseases ranging from tuberculosis to ebola.

Of course, one does not need an evolutionary perspective to develop a taxonomy of threats, or to assert the relation between threats and prejudices (see Stephan et al., 1998, for example). What an evolutionary perspective adds, however, is a deeper conceptual texture. This texture is useful. It helps explain why specific categories of people arouse certain forms of threat, and why specific threats arouse specific expressions of prejudice. And it helps to predict the specific circumstances in which each of those forms of prejudice is especially likely to occur.

Specificity of prejudice processes

The concept of specificity is important to these evolutionary approaches to prejudice. This fits with a fundamental tenet underlying many inquiries within evolutionary psychology: The human mind is modular. Many different—and psychologically independent—cognitive mechanisms evolved in response to the many distinct problems bearing on survival and sexual reproduction in the ancestral past. From this perspective, the psychology of prejudice might more accurately be construed as the psychology of prejudices. It is unlikely that there is any single general-purpose process compelling us to judge all different kinds of outgroups in any sort of generally negative manner. Instead, there are many different and independent processes that, when triggered, lead us to judge specific types of others in specific types of disapproving ways.

Some of these different forms of disapproval are illustrated by the results of some of the studies reviewed above. These domain-specific results reveal a level of complexity that is often overlooked in the study of prejudice. Because prejudice so clearly implies negative affective and evaluative reactions, it is easy to forget that there are many different negative reactions that can comprise a prejudice. Recent research has begun to probe more deeply into the psychological processes underlying the distinct affective responses associated with different prejudices (e.g., Mackie, Devos, & Smith, 2000), and these lines of inquiry are nicely complemented by an evolutionary approach to prejudice. By calling attention to different types of negative reactions and their functional implications, the evolutionary approach offers a set of useful conceptual tools to formulate questions and answers about the specific contents of specific prejudices (Neuberg & Cottrell, 2002).

The evolutionary approach is also useful in reminding us that many prejudice processes are target-specific. We do lump people into categories, yes, and the mere fact of categorisation has psychological implications that generalise across all kinds of social categories. But not all groups and social categories are the same. (In fact, not all social categories qualify psychologically as groups.) Different types of social categories were associated with different adaptive problems—and different solutions to those problems—in ancestral environments (Bugental, 2000; Caporael, 1997; Kurzban & Leary, 2001). Consequently, in contemporary times, different categories elicit very different prejudices, and the processes that govern prejudice against one particular category of people may be irrelevant to prejudices against other categories of people.

Implications for effective interventions

If indeed there are psychologically distinct processes that account for the different prejudices against different targets, then the tactics we devise to fight prejudice must be target-specific as well. Interventions designed specifically to overcome sexist attitudes are unlikely to have much impact on prejudices based on national, racial, or ethnic difference. Interventions designed specifically to overcome racism or ethnocentrism are unlikely to have much impact on prejudices against individuals with disfigurements or disabilities. If we wish to intervene effectively, it will help to attend to the specific functional origins of the many prejudices that exist.

Attention to these evolutionarily functional origins should compel us to approach intervention in a more realistic, multi-faceted manner. But it should not compel us to be pessimistic. Many prejudices may have deep evolutionary roots, but that doesn't mean we can't do something about them. An evolutionary perspective reminds us that these prejudice processes are flexible, and are responsive to the input from many different variables. If a prejudicial response to unusual-looking people is triggered by cues connoting personal vulnerability to disease, then that response may be inhibited by cues connoting invulnerability or immunity. Interventions designed to reduce individuals' real or imagined risk of contracting infectious diseases may therefore help to reduce this particular prejudice. Similarly, if a prejudice against ethnic outsiders is triggered by cues connoting vulnerability to interpersonal injury, then this prejudice might be inhibited by interventions designed to enhance feelings of safety and security. In fact, results showing exactly this effect have been reported by Mikulincer and Shaver (2001): When Israeli participants were subliminally primed with words connoting safety, they expressed less prejudice against potential immigrants.

CONCLUDING REMARKS

A common critique of theories within evolutionary psychology is that they are unnecessary—that observed relations between psychological variables can be explained without reference to the prehistoric operation of evolutionary processes. This type of critique is almost always right. It is also almost entirely irrelevant to the real value of an evolutionarily informed approach to psychology.

Observations obtained through psychological research methods refer most directly to concepts defined at a psychological level of analysis. Psychologists typically are satisfied by explanations based on processes operating strictly within this level of analysis. The plausibility of any such explanation renders additional theoretical constructs to be subjectively unnecessary, especially if those additional theoretical constructs operate—as evolutionary constructs do—at a different level of analysis entirely (Conway & Schaller, 2002).

Explanatory necessity, however, is a very limited standard against which to judge the value of any theory (Schaller, 2002). If we limit our theoretical horizons to just those constructs necessary to explain the existing psychological database, then we limit our ability to address more ambitious questions about human nature and its origins. We also limit our access to conceptual tools that can lead us to new empirical discoveries. Ultimately, the primary scientific utility of any theory is not merely to explain existing empirical facts, but to generate new ones.

It is for exactly this reason that evolutionary perspectives on prejudice provide valuable scientific tools. By availing ourselves of these tools, and applying them rigorously, we may be able to chart more completely the complex workings of the many prejudices that lurk within the dark waters of the human psyche. Consequently, these tools can help us to navigate our way past these hazards, and more effectively minimise the damage that they do.

REFERENCES

Adorno, T. W., Frenkel-Brunswik, E., Levinson, D. J., & Sanford, R. (1950). *The authoritarian personality*. New York: Harper.

Alexander, M. G., Brewer, M. B., & Herrmann, R. K. (1999). Images and affect: A functional analysis of out-group stereotypes. *Journal of Personality and Social Psychology, 77*, 78–93.

Allport, G. W. (1954). *The nature of prejudice*. New York: Addison-Wesley.

Altemeyer, B. (1988). *Enemies of freedom*. San Francisco: Jossey-Bass.

Barkow, J., Cosmides, L., & Tooby, J. (1992). *The adapted mind: Evolutionary psychology and the generation of culture*. New York: Oxford University Press.

Blascovich, J., Mendes, W. B., Hunter, S. B., Lickel, B., & Kowai-Bell, N. (2001). Perceiver threat in social interactions with stigmatized others. *Journal of Personality and Social Psychology, 80*, 253–267.

Brewer, M. B. (1979). In-group bias in the minimal intergroup situation: A cognitive-motivational analysis. *Psychological Bulletin, 86*, 307–324.

Bugental, D. B. (2000). Acquisition of the algorithms of social life: A domain-based approach. *Psychological Bulletin, 126*, 187–216.

Burnstein, E., Crandall, C., & Kitayama, S. (1994). Some neo-Darwinian decision rules for altruism: Weighing cues for inclusive fitness as a function of the biological importance of the decision. *Journal of Personality and Social Psychology, 67*, 773–789.

Buss, D. M. (1995). Evolutionary psychology: A new paradigm for psychological science. *Psychological Inquiry, 6*, 1–30.

Caporael, L. R. (1997). The evolution of truly social cognition: The core configurations model. *Personality and Social Psychology Review, 1*, 276–298.

Conway, L. G. III, & Schaller, M. (2002). On the verifiability of evolutionary psychological theories: An analysis of the psychology of scientific persuasion. *Personality and Social Psychology Review, 6*, 152–166.

Crandall, C. S., & Moriarty D. (1995). Physical illness stigma and social rejection. *British Journal of Social Psychology, 34*, 67–83.

Crawford, C., & Krebs, D. L. (1998). *Handbook of evolutionary psychology: Ideas, issues, and applications*. Mahwah, NJ: Lawrence Erlbaum Associates Inc.

Cummins, D. D., & Allen, C. (1998). *The evolution of mind*. New York: Oxford University Press.

Diamond, J. (1999). *Guns, germs, and steel*. New York: Norton.

Esses, V. M., Jackson, L. M., & Armstrong, T. L. (1999). Intergroup competition and attitudes toward immigrants and immigration: An instrumental model of group conflict. *Journal of Social Issues, 54,* 699–724.

Faulkner, J., Schaller, M., Park, J. H., & Duncan, L. A. (2003). *Evolved disease-avoidance processes and contemporary xenophobic attitudes.* Unpublished manuscript, University of British Columbia, Canada.

Fein, S., & Spencer, S. J. (1997). Prejudice as self-image maintenance: Affirming the self through derogating others. *Journal of Personality and Social Psychology, 73,* 31–44.

Fox, R. (1992). Prejudice and the unfinished mind: A new look at an old failing. *Psychological Inquiry, 3,* 137–152.

Gaertner, S. L., & Dovidio, J. F. (2000). *Reducing intergroup bias: The Common Ingroup Identity model.* Philadelphia: Psychology Press.

Gaertner, S. L., Dovidio, J. F., Anastasio, P. A., Bachman, B. A., & Rust, M. C. (1993). The Common Ingroup Identity model: Recategorization and the reduction of intergroup bias. In W. Stroebe & M. Hewstone (Eds.), *European review of social psychology* (Vol. 4, pp. 1–26). Chichester UK: Wiley.

Gangestad, S. W., & Buss, D. M. (1993). Pathogen prevalence and human mate preferences. *Ethology and Sociobiology, 14,* 89–96.

Gangestad, S. W., & Simpson, J. A. (2000). The evolution of human mating: Trade-offs and strategic pluralism. *Behavioral and Brain Sciences, 23,* 573–644.

Garcia, J. (1981). Tilting at the paper mills of academe. *American Psychologist, 36,* 149–158.

Greenwald, A. G., McGhee, D. E., & Schwartz, J. L. K. (1998). Measuring individual differences in implicit cognition: The Implicit Association Test. *Journal of Personality and Social Psychology, 74,* 1464–1480.

Grillon, C., Pellowski, M., Merikangas, K. R., & Davis, M. (1997). Darkness facilitates acoustic startle reflex in humans. *Biological Psychiatry, 42,* 453–460.

Haidt, J. (2001). The emotional dog and its rational tail: A social intuitionist approach to moral judgment. *Psychological Review, 108,* 814–834.

Harmon-Jones, E., Greenberg, J., Solomon, S., & Simon, L. (1996). The effects of mortality salience on intergroup bias between minimal groups. *European Journal of Social Psychology, 26,* 677–681.

Haselton, M., & Buss, D. (2000). Error management theory: A new perspective on biases in cross-sex mind reading. *Journal of Personality and Social Psychology, 78,* 81–91.

Hewstone, M., Rubin, M., & Willis, H. (2002). Intergroup bias. *Annual Review of Psychology, 53,* 575–604.

Judd, C. M., & Park, B. (1988). Out-group homogeneity: Judgments of variability at the individual and group levels. *Journal of Personality and Social Psychology, 54,* 778–788.

Kenrick, D. T., Li, N. P., & Butner, J. (2003). Dynamical evolutionary psychology: Individual decision rules and emergent social norms. *Psychological Review, 110,* 3–28.

Kenrick, D. T., Sadalla, E. K., & Keefe. R. C. (1998). Evolutionary cognitive psychology: The missing heart of modern cognitive science. In C. Crawford & D. L. Krebs (Eds.), *Handbook of evolutionary psychology* (pp. 485–514). Mahwah NJ: Lawrence Erlbaum Associates Inc.

Ketelaar, T., & Ellis, B. J. (2000). Are evolutionary explanations unfalsifiable? Evolutionary psychology and the Lakatosian philosophy of science. *Psychological Inquiry, 11,* 1–21.

Kingsolver, B. (1995). *High tide in Tucson: Essays from now or never.* New York: HarperCollins.

Krebs, D. L., & Denton, K. (1997). Social illusions and self-deception: The evolution of biases in person perception. In J. A. Simpson & D. T. Kenrick (Eds.), *Evolutionary social psychology* (pp. 21–47). Mahwah, NJ: Lawrence Erlbaum Associates Inc.

Kurzban, R., & Leary, M. R. (2001). Evolutionary origins of stigmatization: The functions of social exclusion. *Psychological Bulletin, 127,* 187–208.

Mackie, D. M., Devos, T., & Smith, E. R. (2000). Intergroup emotions: Explaining offensive action tendencies in an intergroup context. *Journal of Personality and Social Psychology, 79,* 602–616.

Marr, D. (1982). *Vision.* San Francisco: Freeman.

Mikulincer, M., & Shaver, P. R. (2001). Attachment theory and intergroup bias: Evidence that priming the secure base schema attenuates negative reactions to out-groups. *Journal of Personality and Social Psychology, 81,* 97–115.

Moller, A. P. (1992). Parasites differentially increase the degree of fluctuating asymmetry in secondary sexual characteristics. *Journal of Evolutionary Biology, 5,* 691–700.

Mullen, B., Brown, R., & Smith, C. (1992). Ingroup bias as a function of salience, relevance, and status: An integration. *European Journal of Social Psychology, 22,* 103–122.

Murphy, D. (2003). Adaptationism and psychological explanation. In S. J. Scher & F. Rauscher (Eds.), *Evolutionary psychology: Alternative approaches* (pp. 161–184). Boston: Kluwer Academic Publishers.

Neuberg, S. L., & Cottrell, C. A. (2002). Intergroup emotions: A biocultural approach. In D. M. Mackie & E. R. Smith (Eds.), *From prejudice to intergroup relations: Differentiated reactions to social groups* (pp. 265–283). Philadelphia: Psychology Press.

Neuberg, S. L., Smith, D. M., & Asher, T. (2000). Why people stigmatize: Toward a biocultural framework. In T. Heatherton, R. Kleck, J. G. Hull, & M. Hebl (Eds.), *The social psychology of stigma* (pp. 31–61). New York: Guilford Press.

Öhman, A., & Mineka, S. (2001). Fear, phobia, and preparedness: Toward an evolved module of fear and fear learning. *Psychological Review, 108,* 483–522.

Park, J. H., Faulkner, J., & Schaller, M. (2003). Evolved disease-avoidance processes and contemporary anti-social behaviour: Prejudicial attitudes and avoidance of people with disabilities. *Journal of Nonverbal Behavior, 27,* 65–87.

Phelps, E. A., O'Conner, K. J., Cunningham, W. A., Funayama, E. S., Gatenby, J. C., Gore, J. C. et al. (2000). Performance on indirect measures of race evaluation predicts amygdala activation. *Journal of Cognitive Neuroscience, 12,* 729–738.

Pinker, S. (1997). *How the mind works.* New York: Norton.

Pratto, F., Sidanius, J., & Stallworth, L. M. (1993). Sexual selection and the sexual and ethnic basis of social hierarchy. In L. Ellis (Ed.), *Social stratification and socioeconomic inequality: A comparative biosocial analysis* (pp. 111–137). Westport CT: Praeger.

Rothbart, M., & Park, B. (1986). On the confirmability and disconfirmability of trait concepts. *Journal of Personality and Social Psychology, 50,* 131–142.

Rothgerber, H. (1997). External intergroup threat as an antecedent to perceptions of in-group and out-group homogeneity. *Journal of Personality and Social Psychology, 73,* 1206–1212.

Rozin, P., Haidt, J., McCauley, C., & Imada, S. (1997). Disgust: Preadaptation and the cultural evolution of food-based emotion. In H. MacBeth (Ed.), *Food preferences and taste* (pp. 65–82). Providence, RI: Berghahn.

Schaller, M. (2002). Any theory can be useful theory, even if it gets on our nerves. *Personality and Social Psychology Review, 6,* 199–203.

Schaller, M. (2003). Ancestral environments and motivated social perception: Goal-like blasts from the evolutionary past. In S. J. Spencer, S. Fein, M. P. Zanna, & J. M. Olson (Eds.), *Motivated social perception: The Ontario Symposium* (pp. 215–231). Mahwah NJ: Lawrence Erlbaum Associates Inc.

Schaller, M., Asp, C. H., Rosell, M. C., & Heim, S. J. (1996). Training in statistical reasoning inhibits the formation of erroneous group stereotypes. *Personality and Social Psychology Bulletin, 22,* 829–844.

Schaller, M., & Crandall, C. S. (2003). *The psychological foundations of culture.* Mahwah NJ Lawrence: Erlbaum Associates Inc.

Schaller, M., Park, J. H., & Mueller, A. (2003). Fear of the dark: Interactive effects of beliefs about danger and ambient darkness on ethnic stereotypes. *Personality and Social Psychology Bulletin, 29,* 637–649.

Scher, S. J., & Rauscher, F. (2002). *Evolutionary psychology: Alternative approaches.* Dordrecht: Kluwer.

Schiefenhövel, W. (1997). Good tastes and bad tastes: Preferences and aversions as biological principles. In H. MacBeth (Ed.), *Food preferences and taste* (pp. 55–64). Providence, RI: Berghahn.

Simpson, J. A., & Kenrick, D. T. (1997). *Evolutionary social psychology.* Mahwah NJ: Lawrence Erlbaum Associates Inc.

Snyder, M. L., Kleck, R. E., Strenta, A., & Mentzer, S. J. (1979). Avoidance of the handicapped: An attributional ambiguity analysis. *Journal of Personality and Social Psychology, 37,* 2297–2306.

Stephan, W. G., Diaz-Loving, R., & Duran, A. (2000). Integrated threat theory and intercultural attitudes: Mexico and the United States. *Journal of Cross-Cultural Psychology, 31,* 240–249.

Stephan, W. G., Ybarra, O., Martinez, C. M., Schwarzwald, J., & Tur-Kaspa, M. (1998). Prejudice toward immigrants to Spain and Israel. *Journal of Cross-Cultural Psychology, 29,* 559–576.

Suedfeld, P., & Schaller, M. (2002). Authoritarianism and the Holocaust: Some cognitive and affective implications. In L. S. Newman & R. Erber (Eds.), *What social psychology can tell us about the Holocaust: Understanding perpetrator behaviour* (pp. 68–90) Oxford: Oxford University Press.

Wright, S. C., Aron, A., McLaughlin-Volpe, T., & Ropp, S. A. (1997). The extended contact effect: Knowledge of cross-group friendships and prejudice. *Journal of Personality and Social Psychology, 73,* 73–90.

Zebrowitz, L. A., & Collins, M. A. (1997). Accurate social perception at zero acquaintance: The affordances of a Gibsonian approach. *Personality and Social Psychology Review, 1,* 204–223.

EUROPEAN REVIEW OF SOCIAL PSYCHOLOGY, 2003, *14*, 139–170

The effects of being categorised: The interplay between internal and external social identities

Manuela Barreto and Naomi Ellemers

Leiden University, The Netherlands

In this chapter, we consider the independent and interactive effects of internal categorisations (how people see themselves) and external categorisations (how they are categorised by others) on social behaviour. Our point of departure is that people do not necessarily accept external categorisations that are imposed upon them (regardless of whether these refer to artificially constructed or naturally occurring groups) and that this affects their willingness to invest in the group. We first outline different reasons people may have to behave in line with externally imposed group memberships. Subsequently, we examine how self-presentation motives may interfere with identity expression, as people consider different social norms, different audiences, and the psychological costs associated with the management of their social identities. We conclude by delineating the conditions under which external categorisations can be internalised by targets, depending on the interplay of multiple identities as well as the way people are treated by others.

In social psychology, considerable effort is devoted to examining whether it is possible to derive a better understanding of complex social phenomena by analysing them in terms of individual processes. One complication is that in real social situations, more often than not groups instead of individuals are the social actors, as a result of which people are likely to perceive themselves and others as well as behave in terms of their membership in these groups (for overviews see: Oakes, Haslam, & Turner, 1994; Spears, Oakes, Ellemers, & Haslam, 1997). The translation from individual to group-level phenomena, however, involves more than substituting individuals with groups as the relevant social entities. That is, in addition to establishing how interpersonal processes can be represented at the (inter-)group level, it is

Address correspondence to: Manuela Barreto, Social and Organisational Psychology, Leiden University, PO Box 9555, 2300 RB Leiden, The Netherlands. Email: barreto@fsw.leidenuniv.nl.

Part of the research reviewed in this paper was made possible by a fellowship from the European Community (Marie Curie Fellowship, Program for Training and Mobility of Researchers).

http://www.tandf.co.uk/journals/titles/99998080.asp   DOI: 10.1080/10463280340000045

crucial to understand how the individual is *connected to* the group, as this may moderate and interact with other relevant processes in important ways (see also Ellemers, Spears, & Doosje, 1999c, 2002).

When we look at the theoretical and research literature on group processes and intergroup relations, it is striking how little the interface between the individual and the group as such has been a focus of explicit consideration. More often than not people's membership in particular groups (either ad hoc laboratory groups or real-life social categories) has been taken as a given, on the basis of which it is assumed that they will then, almost automatically, perceive their social environment and act in terms of that group membership. Those who examine the position of different individuals within the group, usually do this by considering how individual features (such as individual behaviour, personality traits, perceived competence, or task performance, e.g., Emler & Reicher, 1995; Marques, Yzerbyt, & Leyens, 1988; Seta & Seta, 1996) objectively compare to group characteristics (cf. the notion of prototypicality, Hogg, 1996). Instead, our approach in this chapter is that of differentiating between different ways in which individuals *subjectively relate* to the group, and examining how this may influence their responses (see also Hinkle & Brown, 1990).

Specifically, our aim in the present chapter is to review the empirical evidence relevant to the issue of how discrepancies between internal (perspective of self) and external (perspective of others) social categorisations may influence people's subjective identities and social behaviour. On the basis of theoretical notions of social categorisation and social identification that are relevant to the examination of the interplay between internal and external social identities, we develop the general proposition that while subjective identification is a primary predictor of the tendency to invest in group outcomes, external categorisations can often importantly influence how and when this behaviour is expressed. To illustrate the implications of this reasoning, we first explore what leads people to bring their behaviour in line with external categorisations. Second, we consider how self-presentational concerns impact upon identity expression by examining the effects of conflicting social norms, different audiences, and psychological costs of social identity management. Finally, we delineate how people may come to adapt their internal identities to external definitions of self, depending on the feasibility of maintaining multiple identities as well as the way they are treated by others.

INTERNAL VERSUS EXTERNAL SOCIAL IDENTITIES

Both social identity theory (Tajfel, 1978, 1981; Tajfel & Turner, 1979) and self-categorisation theory (Turner, 1987, 1999) postulate that subjective identities stem from a process of internalisation of group memberships.

According to both these perspectives, neither identification (or self-categorisation) nor pro-group behaviour can be simply inferred from an external observation of which group an individual appears to belong to. Instead, social identification constitutes a subjective process through which externally assigned category distinctions are accepted and ingroup characteristics are adopted to help define the self. Although the distinction between internal identities and external categories is at the heart of these theories, the relationship between these two concepts has not been systematically investigated. Social identity theory tends to assume this internalisation and then addresses the motivational consequences of the acquired identity. Whereas self-categorisation theory focuses more explicitly on the activation of internal identities (e.g., Turner, 1982), as such the relationship between external and internal categorisations has not constituted a topic of systematic investigation.

Although theoretical statements do refer to possible differences in the way a particular individual is categorised by the self and by others, they mainly address mechanisms that may lead internal and external categorisations to *converge* in the end. For instance, Tajfel (1978) pointed out that when people are repeatedly treated by others in terms of a particular group membership, they are likely to internalise this definition of themselves eventually. For example, whereas migrants may initially aim to integrate with the host group, they may come to adopt or even embrace their ethnic identity in response to systematic ethnic categorisation by others, which will reinforce their segregation. Turner (1987) conversely, has argued that people may actively try to bring external perceptions of self in line with internalised self-categorisations, by behaving in terms of norms that are prototypical for the group that constitutes an important part of their self-definition. This process is illustrated by the general phenomenon that we tend to adapt our clothing or speech styles to induce others to perceive us as belonging to certain regional, professional, or age groups rather than others.

At the same time, it is obvious that there are many circumstances under which a particular social categorisation (by others) does not automatically elicit the corresponding social identification (of the self), or vice versa. The possibility that internal identities may not coincide with external categorisations stems from the fact that each individual can potentially be categorised in multiple ways (e.g., Van Rijswijk & Ellemers, 2002; Zarate & Smith, 1990), and the categorisation that is seen as important by oneself may not be the one that is salient for others. Indeed, these two categorisations often emerge from different processes, with motivational considerations coming into play when one's own identity is at stake, while the cognitive salience of a particular category membership tends to determine its use by others. That is, external categorisations are most often elicited by the accessibility of visible cues, or the numerical distinctiveness of group membership (Ellemers, Kortekaas, & Ouwerkerk, 1999b; Fiske, 1998; Hamilton & Gifford, 1976; Kanter, 1977). At a cognitive level, these factors may have similar effects when looking from the perspective of the targets involved (e.g., McGuire, McGuire, Child, & Fujioka, 1978). However, it is not self-evident that subjective identities are primarily determined by those group memberships that are most visible or distinctive (see also Deaux, 1996; Tajfel, 1981). For instance, for a female executive, her gender is both clearly visible and likely to be numerically distinctive, making this a salient categorisation cue for herself as well as others around her. At the same time, in a work context, she may prefer to think of herself primarily in terms of her professional role, and focus on ways in which she is different from other women (e.g., Ellemers, Van den Heuvel, De Gilder, Maass, & Bonvini, in press; Young, Van Knippenberg, Ellemers, & De Vries, 1997).

Because the different parties involved have another perspective on the social situation, they essentially judge the same target in a different comparative context (Oakes et al., 1994). In many situations, divergent categorisations of the same target are further encouraged because *criteria* for group membership are ambiguous (e.g., when inclusion in a particular religious group can alternatively be defined by birth, participation in childhood rituals, or adult religious activity), or because it is hard to unequivocally establish *fulfilment* of these criteria (when membership cues are not visible, as may be the case among homosexuals). However, even in the absence of such uncertainties, discrepancies between external categorisations and internal identities can emerge because people may have idiosyncratic views on how they wish to define the self in relation to others. That is, people take an active role in how they define themselves, by choosing whether or not they endorse an externally assigned categorisation, and by expressing this choice in their social interaction with others. As a result, it is even possible to define oneself on the basis of a category when one fulfils few of the criteria traditionally considered to define that identity. For instance, one can claim an organisational identity solely on the basis of a newly acquired employment position, without much membership history, or awareness of the norms that characterise this group.

In sum, one's own definition of self (who you think you are: internal categorisation) does not necessarily correspond to the way one is perceived by others (who others think you are: external categorisation). This discrepancy can constitute a threat to the self—a categorisation threat (Branscombe, Ellemers, Spears, & Doosje, 1999; Ellemers et al., 2002). The experience of a categorisation threat cannot be assumed by outside observers, as it is intrinsically connected to the target's subjective sense of self. For instance, we cannot assume that being treated as a woman will necessarily constitute an identity threat to a female executive, even in a professional setting. She may regard her gender either as essential to her work, if she perceives herself as a role model for other working women, or as irrelevant, if she sees herself as "one of the boys", while she may adopt yet another definition of self (e.g., as a parent or as a friend) in other settings.

Research into how people deal with such discrepancies between internal and external sources of identity is scarce. An understanding of this process requires the examination of how people express their identities to others, as it is through identity expression that internal and external self-views are confronted. In the next section we illustrate the powerful role of internalised identities in determining whether or not individuals are motivated to behave as members of a given social category. Later we examine how people take into account external categorisations when they express their identities to others.

THE ROLE OF INTERNAL IDENTITIES

Identification with minimal and natural groups

Previous concerns that were raised regarding the possibility that externally assigned social categorisations are not internalised by the group members involved, have usually focused on the issue of whether results obtained with externally imposed laboratory groups (such as: analytic vs synthetic thinkers, global vs detailed perceivers, or simply the blue vs green group) have predictive value for the processes that are likely to occur with more internalised and meaningful group memberships (e.g., national groups, study majors, political interest groups). Indeed, previous attempts to systematically compare between these research paradigms suggest that different effects may emerge with minimal laboratory groups as compared to natural social categories (e.g., Mullen, Brown, & Smith, 1992). While various explanations have been advanced (e.g., referring to multiple vs single comparison dimensions, Hinkle & Brown, 1990; Mummendey & Schreiber, 1983, 1984, or to an "open" situation vs social reality constraints; Ellemers, Barreto, & Spears, 1999a), some have argued that the crucial difference is that people are generally less inclined to define the self as members of laboratory groups than in terms of natural social categories (Jetten, Spears, & Manstead, 1996).

It has to be acknowledged that minimal groups are unlikely to reflect in important ways upon the identity of the individuals outside the research laboratory. However, it is important to note that similar problems may emerge with natural groups. That is, while people may be unable to deny that they can be categorised in terms of a naturally occurring group membership (such as their national group, or their work organisation) this does not necessarily imply that they consider this an important part of their self-definition. Thus, we would argue that these different kinds of groups and categories should be seen as interchangeable from a theoretical point of view, in the sense that—given the appropriate circumstances—it should be possible to observe similar social identity processes in each of these kinds of groups (e.g., Diehl, 1990).

Indeed, empirical data show that—in natural as well as laboratory groups—only those who actually identify as group members are inclined to describe themselves and act in terms of that group membership (e.g., Ellemers, Spears, & Doosje, 1997; Spears, Doosje, & Ellemers, 1997). Conversely, those who express lack of identification with the group emphasise intra-group heterogeneity and differentiate the self from the group, thus effectively undermining the usefulness of that categorisation as a source of information about the self (Doosje, Ellemers, & Spears, 1995; Yzerbyt, Castano, Leyens, & Paladino, 2000). At the behavioural level, group members who fail to incorporate the external categorisation into their sense of self are more inclined to operate according to what best serves their personal self-interest, relatively independently of their group membership or the implications this may have for them. Again, these differential responses depending on the degree of identification emerge regardless of whether artificially constructed and temporary laboratory groups are examined or whether reference is made to membership in more enduring and naturally occurring social groups (for an overview see Ellemers et al., 1999c).

Instead of focusing on the difference between laboratory groups and natural groups as such, we therefore argue that it is important to consider whether the social categorisation that is externally imposed by the researcher (or by others outside the self) actually refers to those identity aspects that have been internalised as relevant for the self, or conversely, whether people can be expected to ignore or even resist being considered in terms of that particular group membership. Thus, the perceived self-relevance of the category under consideration should affect the likelihood that people respond in terms of that group membership, independently of whether artificially constructed or naturally occurring group memberships are examined. To illustrate the implications of this reasoning, we will now review research examining the circumstances under which individuals are willing to invest in group outcomes.

Individual investment in group outcomes

Our argument so far would suggest that—in itself—an externally imposed categorisation provides insufficient reason for individuals to act in terms of their group membership, and that subjective identification with the group is necessary to induce such behavioural engagement. In an attempt to examine this proposition, in two studies Ellemers et al. (1997) categorised research participants either as "inductive thinkers" or as "deductive thinkers", allegedly on the basis of their performance at a cognitive association test. Additionally, participants were led to believe that they either identified with or felt no particular ties to the group they had been assigned to. This manipulation was realised by informing research participants that the extent to which they identified with their group was indicated by the level of physiological arousal they displayed while working on a group decision task, which could be assessed through electrodes that had been attached to their hand at the outset of the experiment.

Regardless of whether the collective performance of the group had been worse than that of the other group (Study 1) or whether it remained unclear how the group had performed on the decision task (Study 2), the results of both studies consistently revealed that people's responses to the externally imposed categorisation depended on whether or not they had been induced to identify with the group they had been assigned to. That is, mediational analyses showed that when the experimental instructions induced identification with the group, research participants reported feeling committed to the group, and as a result wanted to continue working with the group even when it had been unsuccessful in the past. Conversely, when the manipulations led participants to believe their identification with the group was lacking, they indicated less subjective commitment to the group, and accordingly expressed their preference to leave.

Similar observations were made by Doosje, Spears, and Ellemers (2002), in a study that examined how group members respond to temporal changes in a group status structure, that is, when changes in their subjective involvement in the group could actually be monitored as the group evolved over time. In this study too, research participants were categorised by the experimenter into temporary groups in which they performed a group problem-solving task. According to the bogus feedback they received, the initial position of their group was relatively low, however it was made clear that there was a concrete possibility of improving the group's standing through concerted effort during the experiment. Again, only those who had accepted their inclusion in the group and actually identified with it displayed a willingness to work with the group. By contrast, those who failed to identify with the group they had been assigned to were less inclined to behave in terms of their group membership.

A correlational study among members of natural groups (defined according to study major), which asked psychology students to document the amount of time they spent on a variety of activities, shows converging results (Ellemers, Spears, & Doosje, 1998). Those who identified strongly as psychology students reported spending more time on study-related behaviour (such as studying to prepare exams, attending classes), while students who considered the categorisation as psychology majors as less self-relevant were more likely to engage in other kinds of activities that were not related to their subject of study (e.g., socialising with friends).

In a series of experiments Ouwerkerk and his colleagues went one step further, as they assessed people's actual performance on a collective task, in order to assess the conditions under which individual group members would exert themselves on behalf of the group (see Ouwerkerk, Ellemers, & De Gilder, 1999, for an overview). In these experiments, using artificially constructed ("global" vs "detailed" perceivers) as well as natural category memberships (based on study majors), it consistently turned out that only those who identified strongly with the group intended to exert themselves on behalf of the group (Ouwerkerk & Ellemers, 2002), and actually showed an improved performance at a collective task (Ouwerkerk, De Gilder, & De Vries, 2000). Again, a lack of identification with the group in which they were categorised resulted in unwillingness to engage in behaviour that might benefit the group.

WHY BEHAVE IN LINE WITH EXTERNAL CATEGORISATIONS?

In the previous section we have argued that internal categorisations do not necessarily reflect externally imposed group memberships, and we have shown that people are generally more inclined to behave in terms of a particular categorisation to the extent that they consider it more subjectively self-defining. However, in many social situations we cannot avoid being aware of how we are considered by others, and as a result feel pressure to present the self in line with external expectations. Therefore, we now consider the possibility that people may be induced to comply with what is normative for the group to which they are externally assigned, for socially instrumental reasons, rather than because of internal definitions of self. We argue that this may be the case both when associating the self with the group is profitable for the individual in question (e.g., because inclusion in the group yields social or material benefits, see also Cialdini, Borden, Thorne, Walker, Freeman, & Sloan, 1976), and when a failure to comply with group norms might be sanctioned by others (i.e., to avoid deviance or exclusion from the group, see also Goffman, 1963). We now address each of these conditions in turn, in an attempt to specify different psychological mechanisms that might elicit group-normative behaviour among those who lack an intrinsic motivation to do so.

Personal profitability

For those who do not define the self as a group member, achieving prestige by associating with a prestigious group may provide an alternative reason to align with that group and adopt group norms. Indeed, it has been pointed out that membership in socially valued groups may contribute to the social standing and hence the self-esteem of individual group members (e.g., Abrams & Hogg, 1990; Crocker & Luhtanen, 1990). Accordingly, research has consistently revealed that—regardless of the extent to which this group membership is intrinsically meaningful to them—people are generally quite willing to present themselves as group members and behave in accordance with group norms when the group has high social standing or is otherwise positively distinct from other groups (see Ellemers, 1993; Ellemers & Barreto, 2000, for overviews).

This was also found by Finchilescu (1986), who directly examined whether people would be willing to behave in line with an external category to which they had not chosen to belong, as a function of the relative status of the chosen and the external categories. In this study, participants were first asked to which group they wished to belong, and were subsequently categorised either in the group of their choice or in another group. The relative status of the groups was manipulated, so that one of the two groups had higher status than the other. Participants who were categorised in the group of their choice displayed ingroup favouring bias regardless of the group's status. By contrast, participants categorised into the group to which they had not chosen to belong only displayed ingroup bias when the group in which they had been categorised had high status, and not when it had low status.

Our interpretation that this response stems from individual instrumentality considerations, instead of from the inherent self-relevance of the group, is supported by additional data from the study by Doosje et al. (2002) on group status evolution over time that we described above. In a later phase of this study, we led participants to believe that, while their group's performance had initially been worse than the performance of the other group, this had in the meantime improved so that their group now outperformed the other group. Those who had initially identified strongly with the group remained highly identified, regardless of whether the group's performance had improved or remained the same, again attesting to the intrinsic nature of their involvement. By contrast, however, participants who had declined to identify with the group as long as its performance was inferior, were suddenly eager to define themselves as group members after the group had improved its standing. These data clearly show that, when membership in the group may reflect positively upon individual members, this may lead them to align with the group even when they do not consider their membership in the group as intrinsically meaningful.

Another way in which individuals may benefit from the group, and therefore may be inclined to attach more importance to their membership in the group, is when they derive interpersonal esteem from other group members which they are less likely to obtain in another group. This possibility was examined in a recent study by Branscombe, Spears, Ellemers, and Doosje (2002). They classified research participants into experimental groups but then had group members allegedly exchange personal information and rate each other on the basis of this information. In this way, Branscombe et al. (2002) orthogonally manipulated the amount of interpersonal respect individual participants received from other group members as well as the prestige accorded to their group by members of the other group. Subsequently, Branscombe et al. assessed the amount of additional time participants were willing to invest in their group. The results of this study revealed that when the group in itself was not attractive (because it had low prestige) people were nevertheless quite willing to invest time in serving the group's interest when they were individually respected by their fellow group members. Thus, when aligning with the group may yield desirable individual outcomes (such as group-based prestige or interpersonal respect) people will tend to more willingly adapt their behaviour to external categorisations, even if these have not been internalised.

Possibility of sanction

An alternative reason for complying with group norms has to do with the likelihood that others may be able to *sanction* behaviour that is not group-normative, depending on the identifiability vs anonymity of group members. While external categorisations do not elicit internal motivations to follow group norms, they are associated with group-based expectations as to how one should behave. When one is perceived as belonging to a specific group, the norms associated with that group determine the behavioural expectations that apply to the individual in question. Lack of compliance with these norms will tend to reflect negatively upon the self (e.g., Marques et al., 1988) and hence constitutes an important threat to social acceptance (Baumeister, 1982; Leary & Kowalski, 1990). Therefore, we argue that situations that foster behavioural control by others create normative pressures that may lead group members to endorse group norms even when they are not privately inclined to do so.

The idea that people's concerns with self-presentation affect the way they behave is included in most traditional models of social influence (see Turner, 1991, for a review). It is generally assumed that people tend to adapt their behaviour to what they deem normative for the situation at hand, even if this is not reflected in a private change of attitudes (e.g., Deutsch & Gerard, 1955). However, research examining the behavioural consequences of social category memberships usually relies on paradigms that ensure the confidentiality of group members' responses, so that self-presentational motives are unlikely to emerge. Therefore, we set out to explicitly create conditions that would enable us to assess whether the possibility of social sanctions might induce people to comply with group norms. For this purpose, we conducted a series of studies that systematically compared public vs private expressions of group-relevant responses, in order to test whether group members would consistently display the same behaviour regardless of its public or private nature (which would be indicative of an internal motivation to behave in this way), or whether they would strategically adapt their responses depending on the extent to which others were in a position to monitor and perhaps even sanction their behaviour (consistent with the notion that external, self-presentational considerations may play a role).

In a first study (Barreto & Ellemers, 2000, Study 1), individual participants were assigned to groups, allegedly on the basis of their problem-solving style, and a distinction was made between those who had internalised this categorisation (high identifiers) and those who were less inclined to regard their membership in this group as self-relevant (low identifiers). Participants then performed a group problem-solving task, and received feedback conveying that their group's performance had been below average. Subsequently, they were given the choice to work over eight trials either at the improvement of their group's performance, or at the improvement of their personal performance. It was made clear that the group as a whole would benefit most if group members would opt to work on the improvement of their collective performance. Furthermore, the behavioural choices that had to be made (either to work with the group or individually), would either remain completely confidential, or would be open to scrutiny from fellow ingroup members.

The results of this study showed that those who had internalised their group membership (high identifiers) opted to work with the group regardless of the experimental condition they were in, thus testifying to their internal motivation to adapt their behaviour to what would benefit the group. However, participants who primarily experienced the categorisation as externally imposed (low identifiers), adapted their behaviour, depending on whether it was private or public (see top panel of Table 1). That is, when they were convinced that their choices would remain anonymous, these participants declined to work at the improvement of their group's performance, and instead opted to work for themselves. However, in the condition where they thought they might be accountable for their choices towards other ingroup members, they brought their behaviour in line with

TABLE 1
Effect of degree of ingroup identification and response mode on displays of group-focused behaviour

	Response mode			
	Anonymous		Accountable to ingroup	
	Degree of identification			
	Low	High	Low	High
Study 1	2.83 [b]	5.60 [a]	4.29 [a]	4.47 [a]
	(2.07)	(2.09)	(2.51)	(2.42)
Study 2				
Norm:				
Working with the group	2.93 [b]	5.75 [a]	5.25 [a]	5.50 [a]
	(1.67)	(1.49)	(1.42)	(1.27)
Undifferentiated	3.29 [b]	3.67 [b]	3.27 [b]	3.55 [b]
	(1.86)	(1.75)	(1.87)	(2.28)

Adapted from Barreto and Ellemers (2000), *Personality and Social Psychology Bulletin* (pp. 897–898), copyright © by the Society for Personality and Social Psychology, reprinted by permission of Sage Publications. Scores range from 0 (only choices to work individually) to 8 (only choices to work with the group). Only differences between means with different superscript are significant ($p < .05$). Standard deviations are presented in parentheses.

group goals, resulting in a display of group-oriented behaviour that did not differ significantly from that of high identifiers. This supports our contention that, even when the internal motivation to do so is lacking, those for whom the group is not inherently meaningful might nevertheless be sensitive to external normative pressures to follow group norms. Additionally, response latencies revealed that while in the ingroup accountable condition there was no difference between high and low identifiers in terms of their choice behaviour, compared to high identifiers, low identifiers actually took more time to solve the problems. This was interpreted as a sign that they worked less hard at the group task, which is consistent with the notion that their motivation to opt for the group task was determined by external factors, while high identifiers are more internally driven.

These findings were replicated and extended in a second study (Barreto & Ellemers, 2000, Study 2). In addition to distinguishing between high and low identifiers, and studying their behavioural choices under different conditions of accountability/anonymity, this time the *content* of the group norm was also varied. That is, depending on the experimental condition, group members were either led to believe that other group members expected them to work for the group, or that both behavioural options (working for the group or working individually) were accepted by the group. As can be seen in Table 1 (bottom panel), when the norm was to work with the group, the previously observed pattern was replicated: those who identified strongly with the group opted to work for the group regardless of whether their choices were made privately or in public, while low identifiers whose private preference was to work individually adapted their behaviour to the group norm when accountable to other ingroup members. However, when there was no such clear group norm these differences disappeared. Importantly, while in the ambiguous norm condition the overt behaviour of high and low identifiers was similar, only high identifiers reported that they had made their choices out of a concern with group goals. Thus, the comparison between situations with different social norms confirms that public accountability *per se* is not enough to elicit group-oriented behaviour. Instead, the notion that others may monitor and sanction one's behaviour makes group members more aware that their behaviour may be checked against group norms. However, the *content* of these norms determines the nature of the behaviour that is shown.

To summarise, the studies reviewed above show that in addition to internal considerations, external factors may also lead people to behave according to group norms. Previously we have seen that when the group constitutes an important part of one's individual identity, this provides an intrinsic motivation to do what seems best for the group. In this section we have argued that when such internal motivation is lacking, the awareness that others perceive the self as a group member may still elicit group-normative behaviour, either because aligning with the group may yield individually attractive outcomes (e.g., high group status, interpersonal respect), or because it may help avoid social disapproval or exclusion.

BALANCING IDENTITY EXPRESSION WITH SELF-PRESENTATION

Now that we have demonstrated that concerns with positive presentation of the individual self may lead people to act as group members, we will examine how self-presentational concerns can interfere with the expression of internalised social identities. Our reasoning here is based on a recently developed theoretical model proposing that social behaviour tends to be informed by self-presentation considerations that can refer to different levels of self (Social Identity model of Deindividuation Effects – SIDE, Reicher, Spears, & Postmes, 1995; Spears & Lea, 1994). According to this view, people are not only concerned with their individual reputation, but they also care about how others see their social self, which may cause them to engage in impression management targeting their individual as well as their social identity.

The idea that we care about how we present ourselves to others is also implied in the central tenets of social identity theory. Indeed, Tajfel's early work postulates that we are motivated to establish a positive social identity, implying that we not only wish to think positively about ourselves, but also aim to achieve recognition of these self-views from others (Tajfel, 1981; Tajfel & Turner, 1979; see also Crocker & Luhtanen, 1990). Indeed, the strategies that people may follow to secure a positive identity all aim to improve external views of the self, even though some focus primarily on managing the individual's standing in relation to positively evaluated groups (e.g., individual mobility), while others aim at securing a positive evaluation for the group as a whole (e.g., social creativity). Further developing the social identity perspective, Reicher and colleagues (e.g., Reicher & Levine, 1994a, 1994b; Reicher, Levine, & Gordijn, 1998) have focused on the expressive context in which identities are enacted (Reicher, 2000), in order to understand how people manage their social identities when communicating to different audiences. Based on and extending this work, the research reviewed in this section illustrates three different reasons why identity expression is often balanced with self-presentation: because when expressing their identity people need to take into account the various norms present in a given context, because they need to manage multiple identities to different audiences, and because there are psychological costs involved in the management of one's social identity.

Identity expression and outgroup norms

A concern with how one is regarded by others may lead people to tailor the way they characterise their group-based identity to take into account the social norms that are salient in a given context (see also Ellemers et al., 1999a). However, in many social situations different groups are present, involving not just one, but rather multiple and possibly contradictory behavioural norms. As a result, the desire to act in ways that are normative for the ingroup may be curbed by the awareness that this goes against other and perhaps more broadly held social norms. To examine this process, Reicher and Levine (1994a, 1994b) compared endorsement of group norms in the presence of ingroup members only, and in front of both ingroup as well as outgroup members. They found that group members avoided defending group normative attitudes that were likely to be sanctioned by the outgroup when communicating with the mixed audience (see also Klein & Azzi, 2001; Reicher et al., 1998). In a similar vein, Plant and Devine (1998) showed that endorsement of negative stereotypes held by the ingroup (White Americans) about the outgroup (Black Americans) was constrained when stereotype endorsement was made in public conditions (see also Stangor, Swim, Van Allen, & Sechrist, 2002).

However, not all ingroup characteristic attitudes or behaviours will meet with disapproval of others outside the group. For instance, whereas the management of Schiphol Airport (Amsterdam) reject environmentalist views that they should refrain from building another airport terminal, the airport works together with environmental groups in projects to improve air quality and plant life around the airport. Thus, as long as core values of other groups are not challenged, members of other groups will tend to accept ingroup normative behaviour. As a consequence, the awareness that other groups hold different norms will only constrain identity expression in domains that are central to the identity of those other groups. In fact, Reicher and Levine (1994a, 1994b) found that in the presence of ingroup and outgroup members, research participants actually enhanced endorsement of those ingroup norms that seemed acceptable to the outgroup. This illustrates how people take into account outgroup norms when expressing their identity: identity expression involves affirming what is normative for the ingroup, while avoiding public violation of outgroup norms.

In a similar vein, Ellemers, Van Dyck, Hinkle, and Jacobs (2000) examined how group members portray their group, depending on the social norms that are relevant in a given context. They assessed how members of different student sports societies described their group's performance as a function of whether these ratings remained private, or were shared with other participants (Ellemers et al., 2000, Study 1). Results of this study revealed that students who were aware that the perceived status of their group was relatively low, maintained that their group was superior to other groups when their responses remained private. However, when they expected their ratings to be made public, exposing them to the norms held by others outside the group, no such ingroup-favouring ratings were given. That is, participants adapted their descriptions of what was characteristic of the group depending on whether or not their judgements were likely to violate normative views held by others.

In a second study, using a similar methodology (Ellemers et al., 2000, Study 2), the authors went one step further to examine whether differential sensitivity to ingroup and outgroup norms was displayed depending on the extent to which research participants actually identified with the group (in this case, the university where they studied). It turned out that low and high identifiers presented the ingroup differently when outgroup norms were salient. Those who identified strongly with their university resisted evidence suggesting that students of their university might be inferior, and maintained that both groups of students were equally competent regardless of whether or not they were exposed to outgroup norms. While low identifiers also rated students from their own university equally favourably as students from the other university under private circumstances, they conceded their group's alleged inferiority when outgroup members were present. That is, they adapted their responses to outgroup norms when giving their ratings in public. These results show that while high identifiers behave in line with what is normative for the ingroup without yielding to alternative norms, low identifiers in particular tend to avoid the social costs that they may incur when such behaviour violates outgroup norms.

Expression of multiple identities to multiple audiences

We now examine how people monitor the interplay between internal identities and external categorisations by adapting expressions of group allegiance when communicating their identity to different audiences (see also Barreto, 2000). In particular, we focus on issues of self-presentation that emerge when managing self-descriptions by reference to the multiple group memberships that can characterise one's identity. In line with the argument drawn here, we posit that to avoid making claims that are not accepted or deemed credible by the audience, people are likely to adapt the way they describe their identity to the specific audience they address (Schlenker, 1980). We have argued that people refrain from making identity claims that can violate the norms of the particular audience they address, while they may maintain such claims when the audience is not expected to challenge them. According to the SIDE model, this is particularly likely to happen when group members are *personally identifiable*, because these circumstances heighten the possibility that social costs will actually be incurred by the individual in question (Spears & Lea, 1994; see also Spears, Jetten, & Doosje, 2001).

To examine this issue, we assessed statements of identification with native and host communities among Portuguese migrants in the Nether-lands, depending on whether they communicated with a Portuguese or with a Dutch audience (Barreto, Spears, Ellemers, & Shahinper, 2003, Study 2). The nature of the audience was manipulated by varying the language in which the questionnaires were written (Portuguese vs Dutch). In addition, orthogonal to the manipulation of group audience, we manipulated whether or not respondents were personally identifiable to the audience in question (anonymous vs identifiable). The results showed that when personally identifiable to a particular audience, migrants downplayed claims to group memberships that they thought the audience might question. Indeed, migrants do not satisfy all criteria that contribute to defining membership in either native or host groups (e.g., residence and place of birth, respectively), and since personal identifiability allows fulfilment of these criteria to be scrutinised, it functions so as to constrain identity claims. That is, compared to the condition where they were anonymous, identifiable Portuguese migrants downplayed their Portuguese identity to a Portuguese audience, and refrained from claiming a Dutch identity to a Dutch audience (see Table 2), although identification with the Portuguese always remained stronger than identification with the Dutch. Importantly, in the anonymous condition, that is when there was no threat of having one's identity claims disregarded as invalid or not credible, people felt more free to describe themselves in ways that challenge externally imposed category boundaries (see also Spears et al., 2001).

In sum, when migrants experience a potential discrepancy between their internal sense of identity and the way in which they are externally categorised by others (see also Deaux & Ethier, 1998; Hutnik, 1991; LaFromboise, Coleman, & Gerton, 1993; Phinney, 1990; Verkuyten, 1997), these data suggest that their expressions of group allegiances take into account both the enhancement *opportunities* that public expressions provide, and the *constraints* that specific audiences may present. On the one hand, as long as individuals are not personally identifiable, public identity expressions provide the ideal stage to express one's internal definition of the social self. On the other, identity expressions may be constrained when one is personally identifiable to an audience that is in a position to scrutinise the validity of these identity claims. Thus, similar to the power of sanction an audience may have according to Reicher and Levine (1994a, 1994b) we propose that an audience may also constrain identity expression with the "power of knowledge", referring to the awareness that the audience is in the position to know the limits of one's identity claims (see Barreto et al., 2003).

TABLE 2

Expressions of Portuguese and Dutch identity as a function of audience and identifiability among Portuguese migrants in the Netherlands

	Identity expression			
	Portuguese		Dutch	
	Audience			
	Portuguese	Dutch	Portuguese	Dutch
Anonymous	6.29 [a]	5.22 [b]	2.80 [e]	3.88 [c]
	(.97)	(1.54)	(1.39)	(1.41)
Identifiable	5.38 [b]	5.90 [b]	3.53 [d]	2.64 [d]
	(1.29)	(1.14)	(1.38)	(1.23)

Adapted with permission from the *British Journal of Social Psychology* © 2003 by the British Psychological Society (Barreto et al., 2003; Study 2). Scores range from 1 (not at all identified with the group) to 7 (very much identified with the group). Only differences between means with different superscripts are reliable ($p < .05$). Standard deviations are presented in parentheses.

The psychological costs of social identity management

We have argued that the public expression of internal identities can be adapted to avoid violation of (outgroup) norms, or to convey one's perception of self to different audiences. Both types of situations thus imply that people are able to selectively focus on those parts of their identity that they wish to convey to others present in the situation. When the essence of one's social identity is strongly devalued by others (e.g., for homosexuals), the resulting *threat to the value* of the target's identity (Branscombe et al., 1999; Ellemers et al., 2002), can exacerbate the threat of categorisation. This may lead people to distance the self from the devalued identity in order to enhance self-presentation, such as when they emphasise their difference from the remaining group members (e.g., Spears et al., 1997). In extreme cases, people may even choose to hide the devalued identity and pass as members of a category to which they do not belong (on the basis of internal and external membership criteria), but which provides them with a more positive identity (Goffman, 1963; Katz, 1981; Tajfel, 1981). For instance, people with a severe mental or physical illness sometimes hide their devalued identity from their colleagues at work, because they wish to be regarded as regular co-workers (e.g., Holmes & River, 1998; Lee & Craft, 2002). In these cases, people hide a "real" identity—in the sense that it stems from fulfilment of objective criteria, and is granted with psychological significance—and falsely try to present themselves on the basis of another identity.

In the literature, such passing attempts are often seen to represent a primary identity-management strategy to cope with membership in devalued groups (see also Taylor & McKirnan, 1984). Although use of this strategy has been documented, it is unclear what the identity consequences are when people aim for an external categorisation that does not correspond to their internal self-definition. On the one hand, people who choose to pass in this context are likely to do so in the belief that this will improve the expectations that others have of them. According to this belief, passing may help deflect the threat of being associated with the group's negative stereotype (Steele & Aronson, 1995) and thereby improve self-confidence. In fact, whereas members of devalued groups are often aware of the negative expectations that others have of them (e.g., Cohen & Swim, 1995) and report lower self-confidence in performance contexts (e.g., Lord & Saenz, 1985; Stangor, Carr, & Kiang, 1998), categorisation in a more valued group often boosts self-confidence (e.g, Shih, Pittinsky, & Ambady, 1999). It is thus possible that achieving external categorisation as a member of a more positively evaluated group improves self-confidence.

On the other hand, however, there is empirical evidence to suggest that passing can also be associated with psychological costs that can ultimately undermine self-confidence. This can be understood when we consider that passing not only involves falsely claiming a more positive external categorisation, but also implies that people aim to hide an internal identity that is devalued. This latter aspect of passing in particular can be associated with psychological costs, for instance the experience of shame and guilt (Goffman, 1963; Major & Gramzow, 1999; Paxton, 2002; Smart & Wegner, 2000). At the same time, suppression of a stigmatised identity has been associated with increased accessibility of that identity (e.g., Smart & Wegner, 1999, 2000). Thus, attempts to pass can be expected to increase the cognitive salience of one's internal identity, while the awareness that this identity is devalued by others is predicted to elicit emotional distress. In turn, these combined effects may well undermine the self-confidence of those who try to pass.

To examine this issue, we assessed how members of a contextually devalued group felt about themselves and their abilities, and compared the responses of those who were passing as a member of a more positively evaluated group to the responses of those who revealed their devalued identity (Barreto, Ellemers, & Banal, 2003). Participants were asked to perform a task involving writing about pairs of paintings. This task was to be first performed individually, and subsequently with one (Study 1) or two (Study 2) partners. Participants were told that they would not need to know much about Art to be successful at this task, however they were told that the partner(s) had expressed a wish to be paired with a student of Art. In this way, participants' identity was defined as contextually devalued. Half of our participants were induced to hide their real major and indicate to their partners that they studied Art (the desired identity), rather than Psychology (their real identity). The remaining participants were led to reveal their real major (Psychology) to their partners.

The results showed that passing as a member of a more positively evaluated group can indeed have beneficial effects, in the sense that people think this will improve the expectations others hold about them. At the same time, however, our results illustrate the downside of this passing strategy, as it implies denial of one's internal definition of social self. Specifically, compared to participants who exposed their devalued identity, research participants who passed reported more shame and guilt (see also Frijda, 1986). Furthermore, mediational analyses revealed that these negative emotional responses in turn lowered the self-confidence of those who were trying to pass as members of a more positively evaluated group, whereas no such negative effects on psychological well-being were observed among research participants who revealed their devalued identity.

In sum, although trying to change the way one is externally categorised is often considered a primary identity management strategy and its use is well documented, it appears that pursuit of this strategy may carry negative consequences for the self. Thus, in the extreme case that self-presentational considerations would require people to deny or relinquish their internal views of self altogether, the psychological costs they are likely to incur may outweigh the possible social gains. In sum, although, as we have shown at the beginning of this section, people may seek to express their internal identity in ways that are most likely to be socially accepted, our research suggests that such attempts to manage external views of one's identity will be less desirable as they more clearly violate internal definitions of self.

WHEN DO PEOPLE ADAPT INTERNAL IDENTITIES?

The research reviewed in the previous section indicated that people are sensitive to external views of themselves when choosing how to express their identities. However, the influence of external self-views on identity expression is not limited to the introduction of particular self-presentation concerns. In this section, we review evidence indicating that under some circumstances external categories may actually become internalised into an individual's psychological make-up, and hence develop into a consistent basis for social behaviour.

The ability to internalise new identities is fundamental to any process of socialisation, as when people enter a new profession or work organisation. In these cases, it is crucial both for the individuals involved and for the category that incorporates them (e.g., the organisation) that the new identity is internalised successfully. As we have argued above, such internalisation is a necessary condition for normative behaviour to emerge across a variety of contexts, so that people are willing to engage in discretionary efforts for the benefit of the collective, or continue to behave in ways that are normative for the group in the absence of instrumental rewards or direct supervision by others. Importantly, our previous discussion of the instrumental reasons people may have to behave in line with group norms, addresses a different class of situations, where behavioural displays do not reflect privately held beliefs about the self (see also Festinger, 1957). We now examine the circumstances under which people may actually *internalise* an external categorisation.

The importance of multiple identities

We argue that one important factor that may lead people to internalise membership in a group in which they have been categorised is whether they feel that their initial sense of identity *remains valid* (Barreto & Ellemers, 2002). That is, we propose that external categorisations are more likely to be accepted and internalised when they can be incorporated into (instead of having to replace) people's existing definition of self. For instance, a female professional who is suddenly seen as a "mother" after she has her first baby, may be more inclined to accept this new identity when she can think of herself as a "*working* mother" (as in subtyping). Thus, the adoption of external categorisations by others requires a more complex representation comprising multiple identities, so as to avoid resistance resulting from threat to prior identities.

Research on prejudice reduction through the introduction of a common ingroup identity provides some evidence in support of this reasoning. It shows that imposing a super-ordinate categorisation that members of different groups had in common did not reduce intergroup bias, and in certain cases even led to increased antagonism (Gaertner, Rust, Dovidio, Bachman, & Anastasio, 1994; Hewstone & Brown, 1986; Hornsey & Hogg, 2000; see also Haunschild, Moreland, & Murrell, 1994; Terry, Carey, & Callan, 2001 in the context of organisational mergers). However, intergroup competition and bias were successfully reduced when people who were addressed on the basis of a (new) super-ordinate identity were also encouraged to maintain their (prior) sub-group identity (Hornsey & Hogg, 2000; see also Gonzales & Brown, 1999; Huo, Smith, Tyler, & Lind, 1996). This research is consistent with the general idea that people may be prepared to see themselves in terms of an imposed (higher-order) category provided that other (in this case lower-order) identities are also acknowledged.

One of the processes responsible for this response is a threat to the distinctiveness of the ingroup's identity: imposing a super-ordinate category to subsume the ingroup as well as the outgroup threatens the *distinctiveness* of the ingroup's identity, resulting in expressions of ingroup bias. This threat can be avoided when people are addressed on the basis of multiple (subgroup as well as super-ordinate) identities (see also Brewer, 1991; Hewstone & Brown, 1986; Hornsey & Hogg, 2000; Van Leeuwen & Van Knippenberg, 2003). Additionally, imposing an external categorisation to replace internal self-views may represent a *categorisation* threat (Branscombe et al., 1999; Breakwell, 1986; Ellemers et al., 2002), as it implies that one's internalised identity is not acknowledged by others. Here we argue that acceptance of the imposed identity can be facilitated when established identities can also be maintained in a representation of self on the basis of *multiple identities*. By contrast, when people feel they have to choose between a definition of self in terms of one category membership or the other, external categorisation represents a pressure to relinquish their existing identity. Under those circumstances, people will tend to assert their original identity both by behaving in line with their internalised views of self (e.g., by displaying behaviour that is normative for their internalised group membership) and by actively rejecting the categorisation that is imposed upon them.

The importance of treatment by others

When examining whether or not internalisation of a category membership is facilitated if self-chosen identities are also taken into account, and hindered if one's previous identity is discarded, it is important to distinguish between the way a target is externally *categorised* from the way a target is actually *treated* by others (Barreto & Ellemers, 2002). Indeed, these two do not necessarily go together. The particular way in which a target is categorised depends on factors that are often not under conscious control of the perceiver, such as cognitive salience of the category membership, due to visibility of categorisation cues (e.g., gender and race; Fiske, 1998). However, perceivers can still be sensitive to the internalised identities of their targets and treat them with respect for their chosen definitions of self. For instance, although a female's gender identity in a professional context may be highly salient to her colleagues, and hence they may not be able to avoid categorising her as a woman, they do have the choice to either treat her according to her gender identity or approach her in terms of her professional identity.

From the target's point of view, it is the treatment they receive from others rather than the fact that internal and external categorisations are discrepant *per se* that is the crucial determinant of the psychological and behavioural consequences of such discrepancy. Treating a target in terms of an externally assigned category membership may imply categorisation threat and elicit resistance to the imposed group membership, for instance by showing behavioural affirmation of the self-chosen identity. However, as long as the target's internalised identity is acknowledged, such a discrepancy between internal and external categorisations will tend to be less problematic. That is, the female target in the example above may accept that her gender is a highly salient categorisation cue to others, as long as they respect her choice to focus on her professional identity. For instance, she may be perfectly willing to provide "a women's view" on work-related issues. By contrast, when others fail to respect her choice of self-definition, as when they comment on her clothing style when she expects feedback on her work, she is more likely to affirm her professional identity and resist a categorisation on the basis of her gender.

We examined this issue in an experiment with artificially created groups, which allowed us to independently manipulate discrepancy between an internal and an external categorisation on the one hand and respect of others for a self-chosen identity on the other (Barreto & Ellemers, 2002). Participants were given information regarding two styles of thinking (i.e., inductive and deductive thinkers), and asked to choose which style of thinking they considered most self-descriptive. Subsequently, participants took a test that allegedly could help categorise them into one of these two groups, but they were told that neither their own estimate, nor the test, constituted fully reliable means of assessing their style of thinking. The experimental manipulation consisted of either telling people that the result of the test converged with their own estimate (convergent condition), or leading them to believe that the test results disconfirmed their own views on which style of thinking was most characteristic for them (discrepant condition). Furthermore, in the discrepant condition, participants were either informed that they would be placed in the self-chosen group for the duration of the experiment (respect for self-chosen identity), or that they were assigned to the group that seemed most appropriate according to the test (neglect of self-chosen identity).

Reactions to this treatment were subsequently assessed by examining expressions of subjective group identification and monitoring the extent to which participants displayed loyalty to the group in which they were placed. To measure group loyalty, we first provided feedback that the ingroup had performed poorly on a group task, and assessed participants' willingness to work on group improvement. Moreover, in order to make sure that displays of loyalty were indeed specific to the group in question, we manipulated which behavioural strategy for group improvement was seen as normative for the group (see also Barreto & Ellemers, 2000, Study 2).

In line with our predictions, we observed that participants in the discrepant condition who were placed in the group of their own choice (respect for self-chosen identity), identified more strongly with and behaved more in line with the norms of the group in which they were placed than participants who were assigned to work in the group that was appropriate according to the test (neglect of self-chosen identity). In fact, participants in the discrepant condition whose self-chosen identity was respected did not differ from participants in the convergent condition in terms of their responses on these measures. This is consistent with our position that it is the way people are treated by others, rather than the inconsistency between internal and external membership criteria in itself, that determines their psychological group allegiances. Moreover, additional mediational analyses showed that subjective feelings of identification with the group in which they were placed mediated the extent to which participants behaved in line with group norms. That is, participants in the convergent and discrepant/ respected conditions behaved more in line with the norms of the group in which they worked *because they identified* with that group, whereas participants in the discrepant/neglected condition did not follow the norms of the group in which they worked during the experiment because they did not subjectively identify as members of that group.

Furthermore, and crucial to our argument, in all conditions we examined how participants related to the group in which they had been externally categorised by assessing identification and willingness to co-operate with the group that emerged from the test as most appropriate for them. The results revealed that participants whose own choice of identity had been respected *also* identified with the group in which they were categorised by the test, and expressed willingness to co-operate with this group. By contrast, participants whose self-chosen identity had been neglected, neither identified nor expressed willingness to co-operate with the externally ascribed group, but instead directed their effort at affirming the internalised identity that was neglected in the experiment. In sum, participants whose own choice of identity was respected, identified with the internally chosen as well as the externally assigned categorisations, whereas participants whose choice of identity was neglected, resisted identification with the external category while they identified strongly with the internally appropriate category (see Table 3).

These results suggest that the consequences of a lack of respect for important self-identities are not only felt by the target (in his or her sense of identity) but also by the group in which the target is categorised (Barreto & Ellemers, 2002): people try to convincingly demonstrate allegiance to the chosen identity by distancing themselves from the externally ascribed group and refrain from displaying loyalty to that group. To illustrate, a female worker who is frequently addressed on the basis of her gender may downplay her gender identity, and distance herself from any action to promote gender equality, because this is likely to enhance the salience of that identity to others, and therefore may seem to further undermine her possibility of being treated as a regular colleague by her co-workers (see also Ellemers, 2001).

In this section we have shown that, although externally ascribed group memberships may be seen as constraints to valued identities when self-chosen identities are neglected, as long as internalised identities are respected, additional ascribed identities may come to be regarded as

TABLE 3
Identification with internal and external categories as a function of treatment

	Treatment	
	Internal category respected	Internal category neglected
Identification with:		
Internal category	3.94 [ab] (1.00)	4.25 [a] (.73)
External category	3.80 [b] (.89)	3.57 [c] (1.14)

Adapted from Barreto and Ellemers (2002), *Personality and Social Psychology Bulletin* (p. 635), copyright © by the Society for Personality and Social Psychology, reprinted by permission of Sage Publications. Scores range from 1 (not at all identified with the group) to 7 (very much identified with the group). Only differences between means with different superscript are significant ($p < .05$). Standard deviations are presented in parentheses.

possible ways of defining the self. Thus, a discrepancy between internal and external membership criteria in itself is not a sufficient condition for identity threat to be experienced, nor for identity affirmation to occur. Instead, the understanding that one can be categorised on the basis of multiple criteria can alleviate the experience of threat due to external categorisation by others. That is, when identities that are important to the self can be maintained because they are respected by others, an additional assigned categorisation can form the basis of a multifaceted identity.

CONCLUSIONS

In this chapter we have reviewed evidence demonstrating that individuals do not necessarily endorse identities that are externally ascribed to them, and that as consequence displays of group allegiance cannot simply be derived from the knowledge that people satisfy certain external criteria for category inclusion. In times of heightened inter-ethnic vigilance, it is even more important to be aware that as external observers we are often mistaken in our conclusions about who people actually are, what they stand for, or how they are likely to behave. Mistakes of this kind were responsible for several instances of unjustified ill-treatment in the past, such as the frequently reported mistrust and derogation of American Muslims in the aftermath of September 11, irrespective of whether their primary allegiance was to their identity as American citizens or to the Muslim cause. Empirical evidence further illustrates that mistakes such as these are not inconsequential. In an attempt to correct external views on their identity that they consider inappropriate, people often engage in strategies intended to affirm their desired identities. Whether or not this identity affirmation will (further) undermine the relationship between individuals and those who categorise them will depend on the particular strategies that people employ to express their resistance. Thus, a first conclusion is that people try to influence how others see their social identities, by rejecting categorisations that they do not endorse, and affirming identities that they find subjectively meaningful.

We also argue that it would be too simplistic to conclude that external categorisations have no impact on the behaviour of those who are categorised, or even on their identity. We have reviewed evidence showing that at a more superficial level, people may behave in line with group norms because they expect some personal (material or social) gain from such behaviour. Furthermore, we demonstrated some examples of external views impacting upon self-identities in a process of identity negotiation, as the awareness of what will be accepted by others constrains which aspects of self are enacted in public. Thus, the examination of these issues reminds us that identity management is an interactive process that can be adapted to confront the views and expectations held by different audiences (see also

Emler & Reicher, 1995). Therefore, a second conclusion is that while we tend to place great value on our own subjective sense of self, we neither can nor want to ignore what others think of us—we wish to avoid social costs and, whenever and in what ways possible, we wish to persuade others of how we view ourselves.

However, external views of oneself can also have a deeper impact and become internalised into the individual's self-concept. This will only happen if external views are not experienced as a threat to a prior sense of self. The evidence presented in this chapter demonstrates that respect for prior identities can eliminate the threat that elicits resistance to alternative external categorisations. In modern societies, where social cohesion relies on a common identification with nation states rather than with ethnic groups, this means that only a respect for ethnic differences can promote a sense of common citizenship. In this way what starts off as an external, and therefore psychologically meaningless, categorisation may come to represent a valued identity, just as we hope that valued identities will eventually determine the way others categorise the self. In this sense, internal and external categorisations of the self are in constant interaction.

While previous investigations have focused on the relationship between an individual and a particular group as determining whether people are driven to exert themselves in favour of that group, the research reviewed here clearly demonstrates that the relationship between the individual and the group may be affected by identity needs raised by *alternative* group memberships. In this context, it is important to keep in mind that multiple identities also raise multiple identity needs, and that these cannot be seen as isolated from each other. The work reviewed here addresses this issue by examining how people portray themselves by reference to multiple identities, which characterise multiple perspectives on the self. Although the idea that people may simultaneously identify with multiple groups, defined at different levels of abstraction, may appear at first sight to contradict the notion of functional antagonism in social identity, these views can be reconciled when considering that super-ordinate identities may in fact be defined by reference to the inclusion of subordinate ones (Haslam, 2000; Mummendey & Wenzel, 1999). For instance, Europeans are only likely to identify as European as long as this category is defined with reference to the diverse nations and cultures it includes. Although possibly less obvious, similar processes operate when thinking of what can promote citizenship among migrants: identification as a citizen of a host nation requires a definition of this nation's identity as sufficiently diverse to incorporate migrants as well as the indigenous population. Obviously, application of the ideas developed in this chapter to real-life examples raises additional issues and questions underlining that, while this review aims to contribute to our understanding of the more complex processes involved in the interactive functioning of multiple identities, it only constitutes a first step in opening up this new avenue of theoretical development and research.

REFERENCES

Abrams, D., & Hogg, M. A. (1990). Social identification, self-categorization and social influence. *European Review of Social Psychology, 1*, 195–227.

Barreto, M. (2000). *Identity and strategy in pro-group behaviour*. Doctoral dissertation: Free University, Amsterdam.

Barreto, M., & Ellemers, N. (2000). You can't always do what you want: Social identity and self-presentational determinants of the choice to work for a low status group. *Personality and Social Psychology Bulletin, 26*, 891–906.

Barreto, M., & Ellemers, N. (2002). The impact of respect vs. neglect of self-identities on identification and group loyalty. *Personality and Social Psychology Bulletin, 28*, 629–639.

Barreto, M., Ellemers, N., & Banal, S. (2003). *Working under cover: The effect of 'passing' as a member of a more valued group on performance-related self-confidence*. Manuscript submitted for publication.

Barreto, M., Spears, R., Ellemers, N., & Shahinper, K. (2003). Who wants to know? The effect of audience on identity expression among minority group members. *British Journal of Social Psychology, 42*, 299–318.

Baumeister, R. F. (1982). A self-presentational view of social phenomena. *Psychological Bulletin, 91*, 3–16.

Branscombe, N. R., Ellemers, N., Spears, R., & Doosje, B. (1999). The context and content of social identity threat. In N. Ellemers, R. Spears, & B. Doosje (Eds.), *Social identity: Context, commitment, content* (pp. 35–58). Oxford: Basil Blackwell.

Branscombe, N. R., Spears, R., Ellemers, N., & Doosje, B. (2002). Intragroup and intergroup evaluations effects on group behavior. *Personality and Social Psychology Bulletin, 28*, 744–753.

Breakwell, M. (1986). *Coping with threatened identities*. New York: Methuen.

Brewer, M. B. (1991). The social self: On being the same and different at the same time. *Personality and Social Psychology Bulletin, 17*, 4750–4782.

Cialdini, R. B., Borden, R. J., Thorne, A., Walker, M. R., Freeman, S., & Sloan, L. R. (1976). Basking in reflected glory: Three (football) field studies. *Journal of Personality and Social Psychology, 34*, 366–375.

Cohen, L. L., & Swim, J. K. (1995). The differential impact of gender ratios on women and men: Tokenism, self-confidence, and expectations. *Personality and Social Psychology Bulletin, 9*, 876–884.

Crocker, J., & Luhtanen, R. (1990). Collective self-esteem and ingroup bias. *Journal of Personality and Social Psychology, 58*, 60–67.

Deaux, K. (1996). Social identification. In E. T. Higgins & A. Kruglanski (Eds.), *Social psychology: Handbook of basic principles* (pp. 777–798). New York: The Guilford Press.

Deaux, K., & Ethier, K. A. (1998). Negotiating social identity. In J. K. Swim & C. Stangor (Eds.), *Prejudice: The target's perspective* (pp. 302–323). San Diego: Academic Press.

Deutsch, M., & Gerard, H.B. (1955). A study of normative and informational social influences upon individual judgment. *Journal of Experimental Social Psychology, 69*, 642–655.

Diehl, M. (1990). The minimal group paradigm: Theoretical explanations and empirical findings. *European Review of Social Psychology, 1*, 263–292.

Doosje, B., Ellemers, N., & Spears, R. (1995). Perceived intragroup variability as a function of group status and identification. *Journal of Experimental Social Psychology, 31*, 410–436.

Doosje, B., Spears, R., & Ellemers, N. (2002). Social identity as both cause and effect: The development of group identification in response to anticipated and actual changes in the intergroup status hierarchy. *British Journal of Social Psychology, 41*, 57–76.

Ellemers, N. (1993). The influence of socio-structural variables on identity management strategies. *European Review of Social Psychology, 4*, 27–57.

Ellemers, N. (2001). Individual upward mobility and the perceived legitimacy of intergroup relations. In J. T. Jost & B. Major (Eds.), *The psychology of legitimacy* (pp. 205–222). Cambridge: Cambridge University Press.

Ellemers, N., & Barreto, M. (2000). The impact of relative group status: Affective, perceptual and behavioural consequences. In R. Brown & S. Gaertner (Eds.), *The Blackwell handbook of social psychology, Volume 4: Intergroup processes* (pp. 324–343). Oxford: Basil Blackwell.

Ellemers, N., Barreto, M., & Spears, R. (1999a). Commitment and strategic responses to social context. In N. Ellemers, R. Spears, & B. Doosje (Eds.), *Social identity: Context, commitment, content* (pp. 127–146). Oxford: Basil Blackwell.

Ellemers, N., Kortekaas, P., & Ouwerkerk, J. P. (1999b). Self-categorisation, commitment to the group and group self-esteem as related but distinct aspects of social identity. *European Journal of Social Psychology, 29*, 371–389.

Ellemers, N., Spears, R., & Doosje, B. (1997). Sticking together or falling apart: Ingroup identification as a psychological determinant of group commitment versus individual mobility. *Journal of Personality and Social Psychology, 72*, 617–626.

Ellemers, N., Spears, R., & Doosje, B. (1998). *Group identification, group norms and group behaviour*. Unpublished manuscript.

Ellemers, N., Spears, R., & Doosje, B. (Eds.). (1999c). *Social identity: Context, commitment, content*. Oxford: Basil Blackwell.

Ellemers, N., Spears, R., & Doosje, B. (2002). Self and social identity. *Annual Review of Psychology, 53*, 161–186.

Ellemers, N., Van den Heuvel, H., De Gilder, D., Maass, A., & Bonvini, A. (in press). The underrepresentation of women in science: Differential commitment or the Queen-bee syndrome? *British Journal of Social Psychology*.

Ellemers, N., Van Dyck, C., Hinkle, S., & Jacobs, A. (2000). Intergroup differentiation in social context: Identity needs versus audience constraints. *Social Psychology Quarterly, 63*, 60–74.

Emler, N., & Reicher, S. (1995). *Adolescence and delinquency: The collective management of reputation*. Oxford: Basil Blackwell.

Festinger, L. (1957). *A cognitive theory of dissonance*. Stanford, CA: Stanford University Press.

Finchilescu, G. (1986). Effect of incompatibility between internal and external group membership criteria on intergroup behavior. *European Journal of Social Psychology, 16*, 83–87.

Fiske, S. T. (1998). Stereotyping, prejudice, and discrimination. In D. T. Gilbert, S. T. Fiske, & G. Lindzey (Eds.), *Handbook of social psychology* (4th Edn., pp. 357–411). New York: McGraw Hill.

Frijda, N. H. (1986). *The emotions*. London: Cambridge University Press.

Gaertner, S. L., Rust, M. C., Dovidio, J. F., Bachman, B. A., & Anastasio, P. A. (1994). The contact hypothesis: The role of a common ingroup identity on reducing intergroup bias. *Small Group Research, 22*, 267–277.

Goffman, E. (1963). *Stigma: Notes on the management of spoiled identity*. Englewood Cliffs, NJ: Prentice-Hall.

Gonzales, R., & Brown, R. (1999). *Maintaining the salience of subgroup and superordinate group identities during intergroup contact*. Paper presented at the annual meeting of experimental social psychology, St. Louis, MO.

Hamilton, D. L., & Gifford, R. K. (1976). Illusory correlation in intergroup perception: A cognitive basis of stereotypic judgements. *Journal of Experimental Social Psychology*, *12*, 392–407.

Haslam, S. A. (2000). *Psychology in organizations*. London: Sage.

Haunschild, P. R., Moreland, R. L., & Murrell, A. J. (1994). Sources of resistance to mergers between groups. *Journal of Applied Social Psychology*, *24*, 1150–1178.

Hewstone, M., & Brown, R. J. (1986). Contact is not enough: An intergroup perspective on the "contact hypothesis". In M. Hewstone & R. J. Brown (Eds.), *Contact and conflict in intergroup encounters* (pp. 1–44). Oxford: Basil Blackwell.

Hinkle, S., & Brown, R. J. (1990). Intergroup comparisons and social identity: Some links and lacunae. In D. Abrams & M. A. Hogg (Eds.). *Social identity theory: Constructive and critical advances* (pp. 48–70). London: Harvester-Wheatsheaf.

Hogg, M. A. (1996). Social identity, self-categorization, and the small group. In H. Erich & H. James (Eds.), *Understanding group behavior. Vol. 2: Small group processes and interpersonal relations* (pp. 227–253). Mahwah, NJ: Lawrence Erlbaum Associates, Inc.

Holmes, P. E., & River, L. P. (1998). Individual strategies for coping with the stigma of severe mental illness. *Cognitive and Behavioral Practice*, *5*, 231–239.

Hornsey, M. J., & Hogg, M. A. (2000). Assimilation and diversity: An integrative model of subgroup relations. *Personality and Social Psychology Review*, *4*, 143–156.

Huo, Y. J., Smith, H. J., Tyler, T. R., & Lind, E. A. (1996). Superordinate identification, subgroup identification, and justice concerns: Is separatism the problem, is assimilation the answer? *Psychological Science*, *7*, 40–45.

Hutnik, N. (1991). *Ethnic minority identity: A social psychological perspective*. Oxford: Clarendon Press.

Jetten, J., Spears, R., & Manstead, A. S. R. (1996). Intergroup norms and intergroup discrimination: Distinctive self-categorization and social identity effects. *Journal of Personality and Social Psychology*, *71*, 1222–1233.

Kanter, R. M. (1977). *Men and women of the corporation*. New York: Basic books.

Katz, I. (1981). *Stigma: A social psychological analysis*. Hillsdale, NJ: Lawrence Erlbaum Associates, Inc.

Klein, O., & Azzi, A. (2001). The strategic confirmation of meta-stereotypes: How group members attempt to tailor an outgroup's representation of themselves. *British Journal of Social Psychology*, *40*, 279–293.

LaFromboise, T., Coleman, L. K. H., & Gerton, J. (1993). Psychological impact of biculturalism: Evidence and theory. *Psychological Bulletin*, *114*, 395–412.

Leary, M. R., & Kowalski, R. M. (1990). Impression management: A literature review and two-component model. *Journal of Personality and Social Psychology*, *107*, 34–47.

Lee, J. D., & Craft, E. A. (2002). Protecting one's self from a stigmatised disease … once one has it. *Deviant Behavior*, *23*, 267–299.

Lord, C. G., & Saenz, D. S. (1985). Memory deficits and memory surfeits: Differential cognitive consequences for tokens and observers. *Journal of Personality and Social Psychology*, *49*, 681–694.

Major, B., & Gramzow, R. H. (1999). Abortion as stigma: Cognitive and emotional implications of concealment. *Journal of Personality and Social Psychology*, *77*, 735–745.

Marques, J. M., Yzerbyt, V. Y., & Leyens, J. P. (1988). The 'Black Sheep Effect': Extremity of judgments towards ingroup members as a function of group identification. *European Journal of Social Psychology*, *18*, 1–16.

McGuire, W. J., McGuire, C. V., Child, P., & Fujioka, T. (1978). Salience of ethnicity in the spontaneous self-concept as a function of one's ethnic distinctiveness in the social environment. *Journal of Personality and Social Psychology*, *36*, 511–520.

Mullen, B., Brown, R. J., & Smith, C. (1992). Ingroup bias as a function of salience, relevance, and status: An integration. *European Journal of Social Psychology, 22*, 103–122.

Mummendey, A., & Schreiber, H. J. (1983). Better or different? Positive social identity by discrimination against or differentiation from outgroups. *European Journal of Social Psychology, 13*, 389–397.

Mummendey, A., & Schreiber H. J. (1984). 'Different' just means 'better': Some obvious and some hidden pathways to ingroup favoritism. *British Journal of Social Psychology, 23*, 363–368.

Mummendey, A., & Wenzel, M. (1999). Social discrimination and tolerance in intergroup relations: Reactions to intergroup difference. *Personality and Social Psychology Review, 3*, 158–174.

Oakes, P. J., Haslam, S. A., & Turner, J. C. (1994). *Stereotyping and social reality*. Oxford: Basil Blackwell.

Ouwerkerk, J. W., de Gilder, D., & de Vries, N. K. (2000). When the going gets tough, the tough get going: Social identification and individual effort in intergroup competition. *Personality and Social Psychology Bulletin, 26*, 1550–1559.

Ouwerkerk, J. W., & Ellemers, N. (2002). The benefits of being disadvantaged: Performance-related circumstances and consequences of intergroup comparisons. *European Journal of Social Psychology, 32*, 73–91.

Ouwerkerk, J. W., Ellemers, N., & De Gilder, D. (1999). Group commitment and individual effort in experimental and organizational contexts. In N. Ellemers, R. Spears, & B. Doosje (Eds.), *Social identity: Context, commitment, content* (pp. 184–204). Oxford: Basil Blackwell.

Paxton, S. (2002). The paradox of public HIV disclosure. *AIDS-Care, 14*, 559–567.

Phinney, J. S. (1990). Ethnic identity in adolescence and adults: Review of research. *Psychological Bulletin, 108*, 499–514.

Plant, E. A., & Devine, P. G. (1998). Internal and external motivations to respond without prejudice. *Journal of Personality and Social Psychology, 75*, 811–812.

Reicher, S. (2000). Social identity definition and enactment: A broad SIDE against irrationalism and relativism. Proceedings of the conference "*SIDE issues centre stage: Recent development in studies of deindividuation in groups*", Royal Netherlands Academy of Arts and Sciences, Amsterdam, 30 June–2 July, 1999.

Reicher, S., Levine, M. (1994a). Deindividuation, power relations between groups and the expression of social identity: The effects of visibility to the out-group. *British Journal of Social Psychology, 33*, 145–163.

Reicher, S., Levine, M. (1994b). On the consequences of deindividuation manipulations for the strategic considerations of self: Identifiability and the presentation of social identity. *European Journal of Social Psychology, 24*, 511–524.

Reicher, S., Levine, M., & Gordijn, E. (1998). More on deindividuation, power relations between groups and the expression of social identity: Three studies on the effects of visibility to the in-group. *British Journal of Social Psychology, 37*, 15–40.

Reicher, S. D., Spears, R., & Postmes, T. (1995). A social identity model of deindividuation phenomena. *European Review of Social Psychology, 6*, 161–198.

Schlenker, B. R. (1980). *Impression management: The self-concept, social identity, and interpersonal relations*. Monterey, CA: Brooks/Cole.

Seta, J. J., & Seta, C. E. (1996). Big fish in small ponds: A social hierarchy analysis of intergroup bias. *Journal of Personality and Social Psychology, 71*, 1210–1221.

Shih, M., Pittinsky, T. L., & Ambady, N. (1999). Stereotype susceptibility: Identity salience and shifts in quantitative performance. *Psychological Science, 10*, 80–83.

Smart L., & Wegner, D. M. (1999). Covering up what can't be seen: Concealable stigma and mental control. *Journal of Personality and Social Psychology, 77*, 474–86.

Smart, L., & Wegner, D. M. (2000). The hidden costs of stigma. In R. F. Heatherton, R. E. Kleck, M. R. Hebl, & J. G. Hull (Eds.), *The social psychology of stigma*. New York: The Guilford Press.

Spears, R., Doosje, B., & Ellemers, N. (1997). Self-stereotyping in the face of threats to group status and distinctiveness: The role of group identification. *Personality and Social Psychology Bulletin, 23*, 538–553.

Spears, R., Jetten, J., & Doosje, B. (2001). The (il)legitimacy of ingroup bias: From social reality to social resistance. In J. Jost & B. Major (Eds.), *The psychology of legitimacy: emerging perspectives on ideology, justice, and intergroup relations* (pp. 332–362). New York: Cambridge University Press.

Spears, R., & Lea, M. (1994). Panacea or panopticon? The hidden power of computer-mediated communication. *Communication Research, 21*, 427–459.

Spears, R., Oakes, P. J., Ellemers, N., & Haslam, S. A. (Eds.). (1997). *The social psychology of stereotyping and group life*. Oxford: Basil Blackwell.

Stangor, C., Carr, C., & Kiang, L. (1998). Activating stereotypes undermines task performance expectations. *Journal of Personality and Social Psychology, 52*, 613–629.

Stangor, C., Swim, J. K., Van Allen, K. L., & Sechrist, G. B. (2002). Reporting discrimination in public and private contexts. *Journal of Personality and Social Psychology, 82*, 69–74.

Steele, C. M., & Aronson, J. (1995). Stereotype threat and the intellectual test performance of African Americans. *Journal of Personality and Social Psychology, 69*, 797–811.

Tajfel, H. (1978). *Differentiation between social groups: Studies in the social psychology of intergroup relations*. New York: Academic Press.

Tajfel, H. (1981). *Human groups and social categories*. New York: Cambridge University Press.

Tajfel, H., & Turner, J. C. (1979). An integrative theory of intergroup conflict. In W. G. Austin & S. Worchel (Eds.), *The social psychology of intergroup relations* (pp. 33–47). Monterey, CA: Brooks Cole.

Taylor, D. M., & McKirnan, D. J. (1984). A five-stage model of intergroup relations. *British Journal of Psychology, 54*, 101–114.

Terry, D. J., Carey, C. J., & Callan, V. J. (2001). Employee adjustment to an organizational merger: An intergroup perspective. *Personality and Social Psychology Bulletin, 27*, 267–280.

Turner, J. C. (1987). A self-categorization theory. In J. C. Turner, M. A. Hogg, P. J. Oakes, S. D. Reicher, & M. S. Wetherell (Eds.), *Rediscovering the social group: A self-categorization theory* (pp. 42–67). Oxford: Basil Blackwell.

Turner, J. C. (1982). Towards a cognitive redefinition of the social group. In H. Tajfel (Ed.), *Social identity and intergroup relations* (pp. 15–40). Cambridge: Cambridge University Press.

Turner, J. (1991). *Social influence*. Milton Keynes, UK: Open University Press.

Turner, J. C. (1999). Some current issues in research on social identity and self-categorization theories. In N. Ellemers, R. Spears, & B. Doosje (Eds.), *Social identity: Context, commitment, content,* (pp. 6–34). Oxford: Basil Blackwell.

Van Leeuwen, E., & van Knippenberg, D. (2003). Organizational identification following a merger: The importance of agreeing to differ. In S. A. Haslam, D. Van Knippenberg, M. Platow, & N. Ellemers (Eds.), *Social identity at work: Developing theory for organizational practice* (pp. 205–221). Philadelphia: Psychology Press.

Van Rijswijk, W., & Ellemers, N. (2002). Context effects on the application of stereotype content to multiple categorizable targets. *Personality and Social Psychology Bulletin, 28*, 90–101.

Verkuyten, M. (1997). Discourses of ethnic minority identity. *British Journal of Social Psychology, 36*, 565–586.

Young, H., Van Knippenberg, A., Ellemers, N., & De Vries, N. (1997). The effects of group membership and social context on information organization. *European Journal of Social Psychology, 27*, 523–537.

Yzerbyt, V., Castano, E., Leyens, J-P., & Paladino, M-P. (2000). The primacy of the ingroup: The interplay of entitativity and identification. *European Review of Social Psychology, 11*, 257–295.

Zarate, M. A., & Smith, E. R. (1990). Person categorization and stereotyping. *Social Cognition, 8*, 161–185.

EUROPEAN REVIEW OF SOCIAL PSYCHOLOGY, 2003, *14*, 171–201

Social influences on the emotion process

Agneta H. Fischer and Antony S. R. Manstead
University of Cambridge, UK

Ruud Zaalberg
University of Amsterdam, The Netherlands

Philosophical and psychological theory has traditionally focused on intra-individual processes that are entailed in emotions. Recently sociologists, cultural anthropologists, and also social psychologists have drawn attention to the interpersonal nature of emotions. In this chapter we focus on the influence of others on emotional experiences and expressions. We summarise research on social context effects which shows that both emotional expression and experience are affected by the presence and expressiveness of other people. These effects are most straightforward for positive emotions, which are enhanced in the company of others. In the case of negative emotions, the effects of social context depend on the circumstances in which the emotion is elicited, and on the role of other persons in this situation. We discuss these social context effects in the light of a more general theoretical framework of social appraisal processes.

Traditionally, emotions have been described as intra-individual phenomena, characterised by bodily changes, neural patterns, cognitive appraisals, and other aspects of individual subjectivity. James (1890), for example, defined an emotion as the perception of specific bodily changes. Many current theorists have also regarded emotions primarily as an individual motivational system producing behaviours that help an individual to adapt to the environment (e.g., Ekman, 1992; Ekman & Davidson, 1994; Frijda, 1986; Izard, 1977; Levenson, 1999; Leventhal, 1984; Mandler, 1975; Plutchik, 1980; Scherer, 1984). Levenson (1994, p. 123), for example, states that

> Emotions are short-lived psychological-physiological phenomena that represent efficient modes of adaptation to changing environmental demands. Psychologically, emotions alter attention, shift certain behaviors upward in response hierarchies,

Correspondence should be addressed to: Agneta H. Fischer, University of Amsterdam, Department of Psychology, Roetersstraat 15, 1018, WB Amsterdam, the Netherlands. Email: a.h.fischer@uva.nl

http://www.tandf.co.uk/journals/titles/99998080.asp   DOI: 10.1080/10463280340000054

and activate relevant associative networks in memory. Physiologically, emotions rapidly organize the responses of disparate biological systems including facial expression, somatic muscular tones, voice tone, automatic nervous system activity, and endocrine activity to produce a bodily milieu that is optimal for effective response.

This focus on the intra-individual aspects of the emotion process does not necessarily exclude the role of social factors. Indeed, there is broad consensus on the notion that emotions are functional for our well-being because they help us to adapt to changes in the environment, including the social environment (e.g., Abe & Izard, 1999; Dunn, 1999; Frijda & Mesquita, 1994; Keltner & Haidt, 1999; Manstead, Fischer, & Jakobs, 1999b). This social function is inferred from the fact that the expression of emotions has consequences for how others respond to us, and for how we relate to others. Anger expressions, for example, serve to restore the power balance in a relationship (e.g., Averill, 1982; Tiedens, 2001); smiling evokes sympathy from others, but may also signal powerlessness (LaFrance, Hecht, & Paluck, 2003); blushing signals a decrease in trustworthiness (De Jong, Peters, De Cremer, & Vranken, 2002); and so on. Given these social implications, we may assume that emotion expressions help individuals to overcome threats not only to their physical well-being (poison, predatory animals, darkness), but also to their social well-being (transgression of social norms, social exclusion). Emotions can serve social survival, as well as physical survival.

What does this imply for the nature of emotions? It is clear that emotions have an impact on the social environment, but this does not necessarily mean that the social environment has an impact on emotions, which is the thesis we advance in this chapter. Sociologists (e.g., Franks & McCarthy, 1989; Gordon, 1981; Hochschild, 1983; Kemper, 1978; Scheff, 1988, 1997; Shott, 1979) and cultural anthropologists (e.g., Briggs, 1970; Levy, 1973; Lutz, 1988; Lutz & White, 1986; Mead, 1934) have argued that emotions are more social in nature than we tend to assume. From this perspective, emotions are not biological givens, but phenomena that individuals interpret within socially constructed frameworks of meaning (Gordon, 1989). Hochschild (1983), for example, showed that not only emotional expressions but also feelings themselves are affected by feeling rules and display rules that govern our emotional lives within specific professional contexts. Kemper (1978) has argued that power and status relations influence the types of emotion that are elicited in reaction to another person. Other sociologists, like Scheff (1988, 1997) and Clark (1997), have analysed how social bonds are constituted by emotions and vice versa. Cultural anthropologists have shown how emotions in non-Western cultures have different meanings, and are enacted in different practices, compared to emotions in many Western cultures (Schweder & Levine, 1984; White, 2000).

Similar claims about the fundamentally social nature of emotion have also been advanced by psychologists and philosophers, (e.g., Averill, 1980; Baumeister, Stillwell, & Heatherton, 1994; Fridlund, 1994; Harré, 1986; Hatfield, Cacioppo, & Rapson, 1994; Manstead & Fischer, 2001; Parkinson, 1998, 2001; Parrott, 2001; Shields, 2002; Mackie, Devos, & Smith, 2000). However, the assertion that emotions are social means different things for different emotion researchers (see also Parrott, 2001). For example, to what extent does the presence or behaviour of others affect the quality or intensity of the subjective experience, or the ways in which emotions are expressed? Are emotions always directed at others? How different are subjective emotion and emotional expression if one is alone, as compared to in the company of others? How can the effects of social context on emotions best be explained?

What is lacking, in our view, is systematic research on the influence of social factors on emotion, driven by theoretical accounts of the processes that are responsible for such influence. In the present chapter we attempt to fill this gap by reviewing and presenting research on how other persons and our relationships with these others influence our feelings and how we express them, *over and above the emotional stimulus itself*. Before reviewing the empirical evidence, we first sketch a theoretical framework concerning the relation between emotions and social context.

THEORETICAL ACCOUNTS OF SOCIAL CONTEXT EFFECTS ON EMOTION

One of the first authors to present a general, theoretical view that stressed the social nature of emotions was Averill (1980). He characterised emotions as socially constituted syndromes, or transitory social roles. The basic idea is that emotions should not be considered to be unitary or invariant responses, but rather consist of a variety of different elements, depending on the context in which they occur and the social role of the person experiencing this emotion. Averill (1982) elaborates this idea in relation to the example of anger. Someone who is angry may lash out in antagonism, but may also burst into tears, or withdraw from the situation. All these responses may be part of an anger incident, and whether they occur or not depends—among other things—on whom one is angry with, and why, who else is present, and so on.

Other psychologists (e.g., Christophe & Rimé, 1997; Fridlund, 1994; Hatfield et al., 1994; Parkinson, 1998) have developed views of the way in which emotions can be conceived of as social phenomena, and many of these views can be seen as complementary. Parkinson (1998), for example, argues that communicative factors lie at the heart of emotions, and that emotions may therefore be viewed as forms of communication in which evaluative representations are made to others. In other words, "emotions are syndromes of actions and action readiness that are often intrinsically directed towards an audience" (Parkinson, 1998, p. 676). In a similar vein, Fridlund (1994) proposes in his behavioural ecology view that facial displays are predominantly social and instrumental, because displays "evolve in a particular fashion in response to specific selection pressures, and they necessarily co-evolve with others' responsivity to them" (p. 139). Another approach is presented by Hatfield and colleagues (1992, 1994) who introduced the idea of emotional contagion, defined as the tendency to mimic emotional expressions of other persons in order to converge emotionally. Still another perspective is reflected in research on social sharing, suggesting that sharing our emotional experiences—especially our negative experiences—with others has an impact on the emotional experience itself (e.g., Pennebaker, Zech, & Rimé, 2001; Rimé, Corsini, & Herbette, 2002), presumably because doing so helps us to process the event more fully and thereby to come to terms with it better than we can in the absence of such sharing. Moreover, those who listen to such emotional narratives are themselves likely to experience emotions, and in turn to share these emotions with others (Christophe & Rimé, 1997). This line of research thus implies that emotions are reproduced in social relationships.

A common notion in all these accounts is an emphasis on the role of others in the emotion process. The core assumption is that others have an impact on emotions because emotions are often or always *directed at* others, whether these others are physically or imaginally present. Indeed, according to Fridlund all contexts are to some degree social in nature, because of the fundamentally social nature of the self: Even when we are alone, we are inclined to think of situations or events that are associated with other people. Fridlund refers to this as "implicit sociality". We will return to this issue later.

Further questions that arise are when and why social context effects occur. First, it seems reasonable to assume that—although other persons need not be physically present—social context effects should be greater when others are physically present. Second, communication with these others should be possible. Chovil (1991), for example, defined "sociality" as "the extent to which individuals can fully interact with each other through the auditory and visual channels of language" (pp. 143–144). The general idea is that high "sociality" contexts lend themselves to stronger facial displays, because there is a stronger motivation and/or opportunity to communicate with others. High sociality contexts are generally conceived of as situations in which others, preferably friends, are physically present and engaged in the same task. Low sociality contexts are ones in which there is less motivation and/or opportunity to engage in communication (see also Hess, Banse, & Kappas, 1995; Wagner & Smith, 1991).

Third, the participants' respective roles in the emotional situation also seem relevant for social context effects to occur. For example, in some situations others may simply be part of an audience witnessing the emotional event (e.g., when someone receives a gift, or a punishment), whereas in other situations, they may be the object or target of the same emotional stimulus as the protagonist (e.g., a threat, or an insult). It seems reasonable to assume that others will have a greater impact on an individual's emotion when they are also the object and/or target of the emotional event. Moreover, one's relationship with the other persons is also likely to be relevant. Baumeister and colleagues (1994) have shown that individuals experience guilt more frequently towards intimates than towards strangers. The social bond between intimates is something that (a) leads one party to attempt to create feelings of guilt in the other when that bond is damaged through the other's behaviour, and (b) makes one individual more likely to experience guilt when damage appears to have been done to the relationship. Finally, the way that others behave in an emotional situation is also likely to matter. If another person present panics in a dangerous situation, the effects on one's own behaviour are likely to be different than if the other were to remain very calm. Further, if you listen to someone telling you a "close call" story, or about an anxiety-inducing incident, there is a good chance that you will be "infected" by the emotions being portrayed by the story-teller (Chovil, 1991; Coyne, 1976). We conclude that social context effects depend not only on the simple presence or absence of others, but also on the role of these others in the emotional situation. Important aspects of this role would seem to be the extent to which these others share the same emotion as oneself, the strength of one's relationship with these others, and the way in which these others behave in the emotional setting.

This leads us to a consideration of the processes underlying social context effects. We argue that the social context is appraised along with the emotional event, and thus becomes part of one's emotional reaction. Thus, when one appraises an emotional event, the appraisal of the reactions of others present in the situation automatically follows (e.g., Manstead & Fischer, 2001; Parkinson, 2001). This process of social judgement we call social appraisal, which we define as "the appraisal of behaviors, thoughts, or feelings of one or more other persons in the emotional situation, in addition to the emotional event per se" (Manstead & Fischer, 2001, p. 222). Taking social appraisals into account may help to explain why the ways in which a single emotion such as anger is expressed can range from crying or running away to shouting at somebody or slapping someone in the face, depending on how angry others are; on whether unfair treatment emanates from a superior, a friend, a colleague, a stranger, an intimate, a man, or a woman (see e.g., Archer, 2000; Kring, 2000); on how others present in the situation behave; and on cultural ideals of masculinity or femininity (Fischer & Rodriguez Mosquera, 2001).

In short, our basic assumption is that the emotion process does not unfold in a micro-world that only involves the emotional stimulus and the individual concerned, but is always embedded in a broader social context. It is not only that emotions influence the social context; the social context also has an important impact on emotions. In the sections that follow we will review empirical evidence from our own and others' work on social context effects on emotions, showing that variations in the social environment have an impact on the emotional process itself. We start with the role of others in the immediate emotional antecedent event (emotional stimulus), then go on to examine social context effects on emotion expression and regulation, and finally we will discuss whether the social context also influences subjective emotional experience.

EMOTIONAL STIMULI AND EMOTIONAL CONTEXTS

The fact that others play a role in the elicitation of an emotion is self-evident. Friends accuse us unjustly, superiors treat us unfairly, dangerous persons frighten us, relationships break up, intimates die unexpectedly, and so on. However, in considering the role of others in the antecedent event the first question to arise is what exactly constitutes an antecedent event. In most theories of emotion, emotional stimuli are defined as events that precede an emotion. They can be operationalised in terms of abstract categories (e.g., the blocking of goals) or in terms of more concrete events (e.g., failing on a test). When these events are described at this more concrete level, it has been shown that other persons are very frequently involved.

In their study of emotion prototypes, for example, Shaver and colleagues (Shaver, Schwartz, Kirson, & O'Connor, 1987) found that five prototypical emotions (joy, love, anger, fear, and sadness) are mostly seen as elicited by the acts (or absence of acts) of others. Thus fear is caused by threat of social rejection, or being alone; sadness by loss of a valued relationship, the death of a loved one, or rejection, exclusion, and disapproval by others; anger by the perceived harm inflicted by another person, or interference with plans or goals, usually by the acts of another person; and love by attraction to another person. There are of course certain emotion elicitors that do not entail others, such as snakes or heights; however, these non-social types of stimuli appear to form a small percentage of the events that cause emotions. Many other empirical studies (e.g., Baumeister et al., 1994; Campbell & Muncer, 1987; Kemper, 1978; Shaver et al., 1987; Shaver, Wu, & Schwartz, 1992; Tangney, 1992) have yielded evidence that the causes of most of our emotions are to be found in what others have done, or have neglected to do.

We can also identify a broader emotional context that encompasses the social context in which the emotional event occurs. For example, one may be alone when receiving a low mark for one's work, or when being fired from one's job, or when being robbed of one's possessions. Alternatively, friends, colleagues, or strangers may be present when such things happen. Support for this idea that emotions often occur in interpersonal contexts is provided by a large cross-cultural study conducted by Scherer and Wallbott (e.g., Scherer, Wallbott, Matsumoto, & Kudoh, 1988). They coded antecedents of joy, anger, sadness, shame, and disgust and showed that these emotions most often occur in dyads, and to a lesser extent in small groups. The only exception was fear, which (compared to the other emotions) was more often elicited by events in which the experiencer was alone.

Moreover, friends, colleagues, and strangers may or may not also receive bad marks, be fired, or be robbed; and they may or may not provide help and support. In other words, the question is not only whether somebody else has or has not done something to create an emotional stimulus, but also what his or her role in the emotional context is, and what one's relation with the experiencer is.

Drawing on research on emotions in individualistic versus collectivistic cultures (e.g., Markus & Kitayama, 1991), for example, we can assume that in individualistic cultures, one's self (as active agent, or passive victim) would feature more prominently in emotional antecedents, whereas in collectivistic cultures one's relations with others would prevail as cause of emotions. In a study of emotional prototypes (Fischer, Manstead, & Rodriguez Mosquera, 1999), we investigated whether references to others in antecedents of emotion occur more often in collectivistic or honour cultures than in individualistic cultures. We collected free descriptions of the antecedents of shame, pride, and anger in two countries, one (the Netherlands) relatively individualistic, the other (Spain) relatively more concerned with honour. We found that all antecedents were concerned with the self and social relations, but that the main difference between descriptions in the two countries was the role of others in the antecedent event. In Spain, respondents more often referred to the behaviour of or judgements from *others* (for example the enhancement of other people's honour, identification with the achievements of others), whereas the Dutch respondents more often referred to their self-esteem, or to their own achievements and concerns, albeit often in comparison with or relation to others.

In sum, others are involved in the elicitation of an emotion, not only as actors who cause an emotion in others, but also because they are involved in the emotional situation in some other way. Indeed evidence from cross-cultural research suggests that others or one's relations with others are more often seen as instigators of emotion in collectivistic cultures, compared to individualistic cultures. Thus, the social context in which an emotional event takes place can colour the event itself, thereby influencing subsequent appraisal processes.

THE ROLE OF OTHERS IN EMOTION EXPRESSION AND REGULATION

A second question to address is whether there is evidence of social context effects on emotion expressions, in addition to the effects caused by the emotional event itself. Fridlund (1991, 1994) has argued that the presence of others is more relevant than the emotional experience in determining smiling, because smiles are essentially displays of social motives, as opposed to expressions of subjective feelings such as happiness or amusement. In his view, emotions are social signals, and they serve one's social motives in a specific context. For example, crying signals to others the person's need to be comforted. Seen in this way, facial displays are conceived of as social tools, communicating social motives; they are driven by social intentions and, being social tools, they are affected by the social context. On this account, there is no direct relationship between emotions and facial expressions, and underlying emotional states thus cannot "cause" facial expressions. Instead, facial displays relate to a person's motivations and intentions with respect to the social context. This idea was supported in an experiment (Fridlund, 1991) in which Fridlund showed that the presence of others (both implicit and explicit) affected the intensity of smiling but not the intensity of happiness.

In our view, however, the event that instigated the emotion is as important as the social context in which the event is embedded, such that they jointly affect emotional expressions. We tested this idea in a series of studies by systematically manipulating the strength of the emotional stimulus, on the one hand, and the social context in which the emotional stimulus was presented, on the other.

The impact of other people's presence

In order to investigate the extent to which facial displays are influenced by social context and by the nature of the emotional stimulus, we conducted a series of studies in our laboratory (Jakobs, Goederee, Manstead, & Fischer, 1996; Jakobs, Manstead, & Fischer, 1999a, 1999b, 2001) in which respondents viewed various film excerpts under varying social conditions. In a first study (Jakobs et al., 1996) we asked those who signed up to participate in the experiment either to come alone or to bring a friend. The primary participant and friend viewed the same videotape excerpts, either in the same room or in a different room. The facial behaviour of the primary participant was measured in two ways: EMG recordings were obtained by means of electrodes placed over the cheek (*zygomatic major*) region; and respondents' faces were videotaped and later coded using the Facial Action Coding System (FACS; Ekman & Friesen, 1978). We coded AU12 (produced by contraction of the *zygomatic major* muscle) which is generally regarded as a basic marker for smiles.

As expected, smiling as indexed by both measures (EMG and FACS) increased under social conditions, although only the difference between the alone condition and the condition in which friends watched the film together was significant (see Figures 1a and 1b). These effects were only observed when respondents viewed a film clip that had been rated by pilot participants as very funny; a moderately funny film clip did not result in different degrees of smiling in the different conditions. This pattern of results suggests that both the emotional stimulus and the social context influence facial behaviour: The fact that the presence of others leads to more smiling only when we are already amused by something can be accounted for in two ways. First, the moderate film condition produced fewer smiles and less intense emotion anyway, and thus there was relatively little emotion that could have been influenced by social context. Second, because the moderate film did not elicit much smiling, the friend was also not very expressive, and so the friend's expressiveness would have had less impact on the primary participants' facial displays. This second explanation assumes that the other's expressiveness is important. We will return to this issue below.

The finding that the implicit presence of the other person (as operationalised in the separate viewing condition) did not evoke significantly more smiling than did the alone condition suggests that only physical or explicit presence has an effect on smiling. This conflicts with Fridlund's (1991) evidence that implicit sociality evoked as much facial display as explicit sociality. In order to study this issue of implicit sociality further, we replicated Fridlund's (1991) social context manipulations, along with a manipulation of the intensity of the emotional stimulus (Jakobs et al., 1999a). Respondents who signed up for participation were again contacted and invited to come either alone or to bring a friend. The friend was assigned either the same task as the primary participant (i.e., viewing two film excerpts) or a different task (completing a questionnaire); these tasks were performed either in the same room as the primary participant or in another room. We found the same pattern of results as in the first study: There was a significant effect of social context, but smiling was once again primarily affected by the physical presence of the other (see Figure 2).

Whether or not the friend was also watching the same film excerpts did not influence smiling; on the contrary, we observed a tendency for respondents to smile less while watching the film together, as compared with when they were in the company of a friend engaged in a different task.

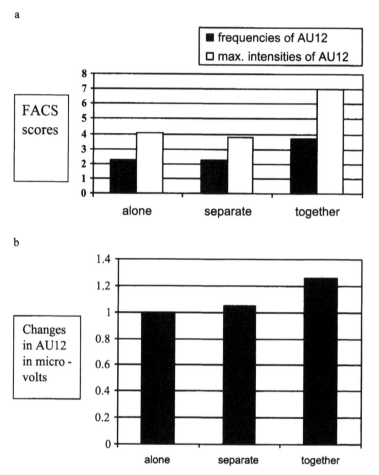

Figure 1. (a) Frequencies and sum of maximum intensities of AU12 (FACS) in reaction to a very funny film clip in three conditions (alone, separate, together). (b) Changes in AU12 EMG-recording in micro-volts in reaction to a very funny film clip in three conditions (alone, separate, together). Source: Jakobs, E., Goederee, P., Manstead, A. S. R., & Fischer, A. H. (1996). De invloed van stimulusintensiteit en sociale context op lachen: Twee meetmethoden vergeleken [The influence of stimulus intensity and social context on laughing: A comparison of two methods of measurement]. In N.K. de Vries, C. K. W. de Dreu, W. Stroebe, & R. Vonk (Eds.), *Fundamentele Sociale Psychologie, Deel 10* (pp. 93–94). Tilburg: Tilburg University Press.

This may have been due to the fact that respondents felt somewhat uncomfortable in this situation, and were uncertain about what was happening. This greater uncertainty may have led to more smiling in the condition where the respondents were engaged in different tasks but in the same room. This explanation is supported by the analysis of facial activity

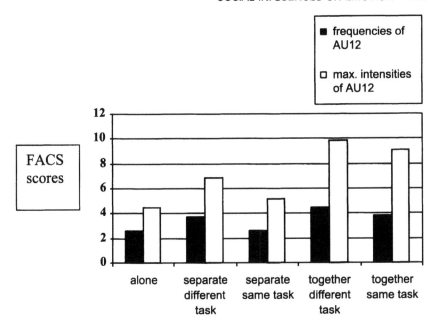

Figure 2. Frequencies and sum of maximum intensities of AU12 in reaction to a very funny film clip in five conditions (alone; separate room, different task; separate room, same task; together, different task; and together, same task). Source: Jakobs, E., Manstead, A. S. R. & Fischer, A. H. (1999a). Social motives and emotional feelings as determinants of facial displays: The case of smiling. *Personality and Social Psychology Bulletin, 25,* 424–435.

simultaneously in the eye and mouth regions (in FACS terms, action units 6 and 12), a pattern that is presumed to reflect enjoyment (see Ekman, Davidson, & Friesen, 1990). For these types of smiles we found a similar or increased degree of activity when respondents were watching the same film clips as opposed to doing another task.

This is also consistent with the results of a third study (Jakobs et al., 1999b), in which we manipulated sociality by creating six different conditions by varying the identity of the co-participant (friend versus stranger) and the way in which the emotional stimulus was presented (communication channel). In one condition respondents listened to the other person telling an amusing story on a tape-recorder, in a second condition they listened to the same story on the telephone, and the third condition was a face-to-face situation in which the other person read the story. Participants' faces were recorded and analysed. No effects of communication channel were found for those respondents who interacted with strangers. For the friends, however, a significant increase in smiling was found in the face-to-face condition.

Several conclusions can be drawn from these studies. First, the physical presence of others affects our smiling more than does imagined or implicit presence. We smile more if we watch amusing videos in the presence of others, rather than when we know that another person is watching in a different room. Second, the type of film or story (i.e., whether it had been established in pilot research as being moderately or very amusing) had a significant effect on the intensity and frequency of facial displays in all three studies. Thus, in contrast to Fridlund's proposal, facial displays vary not only as a function of sociality; they are also shaped by the emotional stimulus and the subjective emotion that it evokes. Third, the identity of other persons affects positive facial displays: More enjoyment smiles are shown in the presence of friends than of strangers. This pattern of results is best explained in terms of sociality: The "high sociality" contexts create or suggest more opportunities to share words and feelings with the other, and it is more pleasant to do this with a friend than with a stranger. The fact that smiling was more affected by the explicit presence of others than by their implicit presence suggests that some observable aspect of how they behave is at least partly responsible for the impact on facial behaviour.

The impact of others' emotional reactions

Indeed, it seems quite likely that the visible behaviour of a friend would affect one's facial behaviour. We have argued that the judgement of other people's reactions in the emotional situation (social appraisals), can have a major impact on emotion experience and expression. Thus the visible behaviour of others constitutes an important basis for social appraisals. However, the potential effects of the other person's *actions* have to date received little research attention.

How expressive someone else is when exposed to the same emotional event is quite likely to influence facial behaviour. Research on emotional contagion (e.g., Hatfield et al., 1994) has examined the impact on emotion of the expressivity of another person. It has been argued that people can "catch" someone else's emotion if there is an outward expression of it by the other person. Various mediating mechanisms have been suggested, ranging from automatic mimicry to more complex cognitive processes such as empathy and imagination. We argue that social appraisal is one of the processes mediating the relation between one's own and another person's expressiveness. In a further experiment (Forrest, Manstead, & Fischer, 1999) we investigated the role of another person's expressiveness on positive facial displays.

We invited female undergraduate students to view each of two video clips in the presence of a co-viewer. The latter was either a female friend or a female stranger who was instructed by the experimenter either to smile and laugh in response to specific parts of the videos, or to remain impassive. One of the video clips was known to be straightforwardly amusing; the other was known to arouse a mixture of amusement and discomfort because of the sexist nature of the humour portrayed. After each clip, the participant and partner completed a questionnaire in which they reported how they felt while watching the video, how they thought their partner felt while watching the video, and how confident they were of their assessments. In addition to the self-report data, the Facial Action Coding System was used to measure the frequency, duration, and intensity of smiling by the participants. We again focused on AU6 (eye region) and AU12 (mouth region).

The results showed that type of emotional stimulus affected facial behaviour, such that participants smiled more and more intensely during the straightforwardly amusing video. Whether the other was a friend or a stranger also had an impact on smiling, but this effect was found only on AU12 activity. Those participating with a friend smiled more often, for longer periods of time, and more intensely. Finally, we found a main effect of expressiveness, such that people smiled more, and more intensely, when the other person was expressive. This effect was found for both AU12 and AU6 + AU12 activity. The effect of expressiveness was mediated by the confidence people expressed in their judgements of the other person's emotions.

These findings are consistent with emotional contagion in that there was more smiling when others were also smiling, independent of whether the others were friends or strangers or how amusing or embarrassing the film fragment was (no interaction effects were found). The fact that the effect of the other person's expressiveness was mediated by the participant's confidence in how expressive the person was suggests that a social appraisal process was operating. Although the precise nature of this process remains unclear, it seems possible that individuals differed with respect to how carefully they scanned others' facial activity during the video; those who paid more attention to the other's expressiveness were more confident in their judgements of this expressiveness and were more influenced by it. The importance of being confident in one's judgement of the other's reaction accords with the results of the studies described earlier, where it was found that only physical presence of others had an effect on facial behaviour. Apparently, behaviour of others generally needs to be overt, and therefore to be able to be judged with confidence, in order to have an impact on one's own facial behaviour.

The impact of social motives

Thus far we have described experiments in which only positive facial displays were elicited. One could argue, however, that smiles may be particularly susceptible to social context effects, because everyday observation suggests they serve multiple social functions (e.g., affiliation, recognition, acknowledgement), as well as signalling happiness, amusement, and enjoyment. This raises the question of whether equivalent social context effects would also be found for negative facial displays. In a further experiment we examined the case of sad displays (Jakobs et al., 2001). We took as a starting point Fridlund (1994)'s proposal that such displays, rather than being expressions of sadness, are a cry for help, signalling a social motive to call for comfort and support. This suggests that sad faces should be more frequently and/or intensely displayed when others are present, because only in these circumstances is a call for comfort effective.

Participants viewed sad film clips. Again five different social conditions were created. Respondents watched two sad film clips (a moderate and a strong clip), either alone or in the company of a friend or a stranger; and the friend or stranger was either in the same or a separate room. Facial activity was recorded and coded using FACS. Here we found a pattern of effects rather different from the one observed in the studies using humorous film clips (see Figure 3).

The same general pattern of effects was observed for the moderate and strong film clips, the only difference being that the strong clip evoked stronger emotions and more intense and frequent expressions. Here we limit ourselves to the results from the strong clip. Facial movements thought to be expressive of sadness (in FACS terms, action units 1 and 4, together producing oblique eyebrows) occurred much more often in the alone condition than in the four social conditions, whereas the intensity of reported sadness was the same across conditions. On the other hand, smiling (as indexed by AU12) showed the opposite pattern: As in the earlier studies, the more social the viewing context, the more smiling was observed.

This pattern implies that displaying a sad face is a spontaneous reaction to sad film clips, but is not regarded as an appropriate response in the company of others, regardless of whether these others are friends or strangers. This suggests the operation of a display rule (Ekman & Friesen, 1978), given that expressing one's sadness is likely to have been regarded as inappropriately weak or sentimental given the nature of the emotional stimulus ("it is only a film"). Participants may have concealed any signs of sadness and smiled, perhaps to hide their real feelings or to demonstrate that they were unaffected by the film excerpts. This pattern of facial displays occurred even more frequently when respondents were in the presence of a friend.

This idea that expressions of sadness in public are regarded as inappropriate is consistent with the results of another study on crying (Fischer & Manstead, 1998), in which participants were asked under different social conditions (namely a "public" condition and an "alone"

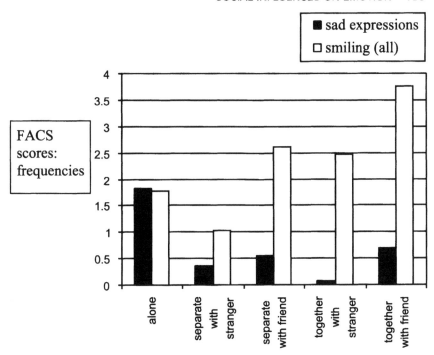

Figure 3. Frequency of sad expressions (AU1 + AU4) and smiling (AU12) in reaction to the strong sad film clip in five conditions (alone; separate room, stranger; separate room, friend; same room, stranger; same room, friend). Source: Jakobs, E., Manstead, A. S. R., & Fischer, A. H. (2001). Social context effects on facial activity in a negative emotional setting. *Emotion, 1,* 51–69.

condition) to answer questions about their crying proneness. In the public condition, a male or female experimenter posed questions, and participants had to give their answers aloud. In order to emphasise the public nature of the situation, the experimenter announced that the answers would be tape-recorded so that they could later be assessed by an expert. In the private condition, participants were asked the same questions in the form of a written questionnaire, and it was emphasised that their answers would remain anonymous. The results clearly demonstrated social context effects on the measures of crying proneness (see Figure 4).

Both men and women reported that their most recent crying episode occurred longer ago in the public condition (higher ratings refer to longer ago) than in the private condition; moreover, in the public condition we found an interaction between sex of experimenter and sex of respondent, such that male respondents reported having cried longer ago when the experimenter was female, whereas female respondents reported having cried

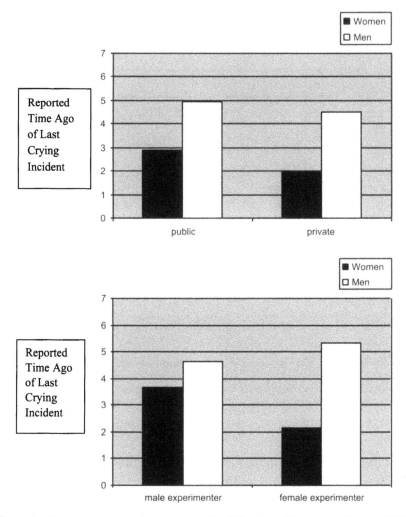

Figure 4. Mean scores on crying proneness in different social contexts. Source: ISRE-proceedings/unpublished data.

longer ago when the experimenter was male. These results suggest the operation of an impression management motive, presumably reflecting the fact that crying is not a desirable image to convey to others. It seems likely that respondents wished to play down their crying proneness, especially when they talked to a stranger of the opposite sex.

Both these studies of negative expressions suggest that social motives affect emotion expressions, albeit in a different way than suggested by

Fridlund (1994). "Sad" displays may sometimes express a need for succour, and thus a motive to be helped, but in certain situations other social motives, such as impression management, may supplant or suppress this motivation. The idea that different social motives are elicited in emotional situations, as a function of the social context, is also supported by the studies described earlier. In these studies we measured different aspects of social motivation, in order to explore the idea that the actual or imagined presence of other persons gives rise to different social motives. We consistently found that social context elicited particular forms of social motivation. Overall, participants are more aware of the other person, more often reported thinking about the reactions of the other person, and more strongly felt the wish to communicate and share their feelings with the other when another person was physically present and watching the same film. Moreover, there was evidence that these social motives, especially the motivation to share one's feelings with and to communicate one's feelings to the other person, mediated the frequency of smiling displays.

In order to explore the role of social motives in emotional expression more explicitly, we conducted a new experiment (Zaalberg, Manstead, & Fischer, in press). Male and female participants were invited to our lab and were asked to sit in a waiting room, apparently for the experimental session to start. A male or female confederate was also in the waiting room, posing as a participant in the same research, and proceeded to tell either a good or a bad joke. This manipulation of joke type was intended to evoke different social motives. The bad joke was assumed to elicit one of the following social motives: a *prosocial motive*, i.e., a motive not to offend the other person, to reassure the other person, or not to be disloyal; or a *motive to hide*, reflecting a wish to conceal one's discomfort or embarrassment. The good joke, on the other hand, was assumed to evoke a *sharing motive*, i.e., a motive to show the other person that one enjoyed the joke. The facial behaviour of the participants was videorecorded for subsequent FACS scoring.

The amount and intensity of smiling were influenced by type of joke, and by the identity of the confederate (see Figure 5). Respondents laughed more (AU6 + AU12) when they heard a funny joke, and they showed more "polite or social smiling" (AU12 without AU6) when the joke was told by the female confederate. Path analyses showed that positive emotions in response to a good joke were associated with an increase in sharing motives and more enjoyment smiling, whereas negative emotions in response to the poor joke (particularly in response to the female confederate), were associated with stronger prosocial motives, which in turn were associated with more polite smiling.

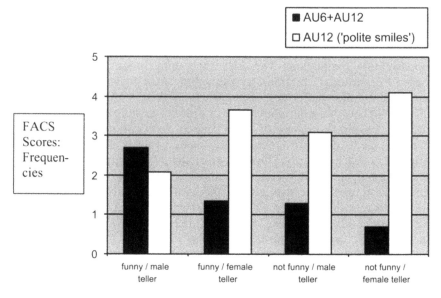

Figure 5.   Intensity of enjoyment smiles (AU6 + AU12) and AU12 smiles ("polite" or "social" smiling) in response to hearing a funny or a not-funny joke, told by a man or a woman. Source: Zaalberg, R., Manstead, A. S. R., & Fischer (in press). Relations between emotions, display rules, social motives and facial behavior. *Cognition and Emotion*.

Gender differences in social motives

Men and women have been shown to differ systematically, particularly with respect to how they express certain emotions (see e.g., Fischer, 2001). These differences can be explained in terms of gender-specific norms (Brody & Hall, 1993; Grossman & Wood, 1993; Shields, 2000; Manstead & Fischer, 2001), but they can also be accounted for in terms of gender-specific social motives that are evoked in emotional situations. It has been argued that women are more oriented to social relationships and more motivated to maintain harmonious relationships, even at the expense of their own power or status (e.g., Chodorow, 1978). Men, on the other hand, have been described as being more oriented to task-related goals and more concerned with status (Eagly, 1987; Fischer & Rodriguez Mosquera, 2001; Tannen, 1990). These different role concerns should give rise to different motives in social interaction and these in turn should lead to differences in emotion expression. If women are less concerned with power and more concerned with relationships, this should result in their expressing emotions that signal vulnerability, like fear, sadness, shame, or guilt. When experiencing such "powerless emotions", one tends to attribute the cause of negative events to oneself, and when one does not know how to cope with an event, the most likely response is to withdraw, hide, or do nothing (e.g., Frijda, Kuipers, & ter Schure, 1989; Roseman, Wiest, & Swartz, 1994). If men are less concerned with harmony in social relationships, and more concerned with status, this should be reflected in a stronger motivation to demonstrate their power and control, and thus to express "powerful emotions", such as anger, disappointment in someone else, pride, or disgust, and to inhibit the expression of powerless emotions.

We tested these assumptions in a vignette study of gender differences in emotion regulation (Timmers, Fischer, & Manstead, 1998). Emotional situations giving rise to anger, disappointment, fear, and sadness were presented and respondents were asked to imagine how they would feel and how and why they would express their feelings in each of these situations. We expected that men and women would report different motives relating to the expression or suppression of these emotions. We further hypothesised that such motives would have different effects in different emotional situations. In the case of anger, for example, we expected women to report stronger relational or pro-social motives, leading them to suppress their anger, whereas men were expected to report impression-management as a motive for expressing their anger. However, for sadness and fear this same impression management motive was expected to lead to the suppression of these emotions in men, whereas the stronger need for social support on the part of women was expected to encourage them to express such emotions more overtly.

To test the influence of these various motives in different situations, we manipulated social context by varying the role of the other person present. In one series of vignettes, the other person present was the target of the emotional expression, but was not the object of the emotion, that is, the other person's behaviour had not caused the emotion in the protagonist; in a second series of vignettes, the target of the expression and the object of the emotion were the same person. Dependent measures included responses to questions about what emotions would be expressed (anger, disappointment, fear, and sadness), and why different emotions would be expressed or suppressed (relational, impression management, seeking comfort, or cathartic motives).

There were significant sex differences in emotion expressions, in the sense that women reported that they would be more likely to cry in all four emotional contexts. They were also more likely than men to say that they felt disappointed, sad, or afraid. The only case where men were more likely to express their emotion was that of anger. Thus women were indeed more likely to display powerlessness. However, there was also an effect of social context in the case of anger: Women were more likely than men to say that they would express their anger more overtly (by yelling, or calling names) if the object of the emotion and the target of the expression were different people. Men, on the other hand, were more likely than women to say that they would express their anger overtly when object and target were the same person (see Figure 6).

This pattern of findings was echoed in differences in the social motives reported by men and women. Women were more likely than men to report wanting to seek comfort, and they were also more likely than men to say that they would find the expression of emotion cathartic in the disappointment and sadness situations. This cathartic motive was stronger in women than in men in relation to all emotion expressions, suggesting that women are less concerned than are men with being seen as emotional. We also found an effect of social context on motives to express emotion, but only in the case of anger. Men were more motivated to control their anger and to engage in impression management than were women in situations where object and target of the anger were not similar. For women the reverse pattern was found. This pattern of results suggests that men are especially motivated to show their anger when they believe that doing so will be functional, in the sense of changing another person's behaviour.

In conclusion, the results of this study suggest that men and women have different social motives for expressing their emotions, and that the way these different motives influence the actual expression of emotion depends in part on the specifics of the social situation. Overall, the motives to seek comfort from others and to give vent to one's emotions are more evident in women

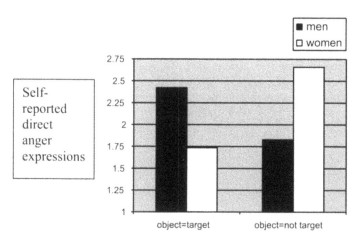

Figure 6.   Mean scores of anger expressions (yelling, calling names) for men and women in different social contexts. Source: Timmers, M., Fischer, A. H., & Manstead, A. S. R. (1998). Gender differences in motives for regulating emotions. *Personality and Social Psychology Bulletin, 24*, 974–985.

than in men, resulting in the expression of powerless emotions or in a tendency to express various emotions in a powerless way, by crying.

The research on social motives described above shows that such motives do have an impact on emotion expression. Individuals who differ in their motivations regarding the expression of emotion express their emotions in different ways; and the way in which emotions are expressed depends on the role of the other person (whether he/she was or was not a cause of the emotion), and on what the individual thought that expressing their emotion would lead to in that specific situation (negative or positive impressions on others, relief, comfort, smooth interactions, etc.).

SOCIAL CONTEXT EFFECTS ON SUBJECTIVE EMOTIONAL EXPERIENCE

Thus far we have focused on social context effects on emotional expressions. An obvious question is whether such effects can also be found in relation to type and intensity of subjective emotional experience.

We first summarise several vignette studies that we have conducted. In each of these studies social context was manipulated in order to examine the effects on subjective emotion. In one study (Jakobs, Manstead, & Fischer, 1996) participants were asked to imagine being the protagonist in a situation in which they were alone, in the company of a stranger, or with a friend. There was a main effect of social context on self-reported emotion, although this was only significant for anger in a situation in which the protagonist had broken some glasses after a birthday party. Angry feelings were more intense if the protagonist was alone or in the company of a stranger than with a friend, perhaps because participants anticipated being distracted or perhaps comforted by the friend. These results suggest that the mere presence of others does not necessarily affect a person's subjective emotion, and that this influence only operates when the other person plays a role in coping with one's emotions.

To test this assumption, in a further study (Jakobs, Manstead, & Fischer, 1997) we manipulated social context in terms of the role and behaviour of the other person present. More specifically, we varied (a) whether the other person was part of the emotional event (co-experiencing) or merely an observer who happened to be present; and (b) whether this person expressed an emotion or not. We found effects of both co-experience and expressiveness in the happiness, sadness, and anger vignettes. Participants reported greater happiness and triumphant feelings, and stronger action tendencies to approach when a friend was co-experiencing the same happy event (both winning a prize in the lottery), and also when this friend expressed happiness. Respondents also reported more intense sadness when a friend also expressed sadness (e.g., when a mutual friend is terminally ill), but whether the friend was a mere observer or not did not make a difference. In the anger situations participants reported less frustration when a friend co-experienced the same event (e.g., both not being hired for a job). All in all, this study suggests that subjective intensity of emotion is especially affected by the other person's *expressiveness*, and less by whether this other person can simply be assumed to experience the same emotion.

In a recent study (Fischer, Manstead, Evers, & Over, 2003), we manipulated the emotional expressions of other persons, by presenting respondents with an emotionally ambiguous situation in which it was plausible to feel either disappointment or anger. The situation description (receiving a low mark by a teacher for a course with difficult study material and a tough exam) included a description of the reaction of fellow students, who were either disappointed by their low marks (the study material had been difficult; disappointment condition) or angry at the teacher (the exam was too tough; anger condition).

The results (see Figure 7) showed that respondents reported more anger than disappointment when others were angry. This suggests that in emotionally ambiguous situations the reactions of other persons can affect one's own emotional experience (see also Schachter, 1959; Schachter & Singer, 1962). However, no differences in self-reported emotion were found in the disappointment condition. The finding that only anger was affected by similar emotional reactions of others may be due to the fact that others' anger helps one to find an explanation for the situation by blaming the teacher, whereas others' disappointment only implies that the event fell short of people's expectations. In other words, the others' anger may have

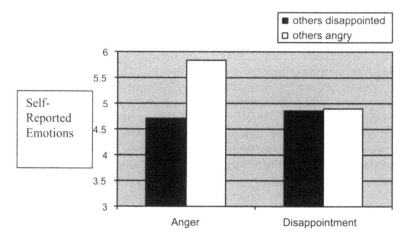

Figure 7. Mean scores of anger and disappointment intensity when others either express disappointment or anger (unpublished data).

been more helpful than others' disappointment in coping with the event and in preventing damage to one's self-esteem.

The effect of social context on emotional experiences was also measured in the studies of social context effects on facial displays described earlier. In all these experiments we found effects of social context on subjective feelings, although these effects were not entirely consistent across studies. In one experiment (Jakobs et al., 1999b), emotional feelings varied as a function of what the other person was doing (i.e., the same task as the participant, or a different one), whereas in the experiment using sad film fragments (Jakobs et al., 2001) there was an effect of physical presence on subjective feelings, such that respondents felt more pleasant and less sad when another person was present, regardless of whether this person was a stranger or a friend.

In sum, these findings demonstrate that social context influences emotional experience, although it is not always clear when or why such effects occur. In some cases it is simply the presence of another person that is influential, but in most cases it is the expressiveness or some specific behaviour of the other that leads to changes in subjective emotion. The fact that these changes were not found to the same degree for all emotions in all situations is probably due to the fact that the relevance of another person's presence and behaviour varies as a function of the specifics of an emotional event. A happy event induces more happiness when that happiness can be shared with a friend who is also visibly happy; a sad event may be experienced as more sad if you are in it with someone else, but perhaps not if the other can provide support. It is evident that more research is needed to establish when and how others have an impact on subjective experience of emotion.

CONCLUSIONS

Emotions serve our survival in a social sense, as well as in a physical sense. Various authors have argued that emotions have social functions because they generally have positive consequences for others or for our relations with others. In previous research emotion expressions have been shown to evoke expressions in others, to lead to inferences by others about one's status or personality, to changes in social relationships, and so on. Here we have argued, however, that the social functions of emotions are also apparent from the ways in which our emotions are influenced by social circumstances. The core issue addressed in this chapter is the effect of the social environment on emotions, rather than the effects of emotions on the social environment.

In the studies described above we have shown that social context extends beyond the mere presence of others. It matters who is present and what this person does. We have argued that others can play different roles in an emotional situation, and that their influence on one's emotions depends on which role they are playing. In our research we have manipulated various aspects of the social context, such as the physical versus imagined presence of others, the role of others as audience or as co-experiencers of the emotional event, and the expressiveness of others. All these facets of the social context can affect both the experience and expression of emotions, but the impact of others was stronger in some situations than in others.

Our findings with respect to the expression of emotion show that whether or not others are physically present makes a difference: In alone conditions, respondents generally smile less, show more negative displays, and report more crying proneness. These results replicate Fridlund's (1991, 1994) findings that the physical presence of others affects emotional displays. However, in contrast with Fridlund's findings, we found significant differences between alone and physically present conditions, and very few differences between alone and implicitly social conditions, which suggests that physical presence of others is a more crucial aspect of the social context than is the mere imagined presence of others.

The effects of physical presence on emotional expressions may appear to be evidence for emotional contagion, in that it was the other's expressiveness that had most effect on the individual's smiling. However, in none of the experiments reported above were participants seated in front of each other. It is therefore difficult to account for the findings in terms of facial mimicry effects. Instead, we argue that they should be explained in terms of social appraisal. Much the same applies to the findings for sadness expressions. Participants apparently took into account the appropriateness of their reactions, and how others responded, and adjusted their expressions accordingly.

The studies described above show that the intensity of subjective experiences is also affected by others in the emotional situation. Thus, being together in a pleasant situation strengthens one's happiness, whereas being together in a sad situation decreases one's sadness. The direction of this influence seems to depend on the role others may play in coping with one's emotions. Further, the way others react to emotionally ambiguous situations appears to encourage people to experience emotions that are consistent with the others' reactions. In sum, others' expressiveness and the emotions we infer from this expressiveness appear to be the major factors influencing the experience and expression of emotion.

The notion that we take into account the fact that we are not alone, or that the other is very powerful, or a complete stranger, or that he or she is smiling or looking sad, implies that we process information beyond the central features of the emotional stimulus itself, however quickly and automatically we do so. We appraise what another will do, and how other persons will react in the same emotional situation.

We argue that these social appraisals are based on expectancies about the other person(s) and recollections of past emotional experiences, and that they require emotion knowledge, which is acquired through direct or indirect socialisation. Thus we know what characterises an emotion, that is, when and how people normally react to an emotional event and how they express and regulate their emotions (e.g., Russell, Fernandez-Dols, Manstead, & Wellenkamp, 1995; Salovey, Hsee, & Mayer, 1993; Shaver et al., 1987). We also have knowledge of the social implications of our emotion and emotion expressions on others. In other words, we have expectations regarding the consequences of an emotional event for oneself and for others (e.g., Averill, 1982; Baumeister et al., 1994; Campbell & Muncer, 1987; Clark & Isen, 1982; Clark & Mehta, 1994; Clark, Pataki, & Carver, 1996; Shaver et al., 1987). For example, in Averill's (1982) research on anger, respondents had no difficulty in reporting the consequences of their anger expressions, such as a greater awareness of their own faults, or a strengthening of their relationship with another person.

This knowledge about how people normally react and what impact their emotional reaction may have on others is likely to be activated when we find ourselves in an emotional situation. It is assumed to form the basis of social appraisal, the process by which we appraise other persons' reactions in an emotional situation, leading to adaptation and regulation of our emotions (see also Fischer, Manstead, Evers, Timmers, & Valk, in press; Manstead & Fischer, 2001). The basic assumption underlying this social appraisal process is the idea that we do not simply appraise the emotional stimulus itself, but we also note who else is present, and how they react.

Social appraisal is part of the appraisal process and serves to modulate the emotional process in the light of the prevailing social context. Just as with the appraisal of the emotional stimulus itself, the appraisal of others' presence and their reactions can be rapid and can take place outside awareness. We suggest that individuals are highly sensitive to others' reactions in emotional settings because such settings are by definition important to the individual and because they are often characterised by a degree of ambiguity regarding either the precipitating event or the most appropriate or effective way to behave. For these reasons, social appraisals are likely to have an impact on the intensity, duration, and/or quality of emotional experience and expression, although we assume that these effects will be most apparent when possible or actual reactions of others are rendered salient in some way.

Social appraisals are typically accompanied by social motives which also play an important role in the expression and regulation of emotions. Social appraisals refer to the anticipated or observed reactions of other persons;

social motives refer to the social goals the individual has in a specific situation. One may, for example, want to re-establish control, to receive comfort, to maintain interpersonal harmony, or to show one's disdain. The relation between social appraisal and social motivation is an important one. We assume that social appraisals direct one's social motives. Thus one may be motivated to receive social support from others, but shedding tears in order to elicit this support only makes sense if one correctly assumes that others will notice the tears and be sensitive to one's need for support. Social appraisals may also activate display rules, partly because the presence of others will automatically sensitise people to the socio-normative implications of their behaviour, and partly because comparing their own emotional reaction to the way that others are behaving will provide information about the appropriateness of that reaction.

Thus, given our assumption that social appraisals underlie social context effects, partly because they trigger social motives, we suggest that context effects are especially likely to occur when the (behaviour of the) other person *matters* for how one copes with one's emotions. For example, the simple physical presence of others is typically not very relevant to how one feels, but it appears to have the capacity to enhance positive emotions (probably because it permits one to implement the action tendency to share positive affect with others). The expressiveness of another person, on the other hand, seems to be relevant in a whole variety of situations, because expressive displays allow one to draw inferences about other persons' emotions, and knowing that another is also happy, or sad, or angry makes one's own reaction more intelligible and may therefore help one to cope with the event. However, this is less likely to be the case if the other is a complete stranger, or is known to be an emotionally volatile person.

We believe that the studies we have described provide a convincing demonstration that our emotions are affected by what we perceive in the social environment, over and above the emotional event itself. The social environment influences our emotions because we know that emotions have interpersonal consequences. Social appraisal processes refer to the anticipation of those consequences, implying that we scan how others react or might react to emotional events, and we manage our own emotions in a way that is consistent with our social objectives. However, we accept that the process underlying this influence requires more research. The studies leave several questions unanswered, in part because there is variation in the findings. Not all emotions, or all aspects of a given emotion, are influenced by social factors in all situations. It is for future research to identify more precisely the content of social appraisals, the conditions under which they exert their influence, and the ways in which they affect our emotional lives.

REFERENCES

Abe, J. A., & Izard, C. E. (1999). The developmental functions of emotions: An analysis in terms of differential emotions theory. *Cognition & Emotion, 13*, 523–549.

Archer, J. (2000). Sex differences in aggression between heterosexual partners: A meta-analytic review. *Psychological Bulletin, 126*, 651–680.

Averill, J. R. (1980). A constructionist view of emotion. In R. Plutchik & H. Kellerman (Eds.), *Emotion: Theory, research and experience* (Vol. 2, pp. 305–339). New York: Academic Press.

Averill, J. R. (1982). *Anger and aggression: An essay on emotion*. New York: Springer Verlag.

Baumeister, R. F., Stillwell, A. M., & Heatherton, T. F. (1994). Guilt: An interpersonal approach. *Psychological Bulletin, 115*, 243–267.

Briggs, J. L. (1970). *Never in anger*. Cambridge, MA.: Harvard University Press.

Brody, L. R., & Hall, J. (1993). Gender and emotion. In M. Lewis & J. Haviland (Eds.), *Handbook of emotions* (pp. 447–461). New York: Guilford Press.

Campbell, A., & Muncer, S. (1987). Models of anger and aggression in the social talk of women and men. *Journal for the Theory of Social Behaviour, 17*, 489–512.

Chodorow, N. (1978). *The reproduction of mothering: Psychoanalysis and the sociology of gender*. Berkeley, CA: University of California Press.

Chovil, N. (1991). Communicative functions of facial displays. *Journal of Nonverbal Behavior, 15*, 141–154.

Christophe, V., & Rimé, B. (1997). Exposure to the social sharing of emotion: Emotional impact, listener responses and secondary social sharing. *European Journal of Social Psychology, 27*, 47–54.

Clark, C. (1997). *Misery and company: Sympathy in everyday life*. Chicago, IL: Chigaco University Press.

Clark, M. S., & Isen, A. M. (1982). Towards understanding the relationship between feeling states and social behavior. In A. H. Hastorf & A M. Isen (Eds.), *Cognitive social psychology* (pp. 73–108). New York: Elsevier North-Holland.

Clark, M. S., & Mehta, P. (1994). Toward understanding emotions in intimate relationships. In A. L. Weber & J. Harvey (Eds.), *Perspectives on close relationships* (pp. 88–109). Needham Heights, MA: Allyn & Bacon.

Clark, M. S., Pataki, S. P., & Carver, V. H. (1996). Some thoughts and findings on self-presentation of emotions in relationships. In G. J. O. Fletcher & J. Fitness (Eds.), *Knowledge structures in close relationships: A social psychological approach* (pp. 247–274). Hillsdale, NJ: Lawrence Erlbaum Associates Inc.

Coyne, J. (1976). Depression and the response of others. *Journal of Abnormal Psychology, 85*, 186–193.

De Jong, P. J., Peters, M., De Cremer, D., & Vranken, C, (2002). Blushing after a moral transgression in a prisoner's dilemma game: Appeasing or revealing? *European Journal of Social Psychology, 32*, 627–644.

Dunn, J. (1999). Making sense of the social world: Mind reading, emotion, and relationships. In P. D. Zelazo, J. Astington, & J. Wilde (Eds.), *Developing theories of intention: Social understanding and self-control* (pp. 229–242). Mahwah, NJ: Lawrence Erlbaum Associates Inc.

Eagly, A. H. (1987). *Sex differences in social behavior: A social-role interpretation*. Hillsdale, NJ: Lawrence Erlbaum Associates Inc.

Ekman, P. (1992). An argument for basic emotions. *Cognition and Emotion, 6*, 169–200.

Ekman, P., & Davidson, R. J. (1994) (Eds.). *The nature of emotion*. New York: Oxford University Press.

Ekman, P., Davidson, R. J., & Friesen, W. V. (1990). The Duchenne smile: Emotional expression and brain physiology. *Journal of Personality and Social Psychology, 17*, 124–129.

Ekman, P., & Friesen, W. V. (1978). *Facial Action Coding System.* Palo Alto, CA: Consulting Psychologists Press.

Fischer, A. H. (Ed.). (2001). *Gender and emotion: Social psychological perspectives.* Cambridge: Cambridge University Press.

Fischer, A. H., & Manstead, A. S. R. (1998). Gender, powerlessness, and crying. In *ISRE '98. Proceedings of the Xth Conference of the International Society for Research on Emotion* (pp. 95–98). Amsterdam, the Netherlands: Faculty of Psychology, University of Amsterdam.

Fischer, A. H., Manstead, A. S. R., Evers, C., & Over, M. (2003). *Social appraisal effects in emotionally ambiguous situations.* Unpublished data.

Fischer, A. H., Manstead, A. S. R., Evers, C., Timmers, M., & Valk, G. (in press). Motives and norms underlying emotion regulation. In P. Phillippot & B. Feldman (Eds.), *Emotion regulation.* Cambridge: Cambridge University Press.

Fischer, A. H., Manstead, A. S. R., & Rodriguez Mosquera, P. M. (1999). The role of honor-related versus individualistic values in conceptualizing pride, shame and anger: Spanish and Dutch cultural prototypes. *Cognition and Emotion, 13*, 149–179.

Fischer, A. H., & Rodriguez Mosquera, P. M. (2001). What concerns men: Women or other men? *Psychology, Evolution, and Gender, 3*, 5–25.

Forrest, J., Manstead, A. S. R., & Fischer, A. H. (1999). Double fun: The role of others on the expression of amusement. In *Abstracts Book XIIth General Meeting of the EAESP* (Oxford, UK).

Fridlund, A. J. (1991). Sociality of solitary smiling: Potentiation by an implicit audience. *Journal of Personality and Social Psychology, 60*, 229–240.

Fridlund, A. J. (1994). *Human facial expression: An evolutionary view.* San Diego, CA: Academic Press.

Franks, D. D., & McCarthy, E. D. (Eds.). (1989). *The sociology of emotions: Original essays and research papers.* Greenwich, CT: JAI.

Frijda, N. H. (1986). *The emotions.* Cambridge: Cambridge University Press.

Frijda, N. H., Kuipers, P., & ter Schure, L. (1989). Relations among emotion, appraisal and action tendency. *Journal of Personality and Social Psychology, 57*, 212–228.

Frijda, N. H., & Mesquita, B. (1994). The social roles and functions of emotions. In S. Kitayama & H. R. Markus (Eds.), *Emotion and culture* (pp. 51–89). Washington, DC: American Psychological Association.

Gordon, S. L. (1981). The sociology of sentiment and emotion. In M. Rosenberg & R. H. Turner (Eds.), *Social psychology: Sociological perspectives* (pp. 562–592). New York: Basic Books.

Gordon, S. L. (1989). Institutional and impulsive orientations in selectively appropriating emotions to self. In D. D. Franks & E. D. McCarthy (Eds.), *The sociology of emotions: Original essays and research papers* (pp. 115–135). Greenwich, CT: JAI.

Grossman, M., & Wood, W. (1993). Sex differences in the intensity of emotional experience: A social role interpretation. *Journal of Personality and Social Psychology, 65*, 1010–1022.

Harré, R. (Ed.) (1986). *The social construction of emotions.* Oxford: Blackwell.

Hatfield, E., Cacioppo, J. T., & Rapson, R. L. (1992). Primitive emotional contagion. In M. S. Clark (Ed.), *Emotion and social behavior [Review of Personality and Social Psychology*, Vol. 14, pp. 151–177]. Thousand Oaks, CA: Sage.

Hatfield, E., Cacioppo, J. T., & Rapson, R. L. (1994). *Emotional contagion.* Cambridge: Cambridge University Press.

Hess, U., Banse, R., & Kappas, A. (1995). The intensity of facial expression is determined by underlying affective state and social situation. *Journal of Personality and Social Psychology, 69*, 280–288.

Hochschild, A. (1983). *The managed heart: The commercialization of human feeling*. Berkeley, CA: University of California Press.

Izard, C. E. (1977). *Human emotions*. New York: Plenum Press.

Jakobs, E., Goederee, P., Manstead, A. S. R., & Fischer, A. H. (1996). De invloed van stimulusintensiteit en sociale context op lachen: Twee meetmethoden vergeleken [The influence of stimulus intensity and social context on laughing: A comparison of two methods of measurement]. In N. K. de Vries, C. K. W. de Dreu, W. Stroebe, & R. Vonk (Eds.), *Fundamentele Sociale Psychologie, Deel 10* (pp. 89–97). Tilburg, the Netherlands: Tilburg University Press.

Jakobs, E., Manstead, A. S. R., & Fischer, A. H. (1996). Social context and the experience of emotion. *Journal of Nonverbal Behavior, 20*, 123–142.

Jakobs, E., Manstead, A. S. R., & Fischer, A. H. (1997). Emotional experience as a function of social context: The role of the other. *Journal of Nonverbal Behavior, 21*, 103–130.

Jakobs, E., Manstead, A. S. R., & Fischer, A. H. (1999a). Social motives and emotional feelings as determinants of facial displays: The case of smiling. *Personality and Social Psychology Bulletin, 25*, 424–435.

Jakobs, E., Manstead, A. S. R., & Fischer, A. H. (1999b). Social motives, emotional feelings, and smiling. *Cognition and Emotion, 13*, 321–345.

Jakobs, E., Manstead, A. S. R., & Fischer, A. H. (2001). Social context effects on facial activity in a negative emotional setting. *Emotion, 1*, 51–69.

James, W. (1890/1950). *The principles of psychology*. (Vol. 2). New York: Dover Publications.

Keltner, D., & Haidt, J. (1999). Social functions of emotions at four levels of analysis. *Cognition and Emotion, 13*, 505–521.

Kemper, T. D. (1978). *A social interactional theory of emotion*. New York: Wiley.

Kring, A. (2000). Gender and anger. In A. H. Fischer (Ed.), *Gender and emotion: Social psychological perspectives* (pp. 211–231). Cambridge: Cambridge University Press.

LaFrance, M., Hecht, M. A., & Paluck, E. L. (2003). The contingent smile: A meta-analysis of sex differences in smiling. *Psychological Bulletin, 129*(2), 305–334.

Levenson, R. W. (1994). Human emotions: A functional view. In P. Ekman & R. Davidson (Eds.), *The nature of emotion: Fundamental questions* (pp. 123–126). New York: Oxford University Press.

Levenson, R. W. (1999). The intrapersonal functions of emotion. *Cognition and Emotion, 13*, 481–505.

Leventhal, H. R. (1984). A perceptual motor theory of emotion. In K. R. Scherer & P. Ekman (Eds.), *Approaches to emotion* (pp. 271–291). Hillsdale, NJ: Lawrence Erlbaum Associates Inc.

Levy, R. I. (1973). *Tahitians: Mind and experience in the society islands*. Chicago, IL: Chicago University Press.

Lutz, C. (1988). *Unnatural emotions: Everyday sentiments on a Micronesian atoll and their challenge to Western theory*. Chicago, IL: Chicago University Press.

Lutz, C., & White, G. M. (1986). The anthropology of emotions. *Annual Review of Anthropology, 15*, 405–435.

Mackie, D., Devos, T., & Smith, E. R. (2000). Intergroup emotions: Explaining offensive action tendencies in an intergroup context. *Journal of Personality and Social Psychology, 79*, 602–616.

Mandler, G. (1975). *Mind and body: The psychology of emotion and stress*. New York: Norton.

Manstead, A. S. R., & Fischer, A. H. (2001). Social appraisal: The social world as object of and influence on appraisal processes. In K. R. Scherer, A. Schorr, & T. Johnstone (Eds.), *Appraisal processes in emotion: Theory, methods, research* (pp. 221–232). New York: Oxford University Press.

Manstead, A. S. R., Fischer, A. H., & Jakobs, E. (1999). The social and emotional functions of facial displays. In P. Philippot, R. S. Feldman, & E. Coats (Eds.), *The social context of nonverbal behavior* (pp. 287–313). New York: Cambridge University Press.

Markus, H. R., & Kitayama, S. (1991). Culture and the self: Implications for cognition, emotion, and motivation. *Psychological Review, 98*, 224–253.

Mead, G. H. (1934). *Mind, self and society*. Chicago, IL: Chicago University Press.

Parkinson, B. (1998). Emotions are social. *British Journal of Psychology, 87*, 663–683.

Parkinson, B. (2001). Putting appraisal in context. In K. R. Scherer, A. Schorr, & T. Johnstone (Eds.), *Appraisal processes in emotion: Theory, methods, research* (pp. 173–186). New York: Oxford University Press.

Parrott, W. G. (Ed.). (2001). *Emotions in social psychology: Essential readings*. Philadelphia, PA: Psychology Press.

Pennebaker, J. W., Zech, E., & Rimé, B. (2001). Disclosing and sharing emotions: Psychological, social, and health consequences. In M. S. Stroebe (Ed.), *Handbook of bereavement research: Consequences, coping, and care* (pp. 517–543). Washington, DC: American Psychological Association.

Plutchik, R. (1980). *Emotions: A psychoevolutionary synthesis*. New York: Harper & Row.

Rimé, B., Corsini, S., & Herbette, G. (2002). Emotion, verbal expression, and the social sharing of emotion. In S. R. Fussell (Ed.), *The verbal communication of emotions: Interdisciplinary perspectives* (pp. 185–208). Mahwah, NJ: Lawrence Erlbaum Associates Inc.

Roseman, I. J., Wiest, C., & Swartz, T. S. (1994). Phenomenology, behaviors, and goals differentiate discrete emotions. *Journal of Personality and Social Psychology, 67*, 206–221.

Russell, J. A., Fernández-Dols, J-M., Manstead, A. S. R., & Wellenkamp, J. C. (Eds.). (1995). *Everyday conceptions of emotions: An introduction to the psychology, anthropology and linguistics of emotion*. Dordrecht: Kluwer.

Salovey, P., Hsee, C. K., & Mayer, D. (1993). Emotional intelligence and the self-regulation of affect. In D. M. Wegner & J. W. Pennebaker (Eds.), *Handbook of mental control* (pp. 258–277). Englewood Cliffs, NJ: Prentice-Hall.

Schachter, S. (1959). *The psychology of affiliation*. Stanford, CA: Stanford University Press.

Schachter, S., & Singer, J. (1962). Cognitive, social and physiological determinants of emotional state. *Psychological Review, 63*, 379–399.

Scheff, T. J. (1988). Shame and conformity: The deference-emotion system. *American Sociological Review, 53*, 395–406.

Scheff, T. J. (1997). *Emotions, the social bond, and human reality. Part/whole analysis*. New York: Cambridge University Press.

Scherer, K. R. (1984). On the nature and function of emotion: A component process approach. In K. R. Scherer & P. Ekman (Eds.), *Approaches to emotion* (pp. 293–317). Hillsdale, NJ: Lawrence Erlbaum Associates Inc.

Scherer, K. R., Wallbott, H. G., Matsumoto, D., & Kudoh, T. (1988). Emotional experience in cultural context: A comparison between Europe, Japan and the United States. In K. R. Scherer (Ed.), *Facets of emotion* (pp. 5–31). Hillsdale, NJ: Lawrence Erlbaum Associates Inc.

Schweder, R. A., & LeVine, R. A. (Eds.). (1984). *Culture theory—essays on mind, self and emotion*. Cambridge: Cambridge University Press.

Shaver, P., Schwartz, J., Kirson, D., & O'Connor, C. (1987). Emotion knowledge: Further exploration of a prototype approach. *Journal of Personality and Social Psychology, 52*, 1061–1086.

Shaver, P. R., Wu, S., & Schwartz, J. C. (1992). Cross-cultural similarities and differences in emotion and its representation. In M. S. Clark (Ed.), *Emotion [Review of Personality and Social Psychology*, Vol. 13, pp. 175–212]. Newbury Park, CA: Sage.

Shott, S. (1979). Emotion and social life: A symbolic interactionist analysis. *American Journal of Sociology, 84*, 1317–1334.

Shields, S. A. (2002). *Speaking from the heart: Gender and the social meaning of emotion.* New York: Cambridge University Press.

Tangney, J. P. (1992). Situational determinants of shame and guilt in young adulthood. *Personality and Social Psychology Bulletin, 18*, 199–206.

Tannen, D. (1990) *You just don't understand: Women and men in conversation.* New York: Morrow.

Tiedens, L. (2001). Anger and advancement versus sadness and subjugation: The effect of negative emotion expressions on social status conferral. *Journal of Personality and Social Psychology, 80*, 86–94.

Timmers, M., Fischer, A. H., & Manstead, A. S. R. (1998). Gender differences in motives for regulating emotions. *Personality and Social Psychology Bulletin, 24*, 974–985.

Wagner, H. L., & Smith, J. (1991). Facial expression in the presence of friends and strangers. *Journal of Nonverbal Behavior, 15*, 201–214.

White, G. M. (2000). Representing emotional meaning: Category, metaphor, schema, discourse. In M. Lewis & J. Haviland-Jones (Eds.), *Handbook of emotions* (2nd ed., pp. 30–45). New York: Guilford Press.

Zaalberg, R., Manstead, A. S. R., & Fischer, A. H. (in press). Relations between emotions, display rules, social motives and facial behavior. *Cognition and Emotion.*

EUROPEAN REVIEW OF SOCIAL PSYCHOLOGY, 2003, *14*, 203–241

The divisive potential of differences and similarities: The role of intergroup distinctiveness in intergroup differentiation

Jolanda Jetten
University of Exeter, UK

Russell Spears
University of Amsterdam, The Netherlands

In this article we examine the relationship between perceptions of intergroup distinctiveness and intergroup differentiation. Research in this area has highlighted two contrasting hypotheses: high distinctiveness is predicted to lead to increased intergroup differentiation (self-categorisation theory), while low distinctiveness or too much similarity can also underlie positive differentiation (social identity theory). We argue for a theoretical integration of these predictions and outline their domains of applicability. In addition to empirical studies from our own laboratory, support for these hypotheses in the literature is examined meta-analytically, and we assess the power of a number of moderators of the distinctiveness–differentiation relation. We focus on group identification and salience of the superordinate category as the most powerful moderators of this relation. We report evidence that low group distinctiveness leads to more differentiation for high identifiers, while high group distinctiveness leads to more differentiation for low identifiers. In addition, our meta-analysis revealed that when the superordinate category was not salient, low distinctiveness tended to lead to differentiation (albeit not significantly so) while high distinctiveness led to differentiation when the salience of the superordinate category was high. A model is proposed integrating our predictions concerning moderators of the distinctiveness–differentiation relation. Theoretical implications of these findings are discussed and we suggest directions for future research.

... the two great empires of Lilliput and Blefuscu. Which two mighty powers have, as I was going to tell you, been engaged in a most obstinate war for six and thirty moons past. It began upon the following occasion. It is allowed on all hands, that the primitive way of breaking eggs before we eat them, was upon the larger end.

Address correspondence to: Jolanda Jetten, School of Psychology, University of Exeter, Exeter EX4 4QG, UK. Email: j.jetten@exeter.ac.uk

© 2003 Psychology Press Ltd
http://www.tandf.co.uk/journals/titles/99998080.asp   DOI: 10.1080/10463280340000063

But his present Majesty's grandfather, while he was a boy, going to eat an egg, and breaking it according to the ancient practice, happened to cut one of his fingers. Whereupon the Emperor, his father, published an edict, commanding all his subjects, upon great penalty, to break the smaller end of their eggs (...). The people have so highly resented this law (...) that there have been six rebellions raised on that account (...). Now the Big-Endian exiles have found so much credit in the Emperor of Blefuscu's court; and so much private assistance and encouragement from their party here at home, that a bloody war hath been carried on between the two empires ...

(Jonathan Swift, *Gulliver's Travels*, 1726, pp. 36/37)

Language, history, and topography – these are probably our defining characteristics. We are a parochial people (...). And we believe that we are different.

(Arthur, in Kerr, 1996: on the conflict in Northern Ireland)

Intergroup relations and intergroup hostility have been at the heart of European research in social psychology ever since it has existed (Brown, 1984a; Ellemers, 1993; Hogg & Abrams, 1988; Tajfel & Turner, 1979; Turner, 1999). The importance of the distinction between "us" and "them" seems to suggest that there are meaningful differences between categories and these assumed differences become the basis of intergroup differentiation. Such intergroup differences can be quite small when groups share many features, or larger when groups are perceived to be distinct on central dimensions of comparison. It is important to distinguish *objective* from *perceived* differences between groups. As illustrated by the above quote from *Gulliver's Travels*, differences and similarities are often as much in the eye of the beholder as in the nature of the groups. While the difference between the Big-Endians and Small-Endians might seem futile and meaningless to most people, in line with research findings obtained with minimal groups (Tajfel, 1970; Tajfel, Flament, Billig, & Bundy, 1971), such trivial distinctions may nevertheless seem important to those involved, and become the basis of differentiation and even fierce intergroup hostility.

Swift's satire on trivial differences becoming the basis for intergroup hostility makes clear that the existence of groups is largely defined by virtue of their distinction from relevant comparison groups. Indeed, several researchers have predicted that too much similarity between groups will be perceived as threatening and will lead to increased intergroup differentiation (e.g., Brown, 1984a; Diehl, 1988; Dovidio, Gaertner, & Validzic, 1998; Tajfel, 1982). Thus, some have concluded that too much similarity breeds contempt. The notion that groups feel threatened by increased intergroup similarity and want to restore clear water between them, was referred to by Freud (1922) as "the narcissism of small differences".

However, as the quote by Arthur (Kerr, 1996) illustrates just as clearly, not only perceived similarities but also the perception of differences between groups can lead to attempts to differentiate one's own group from the other. Intergroup differentiation can also reflect the perception that groups are distinct in terms of race, religion, status, wealth, power, or political views (Staub, 1989). Indeed, such perceived differences are often used to justify intergroup hostility (e.g., "they are different from us"). As we will argue in more detail below, when differentiation occurs on the basis of perceived dissimilarities, the motives for doing so might be purely perceptual and simply reflect existing differences, but it can also be highly motivated and ideological. Examples where the magnitude of religious and political differences are strategically exaggerated and used as the basis for bigotry are alas all too familiar. Thus, paradoxically, intergroup hostility may be exacerbated and even caused by the subjective belief that groups are too different or indeed by the perception that they are too similar. In fact, we argue that both these processes can play a role in intergroup conflict situations. The central questions of this chapter then is when and why are reactions to outgroups driven by the "narcissism of small differences" and when by the "neurosis of large differences"?

Group distinctiveness is defined in the present chapter as the perceived difference or dissimilarity between one's own group and another group on a relevant dimension of comparison (Jetten, Spears, & Manstead, 2001). We examine the effect of group distinctiveness on positive differentiation, which we define as a general tendency to distinguish the own group positively from a relevant comparison group. We use the term positive differentiation rather than intergroup discrimination because this term is closest to the social identity theory motive of maintaining positive distinctiveness. On this view, intergroup discrimination is one particular form of positive differentiation (and indeed it is not always primarily a form of differentiation, when it derives from other motives, such as instrumental concerns, interdependence etc.). The term ingroup bias will be used interchangeably with positive differentiation.

We start the chapter with a theoretical perspective on the distinctiveness–differentiation relation and an outline of the main hypotheses derived from social identity theory (Tajfel & Turner, 1979) and self-categorisation theory (Turner, Hogg, Oakes, Reicher, & Wetherell, 1987). Other theories such as the cognitive differentiation model (Doise, Deschamps, & Meyer, 1978; Eiser & Stroebe, 1972), similarity attraction theories (e.g., belief congruence theory; Rokeach, 1960) and optimal distinctiveness theory (Brewer, 1991, Brewer & Weber, 1994) are also discussed. However, our review of the latter two theories is cursory because we are mainly interested in distinctiveness threat at the group level and these theories examine distinctiveness from a more intragroup and interpersonal perspective. Diehl (1988) has shown that distinctiveness processes at the individual level do not readily generalise to the group level.

Support for both hypotheses is reviewed by reporting evidence from a recently conducted meta-analysis of the relationship between group distinctiveness and differentiation (Jetten, Spears, & Postmes, 2003) as well as studies from our own laboratory. Attempts to reconcile diverging findings and theories focus on identifying the domain of applicability of different distinctiveness processes and by identifying moderators to the distinctiveness – differentiation relationship.

THEORETICAL PERSPECTIVES ON THE DISTINCTIVENESS – DIFFERENTIATION RELATION

In order to understand the effects of distinctiveness on differentiation, we have to distinguish different forms of distinctiveness. We identify two different forms of distinctiveness—reactive and reflective distinctiveness—that are predicted to affect intergroup relations in a different way (Spears, Jetten, & Scheepers, 2002), and we now address these in turn.[1]

Reactive distinctiveness: Similarity as a threat to distinctiveness

This form of distinctiveness is firmly grounded in social identity theory principles. Building on early studies on the accentuation of differences resulting from categorisation (Tajfel & Wilkes, 1963), social identity theory proposed that intergroup comparisons also motivated differentiation in order to create a positively valued identity. Following from this is the prediction that it is more important to differentiate one's ingroup from similar than from dissimilar outgroups (Tajfel, 1982). A lack of group distinctiveness has been explicitly defined as a form of identity threat (Branscombe, Ellemers, Spears, & Doosje, 1999) and it is proposed that the underlying process to maintain group distinctiveness is motivational in character: Ingroup members differentiate their own group positively from relevant outgroups in order to maintain a distinctive sense of the self and to protect the integrity of the ingroup (Brown, 1984a; Tajfel & Turner, 1979). From this, it follows that the more that group distinctiveness is undermined by intergroup similarity, the greater should be the positive differentiation displayed in order to restore group distinctiveness (Brown, 1984a, 1984b; Brown & Abrams, 1986; Henderson-King, Henderson-King, Zhermer, Posokhova, & Chiker, 1997; Moghaddam & Stringer, 1988; Mummendey & Schreiber, 1984; Tajfel, 1982; Turner, 1978).

---

[1] Spears et al. (2002) also identified a third form of distinctiveness—creative distinctiveness—that plays a role when group identity is insufficiently defined. This form of distinctiveness is less relevant in the present analysis and is therefore not discussed in this chapter.

The perception of too much intergroup similarity leading to intergroup hostility is captured well in the Swift's description of the Big-Endians and the Small-Endians. The fact that these groups only differ in the way they break their eggs makes very obvious how similar these groups actually are. The idea that perceptions of too much similarity can instigate attempts to differentiate can be observed in many intergroup encounters. For instance, Freud (1922) states:

> ... Of two neighbouring towns each is the other's most jealous rival; every little canton looks down upon the others with contempt. Closely related races keep one another at arm's length; the South German cannot endure the North German, the Englishman casts every kind of aspersion upon the Scot, the Spaniard despises the Portuguese.

Reflective distinctiveness: Distinctiveness as a cause of differentiation

An opposing hypothesis proposes that differentiation could also be the result of the tendency to preserve and enhance the clarity and distinctiveness of existing social categories (Tajfel & Forgas, 1981; Vanbeselaere, 1996). Indeed, the perception of difference in terms of for instance gender, class, race, age, and sexual orientation is often used to legitimise differentiation and ingroup favoritism (Mummendey & Wenzel, 1999). We distinguished two forms of reflective distinctiveness: Differentiation can reflect real differences between groups (the reality principle) or be the result of instrumental motives associated with group interest (the instrumental function; Spears et al., 2002; Spears, Scheepers, Jetten, Doosje, Ellemers, & Postmes, in press). While most of the studies concerned with group distinctiveness have focused on the first form of distinctiveness by examining the perception of differences between categories (e.g., differences in attitudes of math-science versus social-science students; Hornsey & Hogg, 2000), some work has also examined the second form, namely when differences between groups reflect power differentials or differential access to valued and scarce resources (e.g., the role of distinctiveness when the status of universities differs; Jetten, Spears, Hogg, & Manstead, 2000). In such cases, ingroup bias is likely to reflect instrumental concerns as well as ensuring a distinctive identity.

Self-categorisation principles are theoretically important in helping to explain why distinctiveness can lead to increased differentiation. Self-categorisation theory (Turner et al., 1987) focuses on the cognitive and perceptual aspects of the distinctiveness-differentiation relation. It is predicted that separateness of and distinctiveness between ingroup and outgroup (e.g., high meta-contrast and high comparative fit) increases the perceived intergroup salience of the categorisation. Thus, the more distinct groups are *a priori*, the more salient intergroup differences become, providing a basis for subsequent differentiation (Jetten, Spears, & Manstead, 1996, 1998, 1999; Oakes, 1987).

This form of distinctiveness has also been investigated within the cognitive differentiation model (Doise, 1978; Doise et al., 1978; Eiser & Stroebe, 1972). The main focus of this perspective is on cognitive differentiation processes in intergroup comparisons rather than on the motivational aspects that have been central to social identity theory. Cognitive accentuation processes are assumed to simultaneously enhance perceived similarities within groups and differences between groups. As a result, groups are expected to become homogenised and more distinct following intergroup comparisons. Although the findings of research on cross-cutting categories do not reveal a clear-cut pattern (see Migdal, Hewstone, & Mullen, 1998), there is some evidence that when groups are too similar to be meaningfully distinguished (for instance because they overlap on a particular dimension), the differentiation tendency may be neutralised and intergroup differentiation reduced (Vanbeselaere, 1996). Category differentiation theory predicts that the more distinct the category, the greater the tendency to show intergroup differentiation. Category differentiation processes have mainly been examined in the domain of cross-categorisation research (see Hewstone, Islam, & Judd, 1993; Vanbeselaere, 1991).

Category differentiation theory predictions differ from self-categorisation theory with respect to hypotheses about high levels of distinctiveness and the criterion of comparability. Self-categorisation theory, although emphasising the fit between groups, also requires that they should be *comparable*. Comparability decreases when groups become too distinct, with the result that (positive) differentiation would then decrease (Turner, 1987). For instance, while the French are a distinct and relevant comparison group for the British, the Spanish are a less relevant comparison group for the British and the need to perceptually differentiate from the Spanish would be less evident than differentiation from the French. As we have argued previously (Jetten et al., 1998), it is not clear whether this comparability criterion is also important for the more cognitively based category differentiation model. We assume that this model does not specify the criterion of comparability, and therefore predict a linear relationship from cognitive differentiation models between distinctiveness and differentiation.

While the discussion of reflective distinctiveness has focused so far on relatively "cold" perceptual processes (the reality principle), it is important to point out that reflective distinctiveness can also be highly motivated when it is tied in with longstanding identity conflicts (the instrumental function referred to above; see Spears et al., 2002). When distinctiveness relates to material or realistic concerns (i.e., realistic group conflict), reflective distinctiveness can be highly charged and certainly motivated. For instance, issues relating to deservingness might come into play when groups differ in status or power over resources on important dimensions (e.g., males and females), and groups expect that such differences are reflected in group evaluations and resource distributions. Reflective distinctiveness can also underlie motivated differentiation when high distinctiveness enhances the salience of "us" and "them" which is used to justify differentiation (see also Mummendey & Wenzel, 1999). This is illustrated by former US President Bill Clinton (2001) reflecting on the most extreme form of intergroup hostility: "They [the terrorists who struck the Pentagon and the World Trade Centre] thought that the differences they have with us, political and religious, were all that mattered and served to make all their targets less than human."

INTEGRATING REACTIVE AND REFLECTIVE DISTINCTIVENESS PROCESSES

Considering the opposing predictions, the question of whether we can integrate these opposing processes theoretically becomes all the more important. We have argued in the past that these two forms of distinctiveness should not be seen as being contradictory on this point, but rather as representing different theoretical emphases reflecting somewhat independent processes (Jetten et al., 1996, 1998). Interestingly, both the reactive and reflective process are described in early writings of social identity theory (Tajfel & Forgas, 1981). In fact, Tajfel notes that intergroup differences can sometimes become the basis for differentiation, albeit not always so. Tajfel & Forgas (1981, p. 123) quotes Fishman (1963), a language researcher, who notes that:

> Divisiveness is an ideological position and it can *magnify minor differences*; indeed, it can manufacture differences in language as in other matters almost as easily as it can capitalize on more obvious differences. Similarly, unification is also an ideologized position and it can *minimize seemingly major differences* or ignore them entirely, whether these be in the realm of languages, religion, culture, race, or any other basis of differentiation [italics added].[2]

Tajfel states explicitly that the issue of whether similarity or dissimilarity of an outgroup is associated with greater bias is unresolved (Tajfel, 1981, p.26). Nevertheless, when reviewing the empirical work in this domain it is clear that the prediction that similarity provides a basis for intergroup

---

[2] Note that while the emphasis of this quote is on the importance of differences being exaggerated or played down, the focus in our present analyses is slightly different. We argue that *both* small differences and large differences can be used to feed positive differentiation or an underlying group conflict. Nevertheless, the argument is similar to our reasoning in so far that it depends on other conditions whether intergroup differences lead to increased differentiation.

differentiation (reactive hypotheses) has dominated the empirical research in the social identity theory tradition, whereas research relevant to the reflective hypothesis has been neglected (and addressed more under the rubric of stereotyping than discrimination and ingroup bias).

There have been at least two reasons for this, in our view. First, social identity theory contrasted itself theoretically from the realistic conflict theory tradition of Sherif, Campbell, and others which represented the more instrumental form of the reflective hypothesis. With the focus on the minimal ingroup bias effect, the focus therefore switched to explaining differentiation *without differences*, rather than because of them. Second, the reflective prediction fell from favour among social identity researchers because it was associated with the more individualistic-based belief congruence theory developed by Rokeach (1960), making the same predictions on the interpersonal level. According to belief congruence theory, individuals assume that ingroup members hold similar beliefs and that outgroup members' beliefs differ. On this view, expected differences in belief similarity underlie intergroup differentiation (Byrne, 1971; Insko, Nacoste, & Moe, 1983). Note however that, although similar relations are predicted between distinctiveness and differentiation from a self-categorisation theory and a similarity-prediction framework, different processes are assumed to underlie this relation in these two theories. While category salience and clarity of intergroup distinctiveness are assumed to underlie differentiation for SCT, belief congruence theory is grounded on the assumption that, no different from individuals, groups prefer other groups that hold similar beliefs and attitudes to their own. It seems that research that pitted social identity theory against belief congruence theory associated the reactive hypothesis more and more with social identity theory, while the reflective hypotheses became associated with more individualistic theories.

EMPIRICAL FINDINGS: META-ANALYTICAL EVIDENCE

Given these opposing hypotheses, it is not surprising that empirical studies show mixed support for each of them. Some studies clearly provide support for the reactive distinctiveness processes, some for reflective distinctiveness, while still other studies do not show a clear tendency at all. We recently conducted a meta-analytical review of the effect of perceived intergroup distinctiveness on intergroup differentiation (Jetten et al., 2003) in an attempt to examine in a systematic and quantitative manner the support for these opposing processes. Following an extensive search for published and unpublished papers, studies were included in the analysis which met the criteria that (1) intergroup distinctiveness was manipulated, and (2) the dependent variable had to be some measure of positive differentiation. We distinguished two types of measures: behavioural differentiation (e.g., point or money allocations) and judgemental differentiation (e.g., trait evaluations of ingroup and outgroup, stereotyping of ingroup and outgroup) because findings on these measures have been found to differ in previous research (see for instance Brewer, 1979; Roccas & Schwartz, 1993).

Twenty-nine papers were included in the meta-analysis, providing 79 tests of the distinctiveness–differentiation relation.[3] For each of the 79 tests between intergroup distinctiveness and positive differentiation an effect size (r) was calculated or estimated. Positive effect sizes indicated that low distinctiveness led to more positive differentiation, while negative correlations indicated that high distinctiveness was associated with positive differentiation. The most striking aspect of the meta-analysis was that, while the overall effect size (i.e., averaging across behavioural differentiation and judgemental differentiation measures) was not significantly different from zero, a significant positive effect size was found on behavioural differentiation measures, and a significant negative effect size on judgemental differentiation measures. In other words, "narcissism of small differences" effects were found on behavioural differentiation measures and "neurosis of large differences" effects on judgemental differentiation measures.

In line with recent research (see Spears, 2002), we reasoned that one explanation for this finding may be that behavioural differentiation measures fail to provide content to the identity which may exacerbate any perceived lack of distinctiveness. We predicted that this would lead to increased reactive distinctiveness to establish a sense of distinctiveness because the nature of the dependent measure does not "help" to distinguish the groups in a meaningful way. In contrast, judgemental measures (e.g., evaluative trait ratings) are more likely to provide another way to differentiate meaningfully between groups when distinctiveness is low and we reasoned that this would reduce the need to rely exclusively on judgemental differentiation to establish intergroup distinctiveness. Judgemental measures, because they often contain a descriptive component, may also help to enhance the fit of the categorisation and content, in particular when groups are already distinct, which could explain the dominance of reflective distinctiveness processes on judgemental differentiation measures. This difference in findings on behavioural and judgemental measures is certainly interesting and deserves closer examination in future research. It suggests that dependent measures are differently matched to the needs of different group contexts and that we

---

[3] An extensive overview of the study characteristics and analyses can be obtained on request from the first author of this chapter.

should be aware of the nature of the processes such measures are most likely to pick up.

We also examined in our meta-analysis the role of moderators of the distinctiveness–differentiation relation (to be discussed in more detail below) and whether the relation between distinctiveness and differentiation depends on the nature of the dimension on which distinctiveness is manipulated. Notably, the effect of distinctiveness on differentiation has been examined on a range of different dimensions, including attitudes (e.g., Allen & Wilder, 1975; Diehl, 1988; Hornsey & Hogg, 2000; Jetten et al., 1998; Roccas & Schwartz, 1993), status (e.g., Brown, 1984b; Brown & Abrams, 1986; Sachdev & Bourhis, 1987), group roles (e.g., Brown & Wade, 1987; Deschamps & Brown, 1983), and group norms (Jetten et al., 1996; 2001). While the predictions discussed earlier are usually tailored to the effects of attitude similarity, it is generally assumed that similar predictions can be made when examining the effect of distinctiveness in status between groups or group goals. Specifically, with respect to group status, it is assumed that similarity in status (low distinctiveness) can lead to rivalry for superiority (Brown & Wade, 1987; Mummendey & Schreiber, 1984; Turner, 1978). Alternatively, it has been suggested that similarity in status provides the best conditions for intergroup contact, reducing intergroup conflict (Allport, 1954). The stability of the status relation is predicted to be an important determinant of whether low or high status distinctiveness will lead to increased bias (Tajfel & Turner, 1979). Status differences have been found to cause increased bias when relations are unstable because low-status groups challenge status differences and high-status groups are motivated to protect their status when changes in status relations are likely (Ellemers, 1993).

Related predictions can be derived for the distinctiveness of group goals. There is empirical evidence that role distinctiveness or complementarity minimises threat to social identity when groups are required to cooperate. Thus complementarity is predicted to promote positive effects of interdependence (Brown & Wade, 1987; Deschamps & Brown, 1983). In line with this prediction, Dovidio et al. (1998) found that when the groups' areas of experience were distinct, ingroup bias was lower than when the groups had similar dimensions of expertise. In contrast, Brewer and Miller (1984; see also Marcus-Newhall, Miller, Holtz, & Brewer, 1993) proposed that complementarity of groups enhances the salience of the ingroup and outgroup and will divide the two groups. Our meta-analysis generally confirms that the relationship between distinctiveness and differentiation does not differ depending on the dimension on which distinctiveness was manipulated (e.g., status, attitudes, group roles etc.).

EMPIRICAL FINDINGS: REACTIVE VERSUS REFLECTIVE DISTINCTIVENESS

Our own laboratory research also shows that distinctiveness can both increase and decrease differentiation between groups. For instance, support for the prediction that low distinctiveness increases positive differentiation was found in a study by Jetten et al. (1996; Exp. 2), in which we manipulated group distinctiveness by providing participants with feedback about ingroup and outgroup norms in a natural group setting where the identification with the group was quite high. Participants were University of Amsterdam students whose identity was made salient, while the outgroup consisted of students from the Free University of Amsterdam. Participants received feedback about the reward allocation behaviour of other ingroup and outgroup members. The feedback revealed bias in favour of the ingroup or fairness, and fairness or ingroup favouring behaviour on the part of the outgroup. This resulted in four combinations of ingroup and outgroup behaviour combining into norm similarity (both the ingroup and outgroup have norms prescribing fairness or discriminatory behaviour) or norm distinctiveness (ingroup norm is fairness and outgroup norm prescribes discriminatory behaviour or vice versa). The combination of ingroup and outgroup norms proved to be an important determinant of level of ingroup bias. Similarity of intergroup norms led to more bias than dissimilarity of group norms. This effect was observed on a number of intergroup differentiation measures (e.g., ingroup bias, ingroup favouritism) but was most pronounced on a measure of evaluative bias (see Figure 1a).

However, in a study using the same procedure but using minimal groups rather than natural groups, we found that evaluative and behavioural bias measures were affected quite differently (Jetten et al., 1996; Exp. 1). Analyses of pull-scores derived from allocation matrices (Tajfel et al., 1971) showed on the pull assessing the use of maximising versus positive differentiation strategies that, compared with when ingroup and outgroup had similar norms, distinct norms resulted in greater positive differentiation, although this was especially true for the condition in which the ingroup norm represented discrimination and the outgroup norm fairness (see Figure 1b). This is also logical: a strategy of positive differentiation does not conflict with the ingroup norm in this condition. We reasoned that group distinctiveness helps to define the groups when groups are relatively unestablished, thus increasing the salience of the groups and subsequent bias ("creative distinctiveness"; see Spears et al., 2002).

Although the moderating role of identification was not explicitly examined in this research, it provided some initial support for the idea that reflective distinctiveness processes were prevalent in minimal groups when the identification with the group was low (Exp. 1), while reactive

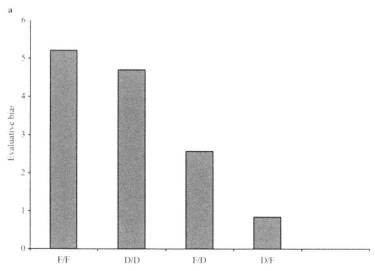

Natural groups: Similarity versus dissimilarity of ingroup and outgroup norms

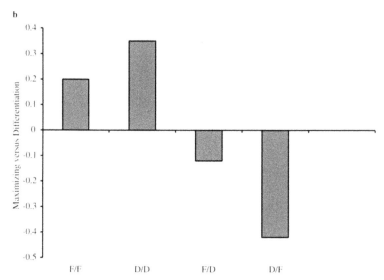

Minimal groups: Similarity versus dissimilarity of ingroup and outgroup norms

Figure 1a. Judgemental differentiation as a function of distinctiveness of ingroup norms and outgroup norms in natural groups. F/F = ingroup norm fair/outgroup norm fair, D/D = ingroup norm discrimination/outgroup norm discrimination, F/D = ingroup norm fair/outgroup norm discrimination, D/F = ingroup norm discrimination/outgroup norm fair.
Figure 1b. Mean use of maximising versus positive differentiation strategies. Scores are factor scores and more negative scores on the maximising versus positive differentiation component represent greater positive differentiation (Jetten, J., Spears, R., & Manstead, A. S. R. (1996). Intergroup norms and intergroup discrimination: Distinctive self-categorization and social identity effects. *Journal of Personality and Social Psychology, 71,* 1222–1233. Copyright © 1996 by the American Psychological Association. Adapted with permission).

distinctiveness processes appeared to dominate in natural groups where the identification was assumed to be higher (Exp. 2). We will discuss the role of identification in the distinctiveness–differentiation relationship in more detail below.

DOMAINS OF APPLICABILITY

In the past, we have tried to integrate the reflective and reactive processes into a broader model by specifying the conditions under which they are expected to occur that would allow integration of the theoretical principles. Importantly, we predicted that the degree to which two groups differ from each other has important implications and may determine which process dominates. Specifically, groups that are too similar can lose their *raison d'être*, and, as a result, reflective processes were predicted to dominate under such conditions. Processes associated with reflective distinctiveness are also predicted to predominate when groups differ a great deal from each other undermining a relevant intergroup comparison. This suggests that there may be a critical point at which perceived group distinctiveness is high enough to make a relevant intergroup comparison possible and at the same time not so low as to undermine the very intergroup distinction. In other words, a critical combination of relatively high reflective distinctiveness (difference) and high reactive distinctiveness (similarity) were predicted to determine intergroup differentiation in such cases.

Two studies were conducted in which we manipulated group distinctiveness at various levels (Jetten et al., 1998). Intergroup distinctiveness was manipulated by providing information about group variability and intergroup distance. The rationale for this procedure was to emphasise that intergroup distance is not only dependent on the absolute distance between ingroup and outgroup, but is also dependent on the perceived variability of these groups, with the two factors in combination determining distinctiveness. Even though the central tendencies of ingroup and outgroup may be quite different (e.g., males and females), if the distribution of ingroup and outgroup scores is heterogeneous, groups can still be perceived as being similar (see also Doosje, Spears, & Koomen, 1995; Ford & Stangor, 1992). Combinations of intergroup distance and group variability created conditions in which groups were (1) clearly distinct (homogeneous and large intergroup distance); (2) overlapping and thus "indistinct" (heterogeneous and small intergroup distance), and; (3) distinct but close (either because the groups were homogeneous and intergroup distance small or because groups were heterogeneous and intergroup distance was large). We predicted that most positive differentiation would be displayed at intermediate levels of group distinctiveness, when groups are distinct but close. Positive differentiation was expected to be lower when groups are too distinct (high intergroup distinctiveness) or not sufficiently distinct because of overlapping group boundaries (low intergroup distinctiveness).

Two studies in which the group setting was varied from minimal groups (Exp. 1) to more natural settings (Exp 2; Jetten et al., 1998) provided consistent support for our hypotheses. For example, we found in our natural group setting that ingroup products (by University of Amsterdam students) were evaluated more positively than outgroup products (by Free University students) and significantly so at an intermediate level of group distinctiveness when groups were distinct but close enough to allow for a relevant intergroup comparison (homogeneous/low intergroup distance and hetero-geneous/high intergroup distance). In contrast, high group distinctiveness (homogeneous/high intergroup distance) and low group distinctiveness (heterogeneous/low intergroup distance) led to low and non-significant levels of positive differentiation (see Figure 2). We concluded that the

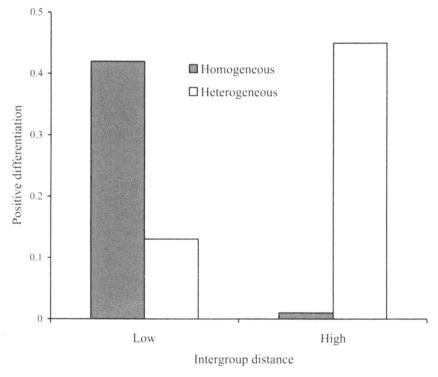

Figure 2. Positive differentiation in product evaluations as a function of intergroup distance and group variability (Jetten, J., Spears, R., & Manstead, A. S. R. (1998). Defining dimensions of distinctiveness: Group variability makes a difference to differentiation. *Journal of Personality and Social Psychology, 74*, 1481–1492. Copyright © 1998 by the American Psychological Association. Adpated with permission).

relation between group distinctiveness and positive differentiation might well be curvilinear (inverted U-shaped).

We argued that the results of these two studies can best be explained by a combination of reflective and reactive processes as derived from social identity and self-categorisation theories. It was suggested that a certain degree of group distinctiveness was necessary in order to define the groups as distinct groups (as predicted by the meta-contrast principle of self-categorisation theory), beyond which point group similarity resulted in attempts to enhance or defend distinctive identity through positive differentiation (as predicted by social identity theory). Note that there is an analogy here with optimal distinctiveness theory (Brewer, 1991), which suggests that there is a critical level where distinctiveness needs and assimilation needs are balanced.

MODERATOR VARIABLES

As Tajfel (1982) pointed out in his discussion of the relationship between group distinctiveness and differentiation: "Any conceptual scheme can only account for a limited part of the variance. Its range of validity and the appearance of alternative patterns can be interpreted adequately only when the relevant processes are looked at in conjunction with the study of their socio-cultural contexts" (p. 27). Indeed, Tajfel and Turner (1979) state in their formulation of social identity theory that the relation between perceptions of distinctiveness and the desire to display positive differentiation in an attempt to maintain or enhance positive distinctiveness is affected by at least three conditions. They predicted that positive differentiation as a reaction to an unsatisfactory identity (e.g., when group distinctiveness is undermined) should only occur when group members identify with their group, when the dimension of comparison is a relevant one, and when the outgroup is perceived as relevant in a particular intergroup context. In addition, Tajfel and Turner (1979) stress the important role of the nature of the intergroup relations and the social context and suggest that positive differentiation must be consistent with the identity and the relation between groups.

Within research on the distinctiveness–differentiation relation, the importance of moderators in helping to explain this complex relationship has played a central role (e.g., Brown & Abrams, 1986). The three most important moderators that have been empirically examined in past research relate to the level of identification with the ingroup, the importance of the dimension of comparison and the nature of the intergroup relations, and specifically the degree of cooperativeness or competition between ingroup and outgroup. If we assume that most researchers focus on the motivational aspects of distinctiveness and examine the potential threat of a lack of distinctiveness, it is not surprising that moderators that are assumed to vary the threat that distinctiveness poses are most often investigated. In addition, in our meta-analysis we examined moderators identified by Tajfel and Turner (1979) that have not yet received any empirical attention, and coded for the fit of the categorisation and the dimension of comparison, the relevance of the outgroup, and the availability of a superordinate categorisation. An overview of the main moderators of the relation between distinctiveness and differentiation is shown in Figure 3.

Importantly, these moderators are not independent and we suspect that there is considerable overlap in the domains that they cover. For instance, when the dimensions of comparisons are more important to group members, it is also likely that the group itself is more important for group members and that identification with the group is higher. We will now discuss each of these moderators identified by Tajfel and Turner (1979) in turn and review the support for them.

Moderation by group identification

The moderator that has been proposed most often in the distinctiveness-bias debate is group identification. When considering the conditions under which group members display positive differentiation, Tajfel and Turner state that: "individuals must have internalized their group membership as an aspect of their self-concept: they must be subjectively identified with the relevant

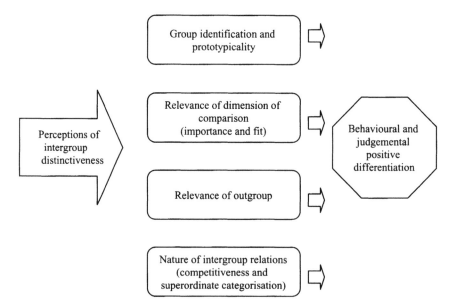

Figure 3. Moderators of the group distinctiveness – positive differentiation relation.

ingroup" (1979, p. 41). In other words, it is not sufficient that individuals are categorised by others as group members; they have to define the self as belonging to the ingroup. However, when we define ourselves, not all groups are equally important to our self-concept. In general, a distinction is made between those who are highly committed to a particular group (high identifiers) and those for whom group membership is less important (low identifiers). A range of research has shown that group identification is important when predicting reactions to threat the group is facing (Branscombe, Wann, Noel, & Coleman, 1993; Doosje, Ellemers, & Spears, 1995; Ellemers, Spears, & Doosje, 1997; Spears, Doosje & Ellemers, 1997). It has been found that high identifiers are more likely to stick to the group, and to defend the integrity of the group when the group is threatened, than low identifiers. Low identifiers are often more strategic in their group behaviour: they might show their loyalty to the group when the group fares well but abandon the group when this group is threatened.

We propose that group identification is also important when predicting how group members will react to low versus high intergroup distinctiveness and it is proposed that different processes underlie low and high identifiers' response to distinctiveness threat. It is argued that high identifiers are most likely to interpret low intergroup distinctiveness as posing a threat to the group, which will motivate them to restore distinctiveness (reactive distinctiveness). In contrast, when group boundaries become unclear because of low distinctiveness, it is predicted that low identifiers will be much less motivated to clarify these boundaries because of their low investment in the group. We predict that low identifiers will accept the superordinate identity to define the self in such conditions. Low distinctiveness should therefore not be perceived by low identifiers as threatening to the group.

An opposing relationship between distinctiveness and differentiation is predicted when group distinctiveness is high. The increased clarity of group boundaries under high distinctiveness conditions is predicted to increase the salience of group membership, which in turn helps low identifiers to define their group more clearly. This latter process is assumed to operate for low identifiers and to a lesser extent for high identifiers because the latter will, because of their greater commitment to the group, already have a clearer idea of how their group is different from other groups (and that there is a basis for its independent existence). Increased salience caused by initial group distinctiveness will therefore not be associated with increased bias, but will allow for a more positive evaluation of the separateness of groups, reducing the need to show bias. Thus, while reflective distinctiveness processes are expected to underlie low identifiers' responses, they are less important in the responses of those whose commitment is higher.

Recent work shows support for the power of group identification to moderate the distinctiveness–differentiation relationship. Group distinctiveness was manipulated by providing Australian participants with false feedback indicating that Australian culture was at present either very distinct, moderately distinct, or not very distinct from American culture (Dwyer, 2000). In line with predictions, it was found that low identifiers stereotyped the outgroup more when cultural distinctiveness was assumed to be high, while high identifiers stereotyped the outgroup more when cultural distinctiveness was low. There were no differences in outgroup stereotyping between low and high identifiers when group distinctiveness was moderate. Interestingly, this study also reveals that the sampling of the dimension of distinctiveness is critical. As shown in the Jetten et al. (1998) research, in which group distinctiveness was manipulated as being low, moderate, and high, we also observed in this study that outgroup stereotyping was quite high at a moderate level of distinctiveness.

In these studies, identification is typically measured and participants are classified as low or high identifiers on the basis of a median-split (or taken as a continuous variable). Recently, we examined in two studies the moderating role of identification not only by measuring identification (Exp. 1) but also by manipulating group identification (Exp. 2, Jetten et al., 2001). In the first study, all participants were students of the University of Amsterdam and this identity was made salient. The outgroup consisted of students of the Free University in Amsterdam. Group identification was measured. Intergroup distinctiveness was manipulated by providing participants with graphs that represented the distribution of scores of ingroup and outgroup members on a relatively neutral comparison dimension, level of extroversion. The intergroup distance between the mean scores of ingroup and outgroup members was identical in both distinctiveness conditions, but the variability of ingroup and outgroup scores was different. Thus, high intergroup distinctiveness was achieved by presenting the ingroup and outgroup distributions as homogeneous, while heterogeneity of ingroup and outgroup caused overlap between distributions and the perceptions of low intergroup distinctiveness. The dependent measure consisted of ingroup and outgroup stereotyping measures tapping the extent to which the ingroup was differentiated from the outgroup.

Similar patterns of results were obtained on both measures, albeit stronger on outgroup stereotyping (outgroup stereotyping as a function of group variability and identification is displayed in Figure 4a). A significant interaction between group variability and identification revealed, in line with predictions, that high identification led to more outgroup stereotyping when group distinctiveness was low (heterogeneous groups) than when it was high (homogeneous groups). Although there was a tendency for outgroup stereotyping to increase when identification decreased and when distinctiveness was high (homogeneous groups), slope analysis revealed that this difference was not significant. Thus, support for the prediction that high

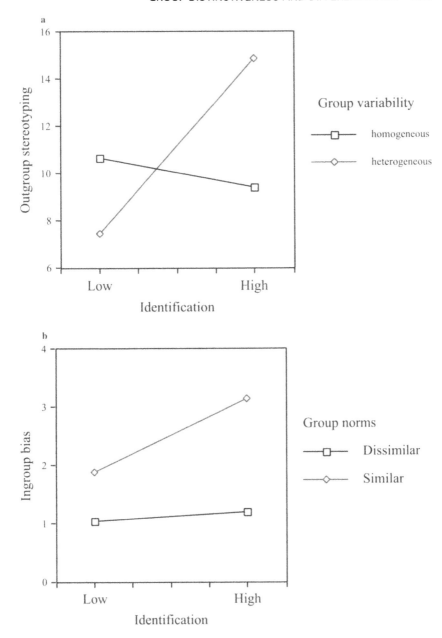

Figure 4a. Outgroup stereotyping as a function of group variability and group identification.
Figure 4b. Ingroup bias as a function of similarity of group norms and group identification
(Similarity as a source of differentiation: The role of group identification, J. Jetten, R. Spears,
and A. Manstead. © 2001 John Wiley & Sons Limited. Reproduced with permission).

identifiers would stereotype the outgroup in order to defend or restore group distinctiveness was stronger than support for the prediction that low identifiers would display more differentiation as distinctiveness increased (and less differentiation as distinctiveness decreased).

Group identification was manipulated in the second study to provide a stronger empirical test, which would allow us to draw causal inferences about the role of identification in the distinctiveness–differentiation relation. Identification was manipulated by means of a bogus pipeline procedure developed by Doosje et al. (1995). The study was run on computers and participants were categorised in minimal groups (detailed versus global perceivers). Electrodes were attached to their hand, which participants were told measured their galvanic skin response (GSR), which in turn provided an indicator of group identification. Part of the cover story was that measurements would be taken during the course of the study that would give an indication of their involvement in the group. False feedback was given that participants were either weakly or strongly identified with their minimal group. The intergroup distinctiveness manipulation involved varying the distinctiveness of ingroup and outgroup norms (see the Jetten et al., 1996, studies). Low group norm distinctiveness was manipulated by informing participants that the ingroup and outgroup were ingroup-favouring. High group norm distinctiveness was manipulated by giving feedback indicating that whereas the ingroup generally favoured their own group, outgroup members were generally fair.

A rather similar pattern of results was obtained on behavioural and judgemental differentiation measures. To illustrate this pattern, Figure 4b displays the mean ingroup bias scores (difference between ingroup and outgroup allocations) on allocation matrices. Contrast analyses revealed, as predicted, that low group norm distinctiveness led to reliably more ingroup bias for high identifiers compared to the high norm distinctiveness condition. However, low identifiers' allocation behaviour was not significantly affected by the norm manipulation.

The fact that there is some evidence that the moderating effect of group identification is similar in a study where identification was measured compared to a study where it was manipulated is reassuring and indicates that generalising findings obtained with both experimental procedures is permissible under some conditions. Both studies reveal that while the predicted interaction between intergroup distinctiveness and group identification emerged on some measures, there was even clearer evidence for a main effect indicating that low distinctiveness rather than high distinctiveness led to more differentiation in general.

Our meta-analysis clearly supports the idea that identification is an important moderator of the distinctiveness–differentiation relationship (Jetten et al., 2003). Each test was coded by two coders for the degree of involvement or identification (low, moderate, or high). We found a significant relationship between group distinctiveness and differentiation when the effect size was regressed on group identification. While the correlation between distinctiveness and differentiation was negative for low identifiers, a positive correlation was found for high identifiers. Thus, when identification was high, differentiation was higher when group distinctiveness was low and thus most threatened. For low identifiers, in contrast, differentiation was lowest under conditions of low distinctiveness, presumably because the groups are difficult to distinguish meaningfully.

Moderation by prototypicality

Another moderator of the distinctiveness – differentiation relationship that we have examined in the past is perceived intragroup position (Jetten et al., 1997). Rather than assuming that all group members react in a similar way to distinctiveness threat, we have argued that the differences in the position of individual group members might help to explain this relationship. We made a distinction between those group members who are more central in the group (prototypical group members) and those who have a more peripheral or marginal position in the group. It should be noted that although group identification and prototypicality will be positively correlated in most social situations and have similar effects, there are some important differences between the two concepts. Prototypicality relates to centrality in the group and this is assumed to be context-dependent (e.g., a soccer player can be prototypical for the group on the field but peripheral when having a drink after the match). Degree of prototypicality is thus largely determined by cognitive processes relating to accessibility and fit (see Jetten et al., 1997; Oakes, 1987; Spears et al., 1997). In contrast, identification relates to the knowledge, value, and emotions attached to group membership (Tajfel, 1978) and has its effect largely through motivational processes.

Nevertheless, processes outlined for those varying in commitment to the group are also predicted to underlie intergroup bias for peripheral and prototypical group members, with peripheral group members being motivated by the same processes as low identifiers and high identifiers resembling prototypical group members. Interestingly, low distinctiveness creates a unique situation for peripheral group members, specifically for those who, because of their peripheral status, are relatively close to the outgroup. Their similarity to the outgroup might even exceed similarity to other more prototypical ingroup members. Although the underlying process for peripheral group members and low identifiers may differ, we predict that, in both cases, low intergroup distinctiveness should enhance the likelihood that superordinate categories become salient for defining the self.

Two studies were conducted to test the prediction that prototypical group members are more likely to show intergroup bias in an attempt to defend threatened distinctiveness than peripheral group members (Jetten et al., 1997). The first study was conducted in a modified minimal group setting in which distinctiveness threat was operationalised as overlapping group boundaries (low distinctiveness) or separateness of ingroup and outgroup (high distinctiveness). Participants were given feedback that they were either prototypical of the group, or that they were peripheral (either near the outgroup or far from the outgroup). Specifically, the "near" peripheral group member was in the middle of the overlap region in the low distinctiveness condition while the prototypical group member was clearly situated in the ingroup. Results showed in line with predictions that differences between prototypical and peripheral group members were especially apparent when group distinctiveness was threatened. Only prototypical group members defended their threatened distinctiveness by engaging in higher levels of ingroup bias than in the low threat condition. Peripheral group members showed less ingroup bias, presumably because they were less motivated to preserve their distinctive identity when this identity was threatened by overlapping group boundaries.

These results were then replicated in a second study, using better-established groups. The university identity of the participants was made salient (University of Amsterdam) and the outgroup consisted of the Free University. Intergroup distinctiveness was manipulated on the dimension "belief in supernatural phenomena" by giving feedback at three levels that attitudes of ingroup and outgroup members were defined as being separated by a large, medium, or small intergroup distance. In the small intergroup distance condition the groups partially overlapped. Participants were asked to allocate resources to ingroup and outgroup (e.g., student apartments, grants to study abroad, and positions in a national student delegation). Ingroup favouritism scores are displayed in Figure 5. In line with predictions, only prototypical group members expressed more ingroup favouritism when group distinctiveness was threatened by a smaller intergroup distance. In line with our predictions, there was a trend that peripheral group members showed more ingroup favouritism than proto-typical group members when intergroup distinctiveness was high, pre-sumably because distinctiveness allowed them to meaningfully differentiate the groups.

Relevance of the dimension of comparison

Another factor that seems important to explain reactions to distinctiveness threats is the degree to which the dimension of comparison is central to the ingroup identity. Intergroup differences can lead in one context to extreme

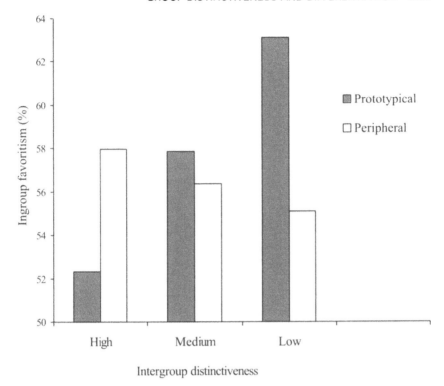

Figure 5. Ingroup favouritism in percentages as a function of intergroup distance and prototypicality (Distinctiveness threat and prototypicality: Combined effects on intergroup discrimination and collective self-esteem, J. Jetten, R. Spears and A. Manstead. © 1997 John Wiley and Sons Limited. Reproduced with permission).

hostility (e.g., Catholics and Protestants in Northern Ireland), while equivalent differences lead to relatively positive intergroup relations in another context (e.g., Catholics and Protestants in the Netherlands). The reason for this is probably that religion has become the central dimension of comparison in Northern Ireland, and as a result of political developments in the past, religious differences are important and have provided the basis of differentiation. Religion is not perceived to be a relevant dimension of comparison within the Netherlands (although William of Orange ironically provides a Dutch connection to Ireland), and consequently, the same distinction is not very salient.

This example points to another aspect of relevance of dimension of comparison in terms of fit between the dimension of comparison and the nature of intergroup relations. Specifically, a dimension can be important, but not match the dimension on which ingroup and outgroup compare themselves (see Roccas & Schwartz, 1993, for a similar point). For instance, in the comparison between left-wing and right-wing political parties the topic of refugees and issues of economic migration better fits the comparison than issues relating to whether life in space is possible. Note that perceived importance of the dimension of comparison and fit are not independent from each other; importance is largely determined by normative fit between the dimension of comparison and the nature of the intergroup relations.

Moderation of the distinctiveness – differentiation relationship by the degree to which the dimension of comparison on which distinctiveness is threatened is considered to be important has been discussed in the past (Brown, 1984b, Brown & Abrams, 1986; Henderson-King et al., 1997; Moghaddam & Stringer, 1988; Mummendey & Schreiber, 1984; Roccas & Schwartz, 1993). However, while most researchers note that the relevance and importance of dimension of comparison will have an effect, it is surprising that there is to our knowledge no research that has empirically investigated this moderator. It seems logical however to predict that distinctiveness threats to dimensions of comparison that are important to the self-definition of a group and that fit the categorisation lead to stronger reactions than threats to less central and less fitting dimensions of comparisons. We predicted that processes relating to reactive distinctiveness might only be triggered when the dimension of comparison is important and normative fit is high. Reflective distinctiveness is predicted to dominate when the central dimension of comparison is less central and fits the categorisation to a lesser extent.

There are a number of studies that have tested the moderating role of importance of dimension of comparison in a less direct way (Moghaddam & Stringer, 1988). For instance, Brown (1984b; Exp. 2; see also Brown & Abrams, 1986) manipulated distinctiveness by providing information that distinctiveness between groups was low on dimensions that were assumed to be relatively important in the school context and relevant for the upcoming task (e.g., mathematics, English and general knowledge). High distinctiveness was manipulated by providing information that the outgroup considered other dimensions more important (e.g., Latin, music, religious knowledge, and art). However, as discussed before, results revealed no straightforward relation between intergroup distinctiveness and intergroup differentiation.

The role of importance of the dimension of comparison was examined in our recent meta-analysis (Jetten et al., 2003). Each test was coded by two independent coders for the importance of the dimension of comparison in the experimental context (low, moderate, or high) and the fit of the categorisation and dimension of comparison (low, moderate, or high). However, the overall evidence for these moderators in the distinctiveness – differentiation relation was rather weak and not significant.

Moderation by the relevance of the outgroup

The third factor identified by Tajfel and Turner (1979) affecting the expression of differentiation is the relevance of the outgroup in the intergroup comparison. Outgroup relevance is determined by three factors; the degree of similarity to the ingroup, proximity to the ingroup, and salience of the outgroup in the intergroup comparison (see McGarty, 1999; Tajfel & Turner, 1979). We coded for all three factors in our meta-analysis and assessed their averaged impact on the distinctiveness – differentiation relation. In line with the prediction, we found a marginally significant positive effect size indicating that increased relevance of the outgroup in the intergroup comparison did enhance reactive distinctiveness processes.

Moderation by the nature of intergroup relations: Cooperative versus competitive relations

In an attempt to tease out when intergroup distinctiveness leads to attraction and when it leads to increased differentiation, Brown (1984b) suggested examining the role of the nature of the intergroup relations. More specifically, a range of studies were conducted to examine the effect of intergroup cooperation versus competition on positive differentiation for attitude and status distinctiveness (Brown, 1984b; Brown & Abrams, 1986). Based on Sherif's (1966) work on group goals, intergroup relations may be influenced by the presence of goal interdependency. We predicted that under cooperative conditions when both groups work towards the same goal, low intergroup distinctiveness should help in the validation of attitudes and beliefs and would have a positive effect on intergroup relations. Hence, low distinctiveness should be associated with less bias in a cooperative setting when group goals are interdependent.

Low distinctiveness is expected to lead to increased bias in a competitive intergroup setting because similarity increases perceptions that group goals clash and this will only enhance intergroup rivalry. A similar argument is derived from the contact hypothesis (Allport, 1954) for equal status interactions. In short, we predicted that similarity of status will be associated with pleasant intergroup relations when the relationship between the groups is cooperative. However, status equality will be perceived as threatening under competitive intergroup relations because it implies an impending change in status (either a loss or gain of status), and leads to instability in perceived status-relations (Brown, 1984b).

Studies examining the moderating role of group goals show little support for this hypothesis. Brown (1984b; Exp 1) found some evidence for low distinctiveness leading to less differentiation when relationships between groups were defined as cooperative. A second study was conducted in which, in addition to a distinctiveness manipulation, cooperation versus competition was explicitly manipulated in a school context (Brown, 1984b; Exp 2). Students were told that the schools worked together on a task or that they worked against another school and that their performance would be compared. Initial analyses did not reveal any effects for whether the task was introduced as cooperative or competitive on an intergroup differentiation measure. Only secondary analyses, in which participants were classified as cooperative or competitive on the basis of a question assessing how competitive they felt towards the other school, revealed support for the moderating role of goal orientation. However, this procedure confounds the independent variable (e.g., competitiveness) with the dependent variable (i.e., the resulting degree of conflict or competitiveness between the groups).

The moderating role of goal interdependence was further examined in a study by Brown and Abrams (1986). School children were told that they either worked jointly with another group or that their relative performance would be compared. Distinctiveness of attitudes and status was manipulated as well. The results revealed no evidence for moderation by goal interdependence and the data suggested that low attitude distinctiveness led to greater liking, regardless of the type of goal relationship. Finally, a study on the relation between task characteristics and ingroup bias (Brewer & Silver, 1978) also revealed no interactive effect between the cooperative versus competitive task structure and the extent to which groups could be distinguished (when categorised as "dark" and "light" group versus categorisation into similar groups) on judgemental and behavioural bias measures.

In an attempt to assess the overall moderating power of group goals, each test of the distinctiveness-bias relationship was coded in our meta-analytical review by independent coders for the degree to which intergroup relations were cooperative, neutral, or competitive (Jetten et al., 2003). This analysis revealed no support for the moderating role of competitiveness of intergroup relations to the distinctiveness – differentiation relation. However, we agree with an observation by Brown and Abrams (1986) that effects of group goals would be stronger when examining actual competition and cooperation instead of their anticipation. Furthermore, it should be noted that cooperation and competition is defined in most studies as group goals being interdependent or independent rather than as outright competition for scarce resources (e.g., a prize or reward). It is likely that moderating effects would be stronger in the latter than in the former case.

Moderation by the nature of intergroup relations: Superordinate categorisations

Importantly, the perception of distinctiveness and comparability is largely defined and evaluated with reference to a shared identity or superordinate group membership. Turner (1987, p.48) states: "... the comparison of different stimuli depends upon their categorization as identical (the same, similar) at a higher level of abstraction, and takes place on dimensions that define their higher level identity." A similar point is made by Mummendey and Wenzel (1999) in their discussion of the ingroup projection model (see also Weber, Mummendey, & Waldzus, 2002). We propose that a salient superordinate category can affect the distinctiveness – differentiation relation in two ways. First, a superordinate category can be an important indicator of whether it is normatively consistent to show positive differentiation (Weber et al., 2002). As recently stated by Turner (1999, p. 22),

> There is often good evidence that the intergroup relationships are not insecure, but relatively positive and that there are powerful superordinate social identifications at work (e.g., as nurses, workers, trade unionists). The latter often imply superordinate values and norms that prescribe that discrimination is not appropriate between the subgroups. This also means that the evaluative direction of the comparison can be ambiguous. Is it positive for a subgroup of nurses to discriminate against another who work together with them in a complementary, cooperative relation as nurses?

Second, superordinate categorisations can affect the perceived comparability of groups; groups are perceived to be more comparable when they share a superordinate category (e.g., the French and British are comparable because they are both members of the European Union, i.e., it is a superordinate category, while the Russians are not, at the time of writing, included in this overarching category and are therefore less comparable). This enhanced comparability, however, is also predicted to affect whether distinctiveness between (sub)groups is valued and appreciated. High distinctiveness can lead to tension when a superordinate category is salient because differences between groups are accentuated and may represent a stumbling block to positive intergroup relations. For instance, when hunters and anti-hunt protesters are categorised into the same superordinate category—those who care for the countryside—groups may on the one hand become more compatible but perceived differences may enhance reflective distinctiveness processes (see Mummendey & Wenzel, 1999, for a similar argument).[4]

---

[4] Note that there is an important difference between our reasoning and Mummendey and Wenzel's (1999) reasoning with respect to intergroup distinctiveness. While we focus on distinctiveness as determined by differences between ingroup and outgroup, intergroup differences are determined in the ingroup projection model as relative prototypicality of the ingroup for the superordinate category. For instance, we would examine perceptions of distinctiveness between German and Dutch while the ingroup projection model would assess the relative prototypicality of German and Dutch for the superordinate category—the European identity. Greater relative prototypicality would thus provide an indirect indication for intergroup distinctiveness: the more Germans perceive themselves to be more prototypical than the Dutch for the European category, the greater the perceived intergroup distinctiveness.

We coded the availability and salience of superordinate categorisations in addition to an assessment of the competitiveness of the intergroup relations in our meta-analysis. We did find a marginally significant effect for this variable. We found that when the superordinate category was not salient, low distinctiveness tended to lead to differentiation (albeit not significantly so) while high distinctiveness led to differentiation when the salience of the superordinate category was high. We interpret this finding as being in line with the ingroup projection model developed by Mummendey and Wenzel (1999): high intergroup distinctiveness is evaluated negatively and leads to more differentiation when being included in a more abstract social category enhances the comparability of groups. In contrast, there was no such tendency when superordinate category salience was low. This suggests that the shared values, norms, and goals that a superordinate categorisation embodies may reduce tendencies to show reactive distinctiveness as a response to low distinctiveness (see Gaertner, Dovidio, Anastasio, Bachman, & Rust, 1993; Terry, 2003).

A MODEL OF THE DISTINCTIVENESS – DIFFERENTIATION RELATIONSHIP

Analysis of moderators of the distinctiveness – differentiation relation revealed that identification was the strongest moderator to this relation, followed by the salience of a superordinate category. In an attempt to integrate the results of the primary research and the results of the meta-analysis we developed the model on moderators of the distinctiveness – differentiation relation (Table 1). Positive differentiation is predicted to be determined by the interaction between group identification (and proto-typicality), level of distinctiveness (low, moderate and high), and the salience of superordinate categories. Parts of this model (in particular those relating to the interaction between identification and level of distinctiveness) have received sufficient empirical support, but there are also aspects of the model that have not been tested yet in great detail and that deserve further attention. In particular, including salience of superordinate categorisations in the model opens up this research to examine contexts in which intergroup distinctiveness takes on a different meaning.

The starting point of the model is to integrate studies showing a curvilinear relation between distinctiveness and differentiation (Jetten et al., 1998) with studies showing moderation by identification and prototypicality (Dwyer, 2000; Jetten et al., 1997, 2001, 2003). Combining these findings, under conditions of low superordinate category salience, we predicted that a curvilinear relation should only be observed for low identifiers or peripheral group members but not for high identifiers or prototypical group members (see Jetten et al., 1999, for a similar integration). This prediction seems at first sight inconsistent with the crossover interaction between distinctiveness and differentiation we found in our meta-analysis and other primary research. Specifically, what differ in our current analysis and our previous research are predictions for low identifiers in the high distinctiveness conditions. We found relatively low levels of differentiation under those conditions in previous work (Jetten et al., 1998) but find relatively high levels of differentiation in research examining the interaction between identification and distinctiveness directly or meta-analytically (Dwyer, 2000; Jetten et al., 2001, 2003). One way to reconcile these findings is by assuming that the levels of distinctiveness sampled in the meta-analysis and primary work are not high enough (or generally as high as the most distinctive condition in Jetten et al., 1998). Indeed, we predicted that low identifiers would show low levels of differentiation when groups are distinct because they are no longer perceived as comparable but that differentiation would be relatively high when distinctiveness is moderate. We do not think extremely high levels of distinctiveness are adequately sampled in the studies included in the meta-analysis (i.e., high distinctiveness is mostly manipulated as moderate distinctiveness such that groups are still comparable). This occurs because most experimental tests focus on distinctiveness-threat (the social identity based prediction) and are therefore more concerned with ensuring a high degree of similarity in the threat condition than a high degree of difference in the non-threat condition. Few if any studies focusing on distinctiveness were designed with the self-categorisation/reflective distinctiveness hypothesis in mind.[5]

Building on the model integrating curvilinear relations with moderation by identification, we added the other important moderator that emerged from our meta-analysis to our model; the role of salience of superordinate identities. To reiterate, we found that high distinctiveness led to more differentiation when a superordinate category was salient while low distinctiveness tended to be associated with differentiation when salience of the superordinate category was low. As outlined in more detail below, we predict that salience of the superordinate category will interact with group identification and degree of distinctiveness to determine differentiation.

---

[5] We were not in a position to explore the possibility of a curvilinear relation between distinctiveness and differentiation directly in our meta-analysis. The reason for this is that it was impossible to sample extremes of the distinctiveness continuum and to code distinctiveness in any other way than as a dichotomous variable.

NEW DIRECTIONS IN THINKING ABOUT DISTINCTIVENESS

While empirical research provides support for the interaction between distinctiveness and identification, there is still much to do to understand how differentiation is affected by distinctiveness when superordinate categorisations are salient or, going one step further, when superordinate categories suppress subgroup identities (e.g., in the case of mergers between groups). Without trying to give an exhaustive list of the possible routes for future research, we would now like to expand on a few of these ideas.

Distinctiveness and superordinate categories

How the salience of superordinate categories is predicted to impact on the distinctiveness – differentiation relation as a function of group identification is illustrated in Table 1.

The salience of superordinate categories was predicted not to affect the distinctiveness – differentiation relation for low identifiers when distinctiveness is low because the superordinate category would not crucially determine the comparability of groups. In other words, when the superordinate category is not salient, low identifiers are expected to accept low intergroup distinctiveness because they are insufficiently invested in the group to assert group identity. Moreover, we predict that low identifiers embrace the superordinate category when such recategorisation at a higher level is possible (high superordinate category salience conditions), again because of low commitment to the group.

We expect that salience of the superordinate category would accentuate differentiation for low identifiers once there is some sense of intergroup distinctiveness (moderate intergroup distinctiveness) compared to when the superordinate category is not salient. If we assume that maintaining clear boundaries between groups is important for low identifiers, the salience of superordinate groups could potentially undermine the perceived separateness of groups, which could stimulate differentiation.

In line with our meta-analytic finding we propose that when distinctiveness is high, the salience of superordinate categories is likely to affect the comparability of groups. Differentiation should be high for low identifiers when the superordinate category is salient and distinctiveness is high because the salience of the superordinate category increases the comparability of the outgroup and reflective distinctiveness processes would come into play under such conditions. However, we predict that high distinctiveness will undermine comparability for those who are not strongly invested in the group when the superordinate group is not salient, which will reduce intergroup differentiation.

TABLE 1
A model of the distinctiveness–differentiation relation moderated by group identification and salience of superordinate categories

Intergroup distinctiveness	Salience of superordinate category	Process	Positive differentiation
	Low identification (peripheral)		
Low	Not salient	Insufficiently invested in the group to maintain independent identity	Low
↓	Salient	Embrace superordinate identity which reduces intergroup salience	Low
Moderate	Not salient	Groups are distinct and comparable	Moderate
	Salient	Salience of the superordinate identity undermines separateness	High
↓	Not salient	Groups are distinct and not comparable	Low
High	Salient	Salience of the superordinate identity increases comparability and salience	High
	High identification (prototypical)		
Low	Not salient	Motivated to maintain or defend and restore low disctinctiveness	High
↓	Salient	Salience of superordinate category enhances perceived sharedness of values, norms and beliefs	Moderate
Moderate	Not salient	Groups are distinct and comparable	Moderate
	Salient	Salience of superordinate category enhances perceived sharedness of values, norms and beliefs	Moderate
↓	Not salient	Groups are distinct and not comparable	Low
High	Salient	Salience of superordinate category increases comparability and quest for prototypicality of the superordinate group.	High

For high group identifiers, we predict that the hypothesis typically derived from social identity theory will apply when a superordinate category is not salient: low distinctiveness should lead to more competitive intergroup relations because low intergroup distinctiveness will form a threat to group distinctiveness. In contrast, we predict that when the superordinate category is salient and group distinctiveness low, perceptions of sharedness of values and norms are enhanced, which would take the sharp edge off positive differentiation. In that case, intergroup similarity should engender a positive connotation which would aid in the development of more cooperative and harmonious intergroup relations.

We predicted that differentiation would not differ for high identifiers as a function of salience of the superordinate category when intergroup distinctiveness is moderate. Moderate distinctiveness would reduce reactive distinctiveness processes compared to low intergroup distinctiveness perceptions. The salience of superordinate categories would also enhance the perceptions of sharedness of values and beliefs under moderate distinctiveness conditions.

Finally, in line with Weber et al. (2002), we predicted that under high distinctiveness conditions high identifiers are more likely to emphasise differences between groups when a superordinate identity is salient and that this will enhance positive differentiation. This leads to the interesting prediction that when distinctiveness is high, those with high investment in the group will interpret distinctiveness in a positive way when the superordinate category is not salient because groups are not comparable, but that the same differences may stimulate differentiation processes when the superordinate category is salient. Note that although a similar pattern of positive differentiation may be observed for low and high identifiers when distinctiveness is high, the underlying processes are expected to differ (i.e., for perceptual and motivational reasons respectively). As mentioned before, these predictions relating to the interaction between salience of super-ordinate groups, identification, and distinctiveness remain largely untested and the full model is in need of empirical examination.

The ultimate threat to distinctiveness: Mergers between groups

We mentioned before that, when examining the relationship between distinctiveness and differentiation, the way the distinctiveness dimension is sampled is of crucial importance. While research has focused on moderate levels of distinctiveness, there has been less attention to social contexts where there is a complete lack of distinctiveness. Specifically, once a critical point is reached beyond which the ingroup cannot be sufficiently distinguished from the outgroup, similarity of ingroup and outgroup can blur the intergroup boundaries and lead to categorisation at a higher level of inclusiveness. We predict that those who identify strongly with the subgroup will feel more threatened than low identifiers when groups have become so similar that they are no longer perceived as separate entities. However, empirical evidence for this hypothesis is generally lacking and most of the research has not explored this form of distinctiveness threat. An exception is a study by Roccas and Schwartz (1993) who manipulated very low distinctiveness by giving high-school students false feedback suggesting that the Ministry of Education was considering merging their school with another school because they were so similar. In line with predictions, it was found that intergroup bias was higher in this condition than in a low and moderately low distinctiveness condition in which the possibility of unification with the other school was not mentioned. However, it was often the anticipation of a merger that was studied and not the actual process of unification and its aftermath. It is clear from research on organisational mergers that group members are very reluctant to relinquish their old identities when anticipating a merger. The new identity is often evaluated using the old identity as a comparison standard or anchor even years after the merger was implemented (Haunschild Moreland, & Murrell, 1994; Terry, 2003).

However, there is some evidence from research on the relationship between subgroup and superordinate identities suggesting that the extent to which the subgroup identity is preserved in the superordinate identity is crucial in predicting the degree to which inter-subgroup bias will be displayed (Hewstone & Brown, 1986; Hornsey & Hogg, 2000). Specifically, when subgroup members are categorised exclusively at the superordinate level and when their subgroup identity is not recognised within the superordinate entity, more negative relations between subgroups are likely to develop. One extension to our model would involve including predictions on the role of subgroup distinctiveness when the subgroup identity is actively played down at the expense of the superordinate identity. In line with the mutual differentiation model (Hewstone & Brown, 1986) and findings by Hornsey and Hogg (2000) we predict that low distinctiveness should lead to increased intergroup differentiation under those conditions. Future research should examine the full spectrum of distinctiveness threat and examine the prediction that high and low identifiers react differently to such threat.

Affective consequences of intergroup distinctiveness

Research on the effect of intergroup distinctiveness has largely focused on the *magnitude* of the perceived differences between ingroup and outgroup but not so much on the *content and meaning* of low or high intergroup distinctiveness. In fact, in order to avoid confounding the magnitude with the content of distinctiveness, researchers have typically examined distinctiveness on relatively neutral dimensions of comparison (e.g., groups differ in the degree to which members believe in supernatural phenomena; see Jetten et al., 1997) or on relatively broad value-free dimensions (e.g., groups are different or similar in their ideas and attitudes regarding the world; see Hornsey & Hogg, 2000). There are only a few studies that have assessed the content of distinctiveness by varying specific values, beliefs, or attitudes of groups. For instance, Jetten et al. (1996) manipulated distinctiveness by providing feedback about ingroup and outgroup norms—ingroup and outgroup were either both discriminatory or fair or differed in their allocation norms—and found that the content of differences and similarities was also affecting positive differentiation (see above for a detailed description).

Given the focus on neutral and value-free dimensions of comparisons in distinctiveness research, it appears that the phenomena are largely explained in cognitive and motivational terms and that affective consequences of distinctiveness threat are largely unexplored (see Smith, 1993). However, we argue that perceptions of low and high distinctiveness may both instigate strong affective responses ("hot" processes). While it is generally acknowledged that reactive distinctiveness processes may induce affective reactions, there has been no research to date documenting specific affective responses (e.g., anger, fear, frustration) when group members perceive that groups are too similar.

We would argue that not only reactive but also reflective distinctiveness processes can be highly charged. For instance, in addition to motivational and cognitive processes, strong affective reactions are likely when group members learn that intergroup distinctiveness is grounded in the perception that core group values are in conflict (e.g., animal rights activists versus hunters). In that case, differentiation may also reflect deeply held convictions and distinctiveness is likely to lead to strong affective responses (e.g., frustration, rage, depression). Group differences may then form a convenient way of justifying differentiation. Greater attention to the role of affective processes and the meaning of distinctiveness in future research should be encouraged to help to provide a full account of distinctiveness processes in accounting for prejudice and discrimination.

CONCLUDING REMARKS

In this chapter we have focused on the role of group distinctiveness in differentiation. The results of a recent meta-analysis on this relationship were discussed and the power of potential moderators was examined. This approach proved successful and, in line with previous research (Jetten et al., 2001), we found that group identification and salience of the superordinate categorisation were the most powerful moderators of this relationship. We conclude that social identity theory and self-categorisation theory should therefore be seen not as contradictory but rather as complementary contributors to this debate. Social identity concerns are dominant when the identification with a group is higher and low distinctiveness is perceived as threatening. Self-categorisation theory principles are more applicable when distinctiveness plays an important role in establishing the groups in the first place but also to justify differentiation on the basis of perceived intergroup differences (Mummendey & Wenzel, 1999). We focused on the importance of being sensitive to the factors that moderate ingroup bias. The path from social categorisation to differentiation is far from direct and the degree to which groups are perceived to differ from each other has important implications for attempts to discriminate between them.

A final word of caution is in order. The conclusion from the above research that both low and high distinctiveness can be the cause of increased intergroup tension should certainly not be interpreted as evidence for the unavoidability of negative intergroup relations. It is important to highlight that similarities or differences between groups do not always lead to negative intergroup relations. Historical examples of mutual respect and of cooperation between groups show that even marked differences in attitudes and beliefs do not necessarily lead to intense intergroup conflict. As Williams (1956) notes with respect to differences between religious groups: "differences could be ignored, passed over, or accepted as matters of slight consequence"(p. 15). Likewise, small differences between groups are often interpreted as evidence that groups share a common ground and provide a fertile starting point for increased intergroup cooperation, enriching both groups without dividing them. As we have argued in the present chapter, it is thus important to determine the factors and conditions that prompt a particular response following the perception of intergroup distinctiveness. Those factors can help us understand the potentially divisive role of distinctiveness by identifying when differences between groups are reconcilable and when they will become or remain causes of intergroup conflict.

REFERENCES

Allen, V. L., & Wilder, D. A. (1975). Categorization, belief similarity, and intergroup discrimination. *Journal of Personality and Social Psychology, 32*, 971–977.

Allport, G. W. (1954). *The nature of prejudice*. Cambridge, MA: Addison-Wesley.

Branscombe, N. R., Ellemers, N., Spears, R., & Doosje, B. (1999). The context and content of social identity threat. In N. Ellemers, R. Spears, & B. Doosje (Eds.), *Social identity: Context, commitment, content* (pp. 35–58). Oxford: Blackwell.

Branscombe, N. R., Wann, D. L., Noel, J. G., & Coleman, J. (1993). In-group or out-group extremity: Importance of the threatened social identity. *Personality and Social Psychology Bulletin, 19*, 381–388.

Brewer, M. B. (1979). In-group bias in the minimal intergroup situation: A cognitive-motivational analysis. *Psychological Bulletin, 86*, 307–324.

Brewer, M. B. (1991). The social self: On being the same and different at the same time. *Personality and Social Psychology Bulletin, 17*, 475–482.

Brewer, M. B., & Miller, N. (1984). Beyond the contact hypothesis: Theoretical perspectives on desegregation. In N. Miller & M. B. Brewer (Eds.), *Groups in contact: The psychology of desegregation* (pp. 281–302). Orlando, FL: Academic Press.

Brewer, M. B., & Silver, M. (1978). Ingroup bias as a function of task characteristics. *European Journal of Social Psychology, 8*, 393–400.

Brewer, M. B., & Weber, J. G. (1994). Self-evaluation effects of interpersonal versus intergroup social comparison. *Journal of Personality and Social Psychology, 66*, 268–275.

Brown, R., & Abrams, D. (1986). The effects of intergroup similarity and goal interdependence on intergroup attitudes and task performance. *Journal of Experimental Social Psychology, 22*, 78–92.

Brown, R., & Wade, G. S. (1987). Superordinate goals and intergroup behaviour: The effects of role ambiguity and status on intergroup attitudes and task performance. *European Journal of Social Psychology, 17*, 131–142.

Brown, R. J. (1984a). The role of similarity in intergroup relations. In H. Tajfel (Ed.), *The social dimension: European developments in social psychology* (pp. 603–623). Cambridge: Cambridge University Press.

Brown, R. J. (1984b). The effects of intergroup similarity and cooperative versus competitive orientation on intergroup discrimination. *British Journal of Social Psychology, 23*, 21–33.

Byrne, D. (1971). *The attraction paradigm*. New York: Academic Press.

Clinton, W. J. (2001, December). *The struggle for the soul of the 21st century* [Television broadcast]. Lecture presented in the Dimbleby Lecture Series. London: BBC. Available from http://www.bbc.co.uk/arts/news_comment/dimbleby/clinton.shtml

Deschamps, J. C., & Brown, R. (1983). Superordinate goals and intergroup conflict. *British Journal of Social Psychology, 22*, 189–195.

Diehl, M. (1988). Social identity and minimal groups: The effects of interpersonal and intergroup attitudinal similarity on intergroup discrimination. *British Journal of Social Psychology, 27*, 289–300.

Doise, W. (1978). *Groups and individuals: Explanations in social psychology*. Cambridge: Cambridge University Press.

Doise, W., Deschamps, J. C., & Meyers, G. (1978). The accentuation of intracategory similarities. In H. Tajfel (Ed.), *Differentiation between social groups* (pp. 159–168). London: Academic Press.

Doosje, B., Ellemers, N., & Spears, R. (1995). Perceived intragroup variability as a function of group status and identification. *Journal of Experimental Social Psychology, 31*, 410–436.

Doosje, B., Spears, R., & Koomen, W. (1995). When bad isn't all bad: Strategic use of sample information in generalization and stereotyping. *Journal of Personality and Social Psychology, 69*, 642–655.

Dovidio, J. F., Gaertner, S. L., & Validzic, A. (1998). Intergroup bias: Differentiation, and a common ingroup identity. *Journal of Personality and Social Psychology, 75*, 109–120.

Dwyer, L. (2000). *The source of ingroup bias: Combined effects of group distinctiveness and identification*. Unpublished Honors Thesis, University of Queensland, Australia.

Eiser, J. R., & Stroebe, W. (1972). *Categorization and social judgment*. London: Academic Press.

Ellemers, N. (1993). The influence of socio-structural variables on identity enhancement strategies. *European Review of Social Psychology, 4*, 27–57.

Ellemers, N., Spears, R., & Doosje, B. (1997). Sticking together or falling apart: Group identification as a psychological determinant of group commitment versus individual mobility. *Journal of Personality and Social Psychology, 72*, 617–626.

Fishman, J. A. (1963). Nationality-nationalism and nation-nationism. In J. A. Fishman, C. A. Ferguson, & J. D. Gupta (Eds.), *Language problems in developing countries*. New York: Wiley.

Ford, T. E., & Stangor, C. (1992). The role of diagnosticity in stereotype formation: Perceiving group means and variances. *Journal of Personality and Social Psychology, 63*, 356–367.

Freud, S. (1922). *Group psychology and the analysis of the ego*. New York: W. W. Norton & Co.

Gaertner, S. L., Dovidio, J. F., Anastasio, P., Bachman, B., & Rust, M. (1993). The common ingroup identity model: Recategorisation and the reduction of intergroup bias. *European Review of Social Psychology, 4*, 1–26.

Haunschild, P. R., Moreland, R. L., & Murrell, A. J. (1994). Sources of resistance to mergers between groups. *Journal of Applied Social Psychology, 24,* 1150–1178.

Henderson-King, E., Henderson-King, D., Zhermer, N., Posokhova, S., & Chiker, V. (1997). Ingroup favoritism and perceived similarity: A look at Russian's perceptions in the post-Soviet era. *Personality and Social Psychology Bulletin, 23,* 1013–1021.

Hewstone, M., & Brown, R. J. (1986). Contact is not enough: An intergroup perspective on the "contact hypothesis". In M. Hewstone & R. J. Brown (Eds.), *Contact and conflict in intergroup encounters* (pp. 1–44). Oxford, UK: Blackwell.

Hewstone, M., Islam, M. R., & Judd, C. M. (1993). Models of crossed categorization and intergroup relations. *Journal of Personality and Social Psychology, 64,* 779–793.

Hogg, M. A., & Abrams, D. (1988). *Social identifications: A social psychology of intergroup relations and group processes.* London: Routledge.

Hornsey, M. J., & Hogg, M. A. (2000). Subgroup relations: A comparison of the mutual intergroup differentiation and common ingroup identity models of prejudice reduction. *Personality and Social Psychology Bulletin, 26,* 242–256.

Insko, C. A., Nacoste, R. W., & Moe, J. L. (1983). Belief congruence and racial discrimination: Review of the evidence and critical evaluation. *European Journal of Social Psychology, 13,* 153–174.

Jetten, J., Spears, R., Hogg, M. A., & Manstead, A. S. R. (2000). Discrimination constrained and justified: Variable effects of group variability and ingroup identification. *Journal of Experimental Social Psychology, 36,* 329–356.

Jetten, J., Spears, R., & Manstead, A. S. R. (1996). Intergroup norms and intergroup discrimination: Distinctive self-categorization and social identity effects. *Journal of Personality and Social Psychology, 71,* 1222–1233.

Jetten, J., Spears, R., & Manstead, A. S. R. (1997). Distinctiveness threat and prototypicality: Combined effects on intergroup discrimination and collective self-esteem. *European Journal of Social Psychology, 27,* 635–657.

Jetten, J., Spears, R., & Manstead, A. S. R. (1998). Defining dimensions of distinctiveness: group variability makes a difference to differentiation. *Journal of Personality and Social Psychology, 74,* 1481–1492.

Jetten, J., Spears, R., & Manstead, A. S. R. (1999). Distinctiveness and intergroup discrimination. In N. Ellemers, R. Spears, & B. Doosje (Eds.), *Social identity: Context, commitment, content* (pp. 107–126). Oxford: Basil Blackwell.

Jetten, J., Spears, R., & Manstead, A. S. R. (2001). Similarity as a source of discrimination: The role of group identification. *European Journal of Social Psychology, 31,* 621–640.

Jetten, J., Spears, R., & Postmes, T. (2003). *Intergroup distinctiveness and differentiation: A meta-analytic investigation.* In press. *Journal of Personality and Social Psychology.*

Kerr, A. (1996). *Perceptions: Cultures in conflict.* Derry, Northern Ireland: Guildhall Press.

Marcus-Newhall, A., Miller, N., Holtz, R., & Brewer, M. B. (1993). Cross-cutting category membership with role assignment: A means of reducing intergroup bias. *British Journal of Social Psychology, 32,* 125–146.

McGarthy, G. (1999). *Categorization in social psychology.* London: Sage.

Migdal, M. J., Hewstone, M., & Mullen, B. (1998). The effects of crossed categorization on intergroup evaluations: A meta-analysis. *British Journal of Social Psychology, 37,* 303–324.

Moghaddam, F. M., & Stringer, P. (1988). Outgroup similarity and intergroup bias. *Journal of Social Psychology, 128,* 105–115.

Mummendey, A., & Schreiber, H. J. (1984). Social comparison, similarity and ingroup favouritism—A replication. *European Journal of Social Psychology, 14,* 231–233.

Mummendey, A., & Wenzel, M. (1999). Social discrimination and the tolerance in intergroup relations: Reactions to intergroup difference. *Personality and Social Psychology Review, 3,* 158–174.

Oakes, P. J. (1987). The salience of social categories. In J. C. Turner, M. A. Hogg, P. J. Oakes, S. D. Reicher, & M. S. Wetherell (Eds.), *Rediscovering the social group: A self-categorization theory* (pp. 117–141). Oxford: Basil Blackwell.

Roccas, S., & Schwartz, S. H. (1993). Effects of intergroup similarity on intergroup relations. *European Journal of Social Psychology, 23*, 581–595.

Rokeach, M. (1960). *The open and closed mind.* New York: Basic Books.

Sachdev, I., & Bourhis, R. Y. (1987). Status differentials and intergroup behaviour. *European Journal of Social Psychology, 17*, 277–293.

Sherif, M. (1966). *In common predicament: Social psychology of intergroup conflict and cooperation.* New York: Houghton Mifflin.

Smith, E. R. (1993). Social identity and social emotions: Toward new conceptualizations of prejudice. In D. M. Mackie & D. L. Hamilton (Eds.), *Affect, cognition, and stereotyping: Interactive processes in group perception* (pp. 297–315). San Diego, CA: Academic Press.

Spears, R. (2002). Four degrees of stereotype formation: Differentiation by any means necessary. In C. McGarty, V. Yzerbyt, & R. Spears (Eds.), *Stereotypes as explanations: The formation of meaningful beliefs about social groups* (pp. 127–156). Cambridge: Cambridge University Press.

Spears, R., Doosje, B., & Ellemers, N. (1997). Self-stereotyping in the face of threats to group status and distinctiveness: The role of group identification. *Personality and Social Psychology Bulletin, 23*, 538–553.

Spears, R., Jetten, J., & Scheepers, D. (2002). Distinctiveness and the definition of collective self: A tripartite model. In A. Tesser, D. A. Stapel, & J. Wood (Eds.), *Self and motivation: Emerging psychological perspectives* (pp. 147–171). Washington, DC: American Psychological Association.

Spears, R., Scheepers, D., Jetten, J., Doosje, B., Ellemers, N., & Postmes, T. (in press). Group homogeneity, entitativity and social identity: Dealing with/in social structure. In V. Yzerbyt, C. M. Judd, & O. Corneille (Eds.), *The psychology of group perception: Perceived variability, entitativity and essentialism.* Hove, UK: Psychology Press.

Staub, E. (1989). *The roots of evil: The origins of genocide and other group violence.* New York: University Press.

Swift, J. (1726/1998). *Gulliver's travels.* Oxford: Oxford University Press.

Tajfel, H. (1978). Interindividual behaviour and intergroup behaviour. In H. Tajfel (Ed.), *Differentiation between social groups: Studies in the social psychology of intergroup relations* (pp. 27–60). London: Academic Press.

Tajfel, H. (1970). Experiments in intergroup discrimination. *Scientific American, 223*, 96–102.

Tajfel, H. (1981). *Human groups and social categories: Studies in social psychology.* Cambridge: Cambridge University Press.

Tajfel, H. (1982). Social psychology of intergroup relations. *Annual Review of Psychology, 33*, 1–39.

Tajfel, H., Flament, C., Billig, M. G., & Bundy, R. P. (1971). Social categorization and intergroup behavior. *European Journal of Social Psychology, 1*, 149–178.

Tajfel, H., & Forgas, J. P. (1981). Social categorization: Cognitions, values and groups. In J. P. Forgas (Ed.), *Social Cognition: Perspectives in everyday understanding* (pp. 113–140). London: Academic Press.

Tajfel, H., & Turner, J. C. (1979). An integrative theory of intergroup conflict. In W. G. Austin & S. Worchel (Eds.), *The social psychology of intergroup relations* (pp. 33–47). Monterey, CA: Brooks/Cole.

Tajfel, H., & Wilkes, A. L. (1963). Classification and quantitative judgement. *British Journal of Psychology, 54*, 101–114.

Terry, D. J. (2003). A social identity perspective on organizational mergers: The role of group status, permeability, and similarity. In S. A. Haslam, D. van Knippenberg, M. J. Platow, & N. Ellemers (2003). *Social identity at work: Developing theory for organizational practice.* New York: Psychology Press.

Turner, J. C. (1978). Social comparison, similarity and intergroup favouritism. In H. Tajfel (Ed.), *Differentiation between social groups* (pp. 235–250). London: Academic Press.

Turner, J. C. (1987). A self-categorization theory. In J. C. Turner, M. A. Hogg, P. J. Oakes, S. D. Reicher, & M. S. Wetherell (Eds.), *Rediscovering the social group: A self-categorization theory* (pp. 42–67). Oxford: Basil Blackwell.

Turner, J. C. (1999). Some current issues in research on social identity and self-categorization theories. In N. Ellemers, R. Spears, & B. Doosje (Eds.), *Social identity: Context, commitment, content* (pp. 6–34). Oxford: Blackwell Publishers.

Turner, J. C., Hogg, M. A., Oakes, P. J., Reicher, S. D., & Wetherell, M. S. (1987). *Rediscovering the social group: A self-categorization theory.* Oxford: Basil Blackwell.

Vanbeselaere, N. (1991). The different effects of simple and crossed categorizations: A result of the category differentiation process or of differential category salience? In W. Stroebe & M. Hewstone (Eds.), *European review of social psychology.* Chichester, UK: Wiley.

Vanbeselaere, N. (1996). The impact of differentially valued overlapping categorizations upon the differentiation between positively, negatively, and neutrally evaluated social groups. *European Journal of Social Psychology, 26,* 75–96.

Weber, U., Mummendey, A., & Waldzus, S. (2002). Perceived legitimacy of intergroup status differences: Its prediction by relative ingroup prototypicality. *European Journal of Social Psychology, 32,* 449–470.

Williams, R. M. (1956). Religion, value-orientations, and intergroup conflict. *Journal of Social Issues, 12,* 12–20.

EUROPEAN REVIEW OF SOCIAL PSYCHOLOGY, 2003, *14*, 243–275

Stereotype threat: When minority members underperform

Anne Maass and Mara Cadinu

University of Padova, Italy

This chapter provides a brief overview of research on stereotype threat, and considers whether this phenomenon is specific to minority groups (defined as low status groups), or whether similar deficits may also be observed in groups that generally enjoy a high status in society but that are negatively stereotyped in a specific domain. We then review a number of individual difference variables that moderate stereotype threat and that may explain why some people are highly vulnerable to stereotype activation while others appear to resist its influence. Next, we consider what processes drive stereotype threat, including anxiety, intrusive thoughts, shift towards caution, expectancy, and disengagement. In the subsequent section we compare the stereotype threat model with other theories dealing with the link between stereotypes and performance, in particular self-fulfilling prophecy and the expectancy value model. The final sections of the chapter concern areas of application in which stereotype threat may account for performance gaps between social groups, and how to prevent it.

In 1954 Allport discussed the pernicious effects of prejudice on the members of stigmatised groups. According to Allport, one of the most insidious of these effects occurs when a member of a stigmatised group confirms with his/her behaviour the negative stereotypes prevalent in the society, thus "reassuring" the prejudiced majority members that their negative stereotypes are indeed justified. Despite this early interest, minority behaviour has subsequently been typically underinvestigated in favour of an extensive effort to investigate attitudes and behaviours held by majority members. However, recent work by Crocker and Major

Address correspondence to Anne Maass, DPSS, University of Padova, Via Venezia, 8, 35139 Padova, Italy. E-mail: anne.maass@unipd.it

We would like to thank Francesco Foroni for his great help in conducting a pilot study in the USA.

http://www.tandf.co.uk/journals/titles/99998080.asp   DOI: 10.1080/10463280340000072

(1989), Steele and Aronson (1995), Swim and Stangor (1998) and others has contributed to a renewed interest in the so-called minority perspective, in an attempt to better understand the effects of stereotypes and prejudice on minority members. One important contribution in this direction has been the recent model of stereotype threat proposed by Steele and collaborators (Spencer, Steele, & Quinn,1999; Steele & Aronson, 1995). These authors claim that negative stereotypes are in part responsible for the underperformance of minority members in stereotype-relevant domains. More specifically, those tasks for which a negative association exists between the task domain and the minority group will represent a threat for minority members; their preoccupation with inadvertently confirming the stereotype will in turn lead to a decrease in performance. For example, women are expected to perform poorly on maths tests if the gender stereotype "Women are poor at maths" becomes salient in the test situation.

In this chapter, we will first provide a brief overview of stereotype threat research, with particular attention to the different research paradigms used to test the model. We will then ask whether stereotype threat is specific to minority groups, defined as low-status groups, or whether similar deficits may also be observed in groups that generally enjoy a high status in society but that are negatively stereotyped in a specific domain (e.g., men with reference to social intelligence). Subsequently, we will review a number of individual difference variables that moderate stereotype threat and that may explain why some people are highly vulnerable to stereotype activation while others appear to resist its influence. We will then ask when and how stereotype threat related deficits may develop during childhood. Subsequently, we will address the question of what processes are driving stereotype threat, an issue that continues to be the prime challenge to researchers; in this section, we will consider a number of hypotheses including anxiety, intrusive thoughts, shift towards caution, expectancy, and disengagement. In the subsequent section we will compare the stereotype threat model with other theories dealing with the link between stereotypes and performance, in particular self-fulfilling prophecy and the expectancy value model. We will ask whether stereotype threat does indeed represent a distinct model or whether it is largely redundant with respect to previous theories. The final sections will be dedicated to the areas of application in which stereotype threat may account for performance gaps between social groups, and to ways of preventing stereotype threat. Throughout this chapter, we will draw both on the general literature and on our own studies, including current work. Unless mentioned otherwise, we will use the term "minority" as referring to a social group that has a relatively low status in society, even if it represents a numerical majority (e.g., women), and that is negatively stereotyped in a specific area of competence (e.g., women in mathematics; Blacks in verbal intelligence; low social class in academics; elderly in memory tasks).

RESEARCH PARADIGMS

In the paradigm originally proposed by Steele and Aronson (1995), minority and majority members were asked to solve a task associated with a negative minority stereotype (e.g., women on maths tasks, Blacks on verbal tasks). In the stereotype threat condition the test was described as diagnostic of the participants' performance, whereas in the control condition it was described as a simple exercise. The typical finding emerging from these studies is that minority members (women, Blacks) show significantly poorer performance when they believe that the test is diagnostic of their abilities than in the control condition. On the contrary, the experimental manipulation does not affect majority members' performance (men, Whites). According to Steele and Aronson, the decline in performance can be attributed to stereotype threat: The diagnostic test will activate the negative stereotype about the ingroup in the relevant domain (mathematics or verbal abilities) so that participants under threat will underperform because they may feel anxious about confirming the stereotype or suffer from evaluation apprehension (Steele & Aronson, 1995; Exps. 2 & 3). However, findings based on this paradigm are open to an alternative explanation. Minorities may simply suffer from greater evaluation apprehension or anxiety whenever a test is diagnostic, and in principle this could occur regardless of whether the test domain is relevant (e.g., verbal for Blacks, as in Steele & Aronson, 1995) or not (e.g., spatial skills for Blacks) to the minority stereotype.

In a second research paradigm, participants were explicitly told that previous research has shown differences in performance between the minority and the majority group. In one study conducted by Spencer et al. (1999; Exp. 2) a group of men and women were given a difficult test of their mathematics abilities. In the "no gender difference" condition participants were explicitly told that previous research has shown that males and females obtain similar results, whereas in the "gender difference" condition participants were told that differences have been found (implicitly suggesting that women were doing more poorly than males). The results for women showed a performance deficit in the "gender difference" condition compared to the "no gender difference" condition, whereas males performed equally well in the two experimental conditions. A subsequent study by Spencer et al. (1999; Exp 3) showed that women assigned to a condition in which no mention of the gender difference was made performed worse than females in a "no gender difference" condition whereas, again, males' performance did not vary across conditions. To put things differently, women taking a difficult maths test showed a performance deficit compared to men even when the maths stereotype was never mentioned whereas their performance was equal to that of men when they were reassured that the prevalent stereotype is incorrect. This study is important because it suggests an explicit threat is not necessary for stereotype threat effects to occur and that the maths test *per se* may implicitly activate the stereotype concerns hypothesised by the model. However, these studies do not clarify whether the performance deficit is obtained only when the task is relevant to the stereotype, which is a crucial feature of the stereotype threat model. In principle, women may underperform in any situation in which they are compared to men or in any difficult testing situation unless they are reassured about the lack of gender differences; if this were the case, being tested in grammar, for example, may in principle represent a threat for women, thus leading to a decrease in performance. This is quite different from the stereotype threat model predicting performance deficits specifically in those domains in which minorities are negatively stereotyped (for example, for women in maths but not in verbal skills). At this point the literature had not demonstrated that stereotype relevance is crucial for obtaining a stereotype threat effect.

In a third research paradigm, before performing a verbal test, participants under stereotype threat were asked to report their race, a request omitted in the control condition (Steele & Aronson, 1995, Exp. 4). Similar to the non-diagnostic condition used in the other experiments, in both conditions the test was described as a simple exercise. Again, a decrease in performance was found under stereotype threat. This study has important implications because it suggests that simply making salient the minority's social category (in this case race) will lead to stereotype threat effects. In other words, a very subtle threat can lead to results similar to those obtained under explicit threat. However, again, one cannot exclude that the activation of race could lead to a generalised deficit in the performance of minority members, so that a decrease in performance could be observed even on tasks that are irrelevant to the minority stereotype.

Taken together, all three paradigms share one important limitation: They do not provide convincing support for the idea that the performance deficit observed in minority members is due to stereotype threat rather than to a more general performance deficit, possibly due to a process of evaluation apprehension in any testing situation and/or whenever the group stereotype is activated. In other words, one cannot exclude the possibility that describing a test as diagnostic, or presenting a difficult test to low-status participants, could lead to a generalised deficit in performance, i.e., depress performance even on tasks irrelevant to the group stereotype. Yet, the stereotype relevance is a key feature of Steele and Aronson's model, according to which performance decrements are driven by stereotype activation and hence are limited to stereotype-relevant domains. To exclude the possibility that people belonging to minorities are simply more vulnerable in any testing situation, one possibility is to keep the diagnosticitiy information constant and vary the nature of the test, i.e., its relevance to the stereotype.

An important step in this direction was made by Inzlicht and Ben-Zeev (2000; Exp. 1). In their study, a group of women performed both a verbal and a maths test either in a gender-balanced context or in a situation in which females were numerically inferior to males. The rationale behind this study is the following: Because unbalanced gender compositions tend to make gender salient, the activation of the gender stereotype will be more likely in the unbalanced than in the balanced gender composition. Consistent with these predictions, results showed a decrease in maths performance for females in the minority compared to the sex-balanced condition (for conceptually similar results see Sekaquaptewa & Thompson, 2003, who found that women who had a solo status in an otherwise all-male group performed more poorly on a maths test than those working in an all-female group). Most important, the gender composition of the group did not affect their performance on the verbal test, suggesting that women's performance is impaired only when the test domain is relevant to the negative stereotype about the ingroup, i.e., the maths domain. Although this study is very informative because it suggests the importance of the stereotype domain in interaction with gender salience, the use of distinctly different tests leaves the stereotype-relevance question open to alternative interpretations, such as differential test difficulty. A similar paradigm was used by Leyens, Désert, Croizet, and Darcis (2000) who had men and women perform an affective and a valence task of similar levels of difficulty (as well as an easier lexical decision task). Before the tasks, in the stereotype threat condition, participants were told that men are not as good as women in dealing with affect and processing affective information, whereas in the control condition the tasks were simply described as aimed at understanding cognitive factors involved in the processing of verbal information. Males made more errors in the threatening condition but only on the affective task, i.e., the task that was relevant to the previous threat manipulation. This study shows very clearly that an explicit threat about men being inferior to women in the domain of affect was effective in decreasing men's affective performance.

Even more convincing is a paradigm used by Stone, Lynch, Sjomeling, and Darley (1999; Exp. 1), who varied the test label while keeping the test constant. Stone and collaborators told Black and White participants that they would perform a sports test based on a game of golf. Black participants' performance was worse when the task was framed as diagnostic of "sports strategic intelligence" (stereotype threat condition for Blacks) compared to a condition in which the test was framed as measuring psychological factors correlated with "general sports performance" (control condition). At the same time, White participants performed worse when the golf task was framed as diagnostic of "natural athletic ability" (stereotype threat condition for Whites) than in the control condition. In other words, although the domain of the task was kept constant, i.e., golf, the task was presented as either testing athletic talent or strategic intelligence (or simply as correlated with general sports performance, in the control condition). What makes this research paradigm very interesting is the constancy of the test across conditions and the subtlety of the experimental manipulation in addressing pre-existing stereotypes, the athletic talent condition being relevant to a negative stereotype regarding Whites (and a positive stereotype regarding Blacks) and the opposite being true for the strategic intelligence condition.

A similar logic was used in one of our experiments (Cadinu, Maass, & Lombardo, 2002) in which we manipulated the stereotype relevance of the test by varying the test domain. We focussed on a very broad performance domain that is closely linked to people's self-definition as well as to their success in life: intelligence. A group of men and women were given the same logic test that was presented as measuring either logical intelligence or social intelligence. Notice that widely held stereotypes associate women with relatively poor logical intelligence and men with relatively poor social intelligence. Results in the two conditions that are of interest here showed that women performed worse when the test allegedly measured logical rather than social intelligence, whereas the opposite was found for men. Thus, both in the study by Stone et al. and in the study by Cadinu et al. Steele and Aronson's model was supported within an experimental paradigm that (a) kept the test constant but implicitly varied the stereotype relevance of the test for each of the two groups, and (b) did not explicitly mention stereotypes regarding one group's inferiority. Because the decrease in performance was only observed in the domain in which a given group is negatively stereotyped, these studies provide strong evidence in support of Steele and Aronson's hypothesis that performance deficits occur specifically in stereotype-relevant domains.

An alternative paradigm was developed by Shih, Pittinsky, and Ambady (1999; see also Ambady, Shih, Kim, & Pittinsky, 2001; Cheryan & Bodenhausen, 2000) who manipulated the salience of participants' social identity (gender vs ethnic) and assessed its effects on performance. In line with the stereotype threat model, Shih et al. found that Asian-American women performed more poorly in a maths test when their gender identity rather than their Asian identity was made salient. Because mathematics is related to negative stereotypes about women and positive stereotypes about Asians, this study provides strong evidence that the stereotype consistency between the task and the relevant social identity is the key factor triggering the decrease in performance.

This brief overview suggests that stereotype threat effects emerge consistently across very different experimental paradigms. In particular, depending on the experimental paradigm, stereotype threat is activated in very different ways, for example by varying test diagnosticity, by activating a socially shared stereotype either explicitly or implicitly, by activating the minority's category membership prior to test taking, or by varying the test label and, hence, its stereotype relevance. Also, stereotype-induced performance deficits have been observed for a variety of minority groups, including ethnic minorities (Stone et al., 1999), women (e.g., Spencer et al., 1999), people with low socio-economic status (Croizet & Claire, 1998), elderly (Maass, Cadinu, Verga, & Crimaldi, 2002), and Southern Italians (Mezzapesa, 1999–2000). Apparently, then, stereotype threat is a very robust phenomenon that occurs across different research paradigms, different minority groups, and different stereotypes.

Since published studies are not always a reliable index of robustness, we also looked at dissertation abstracts (less susceptible to "file drawer losses" than published work). Considering the dissertations on stereotype Threat reported during the last 3 years, the "success" rate is surprisingly high. Out of 18 dissertations that manipulated stereotype threat and measured performance, 11 reported reliable performance decrements as a function of stereotype activation and 2 additional studies provided partial support. Only 3 out of 18 dissertations failed to find stereotype threat effects. Also, stereotype threat effects seem to occur to similar degrees across different minority groups including women, racial or ethnic minorities (Blacks, Mexican American, Jews, etc.), gays, and the elderly. Together, these studies suggest that stereotype threat effects may be quite pervasive.

IS STEREOTYPE THREAT SPECIFIC TO LOW-STATUS MINORITIES?

Several studies have addressed the issue of whether stereotype threat deficits are limited to low-status minority members or can also be observed in the performance of high-status majority members. Results show that, when negative stereotypes about the ingroup are made salient, performance deficits can also be observed on the part of people belonging to dominant or high-status groups. In a study conducted by Aronson, Lustina, Good, Keough, Steele, and Brown (1999) a group of Americans of European descent was told that Asians tend to perform better than Whites in tasks involving mathematics abilities. Participants under threat showed a decrease in performance compared to a control condition in which Asians were not mentioned. Similar results were found by Leyens et al. (2000) in a study discussed earlier. The results showed that men underperformed in affective tasks when their inferiority to women had explicitly been stressed. Both of these studies investigated performance deficits of majority members but did not include minority members. Thus, one question that remains open is whether the stereotype threat deficits suffered by low-status and high-status group members are similar in size. In the research conducted by Cadinu et al. (2002, Exp. 1), stereotype threat effects suffered by minority and majority members were assessed within the same experimental design and results showed that the effects for male participants (under social intelligence threat) were as strong as the results found for female participants (under logical intelligence threat).

Overall, these studies suggest that a history of stigmatisation is not necessary for stereotype threat effects to occur. Moreover, the study by Cadinu et al. (2002) suggests that the stereotype threat phenomenon may be just as strong for dominant social groups as for stigmatised or low-status groups. Yet the processes underlying performance deficits by high- vs low-status groups may not be the same. In a recent study by Cadinu, Maass, Frigerio, Impagliazzo, & Latinotti (2003), a group of Black American soldiers living in Italy were exposed to a manipulation that rendered either their race (low-status group) or their nationality (dominant group) salient. They were told that their in-group generally fared either very well or rather poorly on verbal abilities compared to the outgroup (compared to Whites when the Black identity was salient or compared to Italians when the American identity was salient).[1] Subsequently, they were asked to report their level of expectation regarding their performance on a verbal intelligence test and later performed the test itself. Note that the test was the same in all experimental conditions. Consistent with predictions, participants both in the Black (low-status) and in the American (dominant-status) condition had lower expectations and under-performed after having received negative information about the in-group. However, the level of expectancy was found to mediate the decrease in performance for participants in the Black but not in the American condition. These results suggest that, although comparable performance deficits were found for members in the low-status (Black) and in the dominant-status (American) group, the underlying processes may be different. One possibility is that, in

---

[1]In a pilot test conducted in the US, 22 non-Black participants were asked to indicate which group (Blacks vs Whites and Americans vs Italians) were generally believed to have better verbal abilities. Whites were associated with better verbal abilities than Blacks (3.55 on a 5-point scale, which different significantly from the neutral midpoint of 3, one-sample t-test = 3.46, $p < .01$) and Italians with better verbal abilities than Americans (3.27, different from neutral midpoint of 3, one-sample t-test = 2.02, $p < .06$). Thus, our Black American soldiers apparently belong to a group whose verbal abilities are negatively evaluated both on the basis of race and, to a slightly lesser degree, nationality.

the case of dominant or high-status group members, the stereotype threat effects are simply the result of a temporary situational pressure whereas for low-status minority members a history of stigmatisation leads these individuals to lower their level of expectation which in turn causes the performance decrement. Although no definite conclusions can be drawn on the basis of a single study, the findings by Cadinu et al. (2003) suggest that caution is needed when extending a general stereotype threat model to high-status group memberships because the processes underlying comparable performance deficits may be of quite different nature.

MODERATOR VARIABLES: WHO IS MOST VULNERABLE TO STEREOTYPE THREAT?

Although stereotype threat appears to be a robust and widespread phenomenon, people are not equally susceptible to its debilitating effects. To date, a number of individual difference variables have been identified that render minority members more or less vulnerable to stereotype threat, including domain identification, group identification, and internal vs external control beliefs.

One individual difference variable that is known to moderate stereotype threat effects is the importance that individuals attribute to the relevant performance domain. Starting from Aronson et al.'s research (1999; Exp. 2), there is fairly consistent evidence that a strong identification with the relevant domain constitutes a risk factor that makes people particularly vulnerable to stereotype threat (e.g., Cadinu et al., 2003, Exp. 1; Spencer et al., 1999; Stone et al., 1999, Exp. 1). Those who consider the performance domain important (and who generally tend to be good at it) are the ones that are most strongly affected by stereotype activation, whereas their less motivated and less competent peers seem almost immune to stereotype threat. Indeed, domain identification is considered a necessary condition for stereotype threat to occur and many authors now exclude *a priori* from their experiments those participants who are not highly identified with the performance domain (cf. Marx & Roman, 2002). Although the reasons for the differential susceptibility remain unclear, one plausible explanation is that people with low domain identification may have withdrawn from the domain sometime during their life, possibly as a consequence of repeated experiences with stereotype threat. Their dissociation from the domain may then protect them from any further stereotype threat experience exactly because the performance domain is no longer relevant to their self-concept. We will come back to this possibility when discussing the mechanisms driving stereotype threat.

A second individual difference variable that seems to moderate stereotype threat is the degree to which people identify with the social group to which they belong. Drawing on social identity theory, Schmader (2002) argued that stereotype threat should mainly affect those who are highly identified with the group that is the target of the stereotype. Indeed, in line with this prediction, he found that only women strongly identified with their gender group suffered a performance decline when taking a mathematics test aimed at investigating gender differences. When the test was described as measuring individual abilities (rather than gender differences), women performed just as well as men, regardless of their gender identification. Thus, group identification appears to be an important moderator of stereotype threat, possibly because highly identified individuals feel more apprehensive about confirming a negative stereotype regarding their ingroup (although some other experiments have failed to confirm this prediction, see Cadinu et al., 2003).

A third variable that appears to moderate stereotype threat is locus of control. Cadinu et al. (2002, 2003) have argued that individuals with internal locus of control would be more vulnerable to the effects of stereotype threat than those characterised by an external locus of control. Individuals with internal locus of control tend to believe that their successes and failures depend on themselves. The fact that they feel personally responsible for their actions, in conjunction with the pressure deriving from the stereotype threat condition, will put these individuals under intense pressure, which in turn will impair performance (see Svenson & Maule, 1993, for evidence that excessive stress is related to low performance). In line with this reasoning, Cadinu et al. (2003) found that the performance expectancies of internal control individuals were greatly reduced when exposed to stereotype threat, while external control individuals were unaffected by stereotype activation. However, no corresponding effects were found for actual performance in this study. In contrast, Cadinu et al. (2002) found that internal locus individuals underperformed under stereotype threat compared to external locus individuals. This finding is interesting in view of the fact that students with internal control beliefs have generally been found to perform better than those with external control beliefs (Pintrich, Marx, & Boyle, 1993). Despite this general advantage, individuals with internal locus seem to be at greater risk when exposed to stereotype threat, as evidenced for performance expectancy in Cadinu et al. (2003) and for actual performance in Cadinu et al. (2002).

Together, these studies suggest that some individuals should be considered at high risk for stereotype-related performance deficits, including those who consider the performance domain particularly important, those who identify strongly with their stigmatised ingroup, and those who have internal control beliefs. The role of other potential moderator variables such as high stigma consciousness (Pinel, 2002) remain to be explored.

THE DEVELOPMENT OF STEREOTYPE THREAT

When do stereotype threat effects arise and how early will minority children suffer stereotype-related performance deficits? These questions are extremely important if we want to understand (and possibly prevent) the development of stereotype-driven disadvantages. For stereotype threat effects to occur, children need to have acquired three types of knowledge. First, they need to have developed a concept of social categories (category awareness), second, they need to be able to confidently identify themselves as members of a given category (self-categorisation), and third, they need to be aware of the fact that specific categories are positively or negatively associated with specific domains (stereotype knowledge). When will children meet these criteria? As far as the first prerequisite, category awareness, is concerned, there is evidence that children learn to perceptually distinguish categories such as males vs females by the end of their first year (Fagot & Leinbach, 1993). By age 3, the majority of children are not only able to label social categories correctly but they have also developed a basic awareness of status differences between social groups and start to show ethnic and gender preferences. Thus, although children of that age may not have full understanding of the defining features and the constancy of social groups, they have acquired a basic understanding of social categories (Fagot & Leinbach, 1993).

Turning to the second prerequisite, self-categorisation, 2-year olds still tend to experience uncertainty in defining their own sexual or racial group membership, but by about 3 years of age, children are generally able to confidently identify their own category membership (e.g., Fagot & Leinbach, 1993; Thompson, 1975). Finally, considering stereotype knowledge, there is evidence that, even before 3 years of age, children have some idea about how members of different categories, such as boys and girls, are expected to behave. By the age of 4, they are able to correctly understand specific stereotypic expectancies (Killen, Pisacane, Lee-Kim, Ardila-Rey, 2001; Signorella, Bigler, & Liben, 1993). It is interesting to note that children adopt stereotype-consistent (e.g., gender-appropriate) behaviours long before having mastered group (e.g., gender) constancy (see Fagot & Leinbach, 1993, and Martin, 1993, for overviews). Not surprisingly, such stereotype knowledge is limited to age-relevant domains such as toy/game preferences, appearance, athletic abilities and preferences, future professions, etc; it may not include domains such as mathematics or astrophysics that are beyond the experience of small children. Despite this obvious limit, there is no reason to believe that, in principle, children are unable to experience stereotype threat. By the time they enter school, children have long acquired all of the cognitive prerequisites of stereotype threat including category knowledge, self-categorisation, and stereotype knowledge.

Although it is clear that children acquire these prerequisites very early on, surprisingly little is known about the ways in which this knowledge may affect their performance expectations and their actual performance in stereotype-relevant domains. There is evidence that boys' and girls' achievement beliefs differ in stereotypic ways as early as first grade, and that these beliefs reliably affect subsequent performance. In particular, some studies found that girls already show lower performance expectations in mathematics in their first school year (Eccles, Wigfield, Harold, & Blumenfeld, 1993; Wigfield et al., 1997). Also, both parents' (Tiedemann, 2000) and teachers' gender stereotypes (Keller, 2001) seem to influence the performance expectancies of elementary school children.

More telling about stereotype threat effects in children is a recent series of studies by Ambady et al. (2001) suggesting that stereotypes may directly interfere with performance in relevant domains. In the first study, Asian girls attending elementary or middle school performed worse on a mathematics test when their gender category had been made salient prior to the test than in a no-salience control condition. This was most pronounced for 5-year-olds (K-grade) and for middle school children, whereas upper elementary school children showed a different pattern. Luckily, this same study also suggests that stereotypes may, at times, facilitate performance. An intriguing feature of this study was that in another condition it was the Asian (rather than gender) category that had been activated. In this condition, these girls reformed reliably *better* than in the control condition. In other words, already by 5 years of age, stereotypes may exert either a debilitating or facilitating effect on performance, depending on the positive (Asian–mathematics) or negative (females–mathematics) association between performance domain and social category.

Another, as yet unpublished, study by Good (2001) suggests that gender stereotypes may gain importance with increasing age. Comparing fourth, fifth, and sixth graders, Good found that older girls were particularly concerned about inadvertently confirming the stereotype that associates girls with poor maths performance. Indeed, these older (sixth grade) girls performed worse than boys under stereotype threat, but they actually outperformed boys in the absence of such threat. Taken together, the few available studies on school-aged children suggest that girls may suffer from stereotype threat effects as early as 5 or 6 years of age and that the magnitude of this phenomenon may reach a peak in middle school children (between grade 6 and grade 8). Even very subtle forms of category activation (such as colouring a picture of a girl) seem sufficient to reliably affect performance in stereotype-relevant domains. Unfortunately, nothing is known so far about stereotype-induced performance deficits in children belonging to other stigmatised groups such as Blacks, Hispanics, or Gypsies nor is there any evidence that stereotype threat-induced impediment (or facilitation) is linked to other aspects of cognitive development.

WHAT PROCESSES ARE DRIVING STEREOTYPE THREAT?

While there is little doubt about the pervasiveness and early onset of the phenomenon, the primary challenge currently faced by researchers is the identification of the mechanisms underlying stereotype threat. Different (and often complementary) hypotheses have been formulated, but to this point no single mechanism has emerged as clearly driving stereotype threat.

Anxiety

The first explanation, originally proposed by Steele and Aronson (1995), suggests that minority members are afraid of confirming the stereotype that associates their own group with poor performance in a given domain. In addition to "normal" or baseline anxiety associated with taking difficult tests, minority members may experience further tension due to their preoccupation with inadvertently confirming a negative stereotype. Since high levels of anxiety and arousal have generally been found to be detrimental to task performance on difficult tasks (e.g., Hill & Wigfield, 1984), it is not surprising that stereotype-induced increases in anxiety will interfere with performance. Although the performance-debilitating effects of anxiety are well established in the literature (see Dembo & Eaton, 1997, for an overview), in the earlier work on stereotype threat no effects of stereotype threat on anxiety were found. For example, Steele and Aronson (1995, Exp. 2) measured participants' levels of anxiety immediately after the test and found no effects of stereotype threat on anxiety. Similarly, Aronson et al. (1999) found no effects of stereotype threat on a measure of anxiety taken at the end of the test. Stone et al. (1999) measured anxiety before and after the test and found a general increase in anxiety but this increase was no stronger in the stereotype threat than in the control condition. However, a more promising finding was reported by Spencer et al. (1998, exp. 3), who found that stereotype threat had a marginal effect on anxiety which in turn had a negative effect on performance.

Two recent studies have also provided suggestive evidence that anxiety may play a role in stereotype threat. Osborne (2001) found that race differences in test performance were mediated by anxiety. However, no strong conclusions can be drawn from this study because the mediator variable (anxiety) was measured after the outcome variable (performance).

More telling is a study by Blascovich, Spencer, Quinn, and Steele (2001) who found that African Americans exhibited larger increases in mean arterial blood pressure under stereotype threat than European Americans, a finding that is clearly in line with the anxiety hypothesis. Thus, although empirical proof is limited at this point, there is preliminary evidence that anxiety may play a causal role in stereotype threat.

Intrusive thoughts

A second way in which the fear of confirming negative stereotypes may interfere with performance is via intrusive thoughts. When put under stereotype threat, minority members are subject to dual cognitive demands: on one side, their cognitive resources are occupied by a challenging task, on the other side, they are occupied by thoughts related to the activated stereotype. Thoughts about inadvertently confirming the stereotype are likely to distract the minority member from what should be his or her primary task. So far, there is some evidence that the stereotype is cognitively activated under stereotype threat (see Steele & Aronson, 1995, Exp. 3); what remains to be demonstrated is that stereotype activation reduces cognitive resources available for the primary task, as hypothesised in Steele's model. Although the divided attention hypothesis remains, in our opinion, a strong candidate for explaining stereotype threat, it is still awaiting empirical confirmation.

Shift towards caution

A third possibility is that the activation of the stereotype will increase people's evaluation apprehension in the stereotype-relevant domain which in turn will lead them to be more cautious when providing responses. In other words, the concern about how they will be evaluated, together with a desire to avoid failure, will motivate minority members to exert excessive caution when performing the task. This explanation differs from the previous ones in an important way: Rather than focusing on reduced problem-solving capacities under stereotype threat, this approach hypothesizes a criterion shift when guessing.

Although there is only weak evidence for the mediating role of evaluation apprehension in stereotype threat (e.g., Aronson et al., 1999; Spencer et al., 1999), there is some support for the idea that participants under stereotype threat are reluctant to take risks when responding, resulting in a high number of blank responses (e.g., Aronson et al., 1999, Exp. 2; Croizet & Claire, 1998: Steele & Aronson, 1995). For instance, an unpublished thesis by Mezzapesa (1999–2000) conducted in collaboration with our research team supports the hypothesised shift towards caution.

In this study, Southern Italian high-school students took a difficult logical-mathematical test under three different conditions. In the control condition, no mention was made of their category membership. In the explicit threat condition, they were told that Southern Italian students generally performed worse on this kind of test than Northern Italians. Most importantly, in the implicit threat condition they were required to identify their own category membership ("Southern" vs "Northern") prior to the test, but no explicit mention was made of performance differences. This manipulation is believed to activate, in a subtle way, the widely held stereotype that associates Southern Italians with lower status and lower performance compared to Northern Italians. The results showed that the number of correct responses was reliably lower under stereotype threat, especially when threat was of the implicit kind. These same participants also provided fewer responses and left more problems blank. However, when we looked only at those items for which participants attempted to give a response, then the success rate was at least as good as that in the control group. In other words, threatened students did not make any more mistakes, but they were much more cautious in providing responses and indeed failed to provide responses on a great number of items. Presumably, participants under stereotype threat were more reluctant to provide "educated guesses" whenever they felt uncertain about their responses. Obviously, these data are open to alternative explanations such as effort withdrawal and hence are in need of additional testing. Despite this limit, these findings are in line with the idea that the performance decrement of threatened individuals may be attributable to a more cautious decision criterion rather than to poorer task performance.

Interestingly, Leyens et al. (2000) found a very different pattern for dominant group members exposed to stereotype threat. Threatened men showed impaired performance under threat, attributable to commission (rather than omission) errors. When asked to identify affective words, they shifted their threshold criterion, trying as hard as possible not to miss any such words; this resulted in a great number of false positive responses. One possibility is that low-status and high-status group members use different coping strategies under stereotype threat, the former becoming more cautious, the latter taking greater risks. However, because caution and risk taking have been operationalised differently in the different studies, no conclusion can be drawn at this point.

On the methodological side, the results of the above studies suggest that researchers should construct performance measures so that erroneous responses can be clearly distinguished from non-responses, as they may reflect distinct psychological processes.

Performance expectancy

A fourth potential mechanism of the stereotype threat effect is the individual's level of expectancy regarding his or her performance. According to this perspective, stereotype threat may decrease performance expectancies that in turn may impair performance. Such a self-fulfilling cycle assumes (a) that stereotype threat reduces minority members' level of expectancy regarding their task performance and (b) that reduced expectancies will produce a performance decrement. Distinct from other explanations of stereotype threat, this explanation focuses on the initial stage in which people evaluate the subjective likelihood of success depending on their personal resources. Because personal resources are often anchored to group-level expectations, ingroup-threatening information (e.g., "women are less competent in maths") may reduce personal expectancies about doing well. In line with this idea, Stangor, Carr and Kiang (1998) found that participants had consistently lower performance expectancies under stereotype threat even if they had received positive feedback on a previous test. However, Stangor et al.'s research (1998) does not provide any information about the link between expectancy and performance as no actual performance data were collected. To date, there are only a few studies that have investigated the potentially mediating role of performance expectancy in stereotype threat, but findings are not entirely consistent.

The link between expectancy and performance was addressed in two unpublished studies (reported in Steele & Aronson, 1995) in which performance expectations were experimentally manipulated after stereotype threat, but no effects on performance were found. A problem with experimental expectancy manipulations is that they may not only conflict with the stereotype threat manipulation, but they may also be too weak to override the participant's personally held beliefs. Rather than manipulating expectancies experimentally, we have recently focused on the participants' personal performance expectancies and have tried to untangle their relation with performance (Cadinu et al., 2003). In our first study, female university students were assigned to one of three experimental conditions. They were either told that women generally perform worse on logical-mathematical tests than males (stereotype threat condition), or that they perform as well as males (control condition), or that women generally outperform males (counter-stereotypical information).[2] Later, they were given a difficult maths

---

[2]To increase the credibility of the manipulation, participants were told that research investigating performance differences in different areas of cognition generally finds no differences between men and women. However, there are some areas in which differences do emerge. One of them concerns logical-mathematical abilities where women obtain higher (or lower, depending on condition) scores than men. To underline the veridicality of this statement,

test and asked to estimate their performance prior to taking the test. Not surprisingly, participants who considered mathematics *un*important were not affected by the manipulation. In contrast, participants who considered mathematical-logical abilities an important domain were highly sensitive to the manipulation both with regard to performance expectancies and actual performance. They were most optimistic about their future performance after receiving counter-stereotypical information and least optimistic under stereotype threat. Consistent with these expectations, they did indeed perform best after counter-stereotypical, and hence ingroup-favouring, information but showed a sharp decline in performance under stereotype threat. Most important, mediational analyses suggest that actual performance was partially mediated by expectancies.

A second experiment, reported in an earlier section of this chapter, involved Black Americans living in Italy. These participants were either made aware of their Black identity, a category with a long history of stigmatisation, or of their American identity, a high-status category. In both cases, participants were given either favourable or unfavourable information about how well Blacks (compared to Whites) or Americans (compared to Italians) performed on verbal tests. Regardless of whether their Black or American identity had been activated, participants had lower expectations (see Figure 1) and under-performed after receiving negative information about the in-group (see Figure 2). However, the level of expectancy was found to mediate the decrease in performance for participants in the Black but not in the American condition. Together, these two studies suggest that pessimistic performance expectancies may be one mechanism through which stereotypes induce performance deficits. At the same time, both studies suggest that expectancies are not the only process mediating stereotype-related performance decline, considering that there was evidence for partial but not for full mediation. As discussed earlier, our second study has another implication, namely that apparently identical performance deficits in low- (women, Blacks) and high-status groups (men, Whites) may in reality be driven by distinct processes. When there is a history of stigmatisation, ingroup-threatening information (or the mere activation of the category) may be sufficient to induce reduced expectancies which in turn lead to reduced performance. In high status groups, expectancies seem to play no mediating role in threat-induced performance decrements. Thus, although comparable performance deficits are found for low- and high-status group members, the underlying processes may be quite different.

---

a fictional research study was referred to and a graph was shown supposedly summarising "*the results obtained by men and women based on 72 studies, 36 of which employed randomized samples of men and women (Adapted from Taylor, Sheatsley, & Greeley, 1998)*".

Performance expectancy

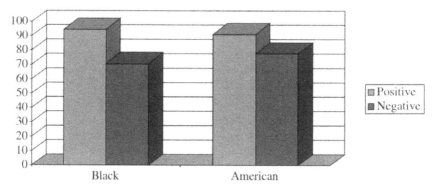

Figure 1. Expectancy as a function of Category Membership (Black vs American) and Type of Information (positive vs negative) (Cadinu et al. 2002, Exp. 2).

Performance

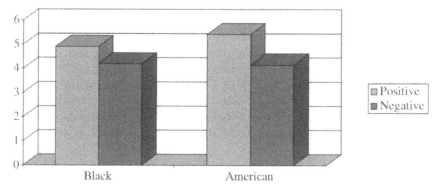

Figure 2. Performance as a function of Category Membership (Black vs American) and Type of Information (positive vs negative) (Cadinu et al. 2002, Exp. 2).

Disengagement and effort withdrawal

Whereas the four processes discussed so far deal mainly with momentary stereotype threat, a fifth and last mechanism, disengagement and effort withdrawal, focuses on long-term effects. According to the stereotype threat model, minorities may, in the long run, "disidentify" from the relevant performance domain. Distancing oneself from a domain fulfills a self-protective function ("maths is irrelevant to my self-concept") but it also implies effort withdrawal and, hence, poor performance. For example, women asked to perform a typically masculine task, such as playing chess, may have learned to consider this domain irrelevant, possibly due to repeated stereotype threat experiences. As a consequence, they may put very little effort into solving a difficult chess problem. Ironically, these women (or low-status group members in general) are not particularly vulnerable to the momentary activation of the stereotype, exactly because they have already disengaged from the domain in prior stages of their learning history. As mentioned earlier, indirect support for this hypothesis comes from different studies showing that stereotype threat effects were only present for participants highly identified with the testing domain (Cadinu et al., 2003, Exp. 1; Spencer et al., 1999). In contrast, participants with high involvement in the domain (for example women who consider chess important and indicative of their intellectual capacities) will suffer momentary stereotype threat effects. It is important to point out that the stereotype threat-induced performance deficit of these women or minority members cannot be attributed to effort withdrawal. To our knowledge, there is no evidence to date that these participants put less effort into the task or that they are less persistent during task performance. Apparently, these women underperform for reasons other than effort withdrawal. Nevertheless, it would be important for future research to measure participants' level of effort and persistence on the task.

In general, demotivation and reduced effort seem to be typical of those low-status group members who have withdrawn from the domain but it does not seem to account for performance deficits of highly involved minorities under momentary stereotype threat. Although the long-term effects of stereotype threat are very interesting, we will not consider them any further as they are beyond the scope of this chapter.

Taken together, there is no definite answer as to which mechanisms are driving stereotype threat. Different authors have hypothesised and tested different potential mediators, but to date none of these has received unequivocal support. To complicate things further, the results obtained so far suggest that not all stereotype threat effects may be attributable to a single process. Thus, we may be faced with a multifaceted phenomenon that is the joint function of different psychological mechanisms.

RELATION TO OTHER THEORIES

More than other sciences psychology has at times been accused of childhood amnesia. Principles and phenomena that had been known in the early years of psychology are no longer accessible to the collective memory of the discipline and are therefore "rediscovered" under new headings and enthusiastically greeted by the forgetful scientific community. At first glance, the stereotype threat model seems to be such a case. Self-fulfilling prophecies have been known to sociologists as well as social and educational psychologists since the 1940s (Merton, 1948). In particular, research conducted on the Pygmalion effect during the 1960s (Rosenthal, 1994; Rosenthal & Jacobson, 1968) has demonstrated the powerful effect of teacher expectations on the (objectively measured) performance of their students. More recently, Eccles and collaborators have extended and integrated these findings within expectancy-value theory of achievement motivation (cf. Eccles, Wigfield, & Schiefele, 1998; Wigfield & Eccles, 2000). Considering this long tradition, one may suspect that stereotype threat is nothing more than a specific case of behavioural stereotype confirmation. We will briefly examine this possibility as it is important to understand to which degree the stereotype threat model contributes beyond previous ones. In particular, there are two previous models, self-fulfilling prophecy and expectancy-value model, that seem to cover the same ground, and a further model, attributional ambiguity, that appears to be a contrasting approach.

Self-fulfilling prophecy

Looking first at self-fulfilling prophecies (Jussim, 1986; Snyder & Haugen, 1995; Snyder & Stukas, 1999), this phenomenon is generally conceptualised as a three-step chain of events. First, person A holds expectations about a target person B that are often (although not exclusively) based on stereotypic beliefs about B's category membership, including race, gender, religion, social class, nationality, etc. Second, these expectations guide A's behaviour in interaction with person B. Third, person A's behaviour, in turn, influences B's behaviour in a way that confirms the initial expectations of person A. Importantly, the target person B is generally unaware of both person A's expectancies and of changes in his/her own behaviour (cf. Vorauer & Miller, 1997). Also, research has consistently shown that it is the low-status or low-power target person who inadvertently confirms the expectancies held by a powerful interaction partner (cf. Copeland, 1994; see Snyder & Stukas, 1999, for an overview). This situation is quite similar to the stereotype threat situation where it is generally the member of a stigmatised minority who suffers the greatest performance deficits. Thus, in many ways, the self-fulfilling cycle described by Snyder and collaborators seems to resemble the stereotype threat model in which stereotypic beliefs (e.g., women are incompetent in maths) produce stereotype-confirming behaviours (decline in performance).

However, there are two important differences between these models. First of all, the self-fulfilling prophecy model requires the presence of an interaction partner who exerts a guiding influence and elicits reactions from the target person that conform to initial expectations. Hence, the behaviour of the interaction partner *A* is essential in modifying the behaviour of target person *B*. Stereotypes exert an influence on the target's behaviour *only* through the mediating role of the person holding the stereotypes. This is quite different from the stereotype threat model, according to which stereotypes, once activated in the mind of the target (low-status group member), can interfere with task performance even in the absence of any other person. Thus, in both cases, stereotypes influence the behaviour of the minority target in a self-confirming way, but the causal link between the stereotype and the confirmatory behaviour are quite different. In the self-fulfilling prophecy cycle, it is the prejudiced interaction partner who mediates this effect, whereas in the stereotype threat model the activation of the stereotype in the mind of the target is sufficient to produce changes in the target's behaviour or performance.

Second, the two models differ in the importance assigned to the target's awareness of stereotypic expectancies. Self-fulfilling prophecies generally occur when the target person is *unaware* of the negative expectancies. When the target person realises that the interaction partner holds negative expectancies, s/he usually makes attempts to disconfirm these expectancies. There is now considerable evidence in the self-fulfilling prophecy literature suggesting that targets of stereotyping are likely to engage in behavioural *dis*-confirmation if they are aware of the stereotypic expectancies held by others (e.g., Hilton & Darley, 1985; Stukas & Snyder, 2002). Thus, self-fulfilling prophecies require that the target be unaware of the negative stereotypic expectancies. To the contrary, stereotype threat effects require awareness. Indeed, stereotypes will not affect performance unless they are activated in the test situation. Taken together, the two models both hypothesise a self-sustaining cycle of stereotypes, but they assume different underlying mechanisms and operate under different boundary conditions.

Expectancy value theory

The second model that seems to overlap with the stereotype threat model is expectancy value theory. According to this model, achievement-related choices and performance are determined by both subjective task value and expectation of success which, in turn, depend on a great number of predictor variables (see Wigfield & Eccles, 2000, for a recent version of the model).

Among these variables are stereotypes. The culturally shared stereotypes, transmitted during socialisation especially by parents, affect the child's self-schemata, goals, and, in particular, his/her ability, beliefs and subjective probability of success in stereotype-relevant domains. Thus, expectancy value theory emphasises, among others, the role of expectancy in determining the level of performance (Eccles et al., 1998; Wigfield, 1994; Wigfield & Eccles, 1992). In this model, people's performance can be explained (a) by their beliefs about how well they will do on a given task and (b) by the extent to which they value the task. Both of these are, in part, determined by stereotypes.

There is obviously considerable conceptual overlap between stereotype threat and the expectancy value model, but again, each theory has distinct features that make it unique. The first concerns the underlying processes. Whereas expectation of success is a critical mediator in the expectancy value model, stereotype threat may or may not be mediated by this same process. As mentioned earlier, there is only limited evidence that stereotype threat is mediated by reduced expectancies, and different alternative explanations remain open, including the possibility that the low-status group member makes a conscious attempt to disconfirm the stereotype. This has potentially important theoretical implications. Whereas the expectancy value framework assumes that the member of a stigmatised group has incorporated the prejudiced world view in his/her self-schemata and values, such an internalisation is unnecessary from the perspective of the stereotype threat model. The stigmatised person may disagree entirely with culturally shared stereotypes, but may still suffer stereotype-induced performance deficits due to intrusive thoughts, anxiety, or a shift towards caution. Another fundamental difference between the two lines of research is that research within the expectancy value model generally focuses on relatively stable, long-term effects of stereotypes (often investigated in longitudinal designs) whereas the stereotype threat model focuses on contextually situated stereotype activation.

In sum, the stereotype threat model seems to make a series of distinct predictions that make it a complementary rather than a redundant model with respect to previous theories.

Attributional ambiguity model

Whereas the self-fulfilling prophecy and the value-expectancy model seem to converge in many aspects with the stereotype threat model, there is another approach that is in apparent contrast. Readers may have noticed a surface contradiction between the stereotype threat model and earlier work on attributional ambiguity. With reference to Dion's (1975) and Crocker and Major's (1989) earlier work, Major et al. argue (in this volume) that stereotype awareness may at times have beneficial consequences for low-status group members. In situations in which stereotypes are salient and low-status group members experience failure, they may be protected against self-esteem loss exactly because they can attribute failure to prejudice rather than to a personal lack of abilities.

At first glance, it may be surprising that the same conditions, namely stereotype activation, may, on the one hand, lead to a performance deficit (or failure) while, on the other hand, bolstering the minority's self-esteem. This apparent paradox represents a challenging question for future research. Unfortunately, we are not aware of any studies in which stereotype threat-induced performance deficits and self-esteem protection have been shown within a single experimental paradigm. Theoretically, it is conceivable that the two effects coexist.

At the same time, we should also point to a number of differences between the two areas of study, stereotype threat and attributional ambiguity, that render a direct comparison difficult. Besides focusing on different aspects of human behaviour (performance vs self-esteem), the two areas also differ in their operational definition of stereotype awareness. Within Major et al.'s paradigm, self-esteem protection is contingent on the belief that the evaluator holds negative stereotypes about the target's own group. In other words, in Major et al.'s model, real or presumed prejudice of the evaluator is essential to protect failing minorities from self-esteem loss. In stereotype threat research, however, stereotype awareness is defined as a more abstract consciousness that there are socially shared stereotypes about one's own group. Stereotype-induced deficits require that the stereotype is activated in the mind of the minority test-taker and may well occur in the absence of any presumed evaluator bias (for example, on an electronically graded maths test). In conclusion, stereotypes have a different conceptual status in the two models and it remains to be seen whether they can simultaneously function as a barrier to performance and a buffer against self-esteem loss.

Taken together, there are multiple conceptual links between stereotype threat and other models including self-fulfilling prophecy, expectancy value, and attributional ambiguity. This brief comparative overview suggests that each of these models has a unique domain of application and makes distinct assumptions about underlying processes, although one may envisage the future development of a more general integrative model.

APPLICATIONS

The areas of application of stereotype threat are virtually unlimited. Whenever members of stigmatised groups engage in a task that is, according to socially shared stereotypes, negatively associated with their social category, there are opportunities for stereotype threat to occur if the category and/or stereotype is made salient. To date, most studies have focused either on Blacks or on women, although stereotype threat effects have also been observed for other stigmatised groups such as low social class (Croizet & Claire, 1998) or elderly people (Maass et al., 2002). With few exceptions (Stone et al., 1999), research has generally analysed stereotype threat effects in different academic domains (maths, verbal tests, etc.), but in principle there is no reason to believe that stereotype threat is limited to these cases. For example, will the widely shared stereotype of female drivers affect the actual driving behaviour of women? What will happen to the concentration of the lonely female chess player faced with 40 male players in a room where an important tournament is taking place? Although females are quite successful in chess as youngsters, how come they are practically absent as chess masters? Does the stereotype of chess as a typically male activity play a role in this? As these few examples illustrate, potential (as yet unexplored) areas of application are practically unlimited.

In our opinion, a particularly interesting and potentially controversial application is affirmative action. There is little doubt that affirmative action is a useful tool to enhance the number of women or minority members in industry, public services, and educational institutions (for an overview see Valian, 1998). At the same time, affirmative action has various negative consequences for those hired under affirmative action rules. In particular, these minority members tend to be less satisfied with their job (Chacko, 1982), they tend to be judged less competent by their colleagues (Heilman, Block, & Lucas, 1992), and they have less trust in their own abilities (Heilman, Lucas, & Kaplow, 1990). One possible explanation of this latter finding is that affirmative action rules activate existing gender and/or race stereotypes. Imagine a woman taking an entrance examination for a prestigious university or to participate in a job selection under affirmative action rules. Affirmative action rules indirectly activate existing gender stereotypes, as they offer legal and institutional protection to members of disadvantaged groups that are subject to discrimination and presumed by some members of society to be less capable. Applying the stereotype threat model to this situation, we would expect women to do less well on admission/hiring tests if they are aware of the affirmative action laws.

First evidence for this possibility comes from a series of studies investigating the effects of (real or presumed) preferential selection on actual performance (Brown, Charnangavej, Keough, Newman, & Pentfrow, 2000; Turner & Pratkanis, 1993). Of particular relevance to our argument is the study reported by Brown et al. investigating the performance of students at the University of Texas belonging to academically stigmatised (Black and Latino) or non-stigmatised groups (White and Asian). The authors found that students belonging to stigmatised groups showed greater suspicion that they *may* have received preferential treatment at admission to the university. Compared to those belonging to non-stigmatised groups, they had also obtained lower GPAs (US college grades) during their first year. Most importantly, the effect of group membership on GPA was reliably mediated by suspicion of preferential treatment. Thus, the mere suspicion of low-status minority members that they may have been admitted to a university (or job) on the basis of affirmative action may be sufficient to impair their performance. Assuming that affirmative action is a potent reminder of stereotypes associating low-status groups with low performance, Brown et al's findings seem consistent with a stereotype threat account, although they are also open to different interpretations.

Along the same line, we have recently conducted a study (Carnaghi, Maass, Benetti, & Callegari, 2003, Exp. 1), in which students were led to believe that they could obtain a desirable short-term job.[3] Job selection was based on a mathematics test, a domain in which women are assumed to do poorly according to socially shared stereotypes. The hiring criterion was varied so that it was either based on merit (the best candidate would be hired) or on an affirmative action rule that either favoured men or women.[4]

We expected that the introduction of an affirmative action rule would make gender highly salient. Indeed, regardless of whether men or women were favoured by the affirmative action rule, a word completion task indicated that gender-related concepts were much more accessible to participants under affirmative action than under the merit rule. Also, overall performance was much better under the merit than under the affirmative action rule. This is not surprising considering that the hiring decision is entirely contingent on the participant's performance under the merit rule, but only partially under the affirmative action rule. Thus, participants should invest greater energy and effort into the task when the decision is purely merit-based. More interesting is another prediction: If affirmative action rules activate stereotypes, then, following Steele's model, women should perform particularly poorly under affirmative action rules regardless of whether the rules favoured women or men. Our data tend to confirm this prediction. Under affirmative action, performance loss (compared to the merit condition) for men was 20% when women were favoured by the affirmative action rules and 23% when men were favoured. For women participants, the performance loss

---

[3]In reality, the money was distributed equally across participants after debriefing.

[4]In both cases, the application of the affirmative action rule was justified on the basis of the information that "the number of men (women) who had applied for this job was inferior to the number of women (men) applicants and that it seemed appropriate to guarantee a reasonable representation of men (women)"

was 38% when men were favoured and reached 47% when their own group, women, were favoured.

If confirmed by future studies, these results suggest that explicit affirmative action rules may activate existing stereotypes which, in turn, may lead to a (stereotype-confirming) decline in performance among minority members. The same minority member who would perform well under merit rules may show considerable deficits under affirmative action. Ironically, the very affirmative action programme that was developed to protect low-status minority members against bias may harm their actual performance.

To be perfectly clear, we do *not* suggest that affirmative action be abolished. On the basis of the above results, we simply want to argue that affirmative action rules may inadvertently activate existing stereotypes in the minority's mind and hence interfere with his or her performance. As Brown et al.'s findings suggest, the mere suspicion of receiving preferential treatment may be sufficient to undermine a minority person's performance. If confirmed by future studies, companies and universities may be well advised to reassure minority members that merit (rather than group membership) played a crucial role in their hiring or admission. Also, it may be wise not to advertise affirmative action in close proximity to the selection procedure since this may hinder (rather than facilitate) the minority's performance. We do believe that affirmative action is a useful tool for increasing minority participation in institutions in which they are under-represented. At the same time, precautions should be taken to protect the target of preferential treatment against the potentially damaging effects of stereotype activation that, unfortunately, are likely to accompany any affirmative action rule.

PREVENTING STEREOTYPE THREAT

The ultimate goal of stereotype threat research is to identify strategies that are able to prevent (or even invert) stereotype-related performance deficits. To date, five different strategies have been investigated. The first, and most straightforward method is to provide counter-stereotypical information (Spencer et al., 1999). For example, in one of our studies we provided information that women are doing better than men (Cadinu et al., 2003). The disadvantage of this method is that the information may at times not be credible enough to override widely held beliefs.

The second strategy is to activate, within the stigmatised group, a different category membership that is not negatively linked to the task domain. This may either be achieved by varying the comparative intergroup context or by having people think about themselves in terms of different category memberships. An example of the former strategy is to tell students that a given maths test is administered with the explicit goal of comparing American vs Canadians (rather than males vs females). This procedure seems able to cancel the gender gap in maths performance (see Walsh, Hickey, & Duffy, 1999). An excellent example of this strategy is also provided by the work of Ambady, Shih and collaborators discussed earlier (Ambady et al., 2001; Shih et al., 1999).

The third prevention strategy is to modify the test label so as to eliminate any link to the category. For example, labelling a logical-mathematical test as measuring "social intelligence" seems sufficient to reliably increase the performance of women (see study by Cadinu et al., 2002, described earlier).

A fourth strategy has recently been proposed by Aronson, Fried, and Good (2002). With reference to Dweck's (1999) model, these authors argued that teaching Black students to endorse an incremental rather than an entity theory of intelligence would make them less vulnerable to stereotype threat. In a very clever design, Black students were made to believe that they were going to tutor younger students with academic problems and hence in need of encouragement. Half of the students were instructed to convince their younger pen pals that intelligence was malleable and may expand with hard work (incremental theory). The remaining participants were also told to encourage their pen pals, but this time the multifaceted nature of intelligence was stressed rather than its malleability. Unbeknown to the participants, the manipulation served to change their own mind set. Results showed that training students to adopt an incremental theory of intelligence reliably improved their attitudes towards academics as well as their actual grades. Thus, reshaping minority members' implicit beliefs about intelligence may protect them against the debilitating effects of stereotype threat, without modifying their perception of stereotype threat itself.

A fifth strategy that has produced promising results is the introduction of a counter-stereotypical role model (Maass et al., 2002; Marx & Roman, 2002; McIntyre, Paulson, & Lord, 2003). Evidence for the potential role of a counter-stereotypical role model as a buffer against stereotype threat comes from a recent article by Marx and Roman (2002, Exps. 2 and 3). The authors tested the hypothesis that learning about a competent female role model would protect women against the debilitating effects of stereotype threat on a difficult maths test. Indeed, in both studies female students performed significantly better after learning about another, similar female student with good (rather than poor) maths abilities.

In McIntyre et al.'s (2003) research, women participants learned about other women's achievements in domains such as architecture or medicine that had no obvious link to mathematics. In the control condition, participants read the same success stories, but this time they were attributed to gender-unspecific companies. The performance of participants exposed to successful female role models was reliably better than that of women who had read the same success stories referred to companies. Thus, it is not the success story *per se*, but the successful female role model that seems to remove stereotype-related barriers.

We have recently extended this reasoning to a very different population, name elderly people. In an as yet unpublished study by Maass et al. (2002), we asked people over 65 years of age (whose age had been made salient) to take a series of memory tests, including a text recall and an object recognition test. In the stereotype threat baseline condition, participants were simply told that these tests measured memory, information that was sufficient to activate the widely held idea of age-related memory deficits. Not surprisingly, our participants performed very poorly in this condition. In the second condition (counter-stereotypical information) they were told that, for the particular type of memory investigated here, there was no age-related decline and, indeed, elderly people often performed better than younger ones. This manipulation strongly and reliably improved performance both on recall and recognition. In the third, and most interesting condition, the same instructions were provided as in the baseline condition, but this time a counter-stereotypical role model was introduced. Participants were told that the study was promoted by the (fictitious) Levi-Montalcini Institute and a recent photograph of the well-known Nobel Prize winner Levi-Montalcini (at the age of 92) appeared on the cover page of the test. Interestingly, the presence of an elderly role model with exceptional intellectual abilities had an enormous, facilitating effect on our participants. When Levi-Montalcini was introduced as a role model, participants not only outperformed those in the baseline condition, they even improved somewhat beyond the condition in which explicit counter-stereotypical information had been provided. A subsequent study showed that the Nobel Prize winner could serve as a role model for our elderly participants only if she was of high age; the model of a younger Nobel Prize winner was unable to improve memory performance. Taken together, these studies suggest that counter-stereotypical role models provide an efficient and easily applicable strategy for reducing undesirable stereotype threat effects.

Although not all of the methods outlined here may be equally appropriate for all applied settings (e.g., it may not be very credible if a maths teacher claims to assess social abilities in a test), we believe that they are a promising starting point for the development of prevention strategies.

CONCLUSION

Only few years have passed since Steele and Aronson's (1995) groundbreaking work on stereotype threat, but during these few years a great number of researchers around the world have been intrigued by this model and by its applied implications. Minority members already face numerous barriers to success including economic and cultural disadvantages and prejudiced attitudes of teachers and employers that may bias performance evaluation, hiring decisions etc. Steele and Aronson's model suggests that, in addition to these external barriers, members of stigmatised groups also seem to be vulnerable to a much more subtle, but equally powerful impact of stereotypes. In many test situations, minority members are disadvantaged simply because their category membership is activated together with the stereotypes that go along with it. The mere activation of stereotypes in the test situation seems sufficient to produce a reliable interference, resulting in greatly reduced performance. As our brief overview of the literature shows, this idea has now received remarkable support in very different paradigms, with different minority populations, and in a wide variety of performance domains. Although many issues, including the identification of the under-lying processes, pose challenges for future research, the fast growing body of literature (including our own work reported here) is largely supportive of the basic predictions of the stereotype threat model. Even a short-lived activation of task relevant stereotypes is sufficient to induce performance deficits in those belonging to stigmatised social groups.

At first sight, the stereotype threat model seems to offer a very pessimistic outlook, as it suggests that even the most subtle reminder of the minority's membership in a stigmatised group reduces its chances of success. But fortunately the very same model can also be read in a positive light as it offers insights into how to explain (apparent) differences in performance and how to remove important barriers to performance. Many social groups such as women, Blacks, and the elderly have been found to perform poorly in specific domains such as chess and maths for women, verbal abilities for Blacks, and memory tasks for the elderly. If Steele and Aronson's model is correct, then such under-performance is, at least in part, attributable to stereotype threat rather than to deeper deficits in domain-relevant capacities. Ultimately, it may be much easier to remove stereotype activation from test situations (e.g., by eliminating gender or race identification, by changing test labels, or by introducing successful role models) than to compensate for profound deficits.

Clearly future research is faced with many difficult tasks. One is to achieve a better understanding of the processes underlying stereotype threat deficits, both for minority and majority members. Second, because not all individuals may be equally vulnerable to the effects of stereotype threat, it is crucial to identify those personal characteristics that may either protect or put individuals at higher risk for stereotype-confirming performance. Third, it is important to identify social contexts and situational constraints (such as unbalanced numerical work settings) that are particularly conducive for stereotype threat effects to emerge. Finally, we are left with the important and most challenging task of proposing applied research and promoting prevention programmes to weaken or override the detrimental effects of stereotype threat.

REFERENCES

Allport, G .W. (1954). *The nature of prejudice*. Reading, MA: Edison-Wesley.

Ambady, N., Shih, M., Kim, A., & Pittinsky, T. L. (2001). Stereotype susceptibility in children: Effects of identity activation on Quantitative performance. *Psychological Science, 12*, 385–390.

Aronson, J., Fried, C. B., & Good, C. (2002). Reducing the effects of stereotype threat on African American college students by shaping theories of intelligence. *Journal of Experimental Social Psychology, 38*, 113–125.

Aronson, J., Lustina, M. J., Good, C., Keough, K., Steele, C. M., & Brown, J. (1999). When white men can't do math: Necessary and sufficient factors in stereotype threat. *Journal of Experimental Social Psychology, 35*, 29–46.

Blascovich, J., Spencer, S. J., Quinn, D., & Steele, C. (2001). African Americans and high blood pressure: The role of stereotype threat. *Psychological Science, 12*, 225–229.

Brown, R. P., Charnangavej, T., Keough, K. A., Newman, M. L., & Pentfrow, P. J. (2000). Putting the "affirm" into affirmative action: Preferential selection and academic performance. *Journal of Personality and Social Psychology, 79*, 736–747.

Cadinu, M., Maass, A., Frigerio, S., Impagliazzo, L., & Latinotti, S. (2003). Stereotype threat: The effect of expectancy on performance. *European Journal of Social Psychology, 33*, 267–285.

Cadinu, M., Maass, A., & Lombardo, M. (2002). *Stereotype threat: The moderating role of individual differences*. Manuscript submitted for publication.

Carnaghi, A., Maass, A., Benetti, A., & Callegari, L. (2003). *Affirmative action: Turning a pro-minority policy into a barrier*. Unpublished manuscript: Padova University.

Chacko, T. I. (1982). Women and equal employment opportunity: Some unintended effects. *Journal of Applied Psychology, 67*, 119–123

Cheryan, S., & Bodenhausen, G. V. (2000). When positive stereotypes threaten intellectual performance: The psychological hazards of "Model Minority" status. *Psychological Science, 11*, 399–402.

Copeland, J. T. (1994). Prophecies of power: Motivational implications of social power for behavioural confirmation. *Journal of Personality and Social Psychology, 67*, 264–277.

Crocker, J., & Major, B. (1989). Social stigma and self-esteem: The self-protective properties of stigma. *Psychological Review, 96*, 608–630.

Croizet, J., & Claire, T. (1998). Extending the concept of stereotype and threat to social class: The intellectual underperformance of students from low socio-economic background. *Personality and Social Psychology Bulletin, 24*, 588–594.

Dembo, M. H., & Eaton, M. J. (1997). School learning and motivation. In G. D. Phye (Ed.), *Handbook of academic learning: Construction of knowledge. The educational psychology series*. (pp. 65–103). San Diego, CA: Academic Press.

Dion, K. L. (1975). Women's reactions to discrimination from members of the same or opposite sex. *Journal of Research in Personality, 9*, 294–306.

Dweck, C. S. (1999). *Self-theories: their role in motivation, personality and development*. Hove, UK: Psychology Press.

Eccles, J. S., Wigfield, A., Harold, R. D., & Blumenfeld, P. (1993). Age and gender differences in children's self- and task perceptions during elementary school. *Child-Development, 64*, 830–847.

Eccles, J. S., Wigfield, A., & Schiefele, U. (1998). Motivation to succeed. In W. Damon (Series Ed.) & N. Eisenberg (Vol. Ed.), *Handbook of child psychology* (5th ed., Vol. III, pp. 1017–1095). New York: Wiley.

Fagot, B. I., & Leinbach, M. D. (1993). Gender-role development in young children: From discrimination to labeling. *Developmental-Review, 1993*, 205–224.

Good, C. D. (2001). *The development of stereotype threat and its relation to theories of intelligence: Effects on elementary school girls' mathematics achievement and task choices.* Unpublished Doctoral Thesis, University of Texas at Austin.

Heilman, M. E., Block, C. J., & Lucas, J. A. (1992). Presumed incompetent? Stigmatization and affirmative action efforts. *Journal of Applied Psychology, 77*, 536–544.

Heilman, M. E., Lucas, J. A., & Kaplow, S. R. (1990). Self-derogating consequences of sex-based preferential selection: The moderating role of initial self-confidence. *Organizational Behaviour and Human Decision Processes, 46*, 202–216.

Hill, K. T., & Wigfield, A. (1984). Test anxiety: A major educational problem and what can we do about it. *Elementary School Journal, 85*, 105–126.

Hilton, J. L., & Darley, J. M. (1985). Constructing other people: A limit on the effect. *Journal of Experimental Social Psychology, 21*, 1–18.

Inzlicht, M., & Ben-Zeev, T. (2000). A threatening intellectual environment: Why females are susceptible to experiencing problem-solving deficits in the presence of males. *Psychological Science, 11*, 365–371

Jussim, L. (1986). Self-fulfilling prophecies: A theoretical and integrative review. *Psychological Review, 93*, 429–445.

Keller, C. (2001). Effect of teachers' stereotyping on students' stereotyping of mathematics as a male domain. *Journal of Social Psychology, 141*, 165–173.

Killen, M., Pisacane, J., Lee-Kim, J, & Ardila-Rey, A. (2001). Fairness or stereotypes? Young children's priorities when evaluating group exclusion and inclusion. *Developmental Psychology, 37*, 587–596.

Leyens, J.-P., Désert, M., Croizet, J.-C., & Darcis, C. (2000). Stereotype threat: Are lower status and history of stigmatization preconditions of stereotype threat? *Personality and Social Psychology Bulletin, 26*, 1189–1199.

Maass, A., Cadinu, M., Verga, S., & Crimaldi, S. (2002). *Preventing stereotype-induced memory deficits among the elderly: The Levi-Montalcini effect* (unpublished manuscript).

Major, B., McCoy, S. K., Kaiser, C. R., & Quinton, W. J. (this volume). Prejudice and self-esteem: A transactional model. *European Review of Social Psychology, 14*, 77–104.

Martin, C. L. (1993). New directions for investigating children's gender knowledge. *Developmental Review, 13*, 184–204.

Marx, T., & Roman, J. S. (2002). Female role models: Protecting women's math test performance. *Personality and Social Psychology Bulletin, 28*, 1183–1193.

McIntyre, R. B., Paulson, R. M., & Lord, C. G. (2003). Alleviating women's mathematics stereptype threat through salience of group achievements. *Journal of Experimental Social Psychology, 39*, 83–90.

Merton, R. K. (1948). The self-fulfilling prophecy. *Antioch Review, 8*, 192–210.

Mezzapesa (1999–2000). *La minaccia legata allo stereotipo: Effetti su un campione di meridionali* [Stereotype threat: Effects on a Southern-Italian sample]. Unpublished Laurea Thesis, University of Padova.

Osborne, J. W. (2001). Testing stereotype threat: Does anxiety explain race and sex differences in achievement? *Contemporary Educational Psychology, 26*, 291–310.

Pinel, E. C. (2002). Stigma consciousness in intergroup contexts: the power of conviction. *Journal of Experimental Social Psychology, 38*, 178–185.

Pintrich, P. R., Marx, R. W, & Boyle, R. A. (1993). Beyond cold conceptual change: The role of motivational beliefs and classroom contextual factors in the process of conceptual change. *Review of Educational Research, 63*, 167–199.

Rosenthal, R. (1994). Interpersonal expectancy effects: A 30-year perspective. *Current Directions in Psychological Science, 3*, 176–179.

Rosenthal, R., & Jacobson, L. (1968). *Pygmalion in the classroom.* New York: Holt, Rinehart & Winston.

Schmader, T. (2002). Gender identification moderates stereotype threat effects on women's math performance. *Journal of Experimental Social Psychology, 38*, 194–201.

Sekaquaptewa, D., & Thompson, M. (2003). Solo status, stereotype threat, and performance expectancies: Their effects on women's performance. *Journal of Experimental Social Psychology, 39*, 68–74.

Shih, M., Pittinsky, T. L., & Ambady, N. (1999). Stereotype susceptibility: Identity salience and shifts in quantitative performance. *Psychological-Science, 10*, 80–83.

Signorella, M. L., Bigler, R. S., & Liben, L. S. (1993). Developmental difffferences in children's gender schemata about others: A meta-analytic review. *Developmental Review, 13*, 147–183.

Snyder, M., & Haugen, J. A. (1995). Why does behavioural confirmation occur? A functional perspective on the role of the target. *Personality and Social Psychology Bulletin, 21*, 963–974.

Snyder, M., & Stukas, A. A. (1999). Interpersonal processes: The interplay of cognitive, motivational, and behavioural activities in social interaction. *Annual Review of Psychology, 50*, 273–303.

Spencer, S. J., Steele, C. M., & Quinn, D. M. (1999). Stereotype threat and women's math performance. *Journal of Experimental Social Psychology, 35*, 4–28.

Stangor, C., Carr, C., & Kiang, L. (1998). Activating stereotypes undermines task performance expectations. *Journal of Personality And Social Psychology, 75*, 1191–1187.

Steele, C. M., & Aronson, J. (1995). Stereotype threat and the intellectual test performance of African Americans. *Journal of Personality and Social Psychology, 69*, 797–811.

Stone, J., Lynch, C. I., Sjomeling, M., Darley, J. M. (1999). Stereotype threat effects on Black and White athletic performance. *Journal of Personality and Social Psychology, 77*, 1213–1227.

Stukas, A. A., & Snyder, M. (2002). Target's awareness of expectations and behavioural confirmation in ongoing interactions. *Journal of Experimental Social Psychology, 38*, 31–40.

Svenson, O., & Maule, A. J. (1993). *Time pressure and stress in human judgement and decision making.* New York: Plenum Press.

Swim, J. K., & Stangor, C. (1998). *Prejudice: The target's perspective.* San Diego, CA: Academic Press.

Tiedemann, J. (2000). Parents' gender stereotypes and teachers' beliefs as predictors of children's concept of their mathematical ability in elementary school. *Journal of Educational Psychology, 92*, 144–151.

Thompson, S. K. (1975). Gender labels and early sex role development. *Child Development, 46*, 339–347.

Turner, M. E., & Pratkanis, A. R. (1993). Effects of preferential and meritorious selection on performance: An intuitive and self-handicapping perspective. *Personality and Social Psychology Bulletin, 19*, 47–58.

Valian, V. (1998). *Why so slow? The advancement of women.* Cambridge, MA: MIT Press.

Vorauer, J. D., & Miller, D. T. (1997). Failure to recognize the effect of implicit social influence on the presentation of the self. *Journal of Personality and Social Psychology, 73*, 281–295.

Walsh, M., Hickey, C., & Duffy, J. (1999). Influence of item content and stereotype situation on gender differences in mathematical problem solving. *Sex Roles, 41*, 219–40.

Wigfield, A. (1994). Expectancy-value theory of achievement motivation: A developmental perspective. *Educational Psychology Review, 6*, 49 – 78.

Wigfield , A., & Eccles, J. S. (1992). The development of achievement task values: A theoretical analysis. *Developmental Review, 12*, 265 – 310.

Wigfield, A., & Eccles, J. S. (2000). Expectancy-value theory of achievement motivation. *Contemporary Educational Psychology, 25*, 68 – 81.

Wigfield, A., Eccles, J. S., Yoon, K. S., Harold, R. D., Arbreton, A., & Freedman-Doan, K. et al. (1997). Changes in children's competence beliefs and subjective task values across elementary school years: A three-year study. *Journal of Educational Psychology, 89*, 451 – 469.

EUROPEAN REVIEW OF SOCIAL PSYCHOLOGY, 2003, *14*, 277–311

Ask, Answer, and Announce: Three stages in perceiving and responding to discrimination

Charles Stangor
University of Maryland, College Park, USA

Janet K. Swim
The Pennsylvania State University, University Park, USA

Gretchen B. Sechrist
University at Buffalo, The State University of New York, USA

Jamie DeCoster
The Free University of Amsterdam, The Netherlands

Katherine L. Van Allen and
Alison Ottenbreit
University of Maryland, College Park, USA

Discrimination towards members of low-status groups takes a variety of forms, and results in a variety of negative consequences for its victims. Furthermore, discrimination may influence its targets either *directly* (for instance, when housing discrimination makes insurance, mortgage rates, or rents higher for African Americans than for whites) or *indirectly*, that is via perceptions on the part of the stigmatised. In the latter case the outcomes are caused or amplified by perceptions on the part of the victim that he or she is the target of discrimination. This chapter focuses on current research concerning factors that influence the perception of discrimination and its indirect influence on individuals. We review work from our own lab as well as from the field more broadly, focusing on research that attempts to explain contextual and individual variability in how events that are potentially due to discrimination are initially perceived, subsequently interpreted, and then publicly reported or withheld.

Address correspondence to: Charles Stangor, Department of Psychology, University of Maryland, College Park, Maryland 20742, USA.

Preparation of this chapter was supported in part by National Science Foundation grant 990722 to Charles Stangor and Janet K. Swim.

http://www.tandf.co.uk/journals/titles/99998080.asp   DOI: 10.1080/10463280340000090

Over the past decades social psychologists have published a substantial amount of research concerning the development, maintenance, and change of stereotypes and prejudice (e.g., Brewer & Brown, 1998; Fiske, 1998). This work is important from a theoretical perspective, because it provides insight into the basic processes of person perception. But the research is also assumed to have practical implications. Social scientists find it important to study stereotyping, prejudice, and discrimination because we assume these beliefs have negative influences on their targets—the stereotyped and the stigmatised.

Discrimination directed at members of low-status groups is expected to take a variety of forms, and to have a variety of harmful effects. At one end of the continuum are overt hostility, violence, and genocide. At the other end are the everyday hassles that, although minor, accumulate over time (Contrada et al., 2000; Kessler, Mickelson, & Williams, 1999; Swim, Hyers, Cohen, Ferguson, & Bylsma, 2003b; Swim, Pearson, & Johnston, 2003d). Even these everyday, "minor" forms of discrimination can be problematic because they may produce anger and anxiety among stigmatised group members. Moreover, over the long term, these hassles, like other daily hassles, can lead to other psychological problems (e.g., Landrine & Klonoff, 1996; Landrine, Klonoff, Gibbs, Manning, & Lund, 1995).

Discrimination may influence its targets either *directly* (for instance, when housing discrimination makes insurance, mortgage rates, or rents higher for African Americans than for Whites) or *indirectly*, that is via perceptions on the part of the stigmatised (Stangor & Sechrist, 1998). The *direct effects* of prejudice and discrimination are commonly observed in employment, income, housing, education, and medical care (Braddock & McPartland, 1987; Cash, Gillen, & Burns, 1977; Neckerman & Kirshenman, 1991; Treiman & Hartmann, 1981; Yinger, 1994). For instance, Blacks are less likely to receive major therapeutic procedures for many conditions and often do not receive necessary treatments, have delayed diagnoses, or fail to manage chronic diseases. In one recent study, Bach, Cramer, Warren, and Begg (1999) found that Blacks die from one form of lung cancer more often than Whites, possibly as the result of their lower rate of surgical treatment, and similar problems have been identified for other minorities (Williams & Rucker, 2000).

Discrimination has been blamed for the large percentage of Blacks living in poverty, and their lack of access to high-paying jobs (Commonwealth Fund, 2001; Williams & Rucker, 2000; Williams & Williams-Morris, 2000). African Americans have elevated mortality rates for 8 of the 10 leading causes of death in the US (Williams, 1999), and have on average less access to and receive poorer-quality health care, even controlling for other variables such as level of health insurance status. Suicide rates among lesbians and gays are substantially higher than that of the general population, and it has been argued that this in part due to the negative outcomes of prejudice, including negative attitudes and resulting social isolation (Halpert, 2002).

Direct effects can occur without the knowledge of the individual who is the target of discrimination. An African American may receive poorer health care than an equivalent white patient would have, for instance, without being aware of this discrimination, or a woman may be assigned a lower salary than an equivalent male employee would have been in equivalent circumstances. Because most instances of discrimination are single events, they are easy for the victims to miss. Indeed, Crosby, Clayton, Alksnis, and Hemker (1986) found that unless the discriminatory events were presented in a format in which the group comparisons were aggregated across a number of individuals, they were not interpreted as due to discrimination.

Although discrimination may in many cases occur out of the awareness of the target, this is not always the case. Indeed, *indirect effects* occur when an individual perceives that he or she is, has been, or will be the victim of discrimination, and these perceptions influence relevant outcomes. The idea that perceptions about being the target of discrimination are important determinants of social judgements has a long literature history within social psychology (e.g. Goffman, 1963). For instance, in a classic study demonstrating the importance of indirect effects, Kleck and Strenta (1980) found that individuals who were led to believe that interaction partners thought that they were stigmatised (either that they had a facial scar or were epileptic) perceived those partners more negatively than those who did not think the partner thought they were stigmatised, even though the partners were in fact entirely unaware of the "stigma", and the partners' behaviour was not actually more negative than their reactions to control participants. More recently, Pinel (2002) found that women who expect to be stereotyped acted more harshly towards a man they believed to be sexist. This behaviour then elicited unfavourable responses from the male participants. Other examples of indirect effects include the recent research on stereotype threat, which demonstrates the potential negative effects of perceptions about the beliefs of others on task performance (e.g., Steele & Aronson, 1995; see Jones & Stangor, 2003, for a review). Individuals who believe that they are the victims of discrimination may also begin to avoid or distrust members of the relevant social category (a sense of "cultural mistrust", e.g., Terrell & Terrell, 1981).

Stigmatised individuals who report experiencing frequent exposure to discrimination or other forms of unfair treatment also report more psychological distress, depression, anger, anxiety, and lower levels of life satisfaction and happiness (Anderson & Armstead, 1995; Corning, 2002; Glauser, 1999; Kessler et al., 1999; Klonoff, Landrine, & Ullman, 1999;

Landrine & Klonoff, 1996; Landrine et al. 1995, Schultz, Israel, Williams, Parker, Becker, & James, 2000; Swim, Hyers, Cohen, & Ferguson, 2001; Williams, Spencer, & Jackson, 1999; Williams & Williams-Morris, 2000). Although the observed correlations between perceptions of discrimination and negative health outcomes are consistent with direct effects, because the results are correlational there are of course a variety of other potential explanations. Particularly, it is possible that indirect effects contribute to the outcomes—that is, the perception of being discriminated against may itself produce negative health outcomes, for instance because it creates anxiety, anger, or control deprivation.

Research from our labs has demonstrated one indirect outcome of expecting to be a victim of stereotyping. We have found that expecting to be a solo member of a group leads people to expect to be stereotyped (Cohen & Swim, 1995). Furthermore, for women whose confidence had been lowered (but not for men), these expectations lead to a desire to avoid participating in such groups. In real-life settings such avoidance may in some cases be adaptive and appropriate, but in other cases it may lead people to self-select out of important social groups.

Expectations of being stereotyped can also potentially explain why people are uncertain about their future performance when they are expecting to be a solo, and why they perform poorly in such contexts. In one study, Stangor, Carr, and Kiang (1998) had participants first complete a word-finding task. Half of the participants were given expectations that they had performed well on this task, whereas the other half were given more ambiguous performance feedback. Then participants were then asked to predict how well they would perform on a similar task if they completed it either alone, or in a group of individuals. Furthermore, the participants who made judgements about their performance in groups were led to believe that the group would be made up of either similar others (those who shared their gender and college major) or different others (individuals who did not share either their gender or major).

As shown in Figure 1, participants expected to perform better in groups than they did if they were to work alone (perhaps because they expected they might get help from others in the group). More importantly, prior expectations about task performance influenced expectations for subsequent performance when individuals expected to work alone or in groups in which they were the majority. In these cases individuals who believed they did well on the first task predicted they would do well on the second task, in comparison to those who received ambiguous performance feedback. However, these prior expectations were completely undermined in the dissimilar other conditions. That is, getting positive feedback was no better than receiving ambiguous feedback when they anticipated being a solo member of their gender or college major in a group of different others. These

Prior Performance Expectations

■ Positive
▨ Ambiguous

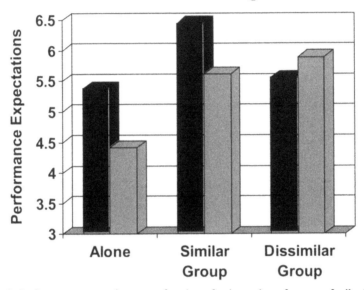

Figure 1. Performance expectations as a function of prior task performance feedback and expected context for task performance. From Stangor et al. (1998).

negative expectations also play a role in leading solos to actually perform poorly (Lord & Saenz, 1985; Sekaquaptewa & Thompson, 2003).

In addition to contextual variables, such as solo status, that can influence the likelihood of perceiving events as related to discrimination, there are also a number of individual difference variables that moderate the occurrence of indirect effects across people. In general terms, individuals who are high in public self-consciousness or who are high self-monitors may be particularly aware of the social situation, and may therefore be particularly likely to notice instances of discrimination. These variables may also influence how people choose to respond to discrimination (Feldman Barrett & Swim, 1998; Swim, Quinliven, Fitzgerald, & Eysell, 2003e). In terms of specific social categories, identification with and salience of the relevant category increases attributions to discrimination on the basis of the category (Operario & Fiske, 2001; Waters, 1994).

Similarly, individuals who are high in sensitivity to rejection based on their racial category have been found to be more likely to report more experiences with negative race events the course of a 3-week diary study (Mendoza-Denton, Downey, Purdie, Davis, & Pietrzak, 2002).

A heightened sensitivity to discrimination can have positive outcomes, for instance if it activates self-protection motivations and leads individuals to select appropriate coping responses (e.g., Hebl & Kleck, 2000; Mallett, 2003). On the other hand, sensitivity may also have negative effects. Race-based sensitivity is associated with more difficult transitions and poorer performance in college, as well as less positive feelings about professors (Mendoza-Denton et al., 2002).

In short, contextual or individual variation in the tendency of stigmatised group members to expect (or not expect) to be the targets of discrimination and to perceive that they have been targets of discrimination may influence their behaviours and psychological outcomes. These behaviours and outcomes may be independent of the actual amount of prejudice and discrimination they currently experience (Feldman Barrett & Swim, 1998). In order to better understand these indirect effects, it is important to understand how and when people initially perceive, make attributions to, and respond to discrimination. Differentiating direct and indirect effects is particularly important from an applied perspective, as interventions to reduce the harmful effects of discrimination would be differentially tailored depending on the underlying mechanisms.

In the remainder of this chapter we will focus on current research concerning factors that influence perceptions of discrimination. We review work from our own lab as well as from the field more broadly. We will focus on research that attempts to explain contextual and individual variability in how events that are potentially due to discrimination are initially perceived, subsequently interpreted, and then publicly reported or withheld. This approach is in keeping with other research programmes that have focused on understanding variability in responses to discrimination (e.g., Crocker, 1999; Friedman & Brownell, 1995; Miller & Downey, 1999).

THE THREE STAGES

In our laboratories, we have assumed that the perceptions of discrimination may influence individuals' cognitions, emotions, and behaviour at any one of three stages, as shown in Figure 2. We assume that one or more perceived "incidents", which refer to behaviours directed towards individuals or groups, and which may or may not constitute discrimination, begin the process. In most of our research the incident involves a single event, although the sequence might be started by a series of events over time, for

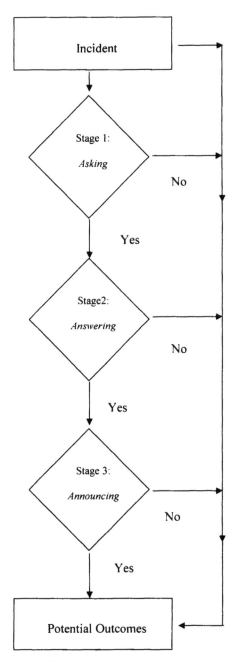

Figure 2. Three stages in perceiving discrimination.

instance the perception that a work environment condones sexism.[1] The sequence ends with one or more "outcomes", which refer to potential effects on the targets.

In addition to presuming the potential for direct effects of incidents upon outcomes, we assume that individual interpretations of and reactions to perceived discrimination may themselves (indirectly) influence outcomes. Furthermore, the nature of these outcomes is assumed to be influenced by the extent to which the perceiver engages in one or more of three information-processing stages. These stages include an initial *asking* stage, a subsequent interpretation or *answering* stage, and a public expression of events (*announcing*). That is, (1) individuals may or may not initially wonder whether an incident might be discriminatory or that an individual or group might harbour prejudice towards them. The asking could be initiated by any of a wide variety of variables, including characteristics of the incident, information about the perceiver, or having the question raised by others. Assuming that the individual questions whether the incident might have involved discrimination, the individual (2) may or may not interpret the behaviour as prejudicial or discriminatory. And finally, assuming that the attribution process leads to an interpretation of the behaviour as due to discrimination (the answer to the question is "yes"), the individual (3) may or may not decide to overtly report to others that he or she has perceived the event as discriminatory, or to confront the perpetrator.

Each of the three stages may have unique effects on perceptions, and may be influenced by both individual-difference and contextual variables. Furthermore, the current approach explicitly allows the possibility that individual or contextual differences may *increase* perceptions of discrimination at one stage, and yet at the same time *decrease* perceptions of discrimination at other stages, and that these discrepancies may predict particular outcomes. For instance, an individual who has low status or power in an organisation may be particularly likely to interpret the negative behaviour of high-status individuals directed at low-status individuals as constituting discrimination, as a result of an *increased* sensitivity to the occurrence of discrimination. Yet at the same time low-status individuals may be particularly unwilling to report the experienced discrimination out of fear of negative consequences, thus decreasing the likelihood of announcing this conclusion to others. This discrepancy between interpreting the event (stage 2) and reporting discrimination (stage 3) may have particularly negative outcomes on the individual, including loss of self-respect or shame resulting from the perception that one has been untrue to one's beliefs.

---

[1]Although we do not address it here, this difference is likely to be critical in terms of how the precipitating event or events are perceived and their effects on subsequent processing.

Although Figure 2 suggests that the three stages are sequential (moving from the top to the bottom of the figure), it is possible that there could also be some reciprocal or inverse influences. For instance, individuals who fail to confront discrimination may publicly agree with another person's conclusions about an incident being the result of discrimination and this public statement may alter, perhaps through cognitive dissonance, the way they personally perceive the incident.

In the following sections we consider research that has addressed each of the three stages outlined in Figure 2. At this point in our research programme we believe that we have documented effects that occur at each of the three stages, although we acknowledge that there is in some cases at least some ambiguity in our research concerning which stage is operating (it has been particularly difficult to disentangle Stage 1 and Stage 2). We have not yet, however, found evidence for either interactions between stages or for reciprocal influences. We expect that these issues will be addressed more fully over the next few years. Despite these limitations, we believe that our approach is heuristic, in the sense that it provides a framework for understanding the relevant processes, makes predictions about how and when contextual and individual difference variables will be important, and specifies the important dependent measures for study.

Stage 1: Asking

Stage 1 involves the initial activation of the question about whether an incident is discriminatory. For instance, when a woman is denied a job in a firm that has predominately male employees, she might (or might not) wonder whether this was a result of gender-based discrimination. Theoretically, this initial asking is expected to be determined by the current construct accessibility of discrimination as an explanatory category. Discrimination, and the resulting tendency to question whether discrimination or prejudice is a cause for an incident, may be accessible either as the result of contextual activation or on the basis of chronic individual differences.

Contextual activation of discrimination

Existing research has focused on delineating the characteristics of behaviours and the social contexts that activate the construct of discrimination. Certain types of discrimination are more prototypical than other types, and thus more likely to be initially recognised. For instance, Marti, Bobier, and Baron (2000) found that race and gender discrimination were more accessible than age and weight discrimination, and were therefore more easily recognised. Furthermore, the role of accessibility in initial detection was indicated by their finding that explicitly priming prejudice only increased the detection of initially less accessible forms of prejudice. Prototypical behaviours are also those that have prototypical perpetrators (Men; Whites) and prototypical targets (Women, Blacks; e.g., Inman & Baron, 1996). As such, these types of behaviours should also result in greater activation of the discrimination construct.

Other research also indicates that particular behaviours vary in the extent to which they are seen as prototypical of discrimination. We (Swim, Mallett, Russo-Devosa, & Stangor, 2003c) have found, for instance, that traditional gender role behaviours (e.g., expressing disapproval for exhibiting behaviour counter to stereotypes about one's group) are more likely to be labelled as sexist than is unwanted sexual attention (e.g., sexual touching when the person knew or should have known that the other person was not interested or it was inappropriate for the situation), suggesting that the former are more likely to activate the concept of sexism than the latter. The use of sexist language may not be perceived as prototypically sexist because it occurs frequently and may not be seen to have negative consequences.

We have also found that exposure to discrimination increases its construct accessibility. Johnston and Swim (1999) had women read about a proposed study in which men would be asked to rate beer advertisements and women would be asked to rate wine advertisements. To activate the construct of discrimination, some of the women were further told that there were either more beer or more wine advertisements to rate, which meant that either men or women would have the opportunity to earn more extra credit. A third group of women was told that men and women would receive equal opportunity to get credit. The participants were then given a word fragment completion task. Imbedded in this task were six words that could be completed as relating to prejudice (e.g., "$p\ r\ e\ \_\ \_\ d\ \_\ \_\ \_$" which could be completed as either *president* or *prejudice*). As expected, participants who read about men being able to earn more points than women ($M = 2.12$) and women being able to earn more points than men ($M = 2.04$) completed more word fragments in terms of their prejudice-related response than those in the control condition ($M = 1.52$).

Differences in the context in which behaviours occur may also influence initial thoughts about discrimination. As we have discussed above, being in solo status increases the accessibility of discrimination (e.g., Cohen & Swim, 1995; Stangor et al., 1998). Research on accessibility of constructs also indicates that recent or frequent activation of the construct is likely to result in the activation of the construct (Higgins & King, 1981). Thus, for example, organisational climates in which sexism is a frequent topic of conversation among individuals is likely to produce an overall increase in asking, and recent or frequent accusations or confrontations with others who are perceived to discriminate will likely also increase accessibility.

Individual differences in the accessibility of discrimination

In addition to contextual variation, some individuals are more likely to have discrimination chronically accessible and should therefore be more likely to question the extent to which incidents are discriminatory. For instance, members of minority racial groups may be more aware of racial disparities and this will likely influence the extent to which they perceive events in racial terms (Waters, 1994; Stangor, Lynch, Duan, & Glass, 1992). Moreover, diary research indicates that individuals for whom discrimination is chronically accessible, such as those who are sensitive to race-based rejection or feel threatened by the possibility of gender stereotyping, are more likely to notice its everyday manifestation of discrimination in comparison to those who are lower in accessibility (Mendoza-Denton et al., 2002; Swim et al., 2001). This sensitivity might be the result of prior exposure to discrimination either directed at oneself or other group members, or may be due to being part of a social milieu in which discrimination is seen as prevalent.

Many analyses of the psychology of the stigmatised argue that members of stigmatised groups will be particularly aware of or sensitive to the potential for discrimination (Crocker & Major, 1989; Swim, Aikin, Hall, & Hunter, 1995). Allport (1954) argued that minority groups might use the "ego defence" of "hypervigilance", and thus overestimate the occurrence of discrimination (p. 144). Not only is such a prediction highly intuitive, but it follows from many considerations of the psychology of being a target of discrimination. Stigmatised individuals are (by definition) typically the targets of discrimination, and since discrimination represents a potential threat to one's well-being, they should be particularly wary of the potential for it (Feldman Barrett & Swim, 1998; Inman & Baron, 1996). Despite this latter possibility, our research has found little evidence that stigmatised groups are hypersensitive about the occurrence of discrimination in their environments. In contrast there appears to be evidence of insensitivity. As one example of this apparent insensitivity, Table 1 shows the results of research from our lab in which we simply asked college students to indicate the categories that they belonged to in terms of which they had experienced discrimination (Stangor, Sechrist, & Swim, 2002). This procedure is based on prior research that has assessed the construct accessibility of categories in terms of priority of activation in thought-listing tasks (Higgins & King, 1981). Participants were allowed to list only one category, and were told that only if they were absolutely unable to think of any category should they

TABLE 1
Percentage of students indicating they had been the targets of discrimination on the basis of various social categories, by gender and ethnicity

Category	Male	Female	Category	Non-white	White
Gender	2%	9%	Ethnicity	48%	9%
Ethnicity	21%	21%	Gender	3%	9%
Religion	10%	11%	Religion	5%	14%
Other	18%	17%	Other	8%	22%
None	50%	42%	None	36%	47%

A. Gender of participant.   B. Ethnicity of participant.

leave the question blank. To help ensure that our measure assessed initial perceptions of the occurrence of discrimination, free of concerns about public reporting, participants were guaranteed complete anonymity.

We coded each response into one of four categories. Table 1a shows the results broken down by gender and Table 1b shows them broken down by race (white vs non-white). Supporting the assumption that stigmatised individuals are more accessible for discrimination in comparison to the non-stigmatised, women were significantly more likely to indicate that they had been discriminated against on the basis of gender in comparison to men, and non-white participants were more likely to indicate that they had been discriminated against on the basis of ethnicity in comparison to white (European American) participants. However, 91% of women did not mention gender and 52% of minorities did not mention ethnicity. Also, almost half of the women and 36% of the minorities indicated that they could not think of a group that they belonged to upon which they experienced discrimination.

These data do not seem consistent with the idea that the stigmatised are hypersensitive to the occurrence of discrimination directed at them. Rather, these students did not report seeing much discrimination at all—with a large proportion finding it impossible to list even a single category. Although it is possible that the participants were embarrassed to report being the targets of discrimination, we attempted to minimise this by encouraging honesty and making the responses entirely anonymous. However, participating in a study that was clearly about discrimination would have been expected to, if anything, increase the accessibility of discrimination and thus increase reporting.[2]

---

[2]These results are not likely a function of college students' lack of experience with or observation of discrimination. When college students were asked to record their observations of sexism and racism in a daily diary they typically reported at least one incident every other week (Swim et al., 2001; Swim, Hyers, Cohen, Fitzgerald, & Bylsma, 2003b).

One limitation of these data is that it is possible that they assess, at least to some degree, the answering as well as the asking stage. That is, if individuals do not perceive that they are the victims of discrimination, we assume that this is because they do not initially see it. However, it is possible that they have in fact been suspicious about events and subsequently reinterpreted them as being due to other factors. However, we have also conducted research that is designed to assess the asking stage more unambiguously.

If there is individual variability in the extent to which people are suspicious about discrimination, then this variability should function as a type of social schema which should influence how they remember events that occur to them. Assessing the impact of schemas on memory for relevant information provides an unobtrusive measure that should assess only Stage 1 processing—the tendency to initially encode or fail to encode information in terms of discrimination.

Using the free-response measure that we have just described, Stangor et al. (2002, Experiment 3) selected women for whom gender discrimination was an accessible construct because they had spontaneously indicated gender as a category upon which they had been the target of discrimination, as well as women who were not accessible because they had not indicated that they had been so discriminated against. The women believed that they would be participating in a study concerning "reactions to the media". After reading and signing a consent form, participants responded to a series of headlines, supposedly extracted from local newspapers, which were presented sequentially via computer. The participants were asked to rate how interested they would be in reading the article that they expected would accompany each of the headlines by rating it on a scale from 1 (not at all interesting) to 7 (extremely interesting). We included this measure only to make sure that the participants paid attention to the headlines.

A total of 48 headlines were presented. Of these headlines 12 dealt with sexual discrimination (for instance, "College women lose battle for equal rights"; "Local employer indicted on sexism charges"), 12 pertained to discrimination against African Americans (for instance, "Country club under scrutiny for denying membership to African-Americans"; "Black males more likely to receive stricter sentencing than white males"), and 24 were about miscellaneous topics ("Stereo equipment stolen from dorm room"; "Marijuana use again increasing on campus"). To reduce the likelihood of any differences in interpretation of the meaning of the headlines, and thus to assure that we were assessing the asking and not the answering stage, the headlines were selected to unambiguously portray discrimination. After reading and rating all of the headlines, the participants were given instructions to complete a short distractor task designed to clear short-term memory. Participants listed as many US states as they could think of for 5 minutes.

After completing the distractor task, participants were provided with a test set of 72 headlines (48 original and 24 new) and asked to rate whether or not they had seen the headline in the first rating session. If they thought the headline had previously been viewed, participants were asked to indicate "old", whereas if they believed the headline had not been previously viewed, they were to indicate "new". The specific headlines that appeared in the initial presentation and those that appeared in the memory test were randomly chosen for each participant, and the order of presentation of the items was also random.

On the basis of signal detection theory, we operationalised both a measure of recognition sensitivity (A') and a measure of response bias (B"), separately for each of the three types of headlines. Sensitivity refers to the ability of the participant to accurately indicate whether a headline had or had not previously been seen, whereas response bias refers to a tendency to set a liberal or conservative criterion for reporting an item as having been seen. We expected that both variables might be influenced by gender prejudice accessibility, but there were no significant effects on the response bias measure. However, on the recognition sensitivity measure, a significant interaction between the two variables was found. As shown in Table 2, women for whom gender discrimination was an accessible category showed better recognition memory for the sexist headlines than did the women for whom sexism was less accessible. In contrast, there were no significant differences between high- and low-accessibility women's memory for race-related or miscellaneous headlines. We again did not find any evidence for hyper-accessibility. The high-accessible women did not show greater sensitivity for the sexist headlines than for the other types. Rather, it was the low-accessible women who had lower perceptual accuracy in comparison to the high-accessible women, and in comparison to memory for the other headline types. We have found similar results in another published study (Stangor, Sechrist, & Swim, 1999).

TABLE 2
Recognition sensitivity by gender discrimination accessibility and headline type

Gender discrimination accessibility	Headline type		
	Sexism	Racism	Miscellaneous
High	.98[a]	.95[a]	.97[a]
	(.02)	(.05)	(.03)
Low	.86[b]	.91[a]	.93[a]
	(.25)	(.12)	(.05)

Standard deviations in parentheses. Means within a column that do not share a superscript are significantly different at $p < .05$ by planned comparison.

Summary

In summary, although they must be made somewhat tentatively, we can nevertheless draw several conclusions about initial asking. There is an array of contextual variables that are likely to influence the accessibility of the construct of discrimination and as such, the likelihood that people will consider the possibility that discrimination has occurred. There are also individual differences in the tendency for individuals to be concerned about discrimination. Moreover, although some groups are more likely to think about discrimination than other groups, many of the college students in our studies indicated that they had never experienced discrimination on the basis of any categories to which they belonged, and those that have discrimination more accessible can be more accurately characterised as sensitive than necessarily biased in their attention to such incidents. Although these variables may also influence the outcomes of Stage 2 and Stage 3 processing, existing research is consistent with the idea that they also relate to initial noticing or asking.

In terms of potential outcomes of Stage 1 processing, if an individual never asks the question—that is, does not even consider an event as potentially due to discrimination—then the path from the incident to the outcome reverts to a direct effect. The event may still have harmful outcomes, but if it does it is independent of any perceptual indirect effects. On the other hand, if the question is asked, the second stage of information processing comes into play, and it is to this stage that we now turn.

Stage 2: Interpretation of potentially discriminatory events

After a behaviour has initially been categorised as potentially being due to discrimination (that is, the outcome of Stage 1 is an initial activation of the possibility of discrimination), an individual will attempt to determine whether they have or have not observed discrimination. A woman may wonder whether a man treated her in a sexist manner, and then learn that he has differentially treated men and women in the past, leading her to be relatively certain that the man is sexist. Alternatively, she may determine that there is an alternative, nondiscriminatory, explanation for his behaviour, for instance deciding that the negative outcomes reflect her lack of ability in the domain, eventually concluding that she was not treated in a sexist manner.

Underlying processes

Whereas Stage 1 processing is assumed to be determined by the category accessibility of discrimination as an interpretive category and to occur relatively automatically, Stage 2 is assumed to be determined by the application of relevant beliefs to a judgement. Which beliefs are activated and applied may be determined by either cognitive (for instance, cognitive load or judgements of what type of information is relevant for making a judgement of discrimination), affective (e.g., mood as information), or motivational (for instance, the denial or enhancement of discrimination to maintain a positive self-image or a sense of a just world) processes.

Stage 2 processing may either increase or decrease the likelihood of interpreting an event as due to discrimination. For instance, according to the attributional ambiguity model of Crocker and Major (1989), stigmatised individuals should in many cases prefer to make attributions for negative events to discrimination rather than to lack of ability, because doing so is self-protective (Major, Quinton, & Schmader, 2003). On the other hand, individuals may also prefer in some contexts to minimise or deny that they or others have experienced discrimination. The conditions under which each of these two processes may occur are summarised by Major, Quinton, & McCoy, 2002, and by Major, McCoy, Kaiser, & Quinton 2003 (this volume). There are many potential variables that could influence the outcome of Stage 2 processing, and we can only consider a relatively limited number here.

Cognitive load. Consistent with existing "dual process" models of decision making, we have found that cognitive capacity can influence the processing of information related to discrimination. DeCoster and Swim (2002) had female participants read a description of a woman who was interviewing for either a stereotypically masculine (electrician) or a stereotypically feminine (daycare worker) job. The male interviewer did not offer her the position, and this decision was justified with either a strong or a weak reason. Crossed with this manipulation of job type, half of the participants made these decisions under high cognitive load (while being asked to count the number of pronouns in the stimuli as they read them), whereas the other half of the participants were not given a cognitive load.

Demonstrating that they were making use of the job description in determining whether the interviewer's behaviour might have been the result of discrimination, the women were more likely to conclude that the boss was prejudiced against women in the masculine job than in the feminine job conditions, regardless of cognitive load. However, the ability to system- atically process the reviewers' justifications varied as a function of the load manipulation. When under cognitive load, participants' conclusions were unaffected by the strength of the interviewer's justifications, indicating that they were unable to systematically process the information about the reason for the decision, and simply categorised the behaviour as discriminatory. However, when participants were *not* under cognitive load, they were more likely to conclude that the interviewer was prejudiced against the woman when he gave a weak argument for not hiring her than when he gave a strong argument. This research illustrates that both heuristic and systematic processing play a role in perceptions of prejudice and discrimination.

Attributional processing.   Stage 2 processing is expected to include, in part, attributional processing of relevant information. The outcome of attributional processing about negative behaviours can be influenced both by assessments of people's intent to engage in the behaviour, as well as by the amount of harm done to the recipient. As Jones (1997), put it, "acts that constitute bias depend, in part on the target's reaction, as well as the actor's intention" (p. 306).

To assess the joint effects of intent and harm in the interpretation of discrimination, Swim, Scott, Sechrist, Campbell and Stangor (2003f) had participants read vignettes about events in which women and men were treated differently. The scenarios varied in terms of the amount of harm done to the woman and the degree to which the man intended to engage in the behaviour. After reading the scenarios, women were asked to rate the extent to which the man was sexist and the action was discriminatory. As Figure 3 illustrates, these results revealed that the degree of both intent and harm influenced the judgement that an event was due to discrimination, although intent was more important than harm, in that harm did not add to perceptions of discrimination when there was evidence of high intent. Furthermore, the results also indicated that when information about either intent or harm was not present, perceivers nevertheless made assumptions about it from the presence of the other. For instance, when a target person was harmed, perceivers tended to assume that the actor intended to discriminate. This finding has potential implications for intergroup relations, because it indicates that different people may draw different conclusions about the causes of an event based on the information they have available to them, and which information they find most important. As an example, targets more than actors may focus more on the harm done to a victim, whereas actors more than targets may focus more on the intent. If this were the case, these different interpretations and emphases could result in misunderstandings and conflict.

Individual differences.   Individual differences are also likely to influence Stage 2 processing, both because of differences in the extent to which individuals are motivated to collect and process information, as well as because of differences in the use and interpretation of information available. For instance, targets of prejudice are more likely than observers to be influenced by the harm that the target experiences when making judgements of prejudice and discrimination (Swim et al., 2003b). This could be because targets have greater access to the extent to which an incident has harmed

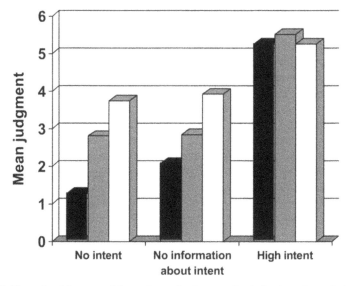

Figure 3. The role of intent and harm in attributions to discrimination. From Swim et al. (2003f).

them than observers. Also, Whites are less likely than Blacks to attribute a White supervisor's negative treatment of Black employee to prejudice when the White supervisor's negative treatment was constrained by circumstances (Johnson, Simmons, Trawalter, Ferguson, & Reed, 2002). This race difference can be explained by race differences in perceptions of the prevalence of racism.

Differences in racial identity can also influence interpretation of incidents. Operario and Fiske (2001) had minority participants, pre-selected as either high or low ethnically identified, interact with a White, female confederate, who after a brief, awkward interaction, left the room and did not return. Operario and Fiske found that individuals who were more identified with their ethnic group made more attributions to prejudice and rated the confederate as significantly more discriminatory than did those low on ethnic identity. Similarly, Major et al. (2002) found that gender identity predicted women's attributions to sexism in situations in which the true causes of the events were ambiguous, and yet in which discrimination had been primed because a confederate had indicated that she had heard that the experimenters treated men and women differently.

The role of affect.   The extent to which an event is interpreted as being the outcome of discrimination may also be influenced by the individual's current affective state. Sechrist, Swim, and Mark (2002) induced women into positive or negative mood states using the Velten Mood Induction procedure. The mood induction involves reading 60 positive ("I feel cheerful and lively") or negative ("My life is so tiresome—the same old thing day after day depresses me") sentences. Then half of the participants were provided with an external attribution for their current mood state. Specifically, half of the participants were informed that their current feelings may have been influenced by previous questionnaires and then were asked to indicate how they currently felt. Thus, they were reminded of the earlier positive or negative mood-producing task before indicating their mood. All other participants were also asked to report their current feelings, but they were not given a potential external attribution for their mood (cf. Schwarz & Clore, 1996; Wyer & Carlston, 1979).

Participants then reported on their perceptions of the extent of discrimination that occurred to themselves and to other women. Specifically, they were asked to indicate on 7-point Likert scales (1 = not at all; 7 = very much) the extent to which they and other women had experienced gender discrimination. Demonstrating that mood was used as information, as shown in Figure 4, results showed that when an external attribution for induced mood was not provided, women in negative moods were more likely to report that they and other women have experienced discrimination than were women in positive moods. When an external attribution for the mood state was available, however, mood had no significant effect on judgements.

Maintaining positive self-regard.   The outcomes of all three stages in our framework—but perhaps most importantly Stage 2—are likely to be influenced by the general goal of maintaining a positive psychological state. The research programmes of Major and her colleagues (Crocker & Major, 1989; Major et al., 2002; Major et al., this volume) and of Branscombe and her colleagues (e.g., Branscombe, Schmitt, & Harvey, 1999; Jetten, Branscombe, Schmitt, & Spears, 2001; Kobrynowicz & Branscombe, 1997; Schmitt & Branscombe, 2002) have both directly addressed this issue, and the important variables in this regard are summarised by Major et al. (2002).

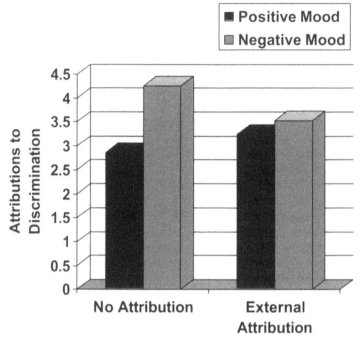

Figure 4. Attributions to discrimination as a function of mood state and opportunity for external attribution. From Sechrist et al. (2002).

In general, both Major and her colleagues as well as Branscombe and her colleagues agree with our general expectation that the outcomes of negative events for members of stigmatised groups are often ambiguous, in the sense that they may or may not be due to discrimination, and that the perceiver must attempt to disambiguate the causes of these events. Crocker and Major (1989) defined this state—*attributional ambiguity*—as an uncertainty about whether the outcomes one receives are indicative of one's personal deservingness or of social prejudices that others have against one's social group. According to this model, attributions to discrimination occur at both the level of cognitive appraisals, and at the level of coping processes.

Prior research has suggested that people may underestimate the extent to which they have personally experienced discrimination, for instance, in comparison to their perceptions of the amount of discrimination that occurs to their social group as a whole (Taylor, Wright, Moghaddam, & Lalonde, 1990). This "personal-group discrepancy" is robust, and has been demonstrated among various stigmatised as well as non-stigmatised groups in a wide variety of laboratory and naturally occurring situations

(Kobrynowicz & Branscombe, 1997; Moghaddam, Stolkin, & Hutcheson, 1997; Taylor, Wright, & Porter, 1994).

Although there are a number of explanations for this individual–group discrepancy in perceiving discrimination, one possibility is that people deny that they personally experience discrimination to maintain a sense of control over their outcomes. Although this seems possible, our research into the role of perceived control (Sechrist, Swim, & Stangor, 2003) was based on the assumption that making attributions to discrimination (rather than to one's lack of ability) may also allow individuals to *reassert* personal control over a situation. People have a fundamental need to maintain control, and will attempt to reassert this perception if they are deprived of it (Burger, 1992). We predicted that individuals with high needs for personal control, who were therefore in need of maintaining or restoring a positive self-image, would be more likely to interpret negative events as due to discrimination. Confirming these predictions, we found that women who were high in dispositional need for control—as assessed using Burger and Cooper's (1979) Desire for Control Scale—were more likely than those low in need for control to conclude that negative feedback about one's own performance on a task was a result of discrimination, rather than ability. Similarly, in a second study, we found that this was also true for women who were placed into a state of control deprivation (using a procedure developed by Pittman & D'Agostino, 1989). Moreover mediational analyses in this experiment showed that making the attribution to discrimination subsequently increased women's level of perceived control.

Although the results of these studies are not entirely consistent with other research suggesting that people may deny discrimination to maintain personal control over outcomes, they are nevertheless consistent with the overall notion that people may either enhance or deny discrimination in order to protect their self-image. The conditions under which needs for control lead people to over-, versus under-estimate the extent to which behaviours reflect discrimination still need to be determined.

Perceiving a "just world". Still another potential determinant of perceptions of discrimination is that people are motivated to maintain perceptions that the world is just—that is, that individuals deserve the outcomes that occur to them. As a result, people show a pervasive tendency to justify existing status hierarchies and outcome distributions, even when those hierarchies and distributions are disadvantageous to themselves or to their group (Jost & Banaji, 1994; Kleugel & Smith, 1986; Major, 1994; Sidanius & Pratto, 1999). Because discrimination is, by definition, unfair to the target of the behaviour, members of disadvantaged groups may be motivated to avoid blaming their negative outcomes on prejudice and discrimination, even when such explanations are likely or even good accounts for their treatment (Crosby, 1984; Olson & Hafer, 2001). Indeed, it has long been argued that social inequality persists because members of low-status groups are victims of *false consciousness*—that is, they fail to recognise the illegitimacy of the status system and of their own disadvantaged position within it (Jost, 1995).

The relationship between Stage 1 and Stage 2 processing

Although Stage 1 and Stage 2 processing are hypothesised to be distinct cognitive stages, they are nevertheless closely linked. For one thing, if a person does not ask whether a situation is discriminatory or a person is prejudiced (Stage 1), she or he will never come to the conclusion that there is discrimination or a person is prejudiced (Stage 2). Moreover, the outcomes of Stage 1 and Stage 2 may both be related to similar individual-difference variables. People who are more chronically accessible for discrimination (Stage 1) are probably also likely to process information in a way that leads them to conclude that an event is discriminatory or a person is prejudiced (Stage 2). For instance, racial identity is associated with perceiving discrimination to be more prevalent—indicating that this construct is likely to be more accessible to these individuals—and is also associated with being more likely to identify specific incidents as racist (Operario & Fiske, 2001). Other variables, such as stigma consciousness, race-based rejection sensitivity, or cultural mistrust, may also increase both Stage 1 and Stage 2 processing (Pinel, 2002, Mendoza et al., 2002: Terrell & Terrell, 1981).

On the other hand, discrepancies between Stage 1 and Stage 2 may be important for accounting for sources of variations in assessments of particular incidents as well as the prevalence of discrimination. For instance, in some cases, constructs may be equally accessible across individuals. This may be why several individual differences, such as racial identity, endorsement of sexist beliefs, and reporting that one actively confronts sexism, were weakly related or unrelated to number of everyday discrimination reported in diary studies (Swim et al., 2001; Swim et al., 2003b). Participating in the diary study may have made discrimination more equally accessible across individuals. This suggests that some individual differences may be principally related to perceptions of the prevalence of discrimination due to differences in the accessibility of the construct more so than difference in the interpretation of the incidents. On the other hand, other individual differences may be more strongly associated with differences in interpretation of incidents rather than accessibility. For instance, in diary studies, women report more incidents of everyday sexism directed at women than do men (Swim et al., 2001). Given that both were attending to such incidents, one explanation for the gender difference may be their interpretation of the incidents. Women are more likely to perceive behaviours and comments as being offensive than men and this accounts for differences in labelling the behaviours as sexist (Swim et al., 2003c).

Summary

In summary, Stage 2 processing involves individual and contextual variation in the tendency to interpret behaviours as discrimination. This variability may be the result of situations that alter the capacity to process information, differences in the tendency to weigh different causal variables when interpreting behaviours, and whether one's mood is used as information when making attributions. Individuals may also be more or less likely to construe events as discrimination in order to maintain a positive sense of self (for instance, to maintain or regain personal control) or a sense that they live in a just world. Thus different types of information are differentially used by different people for different reasons, and the result of this processing may either validate or invalidate initial suspicions that arise from the activation discrimination or prejudice as a possible interpretation of an incident. In general, variability in Stage 2 processing suggests that different people (for instance, perpetrators, victims, and observers) may come to different conclusions about an event based on the information they have available and their interpretations of it. It is also possible (although we have not yet tested this) that how relevant others publicly interpret potentially discriminatory events may also influence the individual's own interpretations. Individuals construe social reality in part on the basis of the perceptions of relevant others' beliefs, and these processes may be particularly important in coming to conclusions about the experience of discrimination. Regardless of their causes, these differences in interpretation may play an important role in perpetuating intergroup misunderstandings.

As shown in Figure 2, if the outcome of Stage 2 processing is a conclusion that an event was not the result of discrimination, the initial event may nevertheless influence individual outcomes. Indeed, continually perceiving discrimination, but then convincing oneself that it is not, may have substantial psychological costs. On the other hand, if the outcome of Stage 2 processing is an affirmation of the initial suspicion, and if there is an opportunity for public expression of this belief, then the individual proceeds to Stage 3.

Stage 3: Overt reporting and confronting

Once an individual has initially asked whether an event was due to discrimination (Stage 1), and subsequently determined that the event really was due to discrimination and not some other factor (Stage 2), they may be faced with a decision about whether to overtly announce the perceived discrimination, by reporting it publicly or confronting it (Stage 3). These decisions are influenced in large part by a target's goals in the interaction (Hyers, 2003). One particularly important goal is a concern to portray a positive impression to others (cf. Noel, Wann, & Branscombe, 1995; Postmes, Branscombe, Spears & Young, 1999).

The costs and benefits of publicly reporting discrimination

Kaiser and Miller (2001) proposed that self-presentation (and particularly the desire to be liked by others) is a motivation for stigmatised individuals to avoid making attributions to discrimination in public. In their research, participants (predominantly white males) read about an African-American student who had received a negative evaluation on a test in a context in which discrimination was either a likely or an unlikely cause. The participants were then presented with a packet containing a survey that had supposedly been filled out by the student, and which concerned his responses to his evaluation. Results showed that the stigmatised student was rated less favourably and perceived as a "complainer" to a greater degree when the student attributed his poor performance to discrimination rather than to ability and effort. Furthermore, this was true regardless of the probability that discrimination was a valid cause of the performance. This tendency to dislike people who complain about discrimination is not limited to African Americans; Dodd, Giuliano, Boutell, and Moran (2001) reported that men liked a woman less if she confronted blatant sexism than if she did not confront it.

One limitation of this prior research is that it focused primarily on the costs of claiming discrimination. But publicly announcing one's opinion that an incident is discriminatory can also have social benefits. Recent research from our lab (Stangor, Van Allen, & Swim, 2003) confirms some of these benefits of confronting. We replicated the Kaiser and Miller study, using the same trait ratings that they had used. However, when we factored the items we found that they represented three variables—perceived likeability, perceived competence, as well as the tendency to complain. The first two factors are remarkably consistent with Fiske's recent conceptualisation of stereotypes (Fiske, Cuddy, Glick, & Xu, 2002; Fiske, Xu, Cuddy, & Glick, 1999) as relating to warmth and competence, and validate the distinction between them in a different context. Replicating Kaiser and Miller (2001), we found that claiming that a negative outcome was due to discrimination, rather than ability, significantly decreased the perceived liking (warmth) of the target, and also made them seem like a "complainer". However, claiming discrimination rather than ability also had a benefit—it significantly increased the target's perceived competence. Furthermore, and suggesting that the tendency to see these costs and benefits was quite general, these patterns held up for both older adults as well as college students, and for both Black and White participants judging both Black and White targets. We also found similar findings for the perception of individuals who claim gender discrimination (both men and women judging both male and female targets).

A second potential advantage of publicly claiming discrimination is that it may increase the likelihood that others become aware of the possibility that events are caused by discrimination. Indeed, Stangor et al. (2003) found that when targets were said to have claimed discrimination, the observers of the event were themselves more likely to label the event as discrimination. Hyers (2003) found that women reported confronting both because they felt that they would appear weak if they did not and because they felt that confronting might educate others. Although confronting, especially by those who are the direct target of prejudice, may not actually end up changing perpetrator beliefs (Czopp & Monteith, 2003), other research indicates that confronting can have other benefits such as altering bystanders' perceptions of events or changing social norms as to what is considered appropriate behaviour (Blanchard, Crandall, Brigham, & Vaughn, 1994; Lalonde & Cameron, 1994).

Discrepancies between Stage 2 and Stage 3 processing

The prior research shows that there are clear costs associated with publicly reporting and confronting discrimination, and this suggests that what one perceives at a private level (i.e., the outcome of Stage 2 processing) may not match what one reports publicly (the outcome of Stage 3 processing). This discrepancy may be important in understanding how people perceive and respond to discrimination. In the following section, we report studies from our lab that have explicitly assessed the discrepancies between Stage 2 and Stage 3 processing.

Differences in stigmatised and non-stigmatised group members' attributions to discrimination. The results of recent research by Stangor, Swim, Van Allen, and Sechrist (2001) suggest that individuals alter their public behaviours based on the potential self-presentation costs of claiming discrimination, and that self-presentation plays a more important role in whether or not stigmatised group members report discrimination than in whether or not non-stigmatised group members report discrimination. In these studies we examined participants' attributions to discrimination after they received negative feedback on a creativity test in public and private settings. The public condition consisted of two participants who were told

Female Participants

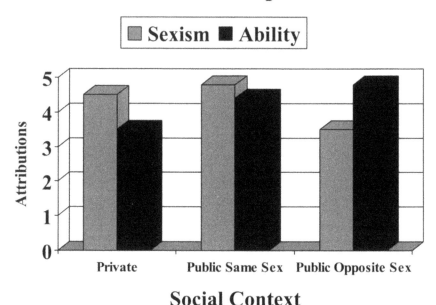

Figure 5. Female participants' attributions to ability and sexism as a function of social context. From Stangor et al. (2001).

that their judgements about the causes of their failure would be reported aloud. In the private condition, participants (who were either alone or in the presence of another participant) were told that all of their responses would remain private and confidential.

As shown in Figure 5, we found that members of stigmatised groups (in this case women) were more likely to report that a failing grade assigned by an opposite-category evaluator (a man) was caused by discrimination, rather than by lack of ability or effort, when judgements were made privately, or when they were made in front of another woman. However, we also found that women were significantly more likely to make ability (rather than discrimination) attributions when they expected to report these responses in the presence of a male student. Male participants, however, were not influenced by the social context. We also found that Blacks were unwilling to report discrimination in front of Whites, although they were quite willing to do so in private and to another Black participant. Again, White participants were not influenced by the social context. Thus, as might be expected given a history of experiencing the negative outcomes associated with claiming discrimination, stigmatised individuals seem particularly aware of the social costs involved in reporting discrimination to non-stigmatised individuals, whereas non-stigmatised group members do not seem to be so concerned. These results are also consistent with the possibility that minimisation is due in part to a desire to avoid negative social consequences from higher-status group members. As Major et al. (2002) put it, "Members of low status groups may fear retaliation (Swim & Hyers, 1999) or being labeled a 'complainer' (Kaiser & Miller, 2001) by members of high status groups but may not have such fears with respect to members of their own group."

Attributing discrimination to the self versus another. Additional research from our lab suggests that self-presentation concerns are particularly salient when they involve reports about one's own experiences with discrimination in comparison to when they involve the experiences of another in-group member. Sechrist, Swim, and Stangor (2003) gave women the opportunity to make an attribution to ability or to discrimination for negative feedback that had occurred either to the self or to another, similar, woman; again these attributions were made either in public or in private. We found that women were equally likely to make attributions to discrimination in public as in private when the negative feedback was directed at another woman. However, when the negative feedback was directed at the self, women were less likely to claim that their outcomes were due to discrimination in public than in private. These results suggest that although individuals may be aware that claiming one has been the victim of discrimination will be seen as complaining, reporting discrimination that has been directed against another person could, in contrast, be seen as a way of supporting them.

Confronting sexism. The previous studies have focused on the conditions that influence stigmatised individuals' willingness to make an attribution to discrimination. The willingness to make such a public attribution can be important in terms of one's willingness to confront sexism. For instance, women who have a tendency to present a different public than private self due to pressure to conform to traditional gender roles are more likely to report having self-silenced to incidents that they report were likely to be sexist (Swim et al., 2003e).

Laboratory studies have explicitly examined public reporting in the form of confronting sexism. Swim and Hyers (1999) observed women's willingness to confront sexist comments made by men in a group setting. Consistent with the findings reported above, they found that women's private thoughts about confronting were unrelated to their public thoughts. Moreover, when the situation these women faced was described to another group of women, this second group of women overestimated

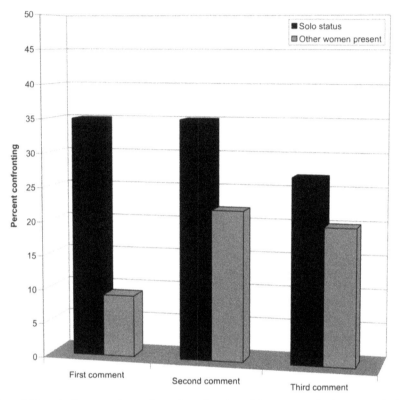

Figure 6. Percent of women who confronted as a function of the presence of other women in the group. From Swim and Hyers (1999).

the likelihood that they would publicly confront the man who made the sexist comment.

The results from Swim and Hyers (1999) also point to specific social conditions that can influence women's willingness to publicly confront sexism. Specifically, we found that women were initially more willing to confront sexism when they were the only women present than if other women were present in the group setting. After they observed the same man making additional sexist comments, however, there was no difference in the context in terms of their willingness to confront (see Figure 6). This suggests that women are looking to other women to decide how to respond and that diffusion of responsibility, rather than, for instance, anticipating social support, directed their behaviour.

Summary. Existing research clearly demonstrates that even though people may in some cases view discrimination when asked to report anonymously and privately, they may nevertheless be unwilling to publicly express that they have been targets or to confront perpetrators. These discrepancies may help us understand variations in people's reports about their own and others' experiences with discrimination, and may help explain why individuals frequently do not report or confront the discrimination that occurs to them. If individuals are not reporting discrimination due to perceived social costs, this may create a type of pluralistic ignorance in which others may erroneously infer that they are not experiencing it. However, although existing research has primarily revealed variables that demonstrate the potential costs of reporting discrimination, there are also potential benefits that accrue when one does so. These include educating others about the possibility that discrimination is occurring and appearing competent to others.

CONCLUSIONS

Our research programme, as well as those of others (see Major et al., 2002; Major et al., this volume; Schmitt & Branscombe, 2002) is focusing on the extent to which members of stigmatised social groups perceive and/or misperceive the discrimination directed at them. The research is based on the assumption that members of stigmatised groups may suffer from discrimination both as a result of its direct negative effects, as well as because of their beliefs that they are, or are not, victims. Thus the stigmatised may hold stereotypes about the attitudes and expected motives of more powerful group members, and these stereotypes may be stronger for some individuals than others, and may or may not be contextually activated. Like all stereotypes, the expectations that the stigmatised hold about those with higher status may be in some senses accurate and in other senses inaccurate. And yet because they are overgeneralised they may be harmful to creating positive intergroup encounters. Indeed, the direct effects of prejudice and discrimination on the stigmatised may reflect only the tip of the causal iceberg. As in virtually every domain studied by social psychologists, perceptions may turn out to be as or more important than reality.

Although individuals may either over- or under-estimate the occurrence of discrimination directed at them, taken together our results seem more consistent with other findings indicating that individuals are often unlikely to perceive and report discrimination that occurs to them personally (Crosby et al., 1986; Magley, Hulin, Fitzgerald, & DeNardo, 1999). Furthermore, this minimisation can occur at different points in the information-processing cycle—because individuals do not initially notice that an incident may be discriminatory, because they do not interpret the event as discrimination, or as a result of anticipated costs to publicly reporting or confronting it.

On a practical level, there are both costs and benefits to underestimating the occurrence of discrimination (Feldman Barrett & Swim, 1998). On the positive side, individuals who are unaware of discrimination may be able to avoid the costs of becoming hostile and angry towards perpetrators, and they will be immune from the negative indirect outcomes of stereotyping, such as stereotype threat. Furthermore, they will avoid the potential costs associated with publicly reporting discrimination. However, if individuals from stigmatised groups underestimate that events that occur to them are discriminatory, they may be unprepared to cope with or respond to true discrimination when it occurs. And, at a social level, when large groups of individuals are unaware of the existence of prejudice, this may result in an unwillingness or inability to challenge the system (Jost & Banaji, 1994).

Because we are in a relatively early stage of the testing of our proposed framework, there are many issues that we have not yet addressed. One issue is that our stage approach predicts that it is not only the outcome of different types of processing that is important, but that dissociations between the stages can also influence psychological responses to discrimination. An interesting research hypothesis, which has been proposed both by us and also by Miller and Kaiser (2001) is that discrepancies between Stage 1 and Stage 2 processing may have important influence on psychological health such that, if individuals do not initially become suspicious about discrimination, this will protect them psychologically. However initially noticing discrimination, but then subsequently denying or reinterpreting events as due to other causes, may produce negative outcomes. Similarly, a dissociation between Stage 2 and Stage 3 might occur such that perceiving discrimination at a private level, but then denying or failing to confront it publicly, could be psychologically costly if it violates a person's need to be true to oneself. There are likely to be large psychological costs when individuals know that they are victims of discrimination and yet do not feel that they can report these experiences or feel helpless to effect social change. These and other interesting questions await our attention and that of others.

REFERENCES

Allport, G. W. (1954). *The nature of prejudice*. Reading, MA: Addison-Wesley.

Anderson, N., & Armstead, C. (1995). Toward understanding the association of socioeconomic status and health: A new challenge for the biopsychosocial approach. *Psychosomatic Medicine, 57*, 213–225.

Bach, P. B., Cramer, L. D., Warren, J. L., & Begg, C. B. (1999). Racial differences in the treatment of early-stage lung cancer. *New England Journal of Medicine, 341*(16), 1198–1205.

Blanchard, F. A., Crandall, C. S., Brigham, J. C., & Vaughn, L. A. (1994). Condemning and condoning racism: A social context approach to interracial settings. *Journal of Applied Psychology, 79*, 993–997.

Braddock, J. H., & McPartland, J. M. (1987). How minorities continue to be excluded from equal employment opportunities: Research on labor market and institutional barriers. *Journal of Social Issues, 43,* 5–39.

Branscombe, N. R., Schmitt, M. T., & Harvey, R. D. (1999). Perceiving pervasive discrimination among African Americans: Implications for group identification and well-being. *Journal of Personality & Social Psychology, 77,* 135–149.

Brewer, M., & Brown, R. (1998). Intergroup relations. In S. Fiske, D. Gilbert, & G. Lindzey (Eds.), *Handbook of social psychology* (4th ed., Vol. 2, pp. 554–594). Boston: McGraw-Hill.

Burger, J. M. (1992). *Desire for control: Personality, social and clinical perspective.* New York: Plenum.

Burger, J. M., & Cooper, H. M. (1979). The desirability of control. *Motivation and Emotion, 3,* 381–393.

Cash, T. F., Gillen, B., & Burns, D. S. (1977). Sexism and beautyism in personnel consultant decision making. *Journal of Applied Psychology, 62,* 301–310.

Cohen, L. L., & Swim, J. K. (1995). The differential impact of gender ratios on women and men: Tokenism, self-confidence, and expectations. *Personality and Social Psychology Bulletin, 21,* 876–884.

Contrada, R. J., Shamore, R. D., Gary, M. L., Coups, E., Egeth, J. D., Sewell, A., et al. (2000). Ethnicity-related sources of stress and their effects on well-being. *Current Directions in Psychological Science, 9,* 136–139.

Corning, A. F. (2002). Self-esteem as a moderator between perceived discrimination and psychological distress among women. *Journal of Counseling Psychology, 49,* 117–126.

Crocker, J. (1999). Social stigma and self-esteem: Situational construction of self-worth. *Journal of Experimental Social Psychology, 35,* 89–107.

Crocker, J., & Major, B. (1989). Social stigma and self-esteem: The self-protective properties of stigma. *Psychological Review, 96,* 608–630.

Crosby, F. (1984). The denial of personal discrimination. *American Behavioral Scientist, 27,* 371–386.

Crosby, F., Clayton, S., Alksnis, O., & Hemker, K. (1986). Cognitive biases in the perception of discrimination: The importance of format. *Sex Roles, 14,* 637–646.

Czopp, A. M., & Monteith, M. J. (2003). Confronting prejudice (literally): Reactions to confrontations of racial and gender bias. *Personality and Social Psychology Bulletin, 29,* 532–544.

DeCoster, J., & Swim, J. K. (2002). *Applying a dual process model to judgments of prejudice.* Manuscript in preparation.

Dodd, E. H., Giuliano, T. A., Boutell, J. M., & Moran, B. E. (2001). Respected or rejected: Perceptions of women who confront sexist remarks. *Sex Roles, 45,* 567–577.

Feldman Barrett, L., & Swim, J. (1998). Appaisals of prejudice and discrimination. In J. K. Swim & C. Stangor (Eds.), *Prejudice: The target's perspective* (pp. 11–36). Santa Barbara, CA: Academic Press.

Fiske, S. T. (1998). Stereotyping, prejudice and discrimination. In D. T. Gilbert, S. T. Fiske, & G. Lindzey (Eds.), *Handbook of social psychology* (4th ed., Vol. 2, pp. 357–414). New York: McGraw Hill.

Fiske, S. T., Cuddy, A. J. C., Glick, P., & Xu, J. (2002). A model of (often mixed) stereotype content: Competence and warmth respectively follow from perceived status and competition. *Journal of Personality and Social Psychology, 82*(6), 878–902.

Fiske, S. T., Xu, J., Cuddy, A. C., & Glick, P. (1999). (Dis)respecting versus (dis)liking: Status and interdependence predict ambivalent stereotypes of competence and warmth. *Journal of Social Issues, 55,* 473–489.

Friedman, M. A., & Brownell, K. D. (1995). Psychological correlates of obesity: Moving to the next research generation. *Psychological Bulletin, 117,* 3–20.

Glauser, A. S. (1999). Legacies of racism. *Journal of Counseling & Development, 77,* 62–67.

Goffman, E. (1963). *Stigma: Notes on the management of spoiled identity.* Englewood Cliffs, NJ: Prentice-Hall.

Halpert, S. C. (2002). Suicidal behavior among gay male youth. *Journal of Gay and Lesbian Psychotherapy, 6,* 53–79.

Hebl, M. R., & Kleck, R. E. (2000). The social consequences of physical disability. In T. F. Heatherton, R. E. Kleck, M. R. Hebl, & J. G. Hull (Eds.), *The social psychology of stigma* (pp. 419–439). New York: Guilford Press.

Higgins, E. T., & King, G. (1981). Accessibility of social constructs: Information-processing consequences of individual and contextual variability. In N. Cantor & J. F. Kihlstrom (Eds.), *Personality, cognition and social interaction* (pp. 69–121). Hillsdale, NJ: Lawrence Erlbaum Associates Inc.

Hyers, L. (2003). *Challenging everyday prejudice: The personal and social implications of women's assertive responses to interpersonal incidents of anti-black racism, anti-Semitism, heterosexism, and sexism* Manuscript submitted for publication.

Inman, M. L., & Baron, R. S. (1996). Influence of prototypes on perceptions of prejudice. *Journal of Personality & Social Psychology, 70,* 727–739.

Jetten, J., Branscombe, N. R., Schmitt, M. T., & Spears, R. (2001). Rebels with a cause: Group identification as a response to perceived discrimination from the mainstream. *Personality and Social Psychology Bulletin, 27*(9), 1204–1213.

Johnson, J. D., Simmons, K., Trawalter, S., Ferguson, T., & Reed, W. (2002). Factors that influence and mediate attributions of "ambiguously racist" behavior. *Personality and Social Psychology Bulletin, 29,* 609–622.

Johnston, K. E., & Swim, J. K. (1999). [*Unpublished raw data.*] Penn State University, USA.

Jones, J. M. (1997). *Prejudice and racism* (2nd ed.). New York: The McGraw-Hill Companies, Inc.

Jones, P., & Stangor, C. (2003). *The moderators and mediators of stereotype threat: A meta-analysis.* Manuscript under review, University of Maryland.

Jost, J. T. (1995). Negative illusions: Conceptual clarification and psychological evidence concerning false consciousness. *Political Psychology, 16,* 397–424.

Jost, J. T., & Banaji, M. R. (1994). The role of stereotyping in system-justification and the production of false consciousness. *British Journal of Social Psychology, 33,* 1–27.

Kaiser, C. R., & Miller, C. T. (2001). Stop complaining! The social costs of making attributions to discrimination. *Personality & Social Psychology Bulletin, 27*(2), 254–263.

Kessler, R. C., Mickelson, K. D., & Williams, D. R. (1999). The prevalence, distribution, and mental health correlated of perceived discrimination in the United States. *Journal of Health and Social Behavior, 40,* 208–230.

Kleck, R., & Strenta, A. (1980). Perceptions of the impact of negatively-valued physical characteristics on social interaction. *Journal of Personality and Social Psychology, 39,* 861–873.

Kleugel, J. R., & Smith, E. R. (1986). *Beliefs about inequality: Americans' view of what is and what ought to be.* Hawthorne, NJ: Aldine de Gruyer.

Klonoff, E. A., Landrine, H., & Ullman, J. B. (1999). Racial discrimination and psychiatric symptoms among Blacks. *Cultural Diversity and Ethnic Minority Psychology, 5,* 329–339.

Kobrynowicz, D., & Branscombe, N. R. (1997). Who considers themselves victims of discrimination? *Psychology of Women Quarterly, 21,* 347–363.

Lalonde, R. N., & Cameron, J. E. (1994). Behavioral responses to discrimination: A focus on action. In M. P. Zanna & J. M. Olson (Eds.), *The psychology of prejudice: The Ontario symposium* (Vol 7, pp. 257–288). Hillsdale, NJ: Lawrence Erlbaum Associates Inc.

Landrine, H., & Klonoff, E. (1996). The schedule of racist events: A measure of racial discrimination and a study of its negative physical and mental heath consequences. *Journal of Black Psychology, 22*, 144–168.

Landrine, H., Klonoff, E. A., Gibbs, J., Manning, V., & Lund, M. (1995). Physical and psychiatric correlates of gender discrimination: An application of the schedule of sexist incidents. *Psychology of Women Quarterly, 19*, 473–492.

Lord, C., & Saenz, D. (1985). Memory deficits and memory surfeits: Differential cognitive consequences of tokenism for tokens and observers. *Journal of Personality and Social Psychology, 49*, 918–926.

Magley, V. J., Hulin, C. L., Fitzgerald, L. F., & DeNardo, M. (1999). Outcomes of self-labeling sexual harassment. *Journal of Applied Psychology, 84*(3), 390–402.

Major, B. (1994). From social inequality to personal entitlement: The role of social comparisons, legitimacy appraisals, and group membership. In M. P. Zanna (Ed.), *Advances in experimental social psychology* (Vol. 26, pp. 293–348). San Diego, CA: Academic Press.

Major, B., McCoy, S. K., Kaiser, C. R., & Quinton, W. J. (this volume). Prejudice and self-esteem: A transactional model. *European Review of Social Psychology, 14*, 77–104.

Major, B., Quinton, W., & McCoy, S. (2002). Antecedents and consequences of attributions to discrimination: Theoretical and empirical advances. In M. P. Zanna (Ed.), *Advances in experimental social psychology*, (Vol. 34, pp. 251–330). San Diego: Academic Press.

Major, B., Quinton, W., & Schmader, T. (2003). Attributions to discrimination and self-esteem: Impact of group identification and situational ambiguity. *Journal of Experimental Social Psychology, 39*, 220–231.

Mallett, R. K. (2003). *Self-protective coping mechanisms used by targets of prejudice*. Unplublished doctorial dissertation, The Pennsylvania State University, USA.

Marti, M. W., Bobier, D. B., & Baron, R. S. (2000). Right before our eyes: The failure to recognize non-protyptical forms of prejudice. *Group Process and Intergroup Relations, 3*, 403–418.

Mendoza-Denton, R., Downey, G., Purdie, V., Davis, A., & Pietrzak, J. (2002). Sensitivity to status-based rejection: Implications for African American students' college experience. *Journal of Personality and Social Psychology, 83*, 896–918.

Miller, C. T., & Downey, K. T. (1999). A meta-analysis of heavyweight and self-esteem. *Personality and Social Psychology Review, 3*, 68–84.

Miller, C. T., & Kaiser, C. R. (2001). A theoretical perspective on coping with stigma. *Journal of Social Issues, 57*, 73–92.

Moghaddam, F. M., Stolkin, A. J., & Hutcheson, L. S. (1997). A generalized personal/group discrepancy: Testing the domain specificity of a perceived higher effect of events on one's group than on oneself. *Personality and Social Psychology Bulletin, 23*, 743–750.

Neckerman, K. M., & Kirschenman, J. (1991). Hiring strategies, racial bias, and inner-city workers. *Social Problems, 38*(4), 433–447.

Noel, J. G., Wann, D. L., & Branscombe, N. R. (1995). Peripheral ingroup membership status and public negativity toward outgroups. *Journal of Personality and Social Psychology, 68*(1), 127–137.

Olson, J., & Hafer, C. L. (2001). Tolerance of personal deprivation. In J. T. Jost & B. Major (Eds.), *The psychology of legitimacy: Emerging perspectives on ideology, justice, and intergroup relations* (pp. 157–175). New York: Cambridge University Press.

Operario, D., & Fiske, S. T. (2001). Ethnic identity moderates perceptions of prejudice: Judgments of personal versus group discrimination and subtle versus blatant bias. *Personality & Social Psychology Bulletin, 27*, 550–561.

Pinel, E. C. (2002). Sigma consciousness in intergroup contexts: The power of conviction. *Journal of Experimental Social Psychology, 34*, 178–185.

Pittman, T. S., & D'Agostino, P. R. (1989). Motivation and cognition: Control deprivation and the nature of subsequent information processing. *Journal of Experimental Social Psychology*, *25*, 465–480.

Postmes, T., Branscombe, N. R., Spears, R., & Young, H. (1999). Comparative processes in personal and group judgments: Resolving the discrepancy. *Journal of Personality and Social Psychology*, *76*(2), 320–338.

Schmitt, M. T., & Branscombe, N. (2002). The meaning and consequences of perceived discrimination in disadvantaged and privileged social groups. *European Review of Social Psychology*, *12*, 167–199.

Schultz, A., Israel, B., Williams, D., Parker, E., Becker, A., & James, S. (2000). Social inequalities, stressors and self reported health status among African American and white women in the Detroit metropolitan area. *Social Science and Medicine*, *51*, 1639–1653.

Schwarz, N., & Clore, G. L. (1996). Feelings and phenomenal experiences. In E. T. Higgins & A. W. Kruglanski (Eds.), *Social psychology: Handbook of basic principles* (pp. 433–465). New York: Guilford Press.

Sechrist, G. B., Swim, J. K., & Mark, M. M. (2002). Mood as information in making attributions to discrimination. *Personality and Social Psychology Bulletin*, *29*, 524–531.

Sechrist, G. B., Swim, J. K., & Stangor, C. (2003). *The self–other discrepancy and its social and personal determinants*. Manuscript submitted for publication.

Sekaquaptewa, D., & Thompson, M. (2003). Solo status, stereotype threat, and performance expectancies: Their effects on women's performance. *Journal of Experimental Social Psychology*, *39*(1), 68–74.

Sidanius, J., & Pratto, F. (1999). *Social dominance: An intergroup theory of social hierarchy and oppression*. New York: Cambridge University Press.

Stangor, C., Carr, C., & Kiang, L. (1998). Activating stereotypes undermines task performance expectations. *Journal of Personality and Social Psychology*, *75*, 1191–1197.

Stangor, C., Lynch, L., Duan, C., & Glass, B. (1992). Categorization of individuals on the basis of multiple social features. *Journal of Personality and Social Psychology*, *62*(2), 207–218.

Stangor, C., Sechrist, G., & Swim, J. (2002). *Gender prejudice accessibility and its effects on perceiving sexism*, Unpublished data, University of Maryland.

Stangor, C., & Sechrist, G. B. (1998). Conceptualizing the determinants of academic choice and task performance across social groups. In J. K. Swim & C. Stangor (Eds.), *Prejudice: The target's perspective*. Santa Barbara, CA: Academic Press.

Stangor, C., Sechrist, G. B., & Swim, J. K. (1999). Sensitivity to sexism and perceptions of reports about sexist events. *Swiss Journal of Psychology*, *58*, 251–256.

Stangor, C., Swim, J. K., Van Allen, K., & Sechrist, G. (2001). Reporting discrimination in public and private contexts. *Journal of Personality and Social Psychology*, *82*, 69–74.

Stangor, C., Van Allen, K., & Swim, J. K. (2003). *There are both costs and benefits in claiming discrimination*. Manuscript in preparation.

Steele, C. M., & Aronson, J. (1995). Stereotype threat and the intellectual performance of African Americans. *Journal of Personality and Social Psychology*, *69*, 797–811.

Swim, J. K., Aikin, K., Hall, W., & Hunter, B. A. (1995). Sexism and racism: Old-fashioned and modern prejudices. *Journal of Personality and Social Psychology*, *68*, 199–214.

Swim, J. K., Chau, P. P., Pearson, N. B., & Stangor, C. (2003a). *The role of feminist attitudes and social context*. Manuscript under review, Penn State University.

Swim, J. K., & Hyers, L. (1999). Excuse me—What did you just say?!: Women's public and private responses to sexist remarks. *Journal of Experimental Social Psychology*, *35*, 68–88.

Swim, J. K., Hyers, L. L., Cohen, L. L., & Ferguson, M. J. (2001). Everyday sexism: Evidence for its incidence, nature, and psychological impact from three daily diary studies. *Journal of Social Issues*, *57*(1), 31–53.

Swim, J. K., Hyers, L. L., Cohen, L. L., Fitzgerald, D. C., & Bylsma, W. H. (2003b). *African American college students' experiences with everyday anti-black racism: Characteristics of incidents and responses to these incidents.* Manuscript under review, Penn State University.

Swim, J. K., Mallet, R., Russo-Devosa, Y., & Stangor, C. (2003c). *Subtle sexism: An assessment of gender-related beliefs and sexist behaviors.* Manuscript in preparation.

Swim, J. K., Pearson, N. B., & Johnston, K. E. (2003d). *Day to day experiences with heterosexism: Heterosexist hassles as daily stressors.* Manuscript under review, Penn State University.

Swim, J. K., Quinliven, E., Fitzgerald, M. J., & Eysell, K. M. (2003e). *Self-silencing to sexism.* Manuscript submitted for publication.

Swim, J. K., Scott, E. D., Sechrist, G. B., Campbell, B., & Stangor, C. (2003f). The role of intent and harm in perceptions of prejudice and discrimination. *Journal of Personality and Social Psychology, 84*, 944–959.

Taylor, D., Wright, S., Moghaddam, F., & Lalonde, R. (1990). The personal/group discrimination discrepancy: Perceiving my group, but not myself, to be a target of discrimination. *Personality and Social Psychology Bulletin, 16*, 254–262.

Taylor, D., Wright, S., & Porter, L. (1994). Dimensions of perceived discrimination: The personal/group discrimination discrepancy. In M. P. Zanna & J. M. Olson (Eds.), *The psychology of prejudice: The Ontario Symposium* (Vol. 7, pp. 233–256). Hillsdale, NJ: Lawrence Erlbaum Associates Inc.

Terrell, F., & Terrell, S. (1981). An inventory to measure cultural mistrust among blacks. *The Western Journal of Black Studies, 5*, 180–185.

Treiman, D. J., & Hartmann, H. I. (1981). *Women, work, and wages: Equal pay for jobs of equal value.* Washington, DC: National Academy Press.

Waters, H., Jr. (1994). Decision making and race. *International Journal of Intercultural Relationships, 18*, 449–467.

Williams, D. R. (1999). Race, socioeconomics status, and health: The added effect of racism and discrimination. In N. E. Adler, M. Marmot, B. S. McEwen, & J. Stewart (Eds.), *Socioeconomic status and health in industrial nations: Social, psychological, and biological pathways* (Vol. 896, pp. 173–188). New York: New York Academy of Sciences.

Williams, D. R., & Rucker, T. D. (2000). Understanding and addressing racial disparities in health care. *Health Care Financing Review, 21*, 75–91.

Williams, D. R., Spencer, M. S., & Jackson, J. S. (1999). Race, stress, and physical health: The role of group identity. In R. J. Contrada & R. D. Ashmore (Eds.), *Self, social identity, and physical health: Interdisciplinary explorations* (Vol. 2, pp. 71–100). New York: Oxford University Press.

Williams, D. R., & Williams-Morris, R. (2000). Racism and mental health: The African American Experience. *Ethnicity and Health, 5*, 243–269.

Wyer, R. S., & Carlston, D. (1979). *Social cognition, inference, and attribution.* Hillsdale, NJ: Lawrence Erlbaum Associates Inc.

Yinger, J. M. (1994). *Ethnicity: Source of strength? Source of conflict?* Albany, NY: State University of New York Press.

Author index

Subject index